JESUS

GEZA VERMES was born in Hungary in 1924. He studied in Budapest and Louvain, where he read Oriental History and Languages and in 1953 obtained a doctorate in Theology with a dissertation on the Dead Sea Scrolls. From 1957 to 1991 he taught at the universities of Newcastle and Oxford. His pioneering work on the Dead Sea Scrolls and the historical figure of Jesus led to his appointment as the first Professor of Jewish Studies at Oxford, where he is now Professor Emeritus. Since 1991 he has been director of the Forum for Qumran Research at the Oxford Centre for Hebrew and Jewish Studies. Professor Vermes is a Fellow of the British Academy and of the European Academy of Arts, Sciences and Humanities, the holder of an Oxford D.Litt. and of honorary doctorates from the universities of Edinburgh, Durham, Sheffield and the Central European University of Budapest.

His books, published by Penguin, include *The Complete Dead Sea Scrolls in English* (most recent edition, 2004), *The Changing Faces of Jesus* (2000), *The Authentic Gospel of Jesus* (2003), *Who's Who in the Age of Jesus* (2005), his trilogy about the life of Jesus, *The Passion* (2005), *The Nativity* (2006) and *The Resurrection* (2007), and *The Story of the Scrolls* (2010). His pioneering work *Jesus the Jew* (1973; most recent edition, 2001) and his autobiography, *Providential Accidents* (1998), are available from SCM Press, London.

GEZA VERMES

Jesus

Nativity – Passion – Resurrection

PENGUIN BOOKS

PENGUIN BOOKS

Published by the Penguin Group
Penguin Books Ltd, 80 Strand, London WC2R ORL, England
Penguin Group (USA) Inc., 375 Hudson Street, New York, New York 10014, USA
Penguin Group (Canada), 90 Eglinton Avenue East, Suite 700, Toronto, Ontario, Canada M4P 2Y3
(a division of Pearson Canada Inc.)
Penguin Ireland, 25 St Stephen's Green, Dublin 2, Ireland (a division of Penguin Books Ltd)
Penguin Group (Australia), 250 Camberwell Road, Camberwell, Victoria 3124, Australia
(a division of Pearson Australia Group Pty Ltd)
Penguin Books India Pvt Ltd, 11 Community Centre, Panchsheel Park, New Dehli – 110 017, India
Penguin Group (NZ), 67 Apollo Drive, Rosedale, North Shore 0632, New Zealand
(a division of Pearson New Zealand Ltd)
Penguin Books (South Africa) (Pty) Ltd, 24 Sturdee Avenue,
Rosebank, Johannesburg 2196, South Africa

Penguin Books Ltd, Registered Offices: 80 Strand, London WC2R ORL, England

www.penguin.com

The Passion first published 2005
The Nativity first published 2006
The Resurrection first published 2008
Published in one volume as *Jesus* 2010

1

Copyright © Geza Vermes, 2005, 2006, 2008
All rights reserved

The moral right of the author has been asserted

Printed in England by Clays Ltd, St Ives plc

ISBN: 978-0-141-04622-8

www.greenpenguin.co.uk

Penguin Books is committed to a sustainable future
for our business, our readers and our planet.
The book in your hands is made from paper
certified by the Forest Stewardship Council.

Contents

v

THE PASSION

THE RESURRECTION

List of illustrations

Woodcuts by Albrecht Dürer (1471–1528):

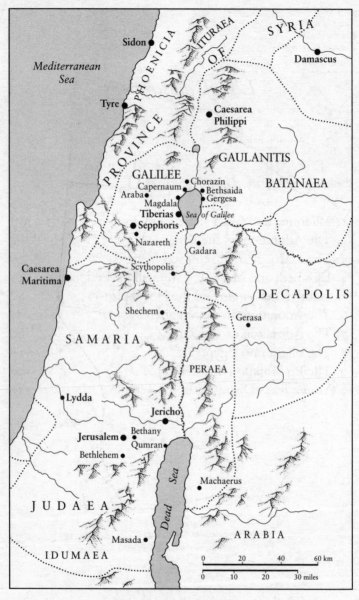

Palestine in the age of Jesus

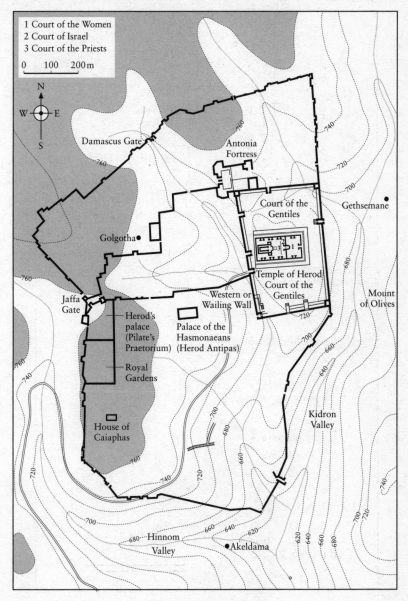

The Jerusalem of Jesus

1 Court of the Women
2 Court of Israel
3 Court of the Priests

0   100   200m

N
W — E
S

Damascus Gate

Antonia
Fortress

Court of the
Gentiles

Gethsemane

Golgotha

3 1

Temple of Herod
Court of the
Gentiles

Western or
Wailing Wall

Mount
of Olives

Jaffa
Gate

Herod's
palace
(Pilate's
Praetorium)

Palace of the
Hasmonaeans
(Herod Antipas)

Royal
Gardens

Kidron
Valley

House of
Caiaphas

Hinnom
Valley

Akeldama

THE NATIVITY

Prologue

Old Christmas – New Christmas

Christmas is no longer what it used to be. It has lost its religious significance in many parts of the Western world and has become the climax of a season of overspending, overeating and uncontrolled merrymaking. The new Christmas mirrors its pagan predecessor which celebrated the winter solstice. Christmas is the children's favourite festival of the year and for the grown-ups it is a time for indulging in sweet old-time memories.

My earliest recollections take me back further than I care to think, to the happy days before the Second World War. I was four years old. My parents, like many assimilated Hungarian Jews before Hitler appeared on the horizon, wanted their little boy to share the seasonal jollification of their Christian friends and neighbours. (Today in progressive Jewish circles the Festival of Lights or Hanukkah has become a substitute Christmas, humorously nicknamed Hanukmas, Chrismukkah or Chrisnukkah.) Hungarian children in those days believed that Christmas presents were brought to them by the Little Jesus or *Jézuska*, who made his rounds on the evening of 24th December, and placed the gifts under the decorated Christmas tree which was delivered from heaven by little angels. I was warned to resist curiosity, for should I peep into the sitting room from my quarters, the angels would be frightened away and that would be goodbye to presents and sweets. I remember how greatly I was tempted to investigate the noises coming from the living room while I was having my afternoon siesta, but wise by nature from the start, I overcame temptation. Then in the evening I was allowed to enter. What a glorious sight it was: the tree with its real candles and little sparklers, which burst into hundreds of bright stars when lit with a match. And there were presents galore, more than I could count. Singing was heard from the street. The doorbell rang and a group of working-class children inquired whether they might bring in their 'Bethlehem', a cardboard crib in which Mary, Joseph and Jesus shared the stable with an ox and a donkey. One of the boys carried the star of Bethlehem on a rod, and other children played the angels, the shepherds and the three kings. Their labour was rewarded with bits of chocolate and a few pennies. Everything was charming and delightful; a naive religious aura filled the place. The red-suited Santa Claus or Father Christmas did not exist. We had 'Uncle' or 'Saint' Nicholas instead, who visited the children much earlier in the month: on the evening of 5th December and stuffed their stockings with goodies. To teach them not to misbehave, he beat with a stick a young companion who played the devil.

A year later matters became slightly more sophisticated in the Vermes household. By then I had learned how to write with capital letters from the headlines of the many newspapers which filled our home, and I used the newly acquired skill to provide 'little Jesus' with a list of toys and books I hoped he would supply. My father, a journalist, put the letter, addressed to 'Jesus in heaven', into his jacket pocket and promised to drop it into the letter-box at the street corner a few days before Christmas. Then catastrophe struck. I did something naughty, I can no longer remember what, and my father decided to teach me a lesson. He fiddled with the knobs of his primitive radio set, his means of communication with the upper world, and to my utmost consternation, he pulled my letter out of his pocket. To punish me for my mischief, little Jesus returned the message to the sender. I burst into tears and firmly promised to amend my ways. Pardon was granted and the much-hoped-for presents somehow materialized.

My wife's early Christmas recollections are of a quite different kind. Though numbering a Jew among her great-grandparents, she grew up in Cracow in a strictly Polish Catholic setting. In her world Christmas was not associated with *large* presents. Those had been delivered by Saint Nicholas during the night of 5th December. (I remember from my student days that in Belgium, too, Saint Nicholas was the chief gift giver, and I gather that in the Netherlands children expect this benevolent ancient bishop of Myra from Asiatic Turkey to arrive by ship from Spain.) The Christmas pleasure of Polish youngsters came from preparing the Christmas tree and attaching to it sweets, oranges, apples and shiny baubles. Less pleasurable were the duties imposed on them by their parents to apologize for all the naughtiness of the past year – promises that they would be well behaved in the future and to convey specific good wishes to each member of the family. But then came the crowning glory of Christmas Eve, a sumptuous meal of twelve courses, accompanied – in other Polish families – by large doses of alcohol among the grown-ups, many of whom found themselves under the influence by the time they had to set off to church to attend midnight mass.

As he remembers it, the experience of the junior member of the family, Ian Vermes, born in Oxford in

1990, does not resemble either mine or his mother's. In the true British way, his Christmas was celebrated on 25th December and not on Christmas Eve, as was the case on the continent. At the age of three and a half he was waiting with burning excitement for the moment when on Christmas morning he could burst into the sitting room and rip the shiny wrapping paper off the many presents left for him not by little Jesus, but by an avuncular white-bearded Santa Claus. The Christmas tree, adorned not with wax candles but with electric lights, held no mystery for him. He never heard that it had been brought to him by angels: he himself helped the previous day to prepare it. A year later even the Father Christmas mystique suffered a deadly blow. Ian, unable to withstand curiosity, quietly crept downstairs from his bedroom late in the evening of 24th December and discovered his mother and me wrapping up the presents and placing them under the Christmas tree. For years he continued to pretend that he believed in Father Christmas, and sent him detailed shopping lists, stating the exact price of the various items in order to ensure that Santa had with him enough money to make all the purchases. His Christmas had become like that of most children in these days: the expectation of toys, videos, DVDs and computer games as seen advertised day in, day out, on television. Now at the age of sixteen he likes to think of himself as an agnostic scientist and claims that he has never associated Christmas with anything religious. 25th December is simply the great day of the increasingly lavish annual bonanza.

But what actually lies behind the feast of the Nativity? To discover the origins of Christmas we must examine the main records that the New Testament places at our disposal – the Infancy Gospels of Matthew and Luke – and

4

endeavour to squeeze the truth out of them. This truth, as we shall see, belongs only very slightly to history and mostly derives from man's hopeful and creative religious imagination.

I

The Nativity in Christian imagination and in the Gospels

There are three versions of the Nativity play. Church-goers of all ages are familiar with the first. It is regularly sketched, Christmas after Christmas, in sermons preached from the pulpit. It can be found and admired on the great Nativity canvasses lovingly created by Christian artists over the centuries. One sees a bearded old man walking beside a donkey on whose back a heavily pregnant young woman rides. The towers of Bethlehem are faintly visible in the distance. In the crowded city the inns are packed and Joseph, after much toing and froing and searching can discover only a modest shed in the neighbourhood for Mary to give birth to her son. The newborn Jesus is laid by his mother in the manger between a cow and an ass. Old Joseph observes the scene with benevolent and detached admiration. Local shepherds are alerted by an angel and learn about the arrival in the world of the Saviour of the Jews. Soon three kings approach, robed in glorious apparel. They have been led from the far-distant Orient via Jerusalem to Bethlehem by a mysterious star. At the royal palace they inquire where the recently born king of the Jews can be seen. First no one knows. So on the advice of experts summoned by Herod the kings are sent to Bethlehem and with the help of the reappearing star they find the stable, greet and worship

Jesus, and offer him regal presents. The curtain falls: end of act one.

Like a child's fairy tale, the Christmas story consists of an admixture of the charming and the dreadful. In act two, generally not featured in Nativity plays, sweetness and joy suddenly vanish and disaster looms on the horizon when bloodthirsty Herod enters the fray. Realizing that the kings have tricked him and slipped out of the country, Herod lets loose his cruel soldiers on the infant boys of Bethlehem. They all perish – from newborn babes to toddlers – except the child who has made Herod so anxious.

Suddenly the scene changes again. Joseph falls asleep and dreams of an angel, who sounds the alarm: father, mother and child must flee at once. Again we see the old man on the road, accompanied by his faithful donkey, but this time it carries the baby and his mother. Cleverly avoiding Herod's frontier guards, they escape from Judaea and reach the safe haven of Egypt, the land of the Nile.

In the last act the scenario gets slightly bogged down. The final phases of the drama become hazy. We are presented with the circumcision of Jesus and with his presentation in the Temple of Jerusalem, but do not learn when these things happened in relation to the escape to Egypt. Nor is the reason and the time of Jesus' move to peaceful Galilee and a happy childhood specified.

The Christian mind does not seem to be greatly bothered by these matters. Its perspective is compact and its chronological framework is foreshortened. For the ordinary faithful all the happenings are squeezed together between Christmas and Candlemas. According to the liturgy of the Church, Jesus was born on 25th December. The innocents of Bethlehem were murdered three days later. Jesus was circumcised on 1st January. In my Oxford

University diary New Year's day is still designated as the feast of the circumcision, but sadly in the Roman Catholic missals, revised after the Second Vatican Council, a solemnity of Mary, Mother of God, has been substituted for the old Latin rite's *Circumcisio Domini* (The circumcision of the Lord) and in consequence the Gospel reading, 'And at the end of eight days, when he was circumcised, he was called Jesus' has disappeared from the day's service. Jesus and Mary (and maybe Joseph) visited the Temple on 2nd February. So the Egyptian episode must have taken place between late December and the beginning of February and the trip to Galilee immediately followed. Everything becomes neat and tidy except ... most of this is legend or fiction.

With all due respect to Christian tradition, some of the essentials of the extended Christmas complex are a million miles away from fact and reality. For instance, the chances that Jesus was born on 25th December are 1 in 365 (or 366 in leap years). This date was invented by the Western church – as late as the fourth century under the emperor Constantine – as a way to replace the pagan festival of the Unvanquished Sun, and is first attested, to be precise, in a Roman calendar in AD 334.[1] Most Eastern Christians celebrate Jesus' birth or manifestation to the world on the feast of Epiphany (6th January), while according to the second-century Church Father Clement of Alexandria other oriental communities commemorated the event on 21st April or 20th May (*Stromateis* [Miscellanea] 1:21).

In our search for clarification let us begin by eliminating the three features of the traditional depiction of Christmas which are without written antecedents in the New Testament. Try as you may, you will find nothing in the Gospels to suggest that Joseph, repeatedly referred to as the father of Jesus, was an old man. We know nothing about his age, when he was born or even when he died. The idea of an elderly Joseph derives from an apocryphal Gospel, the Protoevangelium of James the Brother of the Lord. In it he is described as a widower of advanced years who had sons and daughters from a previous marriage. These are then the members of the household of Joseph and Mary, whom the New Testament designates as the brothers and sisters of Jesus.

Neither do the Gospels contain any allusion to the friendly beasts, the ox and the ass, sharing the stable with Jesus. The imagery of these animals is borrowed from the prophet Isaiah, 'The ox knows its owner, and the ass its master's crib; but Israel does not know, my people does not understand' (Isa 1:3). The Church saw in this passage the prefiguration of the later rejection of Christ by the Jewish people.

Finally, the New Testament nowhere suggests that the oriental visitors who followed the star to Bethlehem were kings. The Greek text of Matthew designates them not as rulers or even 'wise men', but as *magoi*, 'Magi' or magicians (see p. 110). The upgrading of these eastern astrologers to the royal dignity is due to another artificial association of an Old Testament text with this episode of the Infancy Gospel. A passage taken from the Book of Isaiah reads, 'And nations shall come to your light, and kings to the brightness of your rising' (Isa 60:3). It is completed by another verse a few lines further down in the same chapter of the same book, 'They shall bring gold and frankincense, and shall proclaim the praise of the Lord' (Isa 60:6). Nor is it anywhere written that there were *three* kings. This figure is no doubt deduced from the number of gifts listed in Matthew, 'gold and frankincense and myrrh' (Mt 2:11), with the assumption that one present was offered by each visitor.

The two other Christmas pictures are inspired by the New Testament. The first, arising from Matthew's Infancy narrative, begins with the genealogical table of Jesus (Mt 1:1–17), and is followed by Joseph's intention to divorce the pregnant Mary (Mt 1:18–19). His plan is altered when he is reassured by an angel in a dream that his fiancée's condition is due to the miraculous intervention of the Holy Spirit (Mt 1:20). Indeed, the virgin birth is the fulfilment of a prophecy of Isaiah (Mt 1:22–23). Joseph gives credence to this dream-revelation, marries Mary and takes her to his home (Mt 1:24–25).

Jesus' arrival in this world is marked by the apparition of a star on the eastern horizon which leads the 'wise men' of the Orient to Jerusalem (Mt 2:1–2). They go to the royal palace to find out the whereabouts of the newly born king of the Jews (Mt 2:3). The astounded Herod consults the Jewish chief priests who identify Bethlehem as the predicted birthplace of the expected Messiah in conformity with a prophecy by Micah 5:2 (Mt 2:4–6). Herod then extracts from the Magi the time of the first apparition of the star and cannily requires them to share with him whatever they learn about the child (Mt 2:7–8). With the help of the star the Magi find Jesus, and pay homage to him before, in accordance with the instruction they receive in a dream, they return home without retracing their steps to Jerusalem (Mt 2:9–12).

Once more Joseph is instructed by an angel in yet another dream to promptly take Jesus to Egypt in order to escape the massacre of the male children of Bethlehem, decreed by the jealous and enraged Herod, in fulfilment of the prophecy about Rachel, the wife of the Patriarch Jacob, lamenting the loss of her children in Jeremiah 31:15 (Mt 2:13–18). On the death of the king the same angel, in a penultimate dream, orders Joseph to return to the land of Israel, thus bringing to realization another prediction (Hos 11:1), which announces that God will call his Son out of Egypt (Mt 2:19–21). However, when Joseph learns that Archelaus has succeeded Herod, his father, in Jerusalem, a final dream revises the previous instruction and directs him to take up residence in Galilee. An unidentified prophecy, 'He shall be called a Nazarene', is cited to explain Jesus' association with Nazareth (Mt 2:22–23).

In the third version of the events of the Nativity, Luke has a substantially different story to tell. It contains two annunciations. In the first, the elderly priest Zechariah, resident in Judaea, is informed by the angel Gabriel that his aged and sterile wife Elizabeth will miraculously give birth to a son, John the Baptist (Lk 1:5–25). This is followed by a further message by the same Gabriel to Mary, an engaged virgin living in Nazareth, that she will conceive and bear Jesus, and that it is no more difficult for God to make her pregnant and keep her a virgin than to allow her kinswoman Elizabeth to give birth to a son in her old age (Lk 1:26–38). Mary at once visits Elizabeth in Judaea and stays with her until the birth of John the Baptist (Lk 1:39–80). She then travels back to Nazareth, only to take to the road again within a few weeks. The census ordered by the emperor Augustus is given as the explanation of the journey of Joseph and Mary to Bethlehem, where Jesus is born in an animal shelter outside the city of David, the town's hostels being filled to the brim by crowds of people arriving to register (Lk 2:1–7). The newborn child is greeted by local shepherds, and by a heavenly choir singing glory to God (Lk 2:8–20). Eight days later, in conformity with Jewish law, Jesus is circumcised, and on the fortieth day following his birth he is taken to the Temple and the ceremony of the redemption of the first-born is performed, while his mother completes the purification ritual obligatory after giving birth to a male offspring. In the sanctuary Jesus is recognized by two old worshippers as the Messiah of the Jews and the redeemer of the Gentiles (Lk 2:25–38). Their religious duties accomplished, Joseph, Mary and the infant immediately return to Nazareth, their original home town (Lk 2:39–40).

The nature of the material determines the form that our investigation will take. Matthew and Luke seldom furnish the same information in the same order. Sometimes the themes are not unlike in substance, but most frequently the two evangelists offer totally independent data. As a parallel or 'synoptic' approach to the birth accounts is in consequence not feasible, I will deal with the problems as they emerge one after another from the Infancy Gospels of Matthew and Luke.

2

The enigma of the Infancy Gospels

The infancy narratives out of which the traditional Christmas story has arisen constitute a major oddity in the Gospels. They are not attested by all the sources. Only two evangelists felt it necessary to place a very peculiar kind of birth account in front of their theologically motivated biography of Jesus. Neither the oldest nor the most recent of the Gospels contains any reference to the temporal entry of their hero into the world.

Mark, whose work was most probably completed around AD 70, goes without any preamble *in medias res*, and starts straight away with the public appearance of John the Baptist, to be almost immediately followed by the story of the baptism of Jesus. He reports nothing about the historical and geographical circumstances of the birth of Jesus or of his family background and early life. The same is true about the Gospel of John, finally formulated probably in the first decade of the second century, give or take a few years. It has nothing to convey about the earthly beginnings of Christ, except that in some way they were connected to the ministry of a man named John – John the Baptist – but supplies in its magnificent Prologue a mystical-philosophical insight into the eternal pre-existence of the *Logos*, the creative Word of God, that in the fullness of time and for a brief moment appeared in human shape in the person of Jesus to reveal God to mankind.

Matthew and Luke, whose Gospels are thought to have been published in the final two decades of the first century (AD 80–100), appended their birth stories as an introductory supplement to their compilation. The Infancy Gospels stand on their own. All four evangelists begin their main story with an adult Jesus, (in his thirties, according to Lk 3:23), coming from nowhere and suddenly stepping into the limelight in AD 29, in the fifteenth year of the emperor of Rome, Tiberius.

In chronicling Jesus' infancy, Matthew and Luke agree only on a few basic points. The names of the protagonists are the same. The place of birth, the date and the permanent address of the family are identical in both accounts. They also claim, each in his own way, that the pregnancy of Mary was out of the ordinary. But on most other details they completely differ.

Regarding the contradictions between Matthew and Luke, the names of the ancestors of Jesus are irreconcilable. The original place of residence of the parents is the Galilean Nazareth in Luke, but apparently the Bethlehem of Judaea in Matthew. The extraordinary conception of Jesus through the Holy Spirit is announced only to Joseph in Matthew, and only to Mary in Luke. In Matthew, Joseph's first thought on noticing that Mary is expecting a child is that she has misbehaved; hence his intention to divorce her. There is no question in Matthew of Jesus being born in an improvised shelter. The family is found by the wise men in a *house* in Bethlehem. Only Matthew reports the apparition of a prodigious star, the visit of the Magi and the vicious intervention of Herod, the flight of the Holy Family to Egypt and their subsequent choice of Nazareth in Galilee as their permanent place of residence. A final distinctive mark of Matthew's infancy narrative is the presence of five biblical proof texts, Old Testament quotations introduced to demonstrate that in the events connected with the birth of Jesus biblical prophecies have been realized. The first of these – 'Behold, a virgin shall conceive' (Isa 7:14 in Mt 1:23) – is of crucial importance.

Peculiar to Luke is the account relating to John the Baptist. This consists of the annunciation by the angel Gabriel of Mary's pregnancy in Nazareth, the travel of Mary from Galilee to Judaea to visit Elizabeth, the census bringing Joseph and Mary from Nazareth to Bethlehem, the birth of Jesus in a stable, the greeting of the newborn by shepherds and angels, the circumcision of Jesus and his presentation in the Temple, and the return of the family from Jerusalem to their home in Nazareth. Further sections belonging to Luke's special material are the three hymns, known as the *Magnificat*, the *Benedictus* and *Nunc dimittis*, sung respectively by Mary or Elizabeth, Zechariah and Simeon.

Since religious authority dislikes contradictions in its authoritative texts, efforts have been deployed from the early centuries of the Christian era by the official revisers and commentators of the Gospels to eliminate the manifest discrepancies between the infancy narratives of Matthew and Luke. A good example of this unifying tendency is exhibited in the *Diatessaron* or Gospel harmony, a combination of the four Gospels into a single narrative, compiled by the second-century author Tatian, a native of Assyria (Northern Iraq). In his version of the events he first reproduces Luke's account of the birth and circumcision of Jesus and the visit of mother and child to Jerusalem. Then he records the arrival of the Magi, the violent action of

Herod and the precipitate trip of the Holy Family to Egypt. The *Diatessaron* failed to supplant the four Gospels, and at the end the separate narratives triumphed, notwithstanding the problems generated by their contradictions. To attempt a full reconciliation of the two Infancy Gospels is a patently lost cause: squaring the circle would be easier than reducing the two into a single coherent unity.

In view of all the complications, discrepancies and contradictions displayed in the two infancy narratives, without mentioning the substantial number of legendary features contained in them (dreams, angels, a miraculous star, etc.), it is not surprising that they have been a subject of concern for the representatives of the common Christian tradition in modern times more than in antiquity. They have worried not only the literalist or fundamentalist interpreters of the New Testament, but also pious scholars who felt duty-bound to uphold the teaching of the Church. They have all been struggling to produce a smooth and unified version which they have achieved only at a price. These exegetes have been happy to settle the problem of the virginal conception by simply calling it a miracle. They have tried to identify the star of Bethlehem as a genuine comet, falling star or meteor. In the not too far distant past, we quite often encountered around Christmas in the columns of the newspapers academics, no doubt steeped in science, but unquestionably ignorant of ancient literature, who advanced with great conviction half-baked 'definitive' solutions of the dilemma. In the twenty-first century, their discoveries would be publicized in television documentaries in which a computer-reconstructed course of the star of the Magi would be presented as the ultimate optical proof.

As for the census ordered, according to Luke, by the

emperor Augustus and administered by Quirinius, self-appointed defenders of Gospel truth still try to find ways and means to fit it into the end period of the reign of Herod the Great. It seems that sailing between Scylla and Charybdis proves as hazardous today as it used to be in olden times.

Let me select a few typical examples of exegetical acrobatics. In connection with the virgin birth, C. E. B. Cranfield, the noted Protestant New Testament scholar, has committed a double faux pas. First he has presented the issue upside down and has stressed that 'up to the present no proof of its *non-historicity* has been produced',[2] as though the historicity of the virginal conception could be presumed and non-historicity is the alternative that requires demonstration. Furthermore he has used his editorial authority to compel the liberal-minded authors of the relevant volume of the reputable series *International Critical Commentary* to water down the main concluding remark on chapter 2 of the Gospel of Matthew, which they have declared to be 'not the stuff out of which history is made'. Under duress, the two renowned writers W. D. Davies and Dale C. Allison were obliged to add: 'But as the New Testament editor, Dr Cranfield, urges, the readers should note that other critical scholars reckon with the possibility that the narratives contained in this section . . . may have much more substantial factual basis than is envisaged here.'[3] Earlier the commentary on Matthew 1:18–25 carries an additional paragraph in parenthesis: '(We are aware – and the NT editor of this series, Dr Cranfield, has reminded us of this – that other competent critical scholars are firmly convinced of the historicity of the Virginal Conception, though not, of course, supposing that it can be conclusively proved by historico-critical methods, and that careful attention should be paid to their discussions of the relevant evidence as well as to the view expressed here).'[4]

Catholic students of the infancy narratives of Matthew and Luke seem to be particularly stretched between their wish to appear scholarly, yet not to undermine cherished and binding beliefs of their Church concerning the miraculous conception of Jesus and the perpetual virginity of Mary.

Thus John P. Meier, in his monumental work *A Marginal Jew: Rethinking the Historical Jesus*, comforts his readers with the thought that regarding the reliability of the Nativity accounts '*total* skepticism is not in order' (vol. I, p. 205). They are told that stories about angelic annunciations and miraculous births should be taken 'seriously', though not '*necessarily* . . . literally'. Also they are reassured that the tradition concerning the virginal conception does not represent a '*late* legend' (my italics in all three quotations).

For scholarly Catholic ecclesiastics equivocation seems to be the name of the game. The late Raymond Brown, whose monumental book *The Birth of the Messiah* (1993), which runs to 752 pages and is greatly respected by many, is the primary example of the position of 'having your cake and eating it'. He recognizes that angelic appearances, virginal conception and the marvellous star are 'patently legendary themes', that Matthew and Luke contradict each other, and that neither account is likely to be truly historical. But when it comes to the crunch, he opts for what he admits to be a 'retrogressively conservative' position, and is willing to shock his progressive critics even more by affirming that it is easier to explain the New Testament evidence of the virginal conception by positing a historical basis for it than by accepting it as pure theological creation. No surprise that reviewing *The Birth of the Messiah* the celebrated literary scholar Frank Kermode has attributed Brown's refusal to acknowledge the made-up character of Matthew's birth story to his eagerness to secure the Catholic Church's *imprimatur* for his book. Hence the ironical conclusion: 'Giving up the virgin birth might be bad for people'.[5]

Other Christian scholars have felt no reluctance to call a spade a spade. In the considered judgement of Rudolf Bultmann, one of the greatest New Testament exegetes of the last century, the original Semitic report of Matthew's Infancy Gospel contained nothing about the virgin birth. It was a motif unheard of in the Jewish environment of the age, he stated, and it was first added to the Gospel account in the course of its transformation in Hellenism.[6] More recently one of the most respected Jesus scholars, E. P. Sanders, also asserted without the slightest hesitation that the birth narratives are 'the clearest cases of invention' in the Gospels.[7] As for the saying, 'I wouldn't put it past God to arrange a virgin birth if He wanted, but I very much doubt if He would', it is attributed, genuine or apocryphal, to David Jenkins, the outspoken former Anglican bishop of Durham.

In my recent book *The Passion* (Penguin, 2005), devoted to the study of the trial and crucifixion of Jesus, I played the detective who had to confront issues of real history on the basis of ancient literary evidence. I tried to determine the relation of the New Testament story to Jewish and Roman court procedures in first-century Palestine, and to evaluate the reliability of the Gospel portraits of Pilate and Caiaphas compared to parallel Jewish and Roman sources. Facing the Infancy Gospels, writer and reader find themselves in a quite different world. Here the independent investigator's duty is to deal with the birth stories in the

Gospels in the same way as he would deal with any other problem of the history of religions. His first task is to sift the evidence, and separate morsels of fact from legendary accretions. This done, it will be possible to gain an insight into the genesis, purpose and significance of the religious ideas surrounding the birth of Jesus, a Jewish child who was first to be proclaimed the Messiah of Israel, then the Son of God, before rising even higher up on the ladder and being worshipped as God the Son, the Second Person of the Most Holy Trinity.

There is only one safe method to approach an ancient text such as the infancy narrative. We will have to begin with textual interpretation, the analysis of the evidence, verse-by-verse, line-by-line, and when necessary word-by-word. The findings of this investigation will then be compared with all the relevant information assembled from the parallel Jewish documents, biblical and post-biblical, and from the sources of classical literature and history. It is only after the establishment of the significance of the details that we will be able to penetrate the meaning of the New Testament story of the Nativity which in time evolved into the religious complex called Christmas.

3

The genealogies of Jesus

The Bible is full of family trees which strike most readers – apart from addicts of genealogical research – as far from fascinating, not to say plain boring. Yet they can be rich in meaning and in their variations reveal secret purposes. Scriptural genealogies have a threefold significance. When paraphrased, they may serve as an abridged account of history, but can also be used for two practical, legal purposes. The first of these is to demonstrate the legitimacy of kings and priests. Evidence of direct descent from the house of David was indispensable for succession to the throne, and as we will discover from the Infancy Gospels of Matthew and Luke, for the establishment of someone's Messianic status. It was also essential for a Jewish priest, holding a hereditary office handed down from father to son, to be able to prove that he belonged to a family which could trace its line back to Aaron in the tribe of Levi. Without such a pedigree he would lose his livelihood and would not be permitted to function in the Temple of Jerusalem. A genealogical table could also be useful in contested cases of inheritance, that is, when someone claimed entitlement to ancestral property.

As a rule, scriptural genealogies follow the male line, going from father to son. The most elaborate biblical list can be found in the First Book of the Chronicles. No less than nine chapters at the beginning of the book purport to record human and Jewish history starting with Adam, that is to say, in biblical terms from the creation, and going as far as the family of Saul, the first king of Israel, which in our terminology is the end of the eleventh century BC. As one may expect, genealogies usually proceed in a descending order. At the head of the list stands the patriarch, the first forebear of the group, and the family tree descends from father to son in a monotonous sequence of 'begettings'. Sometimes, however, a variation is introduced in that the chronicler reverses the order, beginning at the end and ending with the beginning. For instance, the genealogy of the great post-exilic priestly leader Ezra, who flourished in the fifth century BC, is traced back from him to the brother of Moses, Aaron, who probably lived some eight hundred years earlier in the thirteenth century BC (Ezra 7:1–5). These few snippets of information will come in useful when we turn to the two genealogies of Jesus that figure in the Gospels of Matthew and Luke. As we shall see, neither of them is absolutely straightforward – Matthew's is more exciting than that of Luke – and both have a hidden agenda to pursue.

Matthew's genealogy

As in many other aspects of their recounting of the story of the Nativity, Matthew and Luke follow different paths in their presentation of the pedigree of Jesus. The genealogical table constitutes the opening section of Matthew (Mt 1:1–17), whereas the parallel material in Luke is placed outside the birth narrative and is linked to the account of the baptism of Jesus by John (Lk 3:23–38). As we shall see the two genealogies also proceed in opposite directions.

Mt 1:1–6
The book of the genealogy of Jesus, the son of David, the son of Abraham. Abraham was the father of Isaac, and Isaac the father of Jacob, and Jacob the father of Judah and his brothers, and Judah the father of Perez by **Tamar***, and Perez the father of Hezron, and Hezron the father of Ram, and Ram the father of Amminadab, and Amminadab the father of Nahshon, and Nahshon the father of Salmon, and Salmon the father of Boaz by* **Rahab***, and Boaz the father of Obed by* **Ruth***, and Obed the father of Jesse, and Jesse the father of David the king. And David was the father of Solomon by* **the wife of Uriah***.*

Matthew deliberately imitates the Old Testament when he chooses for the title of his Gospel the familiar biblical heading, 'The Book of the generations'. His model is the biblical Genesis, where the same formula, 'Book of generations', introduces the first family tree of mankind, running from Adam to the sons of Noah, from the creation to the flood (Gen 5:1–32). Matthew at once confronts his readers with two key figures of Jewish history, Abraham, the ancestor of Israel, the father of God's chosen people, and David, the founder of the royal dynasty of Israel, and the forefather of the final ruler, the Messiah. Jesus is characterized straight from the start as Son of Abraham and Son of David, but the main emphasis seems to lie on the second title.

Whilst pretending to offer a direct proof of Jesus' Davidic descent, Matthew's list is far from simple, indeed it is highly artificial. He arranges it so that the ancestors fall for no obvious reason into three periods of fourteen generations. No one so far has come up with a satisfactory explanation for this 3×14. Fourteen has no known significance in Jewish thought apart from being the double of the mystical number seven. It has been suggested that 3×14, being equal to 6×7, would indicate that with Jesus the final seventh period of seven generations would begin, but all this sounds laboured and unconvincing. Why would Matthew choose 14 as his basic unit and not the usual figure of 7?

So if Matthew is to be believed, forty-two generations separate Jesus from Abraham and twenty-eight from David. A preliminary glance at the genealogy of Jesus in Luke reveals striking differences. Matthew's register is considerably shorter even for the period covered by both of them, without taking into account the prehistory added by Luke, which extends far beyond Abraham. Did Matthew artificially shorten the third period in order to reduce it to fourteen generations?

The opening section of the genealogy generally mirrors the Hebrew Bible, but it departs from normal Jewish practice in one important respect: it includes the names of four women. The fifth name, Mary mother of Jesus, will appear in the final generation in the last set of fourteen. This is a remarkable oddity as biblical genealogy always runs on the paternal line. As far as royal succession is concerned, we read in the Book of Ecclesiasticus or Wisdom of Ben Sira, one of the Apocrypha dating to the beginning of the second century BC: 'The heritage of the king is from son to son only' (Ecclus 45:25). A similar rule governs the inheritance of property too. Matthew's reference to women is patently not regular – there are only four, not fourteen, names of females in the first fourteen generations – nor is it accidental. It has an unspecified message to convey. If we discount Mary, who has a very particular role to play, what the other women mentioned have in common is that they all seem to be of foreign stock or have a foreign husband.

Let us look first at the problem of intermarriage with non-Jewish women among the forebears of Jesus. In the patriarchal age the descendants of Jacob, no doubt to avoid inbreeding, chose wives for themselves and their sons from among the daughters of the inhabitants of the country. Judah, who is on Matthew's list, married a Canaanite girl by the name of Shua (Gen 38:2) and Tamar, the wife of his son Er, was also a Canaanite. After she had lost her husband and Judah had refused to marry her to his last surviving son, employing a stratagem she made herself pregnant by Judah and bore him twin sons. Another Canaanite woman, Rahab, also on Matthew's list, was married to one of Joshua's men, Salmon. The latter's son, Boaz, took for wife a Moabite woman, Ruth, who became the great-grandmother of David (Ruth 4:13–22). The fourth person listed in the female ancestry of Jesus was Bathsheba, whom King David acquired as wife after ordering the commander of his army to ensure that Bathsheba's Hittite husband, Uriah, would not return alive from the battlefield.

The other distinguishing feature of three out of the four of the women concerned is some kind of marital irregularity. Tamar, the widowed daughter-in-law of Judah, pretended to be a prostitute on the roadside and seduced her father-in-law, who had sex with her without realizing who she was. Rahab was a professional prostitute from Jericho and Bathsheba committed adultery with David. However, the first two women are held blameless by the Bible and Jewish tradition. In Tamar's case, the guilt lay with Judah, who prevented another of his sons from marrying Tamar. In a rather unusual way she just reasserted her right to bear a son in the family. Rahab redeemed herself when she saved the life of the spies sent by Joshua to reconnoitre the land of Canaan (Josh 6:25). As for the case of Bathsheba, the real culpability lay with David, who not only slept with another man's wife, but to all intents and purposes murdered the husband. The Moabite Ruth was guiltless.

When all these considerations are taken into account, the most likely reason for Matthew to single out these women and record their names in the ancestry of the Messiah is his intention to underline that, although Jesus, the son of Abraham, was Jewish, his remote lineage comprised non-Jews too, at least on the female side, and that in consequence he was of interest to non-Jews also. Here is the first surprise disclosure in a genealogical list which is normally regarded as dull. A bigger one is to follow.

Mt 1:7–16
And Solomon was the father of Rehoboam. And Rehoboam the father of Abijah, and Abijah the father of Asa, and Asa the father of Jehoshaphat, and Jehoshaphat the father of Joram, and Joram the father of Uzziah, and Uzziah the father of Jotham, and Jotham the father of Ahaz, and Ahaz the father of Hezekiah, and Hezekiah the father of Manasseh, and Manasseh the father of Amos, and Amos the father of Josiah, and Josiah the father of Jechoniah and his brothers, at the time of the deportation to Babylon. And after the deportation to Babylon: Jechoniah was the father of Shealtiel, and Shealtiel the father of Zerubbabel, and Zerubbabel the father of Abiud, and Abiud the father of Eliakim, and Eliakim the father of Azor, and Azor the father of Zadok, and Zadok the father of Achim, and Achim the father of Eliud, and Eliud the father of

*Eleazar, and Eleazar the father of Matthan, and Matthan the
father of Jacob, and Jacob the father of Joseph the husband of **Mary**,
of whom Jesus **was born**, who is called Christ.*

From Solomon to Jechoniah, a variant of Jehoiachin (see
Jer 27:20 as against 2 Kings 24:6), Matthew more or less
rigorously excerpts the Books of Kings in the Bible and
lists the royal descendents of David. Luke, as will appear,
follows a totally different path. With Jechoniah's grandson Zerubbabel, the princely leader who brought back a
group of Jews from Babylonia to Judaea in 538 BC, the
evangelist reaches the end of the Old Testament record
serving as the source for his genealogy. From then on,
both Matthew and Luke depend on documents unattested
in, and partly contradicted by, Scripture. For instance, the
son of Zerubbabel in Matthew's genealogy of Jesus is
Abiud, while in Luke the corresponding forefather is called
Rhesa. However, one of the Old Testament books has
preserved a detailed record of Zerubbabel's descendents,
giving the names of no less than seven of his sons: Meshul-
lam, Hananiah, Hashubah, Ohel, Berechiah, Hasadiah and
Jushab-hesed (1 Chr 3:19–20), yet neither Abiud nor Rhesa
figures among them. The other individuals down to Jacob,
the father of Joseph, that is, the grandfather of Jesus, are
totally unknown entities and as will be shown with possibly
one exception they all differ from the corresponding ancestors in Luke's family tree. Short of being held to be entirely
fictitious, the names must have been borrowed from traditions relating to the genealogical table of the house of
David, unknown in the Bible, in Josephus or in rabbinic
literature (see pp. 42–44).

Throughout the whole series, the same formula, 'A was
the father of B', literally, A 'begot' or 'procreated' B, is

employed as befits a Jewish genealogical record always listing fathers and sons. But when Matthew arrives at Mary, the fifth woman on his list, although without hesitation he still calls Joseph her husband (*anêr*), he modifies the standard pattern 'A begot B, B begot C', etc., and changes the linking expression from the active 'begot' to the passive 'was begotten' or 'was born', from the Greek *egennêsen* to *egennêthê*. Clearly the evangelist has a message to pass on. He is determined to avoid an expression which would indicate that Jesus was the normal child of Joseph in a genealogy whose aim is to prove that Jesus descended from David *through Joseph*.

The fluctuating textual tradition reveals that something unusual is afoot here. Significant variations in the Greek codices and in some of the ancient translations of the passage in Matthew indicate that already in the early centuries of Christianity the copyists and interpreters of this verse were aware of problems and difficulties arising from Matthew 1:16. The hesitations they display indicate the pains the copyists have taken to come up with a suitable formula.

The majority of the Greek manuscripts contain the awkward text that has just been quoted: 'and Jacob [was] the father of Joseph, the husband of Mary, of whom Jesus *was born* [or *begotten*], who is called Christ'. What the tradition seeks to obfuscate in this case is the identity of the father. It is not explicitly stated that Joseph, the husband of Mary, did not beget Jesus, but neither are we told who did. In other words the idea of the virgin birth which will be developed a few verses further on is anticipated here by stealth.

Nevertheless, this doctrinal revision was not implemented with full success. Other Greek manuscripts and the Old Latin translation of Matthew 1:16 offer a very different message. They insert a reference to Mary, but safeguard the regular wording of the genealogy which implies that the paternity belongs to Joseph. They read, 'Joseph to whom the virgin Mary was betrothed, *begot* Jesus who was called Christ'. The same plain-speaking has been preserved also in the Dialogue of Timothy and Aquila, a Greek composition dated to the fifth century: 'Joseph *begot* Jesus who was called Christ' (ed. by F. C. Conybeare in *The Dialogues of Athanasius and Zacchaeus*, 1898).

Of all the textual testimonies that run counter to the traditional orthodox stance, perhaps the most significant is the oldest Semitic witness, an early Syriac version of Matthew. It was found in the library of the monastery of St Catherine on Mount Sinai by two learned and adventurous Scottish ladies, Mrs Agnes Smith Lewis and Mrs Margaret Dunlop Gibson and published in 1894. The so-called Sinaitic Syriac or syr[syn] characteristically preserves even in connection with Jesus the formula which runs through the whole genealogy: 'Joseph to whom was betrothed the virgin Mary, *begot* Jesus'. But this is not a one-off accident. Five verses later, in Matthew 1:21, the same Syriac version characteristically supplements the words of the angel addressed to Joseph, 'she [Mary] will bear a son', by adding 'she will bear a son *for you*', which is a commonly used expression to denote paternity. Both passages concur in making crystal clear who the father is meant to be and revealing what must have been the Semitic original subjacent to Matthew 1:16.

The first surprise in Matthew's family tree was the inclusion of women; the second is the compelling case for a genealogy of Jesus transmitted in Jewish-Christian circles in Hebrew or Aramaic, in which just as Joseph is the son of Jacob, Jesus is said to have been 'begotten' by Joseph. Note also that there is no mention of the virginity of Mary in the main tradition and the same silence on Mary characterizes the family tree supplied by Luke too. Jesus is portrayed in Matthew's genealogy as the rightful heir of David, being the son of Joseph, scion of the royal house of Israel. The same position is confirmed, as will be shown in chapter 5, by the doctrine embraced by the Ebionites, a Judeo-Christian community which survived well into the third/fourth century as reported by Church Fathers.

The issue of the paternity of Joseph will be discussed in full detail à propos of the virginal conception of Mary (pp. 62–81).

Mt 1:17

So all the generations from Abraham to David were fourteen generations, and from David to the deportation to Babylon fourteen generations, and from the deportation to Babylon to Christ fourteen generations.

Matthew had to manipulate his list to arrive at a symmetrical periodization of three times fourteen units. The last fourteen generations take us in the post-exilic era of biblical history from Shealtiel, the son of Jechoniah and the father of Zerubbabel, through a line of otherwise unknown individuals to Joseph and to Jesus. But here Matthew, notwithstanding his claim of fourteen generations, supplies only thirteen names: Shealtiel, Zerubbabel, Abiud, Eliakim, Azor, Zadok, Achim, Eliud, Eleazar, Matthan, Jacob, Joseph, Jesus. Has one generation been accidentally dropped by later scribes? If so, it is amazing that no subsequent copyist has tried to remedy the error. Was perhaps the authority of Matthew's textual tradition so great that people turned a blind eye on his apparent lack of elementary arithmetical skill? Or did the ancients realize that in a genre like the Infancy Gospels literal correctness comes second to other, higher purposes?

Luke's genealogy

The first impression we gain when we compare the often discrepant names advanced by Luke with the list of Matthew is that the documents before us are unlikely to be reliable from the point of view of history. As has been pointed out, Luke's genealogy of Jesus is longer than Matthew's. The two coincide only between Abraham and David, where both evangelists directly rely on the information contained in the Hebrew Bible from Genesis to the Books of Kings and Chronicles. However, Luke's genealogy is found outside his Infancy Gospel and contrary to Matthew's it follows an ascending direction starting with Jesus and continues the line, following biblical precedents, beyond Abraham up to Adam, the father of mankind.

Lk 3:23–38

Jesus . . . was . . . the son (as was supposed) of Joseph, the son of Heli, the son of Matthat [Matthan in Mt], the son of Levi, the son of Melchi, the son of Jannai, the son of Joseph, the son of Mattathias, the son of Amos, the son of Nahum, the son of Esli, the son of Naggai, the son of Maath, the son of Mattathias, the son of Semein, the son of Josech, the son of Joda, the son of Joanan, the son of Rhesa, the son of Zerubbabel, the son of Shealtiel, the son of Neri, the son of Melchi, the son of Addi, the son of Cosam, the son of Elmadam, the son of Er, the son of Joshua, the son of Eliezer, the son of Jorim, the son of Matthat, the son of Levi, the son of Simeon, the son of Judah, the son of Joseph, the son of Jonam, the son of Eliakim, the son of Melea, the son of Menna, the son of Mattatha, the son of Nathan, the son of David, the son of Jesse, the son of Obed, the son of Boaz, the son of Sala [Salmon in Mt], *the son of Nahshon, the son of Amminadab, the son of Admin, the son of Arni, the son of Hezron, the son of Perez, the son of Judah, the son of Jacob, the son of Isaac, the son of Abraham, the son of Terah, the son of Nahor, the son of Serug, the son of Reu, the son of Peleg, the son of Eber, the son of Shelah, the son of Cainan, the son of Arphaxad, the son of Shem, the son of Noah, the son of Lamech, the son of Methuselah, the son of Enoch, the son of Jared, the son of Mahalaleel, the son of Cainan, the son of Enos, the son of Seth, the son of Adam, the son of God.*

In order to make possible a comparison between the lists of Matthew and Luke, the order of the names in Luke will be reversed to begin with God and Adam and finish with Joseph and Jesus.

Matthew	*Luke*
	God
	Adam
	Seth
	Enos
	Cainan
	Mahalaleel
	Jared
	Enoch
	Methuselah
	Lamech

Matthew	*Luke*
	Noah
	Shem
	Arphaxad
	Cainan
	Shelah
	Eber
	Peleg
	Reu
	Serug
	Nahor
	Terah
Abraham	**Abraham**
Isaac	**Isaac**
Jacob	**Jacob**
Judah [by *Tamar*]	**Judah**
Perez	**Perez**
Hezron	**Hezron**
Aram	Arni [? **Aram**]
	Admin
Amminadab	**Amminadab**
Nahshon	**Nahshon**
Salmon [by *Rahab*]	**Sala**
Boaz [by *Ruth*]	**Boaz**
Obed	**Obed**
Jesse	**Jesse**
David [by the *wife of Uriah*]	**David**
Solomon	Nathan
Rehoboam	Mattatha
Abijah	Menna

Matthew	Luke
Asaph	Melea
Jehoshaphat	Jonam
	Joseph
	Judah
	Simeon
Joram	Levi
Uzziah	Matthat
Jotham	Jorim
Ahaz	Eliezer
Hezekiah	Joshua
Manasseh	Er
Amos	Elmadam
Josiah	Cosam
	Addi
	Melchi
Jechoniah	Neri
Shealtiel	**Shealtiel**
Zerubbabel	**Zerubbabel**
Abiud	Rhesa
	Joanan
	Joda
	Josech
	Semein
Eliakim	Mattathias
Azor	Maath
	Naggai
Zadok	Esli
	Nahum
Achim	Amos
Eliud	Mattathias

Matthew	Luke
	Joseph
Eleazar	Jannai
	Melchi
	Levi
Matthan	Matthat [?**Matthan**]
Jacob	Heli
Joseph [husband of *Mary*]	**Joseph** [*supposed* father]
Jesus	**Jesus**

A few comments are apposite for the explanation of the two parallel lists. Only the names printed in bold characters are common to both Infancy Gospels. Compared to Matthew, Luke's genealogy is fuller but is also more straightforward. Starting with Jesus, he traces back his line in seventy-seven stages, a multiple of the mystic number 7, to the first man, Adam. Jesus is forty-two generations away from King David (not twenty-eight as in Matthew), and another fourteen generations take him back to Abraham. Between Shealtiel and Jesus twenty-two names are given in Luke against Matthew's thirteen. If we keep Joseph out of the count, the only common ancestor of Jesus in both lists (other than Shealtiel and Zerubbabel) is Matthan, provided that Luke's corresponding name Matthat is considered as a mere scribal variant. But he could just as well be a different person.

On the whole, we seem to be faced in Luke with a less stereotyped, normal genealogy. In Matthew, only the name of Jacob is repeated; in Luke we find Joseph three times, Matthat twice, Matthata and Matthathias once each, but it is not impossible that the last three names, designating four persons, are ultimately one and the same (Mattathias).

It is furthermore significant to observe that no woman is mentioned, not even Mary. The sole departure from a straight list of sons and fathers concerns Luke's qualification that Joseph was the '*supposed*' father of Jesus. But this insertion is patently secondary and parenthetic. Its aim is to make the genealogy conform to the earlier story of the virginal conception and explain away the conflict with the paternal quality of Joseph (Lk 1:26–38; see also chapter 5).

The royal descent is only implicitly asserted insofar as David is given as one of Jesus' many forefathers. Curiously the line of succession is traced not through Solomon and the Jewish kings as in Matthew, but through Nathan, another son of David, whose descendents did not sit on the royal throne. In fact none of them is mentioned in the Old Testament. However, no specific importance should be attached to the absence of emphasis on royal extraction since earlier Luke has already twice characterized Joseph as a member of the house of David (Lk 1:27; 2:4). Nevertheless, the diminished stress on the Davidic connection may insinuate that for Luke Jesus is more than an heir to royalty. He has previously called him '*the Son of the Most High*' (Lk 1:32) and he is in the last resort the counterpart of Adam, also designated as '*the son of God*'. If, as is usually thought, Luke was a disciple of Paul, the ending of Luke's genealogy would echo the Pauline doctrine of the two Adams – the first and the last, the father of mankind and Christ – in 1 Corinthians 15:45–49.

A final remark on the two genealogies. The substantial differences between Matthew and Luke are beyond dispute and have always puzzled the theologians and the Bible interpreters of the Church. New Testament scholars have attempted since time immemorial to iron out the discrepancies and reconcile them, but without visible success. We encounter the first major effort to solve the dilemma as far back as the early third century. It is attached to the name of Julius Africanus, a learned Palestinian Christian. In his opinion the contradictions between the lists of Matthew and Luke must stem from the Jewish law concerning leviratic marriage. Leviratic or brother-in-law marriage entails the moral obligation on a brother to marry his deceased brother's childless widow. The first male issue of the new union becomes by legal fiction the heir of the dead brother, so that his line would continue and his property would remain undivided. If so, Julius Africanus must have surmised, the disagreements between the two genealogical tables arose from one evangelist recording the name of the biological father and the other that of the legal one. At closer inspection, however, this apparently clever idea turns out to be a failure. It could no doubt account for occasional diversity, but it is unsuitable as an explanation for two lists, which disagree with one another so fundamentally and on so many points. In fact between David and Joseph the two genealogies propose only two, or at best three, names (Shealtiel, Zerubbabel and Matthan/ Matthat) that are the same! Other theories accept that complete harmonization is impossible and opt therefore for an entirely new solution. The two lists vary because we are faced with the genealogies of two different persons, namely the two parents. Matthew gives Joseph's family tree and Luke Mary's. But this theory is totally unfounded as there is no hint whatever in Luke that he is dealing with Mary. In fact, not even her name appears anywhere on the list of ancestors. Besides, what possible purpose could a maternal genealogy serve in a Jewish setting?

Unless we assume the not impossible theory that both evangelists largely shaped their documents themselves –

this would not be the only well-meant act of creativity (*pia fraus*) in religious history – the most probable explanation of the enigma is that the aim pursued by Matthew and Luke in compiling their genealogies was doctrinal, and not historical. To prove the Davidic family connection of Jesus, a prerequisite of his Messianic standing, they probably employed documents. But since their records are contradictory, they must have laid their hands on separate registers of David's descendants. All they needed to do was to re-edit them so that they both ended (or started) with Joseph and Jesus (or Jesus and Joseph). This was definitely possible, as we know from Jewish as well as from Christian sources that genealogical lists of this sort were circulating among the Jewish inhabitants of Palestine at the beginning of the Christian era.

Let us start with Jewish parallels. Among these particular attention must be drawn to rabbinic documents that refer to the Scroll of Pedigree or Megillat Yohasin, a written family record which was, we are told, found in Jerusalem purportedly in the first century AD. Its importance lies in the assertion that the famous teacher Hillel the Elder, an older contemporary of Jesus, was a direct descendent of King David (yTaanit 68a). Another rabbinic text gives the same statement concerning Hillel's Davidic connection as an illustration of the messianic prophecy 'The sceptre shall not depart from Judah' in Gen 49:10 (Genesis Rabbah 98:8). Reference to these texts is meant only to imply that a document such as the Scroll of Pedigree actually existed, without taking on board what is asserted in them, namely Hillel's Davidic ancestry. In fact we can nowhere find any trace of Hillel himself alleging that he was the Messiah or that anyone else proclaimed him as such. By contrast, we are told that the head of Babylonian Jewry, Rab Huna (*c.* AD 200) was actually thought to be a member of the Messianic tribe of Judah.

On the Christian side, the second-century writer Hegesippus, whose work, or at least part of it, has been preserved in the *Ecclesiastical History* of Eusebius (3:20, 1–6), reports that the emperor Domitian (AD 81–96), in his effort to wipe out all the Jewish revolutionary movements, decided to rid Palestine of the last surviving representatives of the family of David. Not surprisingly, these Church historians include in the royal house of David some of the late first-century relatives of Jesus. Eusebius testifies to the rumour that the grandsons of Jude, the brother of the Lord, that is to say the great-nephews of Jesus, had to suffer as a result of the Roman persecution. However, assuming that the story is true, such a persecution could not have been organized unless the local authorities had possessed evidence on which to institute charges.

Julius Africanus, who has been cited earlier (p. 42), further asserts that as late as the early third century, some of the inhabitants of Nazareth still paraded as 'The Master's People' (*Desposunoi*). They claimed that they were relatives of Jesus. What is more, they said they could prove this with 'private records' and apparently they 'took pride in preserving the memory of their aristocratic origin' (Eusebius, *Ecclesiastical History* 1:7, 14). Julius Africanus had a critical mind and remained sceptical of the reliability of these tales. Nevertheless Eusebius' records indicate that such documents, however inauthentic, continued to circulate. If that was the case in the third century, it is even more likely that Matthew and Luke at the end of the first century could come across some of them and incorporate them in their Infancy Gospels as evidence of the Messianic entitlement of Jesus.

In sum, since the Davidic descent is an indispensable factor, the claim that Jesus was the son of Joseph 'of the house of David' acquires outstanding importance. However, establishing a justifiable claim to the Messianic title is one thing and the notion of the virginal conception of Jesus quite another. By endeavouring to combine the two, Matthew and Luke unwittingly confused the aim of the genealogies. For if in order to proclaim the virgin birth, they had to deny the real paternity of Joseph, they were unavoidably bound to undermine the royal Messianic claim of Jesus.

4

The idea of miraculous births in Judaism and Paganism

On the essential topics of the Nativity tale both Matthew and Luke concur. God's Holy Spirit is said to have played an essential, though ill-defined, part in Mary's pregnancy and brought about what is termed in traditional Christian parlance a virginal conception. This doctrine of the virginal conception and birth of Jesus forms an essential part of the teaching of the Church and on a more popular level of the Christmas story: Mary became pregnant and gave birth to a son without ceasing to be a virgin and without the participation of a man in the process of impregnation. This dogma is exclusively based on a few verses of the Infancy Gospels; no other section of the New Testament inside or outside the Gospels makes any reference to it either explicitly or even implicitly.

Though such a virginal conception is unparalleled in the Hebrew Bible or in post-biblical Jewish literature in antiquity, stories implying some kind of miraculous birth circulated in abundance in the various corners of the ancient world, both among Jews and among pagans. It is necessary, therefore, to form an idea of the cultural background that conditioned the thinking of the writers and the readership of the New Testament before tackling the Gospel accounts themselves.

To grasp the import of the imagery associated with

miraculous births, we must bear in mind that in the age and in the civilization of Jesus the knowledge of physiology was fairly rudimentary and the mystery of fertility was steeped in religious awe. In pagan antiquity fruitfulness was thought to depend on special gods or goddesses and in biblical Judaism on the one God of Israel. According to the colourful language of the Hebrew Bible, this God had the power to close the womb or to open it. If he closed it, the woman remained sterile. If he opened the womb, she became fertile. In short, in some sense every pregnancy was seen as mediated by God, as a divine gift, but some more so than others. However, in the Jewish view, even a miraculous, i.e. heavenly assisted, conception presupposed prior sexual intercourse. The spouses were expected to play their part in the process.

Extraordinary birth stories in the Old Testament

To begin with, Jesus' birth should be considered against the 'miraculous' or quasi-miraculous pregnancies reported in a number of Old Testament narratives. The women in question are all depicted as barren, having suffered sterility for a long time, and in several instances they are elderly matrons far beyond the childbearing age. The wives of several of the Hebrew Patriarchs are reported to have been infertile for substantial periods. Sarah, the spouse of Abraham, was still childless when she reached the age of ninety. She is expressly described as having passed the menopause – 'it had ceased to be with her after the manner of women' (Gen 18:11) – and to crown her handicaps, in the person of Abraham she had a centenarian for a husband: 'After I have grown old, and my husband is old, shall I have pleasure?' (Gen 18:12). Nevertheless, by virtue of a divine promise Sarah was enabled to give birth to Isaac (Gen 21:1). Isaac's wife, Rebekah, was also barren, but Isaac's persistent prayer made God intervene and the twins Esau and Jacob were 'miraculously' born (Gen 25:21–24). Jacob's hopes of posterity were equally frustrated for a long while and both his wives, Leah and Rachel, remained childless. But God took pity first on Leah, the unloved wife, and 'opened her womb', while her sister Rachel, Jacob's favourite, continued to be without progeny. Exasperated, Rachel tried to blame her condition on Jacob, but he angrily reminded her that barrenness was a woman's failure and that ultimately pregnancy was a divine gift: 'Am I in the place of God, who has withheld from you the fruit of the womb?' Later, in answer to Rachel's supplication, God 'remembered her and opened her womb', and the much beloved patriarch Joseph was born (Gen 29:31; 30:2, 22–23). Likewise Hannah, the mother of the prophet Samuel, was unimpressed by the words of Elkanah, her male chauvinist of a husband, 'Am I not more to you than ten sons?', until her prayers, repeated year in year out, induced God to act and give her a male offspring (1 Sam 1:1–20).

In Luke's infancy narrative the tale of the pregnancy of Elizabeth, the mother of John the Baptist (Lk 1:7, 11–13, 18–20, 57), is modelled on the Samuel anecdote just cited. It is recounted in preparation of the story of the miraculous birth of Jesus. But while the dominant idea of divine participation in procuring pregnancy helps the understanding of the unusual conception of Jesus, the standard biblical solution of female infertility, the removal of long-term sterility through direct action of God, cannot be applied in Mary's case as she was young and unmarried. Neverthe-less, as we shall see (pp. 79–80), youth itself may hold the key to an unforeseen solution to the problem.

'Sons of God' and 'daughters of men'

The Old Testament and Jewish literature of the inter-Testamental age furnish an alternative opening. It consists of legends about progeny born out of the union of heavenly beings or angels and terrestrial women. For the sophisti-cated readers of our age such tales may look exceedingly silly and fanciful, but the Infancy Gospels were composed almost two millennia ago for people steeped in specu-lations of this sort. Weird birth stories, not unlike age-old oriental and Graeco-Roman myths, circulated among Jews in New Testament times, and the Jewish and Gentile public, addressed by the Infancy Gospels both in Palestine and in the Diaspora, was familiar with them. The starting point of the Jewish fables is the biblical Book of Genesis which has preserved the amazing tale of the 'sons of God'. They fell for the charms of the 'daughters of men' and, captivated by their beauty, they abandoned their comfort-able heavenly abode and came down to earth bodily to enjoy female company. As one might guess, the adventure quickly went awry. Their offspring turned out to be giants whose depravity brought on Noah's flood and almost completely destroyed mankind (Gen 6:1–4).

By 'sons of God' the Jews of the age of Jesus understood angels, as we learn from the Greek Septuagint translation of the Bible, the Book of Jubilees, a version of Genesis rewritten in the second century BC, the Dead Sea Scrolls and other ancient Jewish works. The misconduct of these heavenly 'playboys' is described with gusto in the First Book of Enoch (third/second century BC) and in later rabbinic literature. They initiated their girl friends in the use of all kinds of cosmetics, in particular in 'the art of making up the eyes' and as a result fornication entered the world. They also taught them spells, incantations and all kinds of wizardry (1 Enoch 8).

But Jewish thought did not restrict the attractiveness of female beauty to angels of the pre-diluvian age. A second-century BC version of the ordeals of the Patriarch Lamech can be read in the Genesis Apocryphon from Qumran, an Aramaic paraphrase of Genesis. At the sight of the brilliant light that filled the house and surrounded the baby Noah, Lamech began to wonder whether the child produced by Bathenosh was not really the son of an angel with whom his wife had consorted. Lamech's suspicion was soon dispelled by the firm protest of Bathenosh: 'I swear to you by the Holy Great One' – his furious wife expostulated – 'that this seed is yours and that [this] conception is from you. This fruit was planted by you . . . and by no stranger, or Watcher, or Son of Heaven . . .' (Gen Apocryphon 2). The bright light, which according to the story radiated from and around Noah, suggests that in the view of the Jews of that age the offspring of an angel and a woman was not necessarily evil. In the Bible and in post-biblical Judaism, light always had positive associations.

The idea of potential sexual rapport between angels and women continued to float in the air even as late as in New Testament times. Indeed, when St Paul forbade the female members of the church of Corinth to attend Christian assemblies with the head uncovered, he justified this prohibition by his belief that the sight of their hair might lead astray some passing-by sons of heaven: 'That is why a woman ought to have a veil on her head, *because of the angels*', Paul insisted (1 Cor 11:10). The influence of this legend on early Christian thought is attested by the author of the Protoevangelium of James, a New Testament apocryphon dating to the second half of the second century, which is full of popular speculation about Joseph, Mary and the child Jesus. According to Pseudo-James, when Mary was questioned by Joseph about her pregnancy, she protested under oath that she had no idea how it came about. (In this story there is no allusion to the annunciation by Gabriel.) It is not surprising in the circumstances that the first thought crossing Joseph's mind was that she was carrying the seed of an angel (Protoevangelium 13:2–14:1). The idea is clearly odd, but it is not unprecedented.

The metaphor of God 'begetting' humans

Matthew and Luke expressly call Mary's baby 'the Son of God'. In Matthew the designation is derived from biblical prophecy seen as fulfilled in Jesus. In Isaiah 7 the son conceived by the virgin is called Emmanuel or 'God with us', and his return from Egypt realizes the words placed on the lips of the Lord by the prophet Hosea, 'Out of Egypt have I called *my son*' (Hosea 11:1 in Mt 2:15). In Luke the angel Gabriel directly and explicitly announces the birth of 'the Son of the Most High' and 'the Son of God' (Lk 1:32, 35).

It is common knowledge that before the New Testament, the Hebrew Bible and the Dead Sea Scrolls regularly speak of 'Sons of God' and occasionally refer to God in figurative speech as 'begetting' or 'procreating' a human being. In the Bible and in writings produced during the centuries that followed the completion of the Old Testament, 'Son of God' occurs in a variety of meanings. In addition to the angels already discussed, among the humans 'Son of God' was the title of anyone believed in some way to be linked to God. Every male Israelite could pride himself on being a 'son of God', and reciprocally he was in a position to call God his Father. In the course of time the phrase was also applied – more and more restrictively – to the good Jews, to the especially holy Jews, culminating with the king of the Jews and finally with the Messiah, the most holy and powerful future ruler of Israel about whom we read in the Florilegium, one of the Dead Sea Scrolls, 'I will be his Father and he shall be my Son. He is the Branch of David' (see my *Jesus the Jew*, pp. 168–73).

The Jewish king, while the monarchy existed down to 586 BC, and the awaited royal Messiah after the Babylonian exile, were symbolically portrayed as *engendered* by the Deity: 'You are my son, today *I have begotten you*', we read in Psalm 2:7. The Rule of the Congregation among the Dead Sea Scrolls also speaks of God 'begetting' the Messiah (1 QSerekh a 2:11–12). The phrase in the Qumran Aramaic Apocalypse, 'The Son of God he will be proclaimed, and the Son of the Most High they will call him (4Q246, 2:1), whatever its precise meaning may be, is curiously reminiscent of Luke 1:32, 35 (see pp. 75–76).

It is universally agreed among experts that in Judaism the phrase is always used metaphorically; it never designates a person who is believed to be simultaneously man and God, a human being who also shares in some way divine nature. In this respect, from the monotheistic point of view the Jewish inhabitants of the Holy Land found themselves in a privileged position compared to those Jews and Gentiles who lived outside Palestine, in countries imbued with Graeco-Roman religious culture, full of legends about the miraculous, divinely effected birth of heroes and great leaders, past and present.

Miraculous births in the pagan world

Leaving aside classic Graeco-Roman mythology, with half-divine, half-human offspring resulting, for example from the amorous escapades of Zeus, fathering Heracles, Dionysus, Castor and Pollux, and Perseus out of Alcmene, Semele, Leda and Danae, we also encounter numerous allusions to the superhuman origin of historical personalities in ancient Greek and Latin literature. Let us ignore stories relating to early Roman history, such as Romulus having Mars as his father (Ovid, *Metamorphoses*, 14:805–28), and concentrate on figures closer to Jesus' time, who had the reputation of being fathered by a god.

The first of these to mention is Plato, that giant among Greek philosophers, who was believed to be 'not the son of Ariston, but of a visionary figure who came to Amphictione (Plato's mother) in the form of Apollo' (Origen quoting Celsus in *Against Celsus* 6:8). The legend repeated by Celsus further asserts that before Plato was born, 'Ariston [his father] was prevented from having sexual intercourse with Amphictione until she had brought forth the child which she had by Apollo' (Origen, *ibid.* 1:37) – a curious parallel to Matthew's remark concerning Joseph not 'knowing' Mary while she had Jesus in her womb (Mt 1:25, see p. 64).

As one might have guessed, Alexander the Great was also credited with divine origin. Olympias, his mother, is said to have been impregnated not by her husband Philip, king of Macedon, who was apparently afraid of sharing her bed because of her habit of sleeping with snakes, but by Zeus (Plutarch, *Life of Alexander* 3:1, 3). Earlier Plutarch remarked that Philip 'shrank from her embraces in the conviction that she was the partner of a superior being' (*ibid.*, 2:2, 3).

In connection with the emperor Augustus, who ruled the world at the time of the birth of Jesus, Asclepiades of Mendes recounts in his book entitled *Theologoumena* that Atia, Augustus' mother, once attended in the company of certain married women friends a solemn midnight service at the Temple of Apollo, where she had her litter set down, and presently fell asleep: 'Suddenly a serpent glided up, entered her and then glided away again. On awakening, she purified herself, as if after intimacy with her husband . . . The birth of Augustus nine months later suggested a divine paternity' (Suetonius, *Augustus* 94). The divinity of Augustus was derived both from this tale and from his family link with Julius Caesar. He was honoured as *Divi Filius*, or the deified Caesar's son.

It is impossible to establish with any degree of certainty how much the apotheosis of great historical figures in the Graeco-Roman world subconsciously influenced the thinking of Gentile converts to Christianity or even deeply Hellenized Jews in the first and second centuries, but the case of Julius Caesar is worth bearing in mind. The elevation of Caesar to divine status cannot be traced to his birth, but occurred about the end of his lifetime and was completed soon after his death. Shortly before his assassination in 44 BC, he permitted the erection of a statue to himself with the inscription *deo invicto* ('to the Unvanquished God'). 'His immediate deification' – Suetonius tells us –

'was more than a mere official decree since it reflected public conviction' (*Divus Iulius* 88). Indeed in January 42 BC, less than two years after the fatal Ides of March, the Senate inscribed Caesar among the gods of the Roman state, and in 29 BC a temple was erected in his honour on the Forum (Dio, *Roman History* 47:18, 3). It is bizarre to note, but still worthy of consideration, that the sophisticated senators of Rome needed considerably less time to deify Caesar than the supposedly credulous and simple first Gentile Christians required for acknowledging Jesus as God. Nonetheless, the elevation of a human being to divine status was undoubtedly easier for non-Jews than it was for their Jewish contemporaries.

A word needs to be said about the first-century AD Cappadocian Apollonius of Tyana, a Pythagorean sage, often compared to Jesus. He was held by the ordinary folk of his own age to be the son of Zeus (Philostratus, *Apollonius of Tyana*, 1:6). He was also venerated for his miraculous cures and for raising the dead. Later his pagan admirers in their anti-Christian polemics extolled him as a figure greater than Christ.

Finally, we must mention in passing the strange legend, popular in the region of the 'rose-red' desert city of Petra and possibly also in Southern Palestine. It concerns the Nabataean deity Dusares. The Church Father Epiphanius, a native Palestinian who became bishop of Salamis in Cyprus in the fourth century, narrates that on the feast of this god, which like Christmas fell on 25th December, hymns were sung to him and to his mother Kkhbou. Dusares was celebrated, in curious resemblance of Christian ideas, as 'Alone-begotten (*monogenês*) of the Lord' and in Arabic his mother was called *Chaamou*, that is, 'the Virgin' (*Panarion* 51).

No doubt an attempt to explain the virginal conception of Jesus exclusively by means of these pagan stories would be found convincing only by those who are already that way inclined. Nevertheless, these legends are helpful for reconstructing the mentality of the Gentiles who were targeted by the writers of the Gospels, as well as for grasping the turn of mind of those Hellenized Jews who, like Philo, were thoroughly immersed in classical culture and religion.

Hellenistic Jewish birth stories in Philo

While the extramarital affairs of the Olympian gods were nothing out of the ordinary in the context of classical mythology, a similar easy-going behaviour could hardly be contemplated in connection with the God of Israel, not even in Hellenistic Jewish circles accustomed to pagan myths. Nevertheless, an analogous imagery, used in a strictly symbolical context, found its way into the writings of the Alexandrian Jewish philosopher Philo (c. 20 BC– c. AD 50). He has the habit of comparing the virtues and the fruit they produce with the help of divine power to women and their children and occasionally this comparison leads him to strikingly imaginative and innovative allegorization.

For instance, when he speculates about Sarah, the ninety-year-old matriarch, he notices that according to the Bible she conceived Isaac when she was alone with God, and Abraham was absent from the scene (see Gen 21:1). From this Philo deduces that Sarah owed her pregnancy and the birth of Isaac to God, who was 'the Author of her visitation' (*The Cherubim* 45). In other words, Isaac was *begotten* by God, and since the name Isaac derives from the verb to laugh, Philo characterizes him as 'the laughter of the heart, *a son of God*' (*The Change of Names* 131). Elsewhere he goes even further in his figurative treatment of the subject: 'When Happiness [=Isaac] has been born, Sarah says with pride, "The Lord has made laughter for me . . ." (Gen 21:6). Therefore . . . open your ears wide . . ., writes Philo. The *laughter* (=Isaac) is joy, and *has made* is equivalent to "beget", so that what is said is . . . *The Lord begat Isaac . . .*' (*The Allegory of the Laws* 218–19). In short, Sarah conceived of God and gave birth to the Son of God.

Quoting another passage of Genesis which refers to God's opening Leah's womb (Gen 29:31), Philo points out that the Bible attributes to the Deity something that normally 'belongs to the husband', namely impregnation (*The Cherubim* 46). Along the same lines, in connection with Genesis 25:21, Philo recounts that the barren Rebekah became pregnant through the power of God (*The Cherubim* 47), an image that is a straight parallel to Mary's conceiving of the Holy Spirit.

If we bear in mind that in the last resort the Greek story of the virginal conception of Jesus by Mary was transmitted in a Hellenized Jewish and Gentile milieu, one must presume that it had been understood in the meaning to which such a milieu was accustomed.

This summary survey of the thinking of ancient Jews and non-Jews about the supernatural birth of heroes and saints in the age preceding the writing of the infancy narratives of Matthew and Luke will assist the reader in his effort to come to grips with the New Testament message and its complexities dealing with the Virgin and the Holy Spirit.

5

The Virgin and the Holy Spirit

The quintessence of Matthew's message regarding the miraculous birth of Jesus is that Mary was 'found with child *of the Holy Spirit*' (Mt 1:18) and that her offspring was to be called 'Emmanuel' or 'God with us' as predicted in Isaiah's prophecy (Mt 1:23). Likewise, in Luke the *virgin* called Mary learns that she will conceive of '*the Holy Spirit*' and be overshadowed by '*the Power of the Most High*'. As a result her '*holy*' child will be '*the Son of God*' (Lk 1:31, 35). Whatever else these mysterious statements may mean, they certainly describe a child conceived in a way different from the normal and convey that the person to be born will be very specially connected with God.

In Matthew's play the lead actor is Joseph. It is he who learns from an angel appearing in his dream the secret of how Mary has conceived. It is Joseph who has to decide what attitude to take towards her while awaiting the birth of the baby. As far as the geographical setting is concerned, at this stage Bethlehem is the only place mentioned (Mt 2:1). Nazareth is not referred to until the end of Matthew's infancy account.

Matthew's story of Jesus' conception
(Mt 1:18–25)

Now the birth of Jesus Christ took place this way. When his mother Mary had been betrothed to Joseph, before they came together she was found to be with child of the Holy Spirit; and her husband Joseph being a just man and unwilling to put her to shame, resolved to divorce her quietly. But as he considered this, behold, an angel of the Lord appeared to him in a dream, saying, 'Joseph, son of David, do not fear to take Mary your wife, for that which is conceived in her is of the Holy Spirit; she will bear a son, and you shall call his name Jesus, for he will save his people from their sins.' All this took place to fulfil what the Lord had spoken by the prophet: 'Behold, a virgin shall conceive and bear a son, and his name shall be Emmanuel' (which means, God with us). When Joseph woke from sleep, he did as the angel of the Lord commanded him; he took his wife, but knew her not until she had borne a son; and he called his name Jesus.

Matthew's narrative opens with the terse general heading, 'Now the birth of Jesus Christ took place this way', but neither here nor in chapter 2 do we learn anything about the external circumstances in which Jesus was born. Neither the gist of the genealogy consisting of a sequence of procreation, nor the mention that Mary has been engaged to marry Joseph and thus produce children, suggests that in the logic of the original narration an unparalleled birth was contemplated which had nothing to do with sex. Indeed, it can be firmly asserted that there is no trace in biblical or post-biblical Jewish tradition that would anticipate a pregnancy with no male contribution. As has been noted, virginal conception is never contemplated in Judaism, not even in the case of the King Messiah. What follows here is something unexpected, surprising and to a large extent confusing.

The account opens dramatically with Joseph's shock and dismay in discovering that his fiancée is with child. The Gospel of Matthew does not identify the place where Mary and Joseph live, but since there is no question of any change of residence between this moment and the actual birth of Jesus, the conclusion must be that in Matthew's view the couple always resided in Bethlehem. The matter of the pregnancy is so disturbing that the evangelist feels obliged in advance to disclose the reason for it to his readers. They are in the know even before the sleeping Joseph is informed about it by an angelic messenger in his dream. The baffled husband-to-be instinctively imagines the worst and decides that in the circumstances the marital agreement must be terminated. However, being a righteous, that is to say, a decent man, he proposes to do so privately without bringing the case before a law court. In his dream the following night he is reassured that Mary's condition is not due to infidelity, but to a miraculous intervention by God. In a scenario reduced to the strict minimum, Joseph at once proceeds to make Mary his wife and thus call an end to the betrothal. However, to ensure that his readers do not draw erroneous conclusions, Matthew informs them that Joseph is going to abstain from cohabiting with Mary as husband and wife until the birth of Jesus (Mt 1:25). Luke, as we shall see, leaves matters unresolved and says nothing on the subject.

Two issues of Jewish law, betrothal and divorce, are implicated in this account, and they require some clarification. To begin with betrothal, in Matthew (as in Luke) Joseph and Mary are said to be engaged. To appreciate properly the meaning of betrothal, it is to be remembered that in the Jewish society of the age of Jesus, arranged marriage was the established custom. The betrothal of a young girl was the prerogative of her father. If the father was no longer alive, his place was taken by the girl's brother or some other male relative. The head of the family negotiated the financial settlement with the groom and his parents. The girl had no say whatever in the matter. Quite apart from the subordinate status of women in Jewish law, in the rabbinic era and no doubt earlier too, the bride-to-be was by definition a *minor*, a person not yet of age. It should be noted that in the Mishnaic-Talmudic legislation girls attained majority when they started to menstruate, or on the day after their twelfth birthday, whichever came first. In the rabbinic perspective, majority and attainment of puberty were coterminous. By the age of twelve years and six months a young woman became, in the terminology of the rabbis, 'mature' (*bogeret*), and was expected already to be married. In any case, by then her father no longer had the right unilaterally to betroth her.

Once the preliminary requirements laid down in the agreement of betrothal were satisfied, nuptials followed: they were presumed to take place within twelve months from the date of engagement. Then the bridegroom led his bride to his own home amid solemn festivities attended by family, friends and neighbours. The Gospels contain various parables about Jewish weddings (see for example Mt 25:1–13). It would follow from these rules, which appear standard and long-standing, and not some kind of innovation by the redactors of the Mishnah, that at the time of the incidents described in the Gospels of Matthew and Luke, Mary was no more than twelve years old, or conceivably a little less, and by the standards of her society and age, mature enough for marriage.

To understand Joseph's dilemma on noticing Mary's pregnancy, we must bear in mind that Jewish betrothal was as binding as marriage itself and an engaged woman who had sex with a man other than her fiancé became an adulteress. According to Matthew's narrative, Joseph realized before the marriage ceremony had taken place that Mary was expecting a child and since he was at once intent on cancelling the marital arrangements, he is patently depicted as a man who did not consider himself responsible for the pregnancy in question. In the given circumstances the engagement could be nullified either in full legal publicity or without too much fuss. In the first alternative, the young woman would be charged with the crime of adultery before a tribunal, and if the charge was proven, she and her paramour would be condemned to death by stoning. But there was another, less drastic way of terminating the agreement, through issuing a document of repudiation. Matthew's Joseph opted for a quiet divorce (Mt 1:19). The concept of such a private dissolution of a marriage by the husband is associated in Jewish writings from the second century BC with two of the biblical Patriarchs. We learn from the Genesis Apocryphon, one of the Dead Sea Scrolls, that should Sarah have actually been forced to sleep with Pharaoh after she had been abducted to the royal harem in Egypt, Abraham would have been obliged to repel her for good (Gen Apocryphon 20:15). Also the Book of Jubilees relates that Jacob ended cohabitation with Bilhah, his concubine, after she had had sex with his son Reuben even though Bilhah did so innocuously, not realizing that the man in her bed was her stepson Reuben, and not Jacob (Jubilees 33:7–9). In Matthew, Joseph luckily escapes the need to implement his painful decision: the angelic dream vindicates Mary's innocence. He learns that the mysterious impregnation was the work of the Holy Spirit.

The last detail of this part of the story concerns name-giving. Joseph is instructed by the angel to call the child Jesus, accompanied by the explanation of the name – 'Jesus' signifying 'he will save his people from their sins' (Mt 1:21). Such an explanatory gloss is a well-established Jewish custom since biblical times. For example, Hagar, Abraham's concubine, is ordered to call her son Ishmael ('God hears') 'because the Lord has given heed to your affliction' (Gen 16:11).

The virginal conception in Matthew and Isaiah's prophecy

So far Matthew has told a perplexing story. Apart from alluding to some kind of involvement of the Holy Spirit, a phrase designating the power through which God acts in the world, the angel in the dream offers no elucidation of how Mary has become pregnant. The evangelist steps in therefore and sheds new light on the problem with the help of an Old Testament prophecy which predicts that a virgin is to give birth to the Saviour of the Jewish people. In the Gospel's version of the words of Isaiah the prophecy declares: 'Behold, a *virgin* shall conceive and bear a son, and his name shall be *Emmanuel* (which means, God with us)' (Isa 7:14 in Mat 1:23).

This is the first biblical proof text produced by Matthew in his infancy narrative. Luke has none. But this prophetic evidence, the purpose of which is to announce a miraculous pregnancy or virginal conception, is effective on one condition: it works only if we follow the Greek Septuagint version of Isaiah 7:14, intended for Greek speakers and understood as Greek readers would understand it. Needless to say, Matthew's Gospel in its extant form is in Greek and as such it was obviously aimed at a Greek audience. However, the original public for which the tradition of the birth narrative of Jesus was developed was Palestinian Jewish and the language in which it was first transmitted was either Aramaic or possibly Hebrew, *not* Greek. Also it goes without saying that for these Palestinian, mostly Galilean Jews, the text of Isaiah would have been quoted from the Hebrew Bible, and *not* from the Greek Septuagint.

And this leaves us in a real quandary. To allude to the woman who is going to conceive and bear a son, the Hebrew Isaiah 7:14 does not refer to a *virgin*, or a *betulah* in Hebrew, but to an *'almah*, that is to say, 'a young woman', a neutral term that does not necessarily connote virginity. For example, in the Song of Songs 6:8 the term 'young women' (*'alamot*) appears in parallelism with 'queens and concubines', who are surely not virgins. What is more, the *'almah* referred to in Isaiah 7, the young woman who in the near future will conceive and give birth to a son, is most unlikely to be a virgin. The context suggests that she is already married and is the wife of the reigning Jewish king, Ahaz, at the end of the eighth century BC.

By calling her *'almah*, the Hebrew Isaiah nowhere specifies that she is still a virgin or that the conception is foreseen to be miraculous in any way. The prophetic sign in the Hebrew Isaiah 7:14 consists, not in the virginal state of the mother, but in the significance of the name she is to give to her son. The name 'Emmanuel' intimates that the future prince, in conformity with the good omen expressed in his name, 'God with us', will bring divine protection to the inhabitants of Jerusalem, who were threatened at that time by two enemy kings besieging the city (see Isa 7:16). Bearing all this in mind, one is bound to conclude that the Semitic tale underlying the present Greek version of Matthew in no way could comprise a prediction of the *virginal* conception of the Messiah.

How then did this notion enter the Infancy Gospel of Matthew? By sheer accident the Septuagint translator of Isaiah 7:14 rendered the Hebrew term *'almah* by *parthenos*, corresponding to virgin in Greek, though it may also mean maiden or unmarried woman who is not necessarily a virgin. The 'Greek' Matthew or the Semitic Matthew's Greek editor tumbled on this loose translation, and adopted it. This godsend enabled him to present to his Greek-speaking readers the conception of Jesus as unique and towering above all the other miraculous conceptions of the Old Testament.

There is an incontrovertible proof that a substantial proportion of the intended audience of the final text of Matthew consisted of Greeks, who had no knowledge of Hebrew. In Matthew 1:23 the Hebrew name 'Emmanuel' in the Isaiah citation is furnished with a translation to explain that it means 'God with us'. As one may guess, the original Hebrew Isaiah includes no such interpretation, but more important, it also lacks from its Greek rendering in the Septuagint. The Diaspora Jews for whom the Septuagint was produced were expected to know what Emmanuel signified. The Greek gloss in Matthew's quotation, 'which means, God with us', is manifestly the evangelist's own creation for the benefit of his non-Jewish Greek readers. So applied to Mary, the Isaiah prophecy, as worded in Greek, was intended to convey to the Greek-speaking public of Matthew's infancy narrative that

'Jesus—Emmanuel' or 'the Messiah—Son of God' would be conceived of the Holy Spirit and miraculously produced by Mary *as* a virgin.

The Greek Matthew consequently claims that the virginal conception is demonstrated by the Isaiah citation. However, the evangelist's argument is topsy-turvy. He wishes his reader to understand that the event fulfilled the prophecy; in other words, that the conception of Jesus by Mary happened because according to Isaiah it was so predestined by God. The truth is the opposite way around: the idea of the 'conceiving *parthenos*', supplied by the prophecy in Greek, motivated the story. It was the Greek text of Isaiah 7:14 that provided Matthew with a striking formula for expressing the miraculous character of Jesus' birth as the realization of a scriptural prediction.

To repeat it for a last time, the virginal conception is a historicized extrapolation of the words of the Septuagint, proffered to and understood by a Hellenistic Gentile-Christian audience of the Gospel of Matthew. The birth story of Jesus, told in Aramaic or Hebrew and quoting Isaiah in Hebrew, could never have given rise to such an interpretation. But in Greek, combined with the literal exegesis of the name 'Emmanuel=God with us', it became the source out of which arose the concept of the divine Son of a virgin mother. It must be reiterated, even though this may be *ad nauseam*, that such a development was possible only in a Greek-speaking Hellenistic cultural environment. The ideological background of Graeco-Roman mythology and the legends relating to the divine origin of eminent figures in the recent past and in the present (see pp. 55–56) supplied a fertile ground for the growth of what was to become in theological Christian jargon *Christology*. In due course, this original idea evolved via Paul, John and the philosophizing Greek Church Fathers, into the deification of Jesus, Son of the God-bearing (*Theotokos*) Virgin.

That the idea of the virginal conception construed on the text of Matthew with its use of the Septuagint of Isaiah was of *Hellenistic* Gentile-Christian origin can also be argued negatively from the stance adopted on the subject by ancient Judaeo-Christianity. Important facets of the teaching of these Jewish-Christians, known as the Ebionites or the Poor, have been preserved in the writings of Church apologists who sought to refute them. Under the title Ebionites, we have to understand Jewish-Christian communities which after their separation from the main Gentile-Christian Church, probably at the turn of the first century AD, survived for a further two or three hundred years. We learn from the late second-century Church Father Irenaeus, bishop of Lyons, and Eusebius, the fourth-century Church historian from Caesarea, that the Ebionites rejected the doctrine of the virgin birth. Eusebius makes plain that for them Jesus was 'the child of a normal union between a man and Mary' (*Ecclesiastical History* 3:27). Earlier, Irenaeus argued, using phrases borrowed from the New Testament, that the Ebionites were 'unwilling to understand that the Holy Spirit had come to Mary and the power of the Most High had overshadowed her' (*Against Heresies*, 5:1, 3). He further explained that in order to bolster their teaching and pull the rug out from under the feet of Christian orthodoxy, the Ebionites championed the Greek version of Theodotion and Aquila as more correct than the Sepuagint, and substituted for the *parthenos* (virgin) of the Septuagint the term *neanis* (young woman) in their rendering of Isaiah 7:14 (*ibid.* 3:21, 1). In their view, the proof of the unreliability of the Septuagint sounded the death knell of Matthew's and the Christian Church's doctrine of the virginal conception.

Indeed, the *'almah* of the Hebrew Isaiah, and the corresponding *neanis* of Aquila and Theodotion reveal the fragility of the idea of the virgin birth, as conceived by the Greek Matthew. Its adoption by the evangelist (or the final editor of Matthew) necessitated the revision of the straightforward wording of the genealogy (A begot B, etc.) with a view to excluding Joseph's paternity. It also has the unintended effect of spoiling the evidence built up to authenticate Jesus' legitimacy as Messiah directly descended from David through Joseph.

Jesus, the *legal* son of Joseph

Messianic status based on Davidic parentage and virginal conception – excluding Joseph from the real ancestry of Jesus – are forces obviously pulling in opposite directions. How have the Church and traditionally minded Christian scholars tried to overcome the difficulty? The most favoured solution is the theory of legal fiction. Its holders advance the view that it was enough for Joseph to legally acknowledge Jesus as his son to confer on him entitlement to inherit the throne of David. They pinpoint the naming of Jesus by Joseph as the actual act of legal filiation. Indeed, according to Matthew 1:21, it was Joseph who was to call Mary's child Jesus.

It is dubious, however, to say the least, that name-giving amounts to the acknowledgment of paternity and there is uncertainty in the New Testament tradition about the person who was the name-giver. The biblical proof text of Isaiah on which Matthew relies is of no use on this point.

In fact Matthew explicitly departs from the Septuagint which, with its wording, '*you* will call him Emmanuel', would have been pointing at Joseph as the name-giver. But Matthew's Greek quotation of Isaiah reads, '*they* will call him Emmanuel', an impersonal formula with no particular person in mind.

It is often alleged that the legal fiction theory is supported by rabbinic law, but the text of the Mishnah that is usually cited in support of it is of questionable relevance. The passage 'If a man says, "This is my son", he is to be believed' (mBaba Bathra 8:6), is not really concerned with legal paternity, but with a particular aspect of the law governing leviratic marriage. As has been stated earlier (see p. 42), according to the biblical command a brother-in-law is required to marry the widow of his deceased brother if he has died childless. The Mishnah introduces here a clause in favour of the woman. If the husband during his life time has called a boy his son – irrespective of this being true or untrue – his widow will immediately be free to marry any man she wishes, and will no longer be obliged to wait for her brother-in-law to make up his mind whether he is prepared to take her or not.

In short, the legal fiction thesis strikes very much as special pleading. Moreover, the tradition testifying to Joseph being the name-giver clashes with that handed down by Luke. There it is Mary, not Joseph, who is told, 'You will . . . bear a son, and *you* shall call his name Jesus' (Lk 1:31).

Perpetual virginity of Mary?

The doctrine cherished in traditional mainstream Catholic and Eastern Orthodox Christianity of the perpetual virginity of Mary, before, during and after the birth of Jesus, is definitely not buttressed by the account of Matthew. (Luke's corresponding evidence will be discussed later in this chapter on pp. 77–78.) While the Greek Matthew advances the virginal conception of Jesus by Mary, it seems to contradict the belief that her virginity continued after the birth of her child. We must re-read Matthew 1:25. There we are told that after Joseph had accepted the miraculous nature of Mary's pregnancy, that it had come about as the result of the action of the Holy Spirit, he refrained from 'knowing' her *until* she had borne a son'. To unprejudiced readers this verse signifies that, while in Matthew's account during the period of gestation Joseph had kept away from Mary, after the birth of Jesus they assumed life together normally, as man and wife. A similar marital situation is hinted at again by Matthew 1:18, where the evangelist refers to Joseph and Mary *coming together*. The Greek verb *sunerchesthai* (to come together) regularly refers to sexual union. It is used by Josephus (AD 37–*c.* 100) to describe intercourse between Amnon and his sister Tamar and between Absalom and the concubines of his father David (Ant 7:168, 214). St Paul employs the same terminology as Josephus in his advice to Corinthian Christian couples: 'Do not refuse one another except perhaps by agreement for a season . . . but then *come together* again, lest Satan tempt you through lack of self-control' (1 Cor 7:5). From this it would follow that those who are styled by Matthew the brothers and the sisters of Jesus, namely

James, the brother of the Lord, Joses (or Joseph), Judas (or Jude) and Simon, and at least two girls, (Mt 13:55–56; Mk 6:3), were the children produced by Joseph and Mary after the birth of Jesus.

Luke's story of the conception of Jesus

Luke's more extensive Infancy Gospel combines the story of the conception of John the Baptist (see chapter 10), with that of Jesus. The miraculous-birth stories in the Hebrew Bible as well as in inter-Testamental and rabbinic literature suggest that some kind of special divine participation in the birth of the Messiah would have been expected in popular religious circles. Luke, by propounding the wondrous pregnancy of the mother of John the Baptist anticipates, sandwiched between two slices of the Baptist's story, the announcement of the even more wondrous beginnings of Jesus.

The annunciation (Lk 1:26–38)

In the sixth month [of Elizabeth's pregnancy] *the angel Gabriel was sent from God to a city of Galilee named Nazareth, to a virgin betrothed to a man whose name was Joseph, of the house of David; and the virgin's name was Mary. And he came to her and said, 'Hail, O favoured one, the Lord is with you!' But she was greatly troubled at the saying, and considered in her mind what sort of greeting this might be. And the angel said to her, 'Do not be afraid, Mary, for you have found favour with God. And behold, you will conceive in your womb and bear a son, and you shall call his name Jesus. He will be great, and will be called the Son of the Most High;*

and the Lord God will give him the throne of his father David, and he will reign over the house of Jacob for ever; and of his kingdom there will be no end.' And Mary said to the angel, 'How shall this be, since I have no husband?' And the angel said to her, 'The Holy Spirit will come upon you, and the power of the Most High will overshadow you; therefore the child to be born will be called holy, the Son of God. And behold, your kinswoman Elizabeth in her old age has also conceived a son; and this is the sixth month with her who was called barren. For with God nothing is impossible.' And Mary said, 'Behold, I am the handmaid of the Lord; let it be to me according to your word.' And the angel departed from her.

In Luke the principal dramatis persona is Mary, not Joseph as in Matthew, and contrary to Matthew's focus on Bethlehem, Luke chooses Nazareth, the home town of the engaged couple as the original locale of the infancy story. He then moves them from Galilee to Bethlehem and Jerusalem and completes a full circle by bringing the whole family back to Nazareth.

The angel Gabriel, one of the four archangels of Jewish tradition – the other three being Michael, Raphael and Sariel or Suriel – appears to Mary in her family home in some kind of day-time vision, and he informs her that she is to become a mother, and will give birth in due course to 'the Son of the Most High' and the king Messiah, future heir of 'the throne of his father David' (Lk 1:32–33; see also 2:11). To her puzzled question of how such a thing could happen when she does not yet share bed and board with her designated husband-to-be, Gabriel answers that the divine Spirit will play a part in her pregnancy and that she will bear a holy child. To illustrate that such a thing is feasible for God, he informs her about something else humanly impossible, namely that her long-time sterile and elderly cousin Elizabeth is already six months pregnant.

Luke's account about the extraordinary circumstances of Mary is clear-cut in appearance. She cannot understand how she could bear a child as she is without sexual experience. However, after closer inspection the case is less clear-cut than it seems. In fact it is quite equivocal. For contrary to Matthew, Luke never expressly declares that between the annunciation and the birth of Jesus Joseph abstained from 'knowing' Mary. In consequence, in Luke's perspective, the conception of Jesus could be something not unlike the miraculous pregnancies reported in the Old Testament which are all assumed to have been combined with normal sexual intercourse between spouses. Joseph could therefore be the father of Jesus, and the role of the Holy Spirit could consist in the special sanctification of Jesus, making him 'holy' and 'the Son of God'. The courageous words of the well-known Roman Catholic scholar, J. A. Fitzmyer SJ, merit quotation: 'When [Luke's] account is read in and for itself – without the overtones of the Matthean annunciation to Joseph – every detail of it could be understood of a child born to Mary in the usual human way'.[8] Later, it is true, Fitzmyer felt obliged to abandon this statement in favour of a more traditional reading of Luke's text when he had found himself representing in a debate the minority of one against the unanimous verdict of the eleven other Catholic theologians.[9] Some may think that it was a pity, but quite understandable during the papacy of John Paul II.

There are only two references in Luke supporting the idea of the virginal conception. The first figures in his Infancy Gospel where Mary continues to be called Joseph's 'betrothed' – not his wife – at the time of the birth of

Jesus. This has all the appearances of a gauche editorial emendation of the original tradition. The Old Latin and (Sinaitic) Syriac versions of Luke have no hesitation to call her Joseph's wife with all that the word implies. Matthew, as we have seen, is not afraid to designate Joseph as Mary's husband (Mt 1:19). The other passage is in the genealogy (Lk 3:23), discussed earlier (p. 41), where Joseph is downgraded to the rank of the 'supposed' father of Jesus (Lk 3:23), which in the context also appears as another patent retouch made on second thoughts.

The virginal conception in Luke

Luke's description of Mary's miraculous conception, though independent from Matthew and from the Greek Isaiah 7:14, sounds definitely odd in a Palestinian context, but he reveals himself more than once unfamiliar with things Jewish (see pp. 136–7 on Lk 2:22–24). When the angel announces her forthcoming pregnancy, Luke's inexperienced young Mary seems straight away to understand that the words refer to the otherwise unheard-of idea of virginal conception. Hence her astonishment and disbelief: How could such a thing happen to someone who has never 'known' a man (Lk 1:34) and how could she become pregnant and still remain a virgin? But, as many scholars have noted, this question strikes as quite inappropriate in the Jewish historical, social and cultural setting of Mary. On the lips of a girl who is already bound by betrothal to Joseph, and whose wedding day must have been fairly imminent, the question put in her mouth by Luke does not make sense. Should she not have asked the angel to instruct Joseph to hurry up? All he needed to do was to expedite the wedding by taking her to his home at once? Something unsaid seems to lurk beneath the ill-fitting words of Luke.

The secret probably lies in the equivocality of the Jewish concept of virginity. Few if any readers of the New Testament, apart from those versed in rabbinic literature, know that in ancient Judaism there existed two ways to define a virgin. In one of these ways, to which we are all accustomed, a girl is a virgin for as long as she has not experienced sex. The Hebrew term in question is *betulah*, which in the first meaning is the equivalent of *virgo intacta*, a woman with the hymen intact. It is attested both in the Bible, for instance when Rebekah is described as a maiden whom no man has known (Gen 24:16) and in later rabbinic writings (see Tosefta Shebiit 3:15). This first kind of virginity terminates with intercourse. According to the second definition, the girl is a virgin until she reaches puberty. This second kind of virginity comes to an end by the onset of menstruation. The Mishnah, the earliest law code of the rabbis, defines a virgin in the second sense, as a girl 'who has never seen blood' and the text surprisingly adds, 'even though she is married' (Niddah 1:4). The Palestinian Talmud formally distinguishes between the two classes of virginity, one 'in respect of menstruation' and the other in respect of 'the token of virginity' (Niddah 49a).

The matter had practical relevance and was not a mere exercise of clever hairsplitting, even though some rabbis were past masters in the field. In the Jewish society of the age of Jesus, with arranged 'child' marriages, the question could arise whether the bloodstain found on the sheets of a minor (i.e. a young female who previously has not had a period) after her wedding night should be attributed to the breaking of the hymen or to her first menstruation. So if a girl past the legal majority of twelve years was married, although she was still pre-pubertal, it was theoretically possible for her to conceive after her first ovulation, but before her first period. Thus such a person could become – *mirabile dictu* – a virgin mother (virgin as far as the menstrual blood was concerned) and even possibly the virgin mother of more than one child, according to the saying attributed to Rabbi Eliezer ben Hyrcanus in the late first century AD (Tosefta Niddah 1:4).

The practice of child marriage definitely existed in the first century AD. The rule of the marrying branch of the Essene sect as described by the first-century AD Jewish historian Flavius Josephus verifies it. These ascetics, who unlike their celibate brethren accepted marriage, nevertheless expressly prohibited cohabitation between a sexually immature girl and her bridegroom. Marital practice could begin only after the bride had proved by three successive monthly periods that she was physically fit for conceiving. This proof was necessary because sexual intercourse was justified in the view of the marrying Essenes only for the sake of procreation. Consequently sex was prohibited with a girl before she had reached puberty and even with a wife after she knew that she was pregnant, or no doubt after the menopause (Josephus, *Jewish War* 2:161).

In Luke's account, Mary's perplexity about the prospect of her imminent motherhood was alleviated by the angel assuring her that Heaven can cope with such minor matters, as is demonstrated by the case of Elizabeth (Lk 1:34–37). For God, it is no more difficult to enable a post-menopausal woman to bear a child than to allow a virgin, in the sense of a physically immature female, to conceive. In fact a woman beyond the age of childbearing was called a virgin for the second time. Philo, addressing educated

Hellenized Jews, likened the elderly Sarah to someone who had passed 'from womanhood to virginity' (*The Posterity of Cain* 134). The logic of Gabriel's argument dealing with the situation of Mary and Elizabeth makes best sense if by virgin we understand a girl before reaching puberty.

On re-examination the idea of virginal conception must be seen as a late accretion to the infancy narratives. Yet despite its special and unparalleled character, it has made no impact either on Matthew or Luke, or on any other part of the New Testament. Its removal would not create a gap; it would not even be noticed.

We need to take into account the Gentile-Hellenistic context of early Christianity, with its heroes of divine origin, to reconstruct the background of the extraordinary beginnings of Jesus. Far the most important element in the puzzle is Matthew's recourse to the Greek version of Isaiah 7:14: A *parthenos* shall conceive. It served as catalyst in the development of the later notion of Mary as Mother of God.

By the beginning of the second century, when Gentile Christians became accustomed to considering Jesus not just as a metaphorical Son of God, but as a divine person, his unique style of entering the human sphere would no longer create a problem. And when in the age of St Augustine in the late fourth and early fifth centuries a convenient explanation was found for explaining the universal transmission of Adam's original sin – the primeval taint was passed on from generation to generation through the act of procreation – Jesus' asexual conception by a virgin was the last piece completing a mysterious puzzle.

Appendix:
The question of the illegitimacy of Jesus

The idea of the virginal conception and the mention of Joseph's worry about Mary's pregnancy soon produced a very much down-to-earth negative offshoot. Jews hostile to the Jesus movement saw in the birth story a deliberate cover-up invented by the early Christians to conceal the fact that Jesus was illegitimate. The scandalmongers of Palestine must have had a field day. They demanded a more convincing explanation than some fairy-tale story about an angel informing Joseph in a dream of how his fiancée had got in the family way.

Traces of the rumour are concealed under the surface of the New Testament itself. The allegation of illegitimacy probably underlies the altercation, reported in the Gospel of John, between Jesus and his Jewish critics. When his opponents protested that they were not born of fornication, they were tacitly insinuating that Jesus was (Jn 8:41). Also some modern interpreters of the Gospels detect a slur in the designation of Jesus as 'the son of Mary' by the people of Nazareth (Mk 6:3). One would normally expect them to speak of Jesus as 'the son of Joseph'.

The ancient copyists sensed a derogatory meaning in the phrase and sought to paper it over. They substituted the variant, 'Is not this Joseph the carpenter's son and the son of Mary' for the well-established reading, 'Is not this Jesus the carpenter, the son of Mary'. But the proponents of the pejorative interpretation of the phrase, 'the son of Mary', may be mistaken. The occasional metronymic designation of rabbis found in Talmudic literature, i.e. the identification of a man through his mother, such as 'Rabbi

Yose son of the Damascene woman', does not seem to carry any depreciatory connotation.

Clear evidence of Jewish attempts to impugn the reputation of Jesus by attributing to him illegitimate birth may be found in the Acts of Pilate, a Latin New Testament apocryphon dating in its present form to the fourth century, but probably going back to the second. In it the Jews decry Jesus as one born out of adultery (Acts of Pilate 2:3). The same charge is reported by the Church Father Origen, who states that according to the late second-century pagan writer Celsus, hostile Jews depicted Mary as a poor country woman who was forced to earn her living by spinning after her carpenter husband had divorced her for being convicted of an affair with a soldier called Panthera (*Against Celsus* 1:28, 32).[10] Another Church Father, Tertullian, alludes to a hearsay propagated by Jews at the end of the second century about the mother of Jesus being a prostitute (*De spectaculis* 30:6).

The same calumnious charge is conveyed in a variety of forms in rabbinic tradition too. In the Talmud, Miriam, the mother of Jesus, was a hairdresser, the wife of a man called Stada, but she also had a lover by the name of Pandera. Hence Jesus was variously known as the son of Stada or the son of Pandera. For other rabbis Stada was the nickname of the mother and derived from an Aramaic phrase *sotat da*, roughly translatable as 'that adulteress' (Tosefta Hullin 2:23; Babylonian Talmud Shabbat 104b). Similar polemical sarcasms are exhibited in the Toledot Yeshu, the medieval Jewish life of Jesus. The oddest revival of this idea comes from the most unexpected corner, the after-dinner conversations of Adolf Hitler, recorded by Martin Bormann. In them the Führer asserted on a couple of occasions that Jesus' father was a Gallic legionary![11]

More recently, Jesus' conception out of wedlock has become a familiar topic of debate among adherents of the fashionable feminist school of theology,[12] though sometimes it is presented with the addition of a mitigating circumstance, namely that Mary was the victim of rape. In contemporary literary theory the virginal conception is the 'ecclesiastically correct' version of an awkward story about the mistreatment of women.

6

The date and place of the birth of Jesus

So far we have scrutinized what some would call the legendary elements of the conception of Jesus and the aspects of the story which are built on Bible interpretation. Now we can turn to more concrete matters and endeavour to situate his birth in space and time.

A. Matthew's account

The infancy narrative of Matthew mentions only summarily the Nativity itself. The evangelist supplies no details regarding the event (see p. 63). The story of Joseph's discovery that his fiancée was expecting a child is simply prefaced by the heading, 'Now the birth of Jesus Christ took place in this way . . .' (Mt 1:18). A little later he simply repeats: 'Now when Jesus was born in Bethlehem of Judaea in the days of Herod the king . . .' (Mt 2:1). Further elaboration follows when Matthew refers to the consultation of the Jewish chief priests by Herod in answer to the inquiry of the Magi (2:3–6). Herod's Bible experts unhesitatingly cite the words of the Old Testament prophet Micah 5:2, quoting from a Greek translation and not from the Hebrew original, but in a form that differs not only from the Hebrew text of the Bible, but also from the old Greek version of the Scriptures (third–first century BC), attributed to seventy translators and known as the Septuagint (LXX= 70). In fact, among the twenty-four Greek words of the verse in Matthew's quotation and the twenty-one words of the Septuagint only six are in common:

Matthew:
And you, O Bethlehem, **in the land of Judah**,
Are **by no means least** among **the rulers** of Judah;
For from you shall come
A ruler who will **govern** [literally **shepherd**] **my people**
    Israel.

Septuagint:
And you, O Bethlehem, **house of Ephrathah**,
You are **few in number** to count among **the thousands** of
    Judah;
From you shall come for me one
To be **the ruler** of Israel.

To produce a case as strong as possible, the evangelist did not hesitate to rewrite his proof text. He turned into a compliment the prophet's belittling remark, referring to Bethlehem as '*by no means least* among the rulers' instead of a tiny place among the clans or thousands of Judah, attested in the Hebrew Bible and in the Greek Septuagint. Furthermore, Matthew's quotation amalgamates the last line of Micah with 2 Samuel 5:2, with a view to incorporating the pastoral metaphor (shepherding my people), and thus hinting that the Messianic ruler would follow in the footsteps of the young David, the son of Jesse, who was the guardian of his father's flock in Bethlehem (1 Sam 17:15).

For Matthew – and the same remark applies to Luke

too – the geographical setting is crucially important, as it has a major theological significance. Matthew is fully aware of a Jewish tradition according to which the Messiah is expected to come from Bethlehem. In addition to Micah 5:2 concerning the insignificant Bethlehem being the birthplace of the future ruler of Israel, we find, two verses later, an association between ruler and shepherd, and a little earlier (in Micah 4:8) reference is made to 'the Tower of the Flock' or fortified sheepfold as the place where the dominion and the kingdom will be manifested.

The common Jewish interpretative tradition, represented by the Aramaic Targum Jonathan to the Prophets, identifies the 'ruler' with 'the Messiah' (at Micah 5:2; 5:1 in the Hebrew Bible) and the 'Tower of the Flock' (at Micah 4:8) with the locality (Bethlehem) where the Messiah of Israel will inherit the kingdom (see also Targum Pseudo-Jonathan on Gen 35:21). The Palestinian Talmud combines the three elements – Bethlehem, Tower of the Flock, Messianic king – in declaring that the Messiah would arise from 'the royal city of Bethlehem of Judah' (Berakhot 5a). The Church Father Origen (c. 185–c. 254) negatively confirms this tradition when he alleges that the Jews have attempted to undermine the Church's doctrine about Jesus being the promised Christ by attempting to suppress the evidence about Bethlehem as the birthplace of the Messiah. This statement seems of doubtful validity, for if these Jews really tried to efface the Messianic references to Bethlehem, they did a bad job, as a fair amount of testimony has survived until this day.

Luke's account

Lk 2:1–7

In those days a decree went out from Caesar Augustus that all the world should be enrolled. This was the first enrolment, when Quirinius was governor of Syria. And all went to be enrolled, each to his own city. And Joseph also went up from Galilee, from the city of Nazareth, to Judaea, the city of David, which is called Bethlehem, because he was of the house and lineage of David, to be enrolled with Mary, his betrothed, who was with child. And while they were there, the time came for her to be delivered. And she gave birth to her first-born son and wrapped him in swaddling cloths, and laid him in a manger, because there was no place for them in the inn.

Luke, in his turn, while asserting that Nazareth is the home ground of Mary and Joseph, takes the Bethlehem tradition for granted without adducing any biblical proof and makes Bethlehem the second focal point of the infancy narrative. It is there that Joseph and Mary are sent by the imperial census, and Jesus sees the light of day in a shed situated on the outskirts of the town. The word 'stable' is nowhere explicitly mentioned. That the family was staying in an animal shelter is deduced from Luke's reference to a 'manger' where the newborn babe was placed.

Bethlehem as the birthplace of the Messiah being a Jewish, and subsequently Christian *theologoumenon* or doctrinal pre-requirement for the acknowledgment of someone as the Christ, it had to be verified in the case of Jesus. But as we have witnessed apropos of several other points, the theological demands of the infancy narratives – here the identity of the place of origin of the Messiah – remain without echo and support in the remainder of the New Testament.

Whereas Jesus' Davidic descent is a recurrent theme well established in the Gospels, especially in the Synoptics, his Judaean provenance seems to be more than once ignored or contested. People regarded him not as a Southerner, but as a Galilean born and bred. He was called Jesus the Nazarene, that is, stemming from Nazareth, or more fully the prophet Jesus from Nazareth in Galilee (Mt 21:11). Nazareth and the region of the Lake of Galilee were his *patris*, a phrase that can equally mean his place of birth, his home town and his home country (Mk 6:4; Mt 13:57; Lk 4:24; Jn 1:46). Apparently, some local Jews refused to accept him as the Messiah, precisely because they knew that he was from Galilee and not 'from Bethlehem, the village where David was' (Jn 7:41–42). Moreover, they voiced the prejudice, no doubt of Judaean origin, that no great religious leader would ever hail from Galilee (Jn 7:52). So we must recognize that we are in an impasse: the birth in Bethlehem is asserted with theological certainty, but is queried on what seems to be factual knowledge.

When was Jesus born?

As far as the time of Jesus' birth is concerned only negative certainty is attainable; it can be taken for granted that it did not happen in AD 1. The traditional date resulted from a miscalculation far back in the sixth century. A Roman monk, Dionysius the Small, a native of Southern Russia, tried to locate the Nativity in a historical chronology based on the foundation of Rome. However, he erroneously placed the birth of Christ in the Roman year 753 AUC (*ab urbe condita*). It most probably happened, as will appear from the evidence, at least four years earlier. So paradoxically, Jesus was born 'before Christ', 'BC'. This inconsistency is known to most people, but since it would be far too cumbersome to backdate every single event in the current era, the law of the least effort demands that things be left as they are.

Matthew in his birth narrative and Luke both inside and outside his Infancy Gospel supply sufficient information for an approximate dating of Jesus' arrival in this world. Matthew names Herod the Great as the ruler of Judaea at that time ('Now when Jesus was born . . . in the days of Herod the king' (Mt 2:1)), and Herod sat on the royal throne in Jerusalem from 37 to 4 BC. Matthew further alludes not only to Herod's death, which occurred in 4 BC, but also to his replacement by Archelaus, who 'reigned over Judaea in place of his father Herod' (Mt 2:19, 22) during the following ten years, from 4 BC to AD 6. The rough timescale is again confirmed by Luke's allusion to 'the days of Herod, king of Judaea' at the opening of the infancy story of John the Baptist (Lk 1:5), and by his other references to Palestinian and international events associated with John and Jesus. He notes that Jesus was 'about thirty years of age' at the beginning of his ministry, which followed his baptism by John (Lk 3:23). Then he laboriously identifies the start of John's career (Lk 3:1–2). The Baptist stepped into the public arena in the fifteenth year of the emperor Tiberius (AD 28/29), in the course of the governorship of Pontius Pilate (AD 26–36), under the rule of the Herodian princes Antipas (4 BC–AD 39) and Philip (4 BC–AD 33), and the high priesthood of Caiaphas (AD 18–36). (Luke's claim that Caiaphas shared the pontificate with Annas is an error. Annas was high priest from

AD 6–15.) In the light of these combined data, we must conclude that if Jesus was in his thirties in AD 28/29, he must have been born shortly before the turn of the era. However, if Matthew's reference to the succession of Archelaus as ethnarch of Judaea is taken into account, Jesus' birth will have to be put back to some time before Passover in the spring of 4 BC when, according to Josephus, Herod the Great died.

But do we need these vague estimates when Luke clearly attaches the Nativity to what appears to be a major international historical event, the edict of Caesar Augustus ordering a universal census in the Roman empire, an order implemented in Palestine by Quirinius, governor of Syria? If we can fix the date of this *apographê* or census and the period of office of Quirinius as governor or legate of Syria, we will have determined the date of Jesus' birth . . . with the proviso, of course, that Luke was correct in making it coincide with a census by Quirinius in Judaea under Herod.

The event apparently alluded to by Luke is a universal census, or property registration for taxation purposes, imposed by the emperor Augustus on the whole Roman world. The execution of the order must have been entrusted to regional governors and this meant in the case of Palestine Quirinius, the governor of Syria, Publicius Sulpicius Quirinius to give his full name. The evangelist does not explicitly mention Herod in this connection, but the earlier reference to Herod's days (Lk 1:5) implicitly defines the period of the census too. So we have a Roman enrolment, implemented by a Roman official, in the north and the south of the kingdom of Herod the Great, affecting people both in Galilee (Nazareth) and in Judaea (Bethlehem). It further follows that the census described by Luke is of a very special kind. It requires people to make their declaration personally – not in or near the place where they reside and own property – but in the town of their remote origin, that is, the city of their tribal ancestor. For Joseph, purportedly a member of the house of David, this meant, in the tradition represented by Luke, a statutory visit from Nazareth to Bethlehem, the city of David. And from the fact that Mary was in a very advanced stage of pregnancy at the moment of their departure on an approximately seventy-mile-long exhausting journey – she gave birth to Jesus when she arrived in Bethlehem – we must deduce that her attendance in the company of her husband was also thought by Luke to be obligatory. With the help of all these details and in the light of our extensive knowledge of Jewish history in the final stages of Herod's reign and of the ins and outs of Roman provincial administration, we ought to be able to pinpoint the precise date of the Nativity . . . again providing that Luke turns out to be a reliable reporter.

Unfortunately, the Roman census will prove to be less helpful for the dating of the birth of Jesus than one might have expected. Let us begin, therefore, with the clarification of the terms. The Gospel speaks of a registration or enrolment of 'all the world'. Such a census, covering 'the whole world', would deal with the countries of the whole Roman empire under Augustus with a view to furnishing information for levying taxes or enlisting men for military service.

However, there is no evidence that such an empire-wide census was ordered, let alone took place in the time of Augustus. Even if there had been an extensive census, it would not have been universal, as it would not have included Italy, whose Roman citizens by that time were exempted from the payment of taxes and from universal conscription. So the census could have only concerned the provinces of the empire, but no ancient source testifies that a tax registration was imposed on *all* the provinces at any one time. The nearest we come to such an idea is with an edict of Augustus instructing provincial governors to compile a list of Roman citizens (and Joseph and Mary did not belong to this class), but this was issued in AD 6, ten years after the death of Herod the Great, and consequently more than ten years after the presumed birth of Jesus.

So if there was no worldwide operation of any kind, was there at least a provincial census in the kingdom of Herod? The answer must once more be in the negative. Herod was a client king, a *rex socius*, and the Romans did not collect taxes directly from the subjects of such rulers. Moreover, we learn explicitly from Josephus that the Judaean kingdom was *immune* from Roman taxation for as long as Herod lived (Ant 17:27) and that Herod enjoyed independence in fiscal matters – so much so that he was even free to remit taxes when the Jews went through hard economic times. This Judaean immunity seems to have remained in force even after Herod's death during the ten years of the rule of his son Archelaus (4 BC–AD 6). It was only after his deposition that a census became necessary when a new taxation system was required in view of the recently established Roman province of Judaea.

Josephus describes the registration process set into motion in AD 6 by Quirinius, governor of Syria, in the former realm of Archelaus. It was a novelty so unprecedented and shocking for the Jews that it resulted in a major popular rebellion, fomented by Judas of Gamala, surnamed the Galilean. But the AD 6 decree would not have appeared such an innovation if there had already been a census a few years earlier in the final years of Herod. Besides, that particular census in AD 6 concerned only the domain previously governed by Archelaus, that is, Judaea, and would not have affected the Galilee ruled by Herod Antipas, where according to Luke Joseph and Mary had their residence. It is amusing to note that the Protoevangelium of James 17:1 tries to evade this difficulty by limiting the Roman census exclusively to the citizens of Bethlehem, assuming with Matthew that the parents of Jesus lived there!

Nor was it possible for Quirinius to conduct a census in the kingdom of Herod, not only because the realm of a client king was not subject to censuses, but also because Quirinius was not governor of Syria while Herod was alive. Some scholars have sought to argue from a damaged Latin inscription, the so-called Titulus Tiburtinus discovered in Tivoli in the eighteenth century, that the Roman official mentioned there as having twice served as governor, but whose name is no longer extant, was Quirinius. Even if we accepted this purely hypothetical identification, the period of the first supposed Syrian office of Quirinius would fall in 3–2 BC, after the death of Herod. The slots in the governorship of Syria in the final years of Herod's reign are filled by Sentius Saturninus (10/9–7/6 BC) and Quinctilius Varus (7/6–4 BC). Since Herod died in the spring of 4 BC, there is no room left for Quirinius to act as legate in Syria, and definitely none before AD 6.

Finally, Luke's story about Joseph and Mary travelling from Nazareth to Bethlehem to be enrolled there 'because he was of the house and lineage of David' appears to conflict with the sensible rules governing Roman censuses. Owners of property were to make their declaration to the censor in the chief city of the taxation district where they resided. This would have been Sepphoris for people living in Nazareth. They were not required to present themselves in the ancestral city of their clan, the distant Bethlehem for members of the house of David where, according to Luke, Joseph surely had no house or land. If he had owned a place, he would not have been obliged – following Luke's logic – to look for shelter in a stable or a shed. Furthermore, the appearance of the head of the family before the censor sufficed: the presence of wives, especially wives on the point of parturition, was not demanded.

In sum, from whichever angle one looks at it, the census referred to by Luke conflicts with historical reality. According to the great Roman historian Sir Ronald Syme, the New Testament account is based on Luke's confusion of two notable events in Palestinian history, one dating to 4 BC (the death of Herod), and the other to AD 6 (the creation of the Roman province of Judaea). Each led to disturbances. The first followed the passing of Herod, and the second the census of Quirinius. More serious was the rebellion in 4 BC when Varus, the legate of Syria, needed the whole of his army to quell it. However, the crisis of AD 6 was better remembered because the imposition of Roman rule and taxation triggered off a long-lasting insurrection, launched by Judas the Galilean, and continued on and off by his heirs up to the great uprising in AD 66.[13]

The mistaken placement of Quirinius' census in the twilight years of Herod is put to good use in Luke's narrative. It enables him to achieve his main purpose and transfer Joseph and Mary from Nazareth to Bethlehem so that Jesus might be born in the town from where the Messiah was expected to originate. The reliability of Luke from the point of view of historiography falls short of what one might have expected from someone who boasted that he had 'carefully' (akribôs) investigated the records (Lk 1:3).

Incidentally, this is not the only error of Luke in the domain of historiography. In Acts 5:37 he asserts that the revolutionary Theudas, who according to Josephus rose under the procurator Fadus (AD 44–46), *preceded* Judas the Galilean 'in the days of the census'. By putting him before AD 6, Luke predates Theudas by some forty years, a substantive error in what was in his days near-contemporary history.

Where do we stand, therefore, with our inquiry? The precise date of the birth of Jesus is still unknown. It occurred, it would seem, before the spring of 4 BC, and most likely in 5 or a little earlier.

In conclusion, regarding the date of birth of Jesus, we must be content with a *terminus ante quem*, pinpointed as the death of Herod. His birthplace is equally uncertain. Whilst Bethlehem cannot be absolutely excluded, it remains highly questionable. On the whole, a Jesus of Nazareth, the Jesus of the main Gospel tradition, is to be preferred to the Jesus of Bethlehem of the Infancy Gospels. Even in the most factual fields, chronology and geography, the birth narratives leave our historical curiosity rather unsatisfied.

7

Premonitory signs of the Nativity

So far we have examined those parts of the Infancy Gospels which record the annunciation of the conception and birth of the Messiah–Son of God to Joseph in Matthew and to Mary in Luke. However, the good news is not meant to remain a secret entrusted to two persons; it was to be proclaimed by various means to a wider audience too. The means chosen by the evangelists are partly miraculous, partly theological. Herald angels are brought in to inform the shepherds in the fields around Bethlehem, an unknown star is seen by several astrologers in the East, and Jewish chief priests and Bible interpreters are summoned to disclose the meaning of a prophetic prediction relative to the birthplace of the Christ. Wondrous signs and portents, frequently forecasting important births (and deaths), were believed to occur by both the learned and the simple folk in the non-Jewish world too. The accounts relating to Jesus are part of a much wider phenomenon and must be investigated in the general framework of the history of religions. Since Matthew's rich and complex story provides much food for thought and requires a comparative analysis, it is preferable to start with the simpler narrative of Luke.

A. Lk 2:8–20

And in that region [of Bethlehem] *there were shepherds out in the field, keeping watch over their flock by night. And an angel of the Lord appeared to them, and the glory of the Lord shone around them, and they were filled with fear. And the angel said to them, 'Be not afraid; for behold, I bring you good news of a great joy which will come to all the people; for to you is born this day in the city of David a Saviour, who is Christ the Lord. And this will be a sign for you: you will find a babe wrapped in swaddling cloths and lying in a manger.' And suddenly there was with the angel a multitude of the heavenly host praising God and saying, 'Glory to God in the highest, and on earth peace among men with whom he is pleased!'*

When the angels went away from them into heaven, the shepherds said to one another, 'Let us go over to Bethlehem and see this thing that has happened, which the Lord has made known to us.' And they went with haste, and found Mary and Joseph and the babe lying in the manger. And when they saw it they made known the saying which had been told them concerning this child; and all who heard it wondered at what the shepherds told them. But Mary kept all these things, pondering them in her heart. And the shepherds returned, glorifying and praising God for all they had heard and seen, as it had been told them.

Luke recounts a simple tale for simple people. It starts with a heavenly sign, a bright light illuminating the night sky, and it is said to have been witnessed outside Bethlehem by a few guardians of the flock in the fields. They initially believed they saw one angel and afterwards a multitude of them appeared. The first celestial messenger announced to the shepherds the birth of the Lord Messiah in Bethlehem. Then abruptly the whole angelic choir burst into singing glory to God and peace to the chosen among men. The second sign given to the shepherds is less spectacular: they will recognize the newborn king in question when they see a babe lying in a manger. One must presume that the evangelist located the place at the edge of the town or just outside it. This is how the shepherds of the story could quickly find people with whom to share the joyful news before they resumed their watch over their sheep. Luke's bucolic canvas fits well the image of the pastoral city, young David's Tower of the Flock, and evokes a scene of simple rejoicing among village folk at the news of the birth of a baby boy.

Three details in the story deserve further reflection. According to age-old local custom, shepherds kept their flocks out in the fields between March and November. This would place the Nativity not in the winter season of Christmas, but some time between the spring and autumn. As has been noted (see p. 10), Clement of Alexandria (AD 150–215) testifies to traditions fixing Jesus' birthday on either 20th or 21st April or 20th May (*Stromateis* [Miscellanea] 1:21). This observation would be relevant only if Luke's description were historical, but obviously it is not. The second detail to reflect on concerns the end of the angelic praise, 'On earth peace among men with whom he [God] is pleased' (Lk 2:14). The phrase *en anthrôpois eudokias* ('among men of good will') does not allude to people who are nice and kind. It is a Hebraism or Aramaism (see the Hebrew *beney retsônô* or the Aramaic *enôsh re'ûteh*, meaning sons or man of God's good will, in the Dead Sea Scrolls). The difference in the translation may not be of great importance, but it is significant that the expression clearly suggests a Semitic tradition underlying Luke's Greek. Peace on earth is proclaimed only to God's elect. The third point concerns Luke's statement about Mary pondering on 'these things' in her heart. The most likely interpretation of the expression is that she was perplexed and was trying to puzzle out the significance of the arrival of so many unexpected visitors. The same meaning can be detected in a similar phrase appearing at the end of the episode of the twelve-year-old Jesus in the Temple (Lk 2:51). There again Mary is astounded by the words of her precociously wise son. Such an understanding of the verse is to be preferred to the traditionalist claim that Luke's report reflects the testimony of an eyewitness, namely that it derives ultimately from the mother of Jesus.

Luke's low-key birth narrative depicts a simple and unspectacular rural event. Apart from the parents, themselves simple and poor Jews (see p. 136), it brings in only a few shepherds from the country and an anonymous gathering of local inhabitants, if we discount the serenading host of heaven hovering above the scene. This is rather a quiet welcome for the 'Saviour who is Christ the Lord' (Lk 2:11), but it may be a good preparation for the later emphasis in the Gospel on the blessedness of the poor. Matthew, on the other hand, has arranged for the king of the Jews a much more grandiose reception.

B. Mt 2:1–12

Now when Jesus was born in Bethlehem of Judaea in the days of Herod the king, behold wise men from the East came to Jerusalem, saying, 'Where is he who has been born king of the Jews? For we have seen his star in the East, and have come to worship him.' When Herod the king heard this, he was troubled, and all Jerusalem with him; and assembling all the chief priests and scribes of the people, he inquired of them where the Christ was to be born. They told him, 'In Bethlehem of Judaea, for so it is written by the prophet: "And you, O Bethlehem, in the land of Judah, are by no means least among the rulers of Judah; for from you shall come a ruler who will govern my people Israel".'

Then Herod summoned the wise men secretly and ascertained from them what time the star appeared; and he sent them to Bethlehem, saying, 'Go and search diligently for the child, and when you have found him bring me word, that I too may come and worship him.' When they had heard the king they went their way; and lo, the star which they had seen in the East went before them, till it came to rest over the place where the child was. When they saw the star, they rejoiced exceedingly with great joy; and going into the house they saw the child with Mary his mother, and they fell down and worshipped him. Then opening their treasures, they offered him gifts, gold, frankincense and myrrh. And being warned in a dream not to return to Herod, they departed to their own country by another way.

In Matthew, too, the premonitory sign is celestial: a mysterious star appears in the East and leads the so-called wise men westwards to Jerusalem. Matthew recruits a handful of distinguished visitors to pay homage to the Messianic infant. They come, bring their presents and quickly depart. The ingredients of the picture are partly biblical, partly traditional Jewish, with a fair amount of non-Jewish spices and just a dash of dream *à la* Matthew completing the mixture.

The chief point of interest is the star. Ancient and medieval Christian tradition had no doubt about its reality. The simple and the great believed that the star truly appeared, was seen, was followed and, having fulfilled its purpose, vanished from the sky. Even in more recent times, starting with the illustrious Johann Keppler in the seventeenth century, astronomers sought to identify peculiar astral phenomena datable to the presumed period, which could have given rise to the story of the stargazers travelling to Bethlehem from the East under celestial guidance. An odd medley of theories has been proposed over the years to explain the star. It was a supernova; it was Halley's comet; or it was the unusual sight of the conjunction of Jupiter and Saturn. The first of these is pure speculation; the second was visible in 12 BC, a date too early for the birth of Jesus; the third could be observed in 7 BC, still a bit too soon. None of these explications would be very likely even if it could be assumed that the Infancy Gospels dealt with astronomically identifiable scientific facts, but the previous findings would make one feel doubtful in this respect. And what kind of a star, let alone conjunction of planets, could be followed from the Orient to Jerusalem, then for a few miles from Jerusalem to Bethlehem, where it would signal precisely the house among many houses where Jesus happened to be? Already, St John Chrysostom (*Homily on Mt* 6:3), realized that no star could point towards a confined spot from a great height and thought that it must have come down and stayed above the house! Likewise the Protoevangelium of James 21:3 puts the star above the head of Jesus. In fact, all the available evidence shows that the miraculous celestial body, attested in a document most probably dating to the final decades of the first century AD, can be better explained with the help of literary rather than astronomical considerations.

The most likely sources of the star heralding the birth of the Messiah are traceable on the Jewish side to biblical traditions and in a broader Jewish and non-Jewish context to legend, folklore and religious imagination.

In the Old Testament, the principal starting point for our topic is the famous prediction of the Mesopotamian non-Jewish prophet Balaam, contemporaneous with Moses, about a star rising from the Jewish race. The Book of

Numbers 24:17 quotes Balaam as saying: 'A star shall come out of Jacob and a sceptre shall rise out of Israel.' Already the ancient Greek translation of the passage speaks of a 'man' as the realization of the metaphors of star and sceptre. The theme is further developed in the Damascus Document from the Dead Sea Scrolls where the author, who was awaiting the arrival of two Messianic figures, recognized the 'Star' as the priestly Messiah and the 'Sceptre' as the royal Messiah (Damascus Document 7:19–20). Likewise, in the Greek Testament of Levi the 'Star' of the new Priest – the Priest Messiah – is said to arise in heaven similar to that of a king (Testament of Levi 18:3).

The popular interpretation of Numbers 24:17, preserved in the various Aramaic paraphrases or Targumim, expressly includes the word 'king' and even 'Messiah' as the title of the person symbolized by the 'star'. Historically the passage was applied in the second century AD by the most prominent religious teacher of that period to the leader of the second Jewish rebellion against Rome, Simeon ben Kosiba, surnamed Bar Kokhba or Son of the Star. Rabbi Akiba declared that he was the King Messiah (Palestinian Talmud Taanit 68d). In the New Testament itself the Book of Revelation makes Jesus proclaim himself 'the bright morning star' (Rev 22:16; cf. 2 Pet 1:19).

But apart from the Balaam motif, Jewish and Christian traditions associate the birth of other important personalities with extraordinary light portents. We have already encountered the case of the shiny surroundings of Noah (see p. 52 on Genesis Apocryphon 2; see also 1 En 106:2) and rabbinic literature reports the same about Moses, who at the moment of his birth flooded the house of his parents with light (Exodus Rabbah 1:22). The Nativity of Jesus is sketched in similar terms in the Protoevangelium of James:

'[Joseph and the midwife] stood in the cave. And behold, a bright cloud was overshadowing the cave. And the midwife said [plagiarizing Mary and the *Magnificat*], "My soul is magnified this day because my eyes have seen marvellous things; for salvation is born to Israel." And immediately the cloud withdrew itself out of the cave, and a great light spread in the cave . . . And little by little that light withdrew itself until the young child appeared' (Protoevangelium 19:2).

The mysterious star

Although it may have existed in unwritten form throughout the centuries, the theme of stars heralding the birth of the great and the good is attested in Jewish literature only at the medieval stage. The Book of the Upright or *Sefer ha-Yashar*, composed in its present version in the eleventh or twelfth century, reports in chapter 8 the appearance of a new star in the sky at the moment of the birth of Abraham. Examples harvested from classical literature close to the time of the composition of the Infancy Gospel of Matthew provide interesting comparative material. Pliny the Elder testifies to a general popular belief that whenever an important man is born, it is signalled by the apparition of a new bright star (*Natural History* 2:28). Suetonius (*Augustus* 94) cites in turn a certain Julius Marathus reporting that in 63 BC, some months before the birth of Octavian, the future Augustus, the public portent of a star forewarned the senate of Rome about the impending advent of a king. Republican Rome finding the idea intolerable, a decree was tabled in the Senate forbidding the rearing of male infants for the next twelve months, a reaction similar to that of Herod at hearing the news of a newborn king of the Jews (see p. 121). The same child, Octavian, was also acclaimed by the Roman astrologer Publius Nigidius Figulus as the future 'ruler of the world'. The stars continued to be bearers of good news and another astrologer, Scribonius, prophesied an illustrious career for the infant Tiberius (Suetonius, *Tiberius* 14:2). Tacitus too mentions a brilliant comet seen in the sky which led the Romans to imagine that Nero's days were almost over and a new incumbent was on the point of inheriting the imperial throne (*Annals* 14:22).

Stars could deliver a dual message; they could announce death as well as birth. In this connection it is worth recalling that the sudden rise of a comet on the first day of the festivities celebrating the deification of Julius Caesar was interpreted by the Roman people as the heavenly confirmation of the Senate's edict proclaiming his apotheosis: 'A comet appeared about an hour before sunset and shone for seven days running. This was held to be Caesar's soul, elevated to Heaven; hence the star, now placed above the forehead of his divine image' (Suetonius, *Divus Iulius* 88). This is the 'Julian star' (*Iulium sidus*) that is hinted at in one of the poems of Horace (*Odes* I 12, 47) and centuries later it inspired Shakespeare's immortal lines uttered by Calpurnia: 'When beggars die, there are no comets seen; The heavens themselves blaze forth the death of princes' (*Julius Caesar* II, ii).

In considering the star of the Magi, it is worth recalling that about AD 69, shortly before the time of composition of the Infancy Gospels, the established ancient belief in portents announcing the approach of a sovereign became the focus of attention both in Roman and in Jewish circles. The two great Roman historians, Suetonius and Tacitus, allude to a rumour which was going round in the Eastern empire announcing that a ruler of the world would arise from Judaea. The Jews, engaged in war against Rome, took advantage of the prophecy and interpreted it as applying to one of their compatriots, the coming king Messiah. But Suetonius and Tacitus shrugged off, with the customary Roman sense of superiority, the insurgents' claim. They maintained that the oracle was aimed at a Roman, this being realized when the supreme commander of their forces fighting the Jews, Vespasian, was elevated to the imperial throne (Suetonius, *Vespasian* 4:5; Tacitus, *Histories* 5:13, 2). Josephus also refers to this ambiguous prophecy, which his Jewish compatriots erroneously applied to some-one originating from their country. Josephus went further and attributed to himself the interpretation that the bene-ficiary of the oracle would be Vespasian and he personally conveyed to him the news in the presence of Titus and two of his friends (*War* 6:399–401). The story is confirmed by Suetonius who in his account mentions Josephus by name (*Vespasian* 5).

In such a context it is not unreasonable to surmise that the anecdote of the Magi and their star derived from ideas floating in the air among Jews and non-Jews during the gestation period of the Nativity narrative. By the way, we also encounter a star guiding travellers in Virgil's *Aeneid* (2:693), written about the end of the first century BC. The Magi were in good company.

The Magi

After this 'deconstruction' of the star of Bethlehem, what are we to think about the 'wise men' themselves, who observed and followed it from the East to the Holy Land?

'Wise men' is the modern English rendering of the Greek *magoi* used in Matthew's narrative. *Magoi* or Magi were originally Zoroastrian priests among the Medes and Persians who had the reputation in the Graeco-Roman world of being endowed with the gift of interpreting dreams and foretelling the future. Among other things, the forecast of the date of birth of Alexander the Great was attributed to them by Greeks and Romans (Herodotus, *Histories*, 1:120, 128; Cicero, *On Divination* 1:23, 47).

For Greek-speaking Jews the word *magoi* mostly had a pejorative connotation and referred to magicians. It appears in this meaning in the Septuagint and Josephus, synonymous with soothsayers and 'Chaldeans', but it also designated dream interpreters (Dan 2:2; 4:7; *Antiquities* 10:195, 216). Philo in general concurs with the Hellenistic Jewish custom, applying the title for example to the sorcerers and magicians of Egypt (*Life of Moses* 1:92), but at least once he credits the caste of the Persian Magi with the scientific vision of the world (*Special Laws* 3:100).

New Testament Greek in general follows the same path as the Septuagint, Josephus and Philo. In the Acts of the Apostles, Simon Magus was an ex-magician converted to Christianity (Acts 9:9) and the Cypriote Bar Jesus was a magician and Jewish false prophet (Acts 13:6). Rabbinic Hebrew also attributes a derogatory sense to the loan word *magosh*: according to the Babylonian Talmud a Jew choosing a magus as his teacher deserves to be put to death (Shabbat 75a). So in general, the term *magos* has a pejorative meaning. There are, nevertheless, two exceptions to this rule in Jewish writings and in the New Testament: the first concerns Balaam who prophesied about the star rising out of Jacob, and the second the Magi of Matthew.

As regards Balaam, he ended up in Jewish and in Christian traditions as the personification of evil. The rabbis very often designate him as Balaam the Wicked and the various New Testament references are far from complimentary (2 Peter 2:15–16; Jude 11; Rev 2:14). However, we find several flattering comments too. Philo, for instance, depicts him very positively as someone possessed by 'the truly prophetic spirit' which cleansed him of 'his art of wizardry' (*Life of Moses* 1:277). Josephus, in turn, notes that Moses did a high honour to Balaam when he recorded his prophecies and thus perpetuated his memory (*Antiquities* 4:158). Finally the rabbis, who on the whole are deeply critical of the Gentile prophet, nevertheless select him as the opposite number with whom to compare Moses, and remarkably Balaam emerges victorious out of every round of the contest (Sifre on Deuteronomy 34:10).

Now let us try to understand Matthew's thought. Though he never explicitly states it, he must have considered the Magi, who travelled from the East to Bethlehem, as the heirs of Balaam. How could they have recognized the star announcing the birth of the king of the Jews except from Balaam's prophecy about the Messiah which they had handed down among themselves?

Here the words of two Church Fathers deserve to be called to mind. For the understanding of Matthew's vision of the star of the Magi, Eusebius comments: 'In the case of remarkable and famous men we know that strange stars have appeared, what some call comets or meteors or tails of fire, or similar phenomena that are seen in connection with great and unusual events. But what event could be greater or more important for the whole universe than the spiritual light coming to all men through the Saviour's advent, bringing to human souls the gift of holiness and the true knowledge of God?' (*Demonstratio evangelica* 9:1). Origen in turn paints a splendid portrait of the Magi: 'It is said that from Balaam arose the caste and the institution of the Magi which had flourished in the East. They had in their possession in writing all that Balaam had prophesied, including "A star shall come forth from Jacob and a man shall rise from Israel". The Magi held these writings among themselves. Consequently when Jesus was born, they recognized the star and understood that the prophecy had come to fulfilment (*Homily in the Book of Numbers* 13:7).

It is conceivable that another relatively recent event influenced Matthew and prompted him to introduce the Magi into his narrative. This was the visit to Rome in the late 50s or early 60s AD of the Armenian king Tiridates and his courtiers, whom Pliny the Elder designates as Magi (*Natural History* 30:6, 16–17). This Tiridates is said to have come to Rome to worship the emperor-god Nero in the same way as Matthew's Magi came to worship the newborn Messiah of the Jews. A further curious coincidence which may have caught Matthew's attention is a detail noted by the Roman chronicler Cassius Dio. After Tiridates had been confirmed by Nero as king, this group of 'Magi', like the 'wise men' of the New Testament, did not return by the same route as the one they followed coming to Rome (*Roman History* 63:1–7).

Thus putting together Balaam, the Magi from the Orient and a star, which traditionally signals the birth of a great king, the evangelist had all the ingredients of his story. Moreover, as Matthew was keen on involving non-Jews in his tale, demonstrated by his introduction of foreign women into his genealogy of Jesus, the presence of Gentile visitors as the first persons to 'worship' Jesus in Bethlehem

makes the Nativity canvas conform perfectly to his theological intentions.

Matthew first brings the Magi to Herod's palace in
Jerusalem. They are grand enough to have access to the
royal court and their inquiry about the birthplace of Jesus
is answered by the highest doctrinal authority, the Jewish
chief priests in charge of Temple worship, and the scribes
who, according to Josephus, excelled in the 'exact knowledge of the Law and their ability to interpret the meaning
of the Holy Scriptures' (*Antiquities* 20:264; for the corresponding Egyptian commentators of sacred writings, see
p. 123; for the interpretation of Micah 5:2 see pp. 86–88).
The child is found in a house, a more dignified place than
Luke's stable, and the presents are lavish.

At this stage Matthew's plot becomes rather naive.
Herod, instead of calling on his informers and the police
to find the potential rival, passes on the answer of the
chief priests to the Magi and cunningly asks them to report
to him all they have discovered after visiting the new king
of the Jews. Thus the ground is prepared for the next act
of the drama, Herod's decree ordering the massacre of the
infants in Bethlehem.

Led again by their star, the Magi discover the house and
Jesus in it. Curiously, according to the Protoevangelium of
James 21:3 the wise men enter a cave, not a house as
Matthew has it. They 'worship him' there, i.e. pay homage
to Jesus, and offer him 'gold, frankincense and myrrh'. The
gifts have biblical resonance associated with Solomon and
the Temple of Jerusalem. Traditionally incense comes from
Arabia rather than Mesopotamia, the country of the Magi.
In this connection I remember that in my far-distant
student days two of my renowned teachers in Louvain,
Robert de Langhe and Gonzague Ryckmans, argued that

even the gift offered to Jesus, which is designated as gold in Matthew's Greek, could allude to another aromatic substance in the light of a South Arabic inscription engraved on an altar of incense.[14] Be this as it may, later Christian tradition interpreted gold as gold, and together with frankincense and myrrh they were seen as symbols of the kingship, divinity and suffering of Jesus.

Their purpose achieved, the Magi, like the biblical Balaam, returned to their country, but following a dream, as is the wont of Matthew, they chose a different route for the homeward journey, avoiding Jerusalem and Herod. Thus the evangelist found a convenient way to provide a psychological background for the edict issued by the deceived and frenzied king which, according to Matthew's story, led to the massacre of all but one of the male infants of Bethlehem.

8

The murder plot

Matthew takes the opportunity of the clandestine departure of the Magi to inject again an element of high drama into the story, which before the visit of the 'wise men' was confined to the family circle of Jesus. Joseph, after having gone through the agony of deciding what to do with the pregnant Mary, is now faced with a situation in which the life of the newly born baby is threatened by the power of the king. To resolve the matter a dream providentially brings along an angel, who enjoins Joseph to run and escape with the child to Egypt. Duplicitous Herod, who intended to employ the foreign visitors for intelligence-gathering concerning the new king, realizes that he has been let down by them. True to his character, he explodes in fury and orders that at one fell swoop all the male infants in the Bethlehem district be wiped out by his soldiery. This could be history, legend or an amalgam of the two.

Joseph's new dream

Mt 2:13–15
Now when they [the Magi] *had departed, behold, an angel of the Lord appeared to Joseph in a dream and said, 'Rise, take the child*

and his mother, and flee to Egypt and remain there till I tell you;
for Herod is about to search for the child, to destroy him.' And he
rose and took the child and his mother by night, and departed to
Egypt, and remained there until the death of Herod. This was to
fulfil what the Lord had spoken by the prophet, 'Out of Egypt have
I called my son.'

In the plot as devised by Matthew, the solution comes
before the problem. Joseph learns from an angel about the
approaching danger, before Herod has realized that the
Magi have slipped out of the country without reporting
back to him. In consequence, by the time the edict of
massacre is issued, Joseph and his family are already on
their way to Egypt where they are to stay for as long as
Herod is alive. This exodus in reverse brings about the
circumstances which will allow the return of Jesus to the
Holy Land to be proclaimed as the fulfilment of Hosea's
prophecy, 'Out of Egypt have I called my Son' (Hos 11:1).

Matthew's utilization of the proof text is once more
peculiar and serves his special purpose, but it differs in
style from his handling of quotations on the two previous
occasions. With Isaiah 7:14, the evangelist or his editor
relied entirely on the Greek Septuagint against the Hebrew
Bible, conveniently basing his argument on the *parthenos*-
virgin, and not on *'almah*-young woman, phraseology.
Coming to Micah 5:2, Matthew felt free to turn his back
on both the Hebrew and the Greek Scripture in order to
create a new text which would be more suited to underpin
his case. In Hosea 11:1 he was faced with figurative speech
in a poetic passage: in the mind of the prophet the phrase
'my son' does not refer to an individual, but alludes to
the whole people of Israel. The ancient translators, the
Septuagint and the Aramaic Targum of Jonathan, correctly

understood and interpreted the passage in this sense. They distanced themselves from the literal rendering and offered: 'Out of Egypt I have called them [the children of Israel] *sons*': note the plural. However, this true meaning of the text would not have served Matthew's aim. He needed to formulate the prophecy so that it would unequivocally point to a single subject, Jesus. So he preferred to discard the official translation of the Septuagint and substitute for 'sons' his own literal rendering of the Hebrew into Greek as 'son'. Admittedly it is not wholly impossible that an appropriate Greek version of Hosea with a word-for-word translation of the Hebrew text had already existed and was reproduced by Matthew in his Gospel. We know of such a version in the second-century rendering of Hosea by Aquila, the renowned author of a verbatim Greek translation of the Bible. But his work was published some decades after the completion of the Infancy Gospel. However, in the light of Matthew's previous record of manipulating the scriptural text it is more likely that the Greek wording employed in this passage was his own handiwork. In that case one may infer that just as the *parthenos*-virgin formula of the Greek Isaiah 7:14 prompted the story of the virginal conception, the Hosea text thus understood supplied the inspiration for the story of the flight of the infant Jesus to Egypt. Jesus had to be transferred to Egypt in order to allow God to summon his Son from there to his home country.

Herod's murderous decree

Mt 2:16–18
Then Herod, when he saw that he was tricked by the wise men, was in a furious rage, and he sent and killed all the male children in Bethlehem in all that region who were two years old or under, according to the time which he had ascertained from the wise men. Then was fulfilled what was spoken by the prophet Jeremiah: 'A voice was heard in Ramah, wailing and loud lamentation, Rachel weeping for her children; she refused to be consoled, because they were no more.'

On realizing that he had been deceived by the Magi, Herod, instead of establishing which child had been seen by the foreign visitors, a task not beyond the ken even of the dumbest village policeman, ordered the wholesale extermination of the baby boys of the neighbourhood of Bethlehem from newborns to two year olds. This would imply that in Matthew's perspective the star was first seen by the Magi some months before their arrival in Judaea and that Jesus must have gone on living in his home in Bethlehem, perhaps for quite a while.

Once more Matthew wishes to present the event as foreordained by God, as the realization of a prophecy. On this occasion, unlike on the previous ones, he even identifies the prophet and names him Jeremiah, referring to Jeremiah 31:15. The link connecting the prophecy and the murder of the innocents lies in Jeremiah's mention of Ramah, a place not far from Bethlehem where Rachel's tomb was traditionally venerated. It was in Ramah that after the conquest of Jerusalem in the sixth century BC the Babylonians kept their Jewish captives imprisoned before deporting them to Mesopotamia. So poetically, Rachel in her grave was weeping over the boys murdered by Herod at the end of the first century BC, as she had done over their forefathers nearly six hundred years earlier. The Greek citation offered by Matthew is a peculiar abridgement of the Hebrew text of the Bible. It is not in agreement with any of the variations preserved in the Septuagint, but while the quotation is free, there is no sign here of any deliberately twisted application.

Is this story consistent with what we know about Herod's character and volatile temperament? Without any doubt it is. His record of atrocities was a matter of common knowledge in Matthew's time. The list of people whom Herod directly or indirectly put to death is endless: it includes the supporters of the Hasmonaean aristocracy and the members of the Jewish high court who had tried to judge him. A large number of his other victims were his close relations. He was responsible for the execution of his passionately loved wife Mariamme, her mother Alexandra, and her young brother, who was briefly the high priest Aristobulus III. Herod also put to death Mariamme's grandfather, the high priest Hyrcanus II, and Joseph, his uncle, who was also his brother-in-law, the husband of his sister Salome. To cap all this, three of his sons also became the casualties of his insane suspiciousness. Rumour had it that the carnage perpetrated in Herod's family prompted his friend, Caesar Augustus, to utter the famous saying, 'It's better to be Herod's pig than Herod's son' (Macrobius, *Saturnalia* 2:4,11; the emperor knew that trying to appear as a Jew, Herod abstained from pork). As an ultimate gesture of madness, he planned the murder of a crowd of Jewish dignitaries imprisoned in the hippodrome of Jericho to coincide with his own death and thus ensure widespread mourning and lamentation during his funeral ceremony in nearby Herodium. It was due only to his sister Salome's unwillingness to implement the outrageous order that the final blood-bath was avoided.

In the light of Herod's reputation for savagery towards his family, including his children, the legend of the mass-acre of the innocents is provided with a plausible back-ground. Already, the work known as the Assumption of Moses, which probably originated at the turn of the era, depicts Herod as the king who 'shall slay the old and the young, and shall not spare ... And he shall execute judgements on them as the Egyptians executed upon them ...' (Assumption of Moses, 6).

Nevertheless, while the murder of the innocents is con-sonant with Herod's character and consequently could reflect history, there are strong reasons to suppose that Matthew's account primarily derives from a powerful theme embodied in the popular Jewish understanding of the Bible. The Exodus narrative, with Pharaoh's attempt to get rid of all the newborn Israelite boys, observed through the prism of Palestinian and Hellenistic Jewish tradition, supplies the model for Herod's murder plot in Matthew's Gospel. Ancient Jewish literature, represented by Josephus, Pseudo-Philo and the rabbis, recounts the story of how the parents of Moses and Pharaoh were informed in advance about Moses' destiny. From another parallel tale, preserved only in medieval sources, the reader learns about the miraculous sign announcing the birth of Abraham and his escape from the murderous hands of Nimrod. Matthew's narrative must be considered in its literary-historical context.

Let us start with the Bible. In the Book of Exodus the increase of the Israelite population was seen as a threat to the security of Egypt. Their numbers had to be reduced. So, motivated by demographic considerations, Pharaoh issued an atrocious edict ordering Jewish parents to throw their newborn sons into the Nile. Most of the children perished, but little Moses, floating in a reed basket prepared for him by his parents, escaped drowning. He was pulled out of the river and saved by the daughter of Pharaoh. This much is known from Scripture. What did Jewish tradition add to the biblical account?

The Infancy of Moses and Jewish tradition

By the time of Matthew, in the late first century AD, the story had gone through various evolutionary stages.[15] We are informed by one of the evangelist's contemporaries, the first-century AD writer known as Pseudo-Philo, author of what we know now as the *Book of Biblical Antiquities* or *Liber Antiquitatum Biblicarum*, that a significant novel feature entered the picture of the childhood story of Moses – the disclosure of his future role as saviour of Israel and destroyer of Egypt. Within the family circle it was Miriam, the elder sister of Moses, who played the part of prophetess. Like Joseph in Matthew, she first had a dream, and in the light of it she conveyed to her parents the part her unborn brother would play in the future: 'And the spirit of God came upon Maria by night, and she saw a dream, and told her parents in the morning, saying, "I saw this night, and behold, a man in a linen garment [no doubt an angel] stood and said to me, 'Go and tell your parents: behold, he who shall be born of you shall be cast into the water, for by him water shall be dried up, and by him will I do signs, and I will save my people, and he shall be the captain of it always.'" And when Maria had told her dream, her parents did not believe her' (*Biblical Antiquities* 9:10). The same story is repeated in later rabbinic sources with the difference that here Miriam/Maria's prediction was acknowledged by her father after the birth of the child: 'Miriam prophesied, "My mother shall bear a son who shall save Israel".' And when at the birth of Moses the house was filled with light, her father arose and kissed her, saying, "My daughter, your prophecy is fulfilled".' (Exodus Rabba 1:22; Babylonian Talmud Sotah 13a; Megillah 14a).

But the Jewish legend was propagated in various forms and the revelation was not always restricted to the close family circle of Moses. The Egyptian ruler himself, the antitype of Herod, learned what was to happen, and this knowledge carried with it important consequences as far as our perception of the Gospel narrative is concerned. Flavius Josephus supplies the most significant parallel tale in his *Jewish Antiquities*, which was published roughly contemporaneously with Matthew. For Josephus awareness of Moses' part in Israelite-Egyptian relations inspired Pharaoh to sentence to death all the newborn Jewish boys. They had to perish in order to ensure the elimination of Moses. Such an understanding of the affair puts the massacre of the innocents in Bethlehem in an entirely different light, with an Egyptian interpreter of their holy scriptures standing in for the Jewish chief priests approached by Herod. 'One of the sacred scribes [a *hierogrammateus*, a person with considerable skill in accurately predicting the future] announced to the king that there would be born to the Israelites at that time one who would abase the sovereignty of the Egyptians and exalt the Israelites, were he reared to manhood . . .' (*Antiquities* 2:205).

Josephus further recounts (*Antiquities* 2:210–236) that

Amram, the father of Moses, also had a dream in which he was apprised that his son would become the future redeemer of the Jews. Afraid of breaking the royal command, yet intent on doing all he could to save his son, he constructed a papyrus basket and entrusted the fate of the child to God. As in the Bible, little Moses was found by Pharaoh's daughter, who adopted the boy and persuaded her father to make him his heir. The obliging Pharaoh took the baby in his arms, but Moses grabbed the king's crown, threw it to the floor and put his foot on it. The sacred scribe, who had foretold the birth of the liberator of the Jews, then realized who the baby was and advised the king to kill him. However, divine Providence in the person of Pharaoh's daughter quickly stepped in, and Moses survived – as would Jesus too, despite Herod's edict in Matthew's version of the story.

The rabbis were also aware of a similar machination against the life of the baby Moses. Predictably, here too the story commences with a dream. Dreams seem to be essential in infancy tales and in this one the dreamer is Pharaoh. 'The whole land of Egypt' – the story goes – 'lay in one scale of a balance and a *talya*, a lamb, the little one of a ewe, lay in the other scale, but the lamb turned out to be the weightier. Pharaoh immediately summoned all the magicians [the Magi] of Egypt, and repeated to them the dream. At once Yanis and Yimbres – Jannes and Jambres in the New Testament, or Jannes and his brother in the Dead Sea Scrolls (2 Tim 3:8; Damascus Document 5:18) – the chief magicians of Egypt, opened their mouths and said to Pharaoh, "A boy is about to be born in the congregation of Israel by whose hand the whole land of Egypt will be ruined".' (Targum Pseudo-Jonathan on Exod 1:15). In short, the court wizards explained to the king that the lamb symbolized a Jewish infant who would become a lethal threat to Egypt. In Aramaic, the word *talya*, like 'kid' in English, can mean both a young animal and a child.

Jesus as new Moses

When we weigh out the similarities between the Moses/ Jesus and Pharaoh/Herod features in the Jewish texts and in Matthew, their parallelism strikes as compelling. It is especially strengthened by the role played by the official interpreters, the Egyptian sacred scribe on the one hand and the Jewish chief priests and scribes on the other. In the light of the accumulated evidence, we must conclude that Matthew's episode must have been modelled on tales with which both Palestinian and Diaspora Jews of his age were familiar. Its formation was further assisted by Herod's reputation as an insane and bloodthirsty ruler, capable of committing indescribable acts of savagery.

But apart from furnishing material for a gripping episode of the story of the infant Jesus, the Moses link also served an additional purpose. Moses in biblical and Jewish thought was both the deliverer of the Israelites from Egyptian bondage and the great Lawgiver on Mount Sinai. In the main Gospel of Matthew, Jesus performs the part of the new Moses with the Sermon on the Mount and its Beatitudes representing the new Torah (Mt 5:1–7:29). The so-called Golden Rule, 'Whatever you wish that man would do to you, do so to them', to which the evangelist appends, 'for this is the Law and the Prophets' (Mt 7:12) is Matthew's quintessential summary of both the Torah of Moses and the Gospel of Jesus.

Now in the same way as Jesus' identification as the Son

of David, i.e. the royal Messiah, has inspired the Matthean genealogy in the Infancy Gospel, his portrayal with the traits and colours of the infant Moses, prepares the picture of Matthew's final understanding of Jesus as the Revealer of the new law and the Redeemer of the world.

Appendix 1:
Jesus in Egypt in rabbinic tradition

The sojourn of Jesus in Egypt has left no mark in his life story in the Gospels. It was, however, seized on by the rabbis in their anti-Christian polemics in the early centuries of the Christian era. In their view the Egyptian connection persisted long after the infancy period. Jesus' acquaintance with magical science, the negative representation of his miracle-working activity, is ascribed to his contact with Egyptian sorcerers.[16] Origen's Celsus makes these charges in the late second century: 'Because [Jesus] was poor, he hired himself out as a workman in Egypt, and there tried his hand at certain magical powers on which the Egyptians pride themselves; he returned full of conceit because of these powers, and on account of them gave himself the title of God' (*Against Celsus* 1:28). Rabbi Eliezer also asserts that Ben Stada (a nickname of Jesus, see p. 83) smuggled to Judaea, concealed under his skin, formulae of incantation which he had learned in Egypt. The Jesus of the uncommitted Josephus, the 'performer of paradoxical deeds' (Ant 18:63), becomes in hostile rabbinic circles, under the impact of Matthew's Infancy Gospel, Jesus, the Egyptian magician.

Appendix 2:
Abraham's birth signalled by a star

The following rabbinic folk tale, preserved only in the Book of the Righteous or *Sefer ha-Yashar* and other fairly late medieval sources, is similar to the story of the infant Moses. Because of its late date – eleventh or twelfth century – it is unsuitable as comparative material, but is not without interest as a theme of folk legend, exhibiting curious resemblances to the account of the Magi and the royal plan of killing a newborn child. The boy in question is Abraham and the king seeking his life is the legendary Nimrod, 'the first on earth to be a mighty man' (Gen 10:8–9). This is how the story runs. Terah, the father of Abraham, was the commander of the army of king Nimrod. Terah's wife had just given birth to a son and the happy father, surrounded by his servants as well as by the royal sages and magicians, was celebrating the arrival of the baby amid festive eating, drinking and merrymaking. The tale then continues: 'And it came to pass that when they left the house of Terah, the sages and magicians lifted up their eyes towards the heavens that night, towards the stars. They saw a great star come from the east and run through the heavens. [This is the feature that brings the story especially close to the Matthew saga.] And the star swallowed forty stars from the four sides of the heavens. All the sages of the king, and all the magicians were afraid because of this vision, and the sages understood the thing, and knew that it concerned the child. They said to one another: This is nothing but the child, born this night to Terah, who shall grow and flourish and multiply, and shall inherit for himself and his sons the whole earth for ever.

He, and his descendants also, shall kill great kings, and they shall inherit their lands.'

Next day they reported their vision to Nimrod and warned him about the danger and, as is to be expected, the king demanded that Terah hand over the child to be killed. Terah, rather cold-heartedly by our standards, gave the newborn son of one of his concubines to the king and took Abraham and his mother to a hiding place in a cave. He grew up there while the king and his magicians imagined that the dangerous child had been slain.

9

The settlement of Jesus in Galilee

A. Mt 2:19–23

Matthew's birth narrative ends with the departure of the Holy Family from Egypt and their unforeseen and last-minute improvised choice of the Galilean town of Nazareth for their new home. Matthew does not bother to give a hint concerning the duration of the Egyptian episode. But it clearly ended according to his reckoning in 4 BC, the year of Herod's death. A double reason is given by Matthew for selecting Nazareth as the place of settlement of Joseph and his family: the first can be described as historico-political and the second as prophetic.

But when Herod died, behold, an angel of the Lord appeared in a dream to Joseph in Egypt, saying, 'Rise, take the child and his mother, and go to the land of Israel, for those who sought the child's life are dead.' And he rose and took the child and his mother, and went to the land of Israel. But when he heard that Archelaus reigned over Judaea in place of his father Herod, he was afraid to go there, and being warned in a dream he withdrew to the district of Galilee. And he went and dwelt in a city called Nazareth, that what was spoken by the prophets might be fulfilled, 'He shall be called a Nazarene.'

Matthew reverts to the angel-and-dream motif, already used first to explain Mary's condition, and the second time to convey the warning of approaching danger from jealous Herod. Here we hear the all-clear sounding: Herod, the persecutor, is dead, Joseph and the family can go home. But immediately the siren sounds again: Beware Archelaus! He cannot be trusted either. The unexpressed reason for the mention of Archelaus is the assumption that without the danger constituted by his succession as the ruler of Judaea, Joseph would have retraced his steps to his former residence in Bethlehem.

In fact, by order of the emperor Augustus, Archelaus replaced his father as ethnarch, but not as king, of the territory of Judaea from 4 BC to AD 6, and Joseph clearly considered him as great a threat as Herod to the safety of Jesus. The historical truth is that, although Archelaus first tried to ingratiate himself with his Judaean subjects, he nevertheless soon let loose his army on a group of religious Jews, involved in an upheaval in the Temple during the week of Passover in 4 BC. Hence there was genuine reason to fear him. But Matthew offers no specific explanation for his unwillingness to allow for a return of the family to Bethlehem other than the general prejudice that a son is bound to resemble his father.

A final dream, this time without the mention of an angel, directs Joseph away from Judaea towards the north of Palestine, to the district of Galilee. But we know from Josephus that when Augustus reassigned Herod's kingdom to his heirs, the tetrarchy of Galilee was allocated to another son of Herod, Antipas (4 BC–AD 39), who was later described by Jesus as 'that fox', and is said to have plotted against his life (Lk 13:31–32). So why was the presence of Antipas in the northern province not seen as an obstacle for Joseph to take up residence there? Why was only Archelaus regarded as a menace? The evangelist keeps quiet on this issue; he does not seem to have thought out all the implications of Herod's succession.

In fact, Matthew's Joseph had no real choice. He had to opt for Galilee because Jesus had to be associated with Nazareth. As has been noted (pp. 89–90), the entire Gospel tradition and Luke's infancy narrative tie Jesus as well as Joseph and Mary before him to this locality. Yet there was no special reason for preferring Nazareth. It was not famous; indeed, it was a totally insignificant place, never mentioned in the Jewish Bible, or in Josephus (full of Palestinian place names) or in rabbinic literature. Even for St Jerome, who knew Palestine well, having spent many years in Bethlehem in the fourth/fifth century, Nazareth was just a small village, a *villula* in Latin. The earliest non-Christian reference to it comes from a third/fourth century AD inscription found on the floor of a synagogue in Caesarea. There Nazareth is listed as the seat of one of the Jewish priestly divisions, resettled in Galilee after the destruction of the Temple in AD 70. The only conceivable reason for the evangelists (both Matthew and Luke) to bring Joseph and his family to this place of no consequence is that Jesus was generally known for his association with Nazareth, that he actually grew up there, or was possibly even born in that town.

Matthew had a better way of deciding the issue. He proceeded in his usual manner and presented Joseph's choice of Nazareth as a necessary move to fulfil yet another prophecy relative to Jesus, 'He shall be called a *Nazôraios*, a Nazarene'. Some of Matthew's previous biblical proofs have appeared difficult, but this is the slipperiest of them all. There is no single source named: the quotation is vaguely ascribed to several unidentified prophets. As for the prediction 'that he shall be called a Nazarene', these words can nowhere be found in the Old Testament as we have it!

Some scholars argue that Nazarene derives from the Hebrew noun *netser*, meaning 'branch', and cite Isaiah 11:1, 'There shall come forth a shoot from the stump of Jesse, and a *branch* shall grow out of his roots.' But the problem that needs to be faced is that NeTSeR and NaZôRaios do not derive from the same root. Other interpreters seek to base the prophecy on the story of Samson in Judges 13:5, 'For the boy shall be a *nazir* [a holy and ascetic Nazirite who abstains from wine and from cutting his hair]'. However, Samson is not a suitable type for Jesus, and abstemiousness was not one of Jesus' obvious peculiarities. His critics, with usual polemical exaggeration, called him a 'glutton and a winebibber' (Mt 11:19; Lk 7:34).

The solution considered most likely assumes that the two forms of Greek words – *Nazôraios* and *Nazarênos* – are synonymous; both designate someone belonging to, or coming from, Nazareth. The evangelist needed to prove Jesus' connection with Nazareth, and he solved the problem by means of a vague and probably *ad hoc* manufactured prophecy, vaguely assigned to some anonymous prophets. In short, Matthew's odd interpretation of the historical reality gave birth to a prophetic proof whose sole aim was to account for the migration of Joseph, Mary and Jesus from their Judaean home country to obscure Nazareth in distant Galilee. The linking of Jesus to these two localities is the primary task that faced the writers of the Infancy Gospels. Luke had to transfer Joseph and Mary from the north to the south to ensure that Jesus would be born in Bethlehem; Matthew faced the opposite dilemma – how to bring Jesus from the south to the north – from Judaea to Galilee.

B. Lk 2:21–40

In contrast to the display of grandeur associated with the Magi and the element of danger generated by Herod and his men, Luke continues his low-key account of the Nativity of Jesus. After the story of the stable, the shepherds and the ordinary villagers greeting Jesus, he recounts the brief period of peaceful existence of Joseph, Mary and the babe in Judaea – no doubt in Bethlehem – before bringing them back to their home in Nazareth.

And at the end of eight days, when he was circumcised, he was called Jesus, the name given by the angel before he was conceived in the womb.

And when the time came for their purification according to the law of Moses, they brought him up to Jerusalem to present him to the Lord (as it is written in the law of the Lord, 'Every male that opens the womb shall be called holy to the Lord') and to offer a sacrifice according to what is said in the law of the Lord, 'a pair of turtledoves or two young pigeons.' Now there was a man in Jerusalem, whose name was Simeon, and this man was righteous and devout, looking for the consolation of Israel, and the Holy Spirit was upon him. And it had been revealed to him by the Holy Spirit that he would not see death before he had seen the Lord's Christ. And he came in the Spirit into the temple, and when the parents brought in the child Jesus, to do for him according to the custom of the Law, he took him up in his arms and blessed God and said,
'Lord, now you are letting your servant depart in peace, according to your word;

for my eyes have seen your salvation
that you have prepared in the presence of all peoples,
a light for revelation to the Gentiles,
and for glory to your people Israel.'

And his father and his mother marvelled at what was said about him. And Simeon blessed them and said to Mary his mother,

'Behold, this child is appointed for the fall and rising of many in Israel, and for a sign that is opposed and a sword will pierce through your own soul also, so that thoughts from many hearts may be revealed.'

And there was a prophetess, Anna, the daughter of Phanuel, of the tribe of Asher. She was advanced in years, having lived with her husband seven years from when she was a virgin, and then as a widow until she was eighty-four. She did not depart from the temple, worshiping with fasting and prayer night and day. And coming up at that very hour she began to give thanks to God and to speak of him to all who were waiting for the redemption of Jerusalem.

And when they had performed everything according to the Law of the Lord, they returned into Galilee, to their own town of Nazareth. And the child grew and became strong, filled with wisdom. And the favour of God was upon him.

Luke does not tell his readers whether Jesus and his family remained in the shed or moved into some more decent accommodation during the days which followed the birth of the child. The first special event briefly recorded is the circumcision of the week-old boy in conformity with the law laid down in Leviticus 12:3, 'On the eighth day the flesh of his foreskin shall be circumcised'. It was then that Jesus received his name, Yeshua in Hebrew, commonly used among Jews. Who the name-giver was, the father or the mother, is not stated. Tradition would allow either. In Matthew, as has been noted (p. 72), it befell to Joseph to play the role in accordance with the anonymous angel's instruction in his dream (Mt 1:21). In Luke, on the other hand, Gabriel entrusted Mary with the duty to name her son (Lk 1:31).

Naming a male child on the occasion of his circumcision has become traditional in Judaism, but the Bible contains no rules in this respect. Luke refers to the custom twice: first in relation to John, so called both by his mother and by his father, and then to Jesus (Lk 1:59–63; 2:21), and in doing so he supplies the earliest evidence associating the naming of a boy with the ritual of circumcision.

The second family feast day, combining the presentation of Jesus in the Temple and the purification of his mother after giving birth to a boy, severely tested the Gentile Luke's understanding of Jewish customs. The Mosaic law laid down that every first-born male child should become God's property, but he could be redeemed from devoting his whole life to liturgical worship by means of a payment to the Temple of five shekels of silver (Num 18:15–16). Furthermore, a mother who had given birth to a boy had to undergo purification forty days after the event. The sacrifice which was to accompany the purification ceremony consisted of a one-year-old lamb and a young pigeon or a turtledove. However, if a lamb was beyond the family's means, two turtledoves or two young pigeons could be offered as a substitute. Luke mentions only the latter, the pair of birds, and thereby intentionally or unintentionally classifies Mary as not wealthy enough to afford a lamb.

As it happens, Luke gets almost everything slightly off-true. First of all, he refers not to Mary's, but to '*their* purification'. Whether he meant Mary and Joseph or Mary and Jesus, he was mistaken. Only the mother was liable to ritual cleansing. Next, he is unaware of the redemption fee of five shekels and confuses it with the sacrifice to be offered by the mother.

Be this as it may, the main message is that the parents of Jesus stayed in the south undisturbed by Herod – no murder plot, no flight to Egypt – and conscientiously fulfilled all the religious obligations imposed on pious Jews by biblical law. Moreover, the visit to the Temple offers Luke an opportunity to indicate that God-fearing Jews, inspired by the same Holy Spirit who was instrumental in the conception of Jesus, recognized from the very beginning his future greatness. The role assigned to Simeon, apparently an old man, and Anna, a devout widow of eighty-four years, is to proclaim in advance that Jesus would become the future Messiah, the redeemer of Israel. Anna is explicitly introduced as a prophetess and Simeon is portrayed as a man directed by the Holy Spirit. They are portrayed as divinely predisposed to recognize Jesus.

Luke further ensures that his own universalistic message – the Gospel to be preached beyond the boundaries of the Jewish world – finds an early expression. Jesus is to bring salvation not only to God's people Israel, but he will also be the light of revelation to the Gentiles. Luke further inserts a hint about Jesus as a future object of contention, 'a sign that is spoken against', in Israel. Instead of the imminent crisis signalled by Matthew, Luke concludes his infancy account by forecasting the future tragic – as well as glorious – destiny of Jesus.

After the completion of the Temple ceremonies, the pendulum returns to its starting point. Jesus was duly born in Bethlehem thanks to the obliging intervention of Caesar Augustus, and he can now set forth to Nazareth, where according to the prophets he belongs.

At this point the principal part of the Infancy Gospels

abruptly terminates in Matthew, leaving a yawning gap of thirty years in his biography of Christ, and the story is not re-launched until we meet the grown-up Jesus just before he is baptized by John on the shore of the river Jordan. Luke's ending is smoother. As a parting comment, he foresees a happy future for the child blessed by God, and growing in strength and wisdom. He also appends an afterthought in the form of a single further anecdote connected with Jesus, which he dates twelve years later.

Thus the infancy stories reach completion and the real Gospel, as devised by Mark, is ready to spring to life.

Appendix:
Fulfilment interpretation in Matthew

While Luke's Infancy Gospel does not use biblical proof texts to support its statements, Matthew regularly relies on them and his first two chapters exhibit no less than five examples of explicit quotation, of which four are preceded by a formula indicating that the event in question was declared to be the realization of a prophetic prediction. The five citations are: Isaiah 7:14 in Matthew 1:23 (pp. 67–71); Micah 5:2 in Matthew 2:6 (pp. 86–88); Hosea 11:1 in Matthew 2:15 (pp. 117–118); Jeremiah 31:15 in Matthew 2:18 (pp. 119–20) and an unidentifiable text of unnamed prophets in Matthew 2:23 (pp. 132–33).

The procedure is not Matthew's invention; it is common in the Dead Sea Scrolls and is also attested in rabbinic literature. The interpreters, especially those operating in the Qumran community, who created the Scrolls, expound the meaning of a prophetic passage by identifying the persons or occurrences in recent sectarian history, and declaring them to be the implementation of ancient oracles. For example, the Nahum Commentary from Cave 4 claims that Nahum 2:11, 'Whither the lion goes . . .', when properly explained, refers to a Seleucid Greek king's approach to Jerusalem: '[Interpreted, this concerns Deme]trius king of Greece who sought . . . to enter Jerusalem (Nahum Commentary 1:1–2).

The Bible commentators of the Qumran community and the ancient rabbis attached their exegesis to the scriptural text as it stood before them. Sometimes they relied on readings which differ from the traditional wording, but as a rule they did not alter the scriptural sayings to suit their doctrinal purposes. Such a detached objectivity cannot be presupposed in the case of the 'Greek' Matthew. Writing for a Greek-speaking Gentile audience, unfamiliar with the Jewish ways of treating the Bible, he not only felt free to twist the meaning of a passage to underpin his ideas, taking for instance the collective 'son', which in Hosea relates to the people of Israel, as the designation of an individual (Jesus), but purposefully changed the wording of Micah so that instead of deprecating Bethlehem, it extolled its greatness. His free handling of the biblical evidence reaches its climax in the attribution of an otherwise unattested prediction about Jesus being a Nazarene, i.e. a man from Nazareth, to an obscure group of unnamed prophets: 'that what was spoken by the prophets might be fulfilled, He shall be called a Nazarene'.

In our discussion of the citation of Isaiah 7:14 as proof of the virginal conception of Jesus, we have posited that Matthew had been influenced by the Septuagint's imprecise rendering of *'almah* as *parthenos* (virgin), a rendering which was later replaced by *neanis* (young woman) in the versions of Aquila, Symmachus and Theodotion. However, in the absence of pre-Christian manuscripts of the Greek Isaiah 7:14, 'Behold, a *'virgin'* shall conceive . . .', a sneaking uncertainity will persist in one's mind whether the significant use made of *parthenos* by the 'Greek' Matthew might not have played a part in the introduction, from the second century AD onwards, of the word 'virgin' into the *Christian* codices of the Septuagint translation of Isaiah?

10

Luke's supplements to the Infancy Gospel

The basic Infancy Gospel, i.e. the material contained in both Matthew and Luke, entails three topics: the miraculous conception of Jesus, his birth in Bethlehem and the settlement of the family in Nazareth. This main narrative, thought to be traceable to a tradition preceding the Greek Gospels, was transmitted originally in a Semitic language, most probably in Aramaic, in Palestinian Jewish circles. The primitive tradition underwent further changes, first in Aramaic and later in Greek, as can be detected from a comparative study showing the discrepancies between Matthew and Luke. Other differences are attributable to the reworking performed by the two evangelists and/or their editors.

Luke supplies, however, two categories of additional material, totally unknown to Matthew. The first deals with the origin of John the Baptist and the second with a single incident in the life of the young Jesus. Neither of them forms part of the Christmas saga, but for the sake of completeness anyone interested in the Infancy Gospels must give them some consideration.

A. The birth of John the Baptist

The relationship between the birth story of Jesus and that of John is artificial and is undoubtedly Luke's creation. It is based on the purported kinship between Mary and Elizabeth, a kinship that is never again mentioned in the Gospel of Luke or in any other part of the New Testament. In addition to the family link, the common element is the intervention of the Holy Spirit who, after causing Mary's pregnancy, is said to have inspired Elizabeth to greet Mary, and to have mysteriously made one unborn babe (John) recognize another unborn babe (Jesus). Curiously, whereas Jesus is the leading actor of the infancy drama, in the first chapter of Luke the space devoted to John exceeds that given to Jesus. These peculiarities and the prehistory of the material relative to John ask for some clarification.

Lk 1:5–25, 39–80

In the days of Herod, king of Judea, there was a priest named Zechariah, of the division of Abijah; and he had a wife of the daughters of Aaron, and her name was Elizabeth. And they were both righteous before God, walking in all the commandments and ordinances of the Lord blameless. But they had no child, because Elizabeth was barren, and both were advanced in years.

Now while he was serving as priest before God when his division was on duty, according to the custom of the priesthood, it fell to him by lot to enter the temple of the Lord and burn incense. And the whole multitude of the people were praying outside at the hour of incense. And there appeared to him an angel of the Lord standing on the right side of the altar of incense. And Zechariah was troubled when he saw him, and fear fell upon him. But the angel said to him, 'Do not be afraid, Zechariah, for your prayer is heard, and your wife

*Elizabeth will bear you a son, and you shall call his name John.
And you will have joy and gladness, and many will rejoice at his
birth; for he will be great before the Lord, and he shall drink no
wine nor strong drink, and he will be filled with the Holy Spirit,
even from his mother's womb. And he will turn many of the sons of
Israel to the Lord their God, and he will go before him in the spirit
and power of Elijah, to turn the hearts of the fathers to the children,
and the disobedient to the wisdom of the just, to make ready for the
Lord a people prepared.'*

*And Zechariah said to the angel, 'How shall I know this? For
I am an old man, and my wife is advanced in years.' And the angel
answered him, 'I am Gabriel, who stand in the presence of God; and
I was sent to speak to you, and to bring you this good news. And
behold, you will be silent and unable to speak until the day that these
things come to pass, because you did not believe my words, which will
be fulfilled in their time.' And the people were waiting for Zechariah,
and they wondered at his delay in the temple. And when he came
out, he could not speak to them, and they perceived that he had seen
a vision in the temple; and he made signs to them and remained
dumb. And when his time of service was ended, he went to his home.*

*After these days his wife Elizabeth conceived, and for five months
she hid herself, saying, 'Thus the Lord has done to me in the days
when he looked on me, to take away my reproach among men.'*

*In those days Mary arose and went with haste into the hill country,
to a city of Judah, and she entered the house of Zechariah and greeted
Elizabeth. And when Elizabeth heard the greeting of Mary, the
babe leaped in her womb; and Elizabeth was filled with the Holy
Spirit and she exclaimed with a loud cry, 'Blessed are you among
women, and blessed is the fruit of your womb! And why is this
granted me, that the mother of my Lord should come to me? For
behold, when the voice of your greeting came to my ears, the babe in
my womb leaped for joy. And blessed is she who believed that there*

would be a fulfilment of what was spoken to her from the Lord.' And Mary said, 'My soul magnifies the Lord, and my spirit rejoices in God my Saviour, for he has regarded the low estate of his handmaiden. For behold, henceforth all generations will call me blessed; for he who is mighty has done great things for me, and holy is his name. And his mercy is on those who fear him from generation to generation. He has shown strength with his arm, he has scattered the proud in the imagination of their hearts, he has put down the mighty from their thrones, and exalted those of low degree; he has filled the hungry with good things, and the rich he has sent empty away. He has helped his servant Israel, in rememberance of his mercy, as he spoke to our fathers, to Abraham and to his posterity for ever.' And Mary remained with her about three months, and returned to her home. Now the time came for Elizabeth to be delivered, and she gave birth to a son. And her neighbours and kinsfolk heard that the Lord had shown great mercy to her, and they rejoiced with her. And on the eighth day they came to circumcise the child; and they would have named him Zechariah after his father, but his mother said, 'Not so; he shall be called John.' And they said to her, 'None of your kindred is called by this name.' And they made signs to his father, inquiring what he would have him called. And he asked for a writing tablet, and wrote, 'His name is John.' And they all marvelled. And immediately his mouth was opened and his tongue loosed, and he spoke, blessing God. And fear came on all their neighbours. And all these things were talked about through all the hill country of Judea; and all who heard them laid them up in their hearts, saying, 'What then will this child be?' For the hand of the Lord was with him. And his father Zechariah was filled with the Holy Spirit, and prophesied, saying, 'Blessed be the Lord God of Israel, for he has visited and redeemed his people, and has raised up a horn of salvation for us in the house of his servant David, as he spoke by the mouth of his holy prophets from of old, that we should be saved from our enemies, and from the hand of all who hate *us; to perform the mercy promised to our fathers, and to remember his covenant, the oath which he swore to our father Abraham, to grant us that we, being delivered from the hand of our enemies, might serve him without fear, in holiness and righteousness before him all the days of our life. And you, child, will be called the prophet of the Most High; for you will go before the Lord to prepare his ways, to give knowledge of salvation to his people in the forgiveness of their sins, through the tender mercy of our God, when the day shall dawn upon us from on high to give light to those who sit in darkness and in the shadow of death, to guide our feet into the way of peace.' And the child grew and became strong in spirit, and he was in the wilderness till the day of his manifestation to Israel.*

The preliminaries to the miraculous birth of the Baptist are unquestionably modelled on the story of Samuel in the Hebrew Bible (see p. 50). After suffering sterility for many years, Hannah, the mother-to-be of the future prophet, promised God that if he intervened and made her conceive a son, she would dedicate the child to the life of a holy ascetic or Nazirite (1 Samuel 1:11). God listened, fulfilled Hannah's prayer, Samuel was born and became a Temple servant at the Temple of Shiloh.

In Luke history repeats itself. The devout but childless elderly couple, the priest Zechariah and his wife Elizabeth, play the part of the biblical Elkanah and Hannah. When Zechariah was on Temple duty, he saw a vision, and the angel Gabriel told him that his wife would give birth to a male child to be called John. He would be a Nazirite, always abstaining from alcohol, and filled with the Holy Spirit already in his mother's womb, he would be destined to become the new prophet Elijah.

Contrary to the young Mary, who readily trusted the angel, the more sophisticated Zechariah refused to believe what he was told and as a punishment he was struck with dumbness. In due course, John was conceived in the normal but divinely assisted fashion, and Elizabeth thanked God for removing her shame, as did the biblical women before her whose barrenness had been miraculously ended by God (see Gen 30:23).

After the interlude of the Annunciation, with the angel Gabriel's mission to Mary in Nazareth (see p. 75), Luke introduces the episode of the visitation. No particulars are given about how the pregnant young Mary travelled from Galilee to Judaea (alone? in a group?). The traditional place of the meeting of the two women is located at Ain Karim, west of Jerusalem. In the neighbourhood of Ain Karim a cave was discovered in 2004 and Shimon Gibson, the archaeologist in charge of the investigations, believes that the site was used in the early Byzantine period for the cult of John the Baptist. Luke seems to interpret John's joyful kick in his mother's womb as a sign of welcome for the few weeks old embryo, Jesus, whom Elizabeth, no doubt believed to be inspired by the Holy Spirit, subsequently calls 'my Lord'.

The song of praise – the *Magnificat* –which follows, is ascribed in most ancient manuscripts of Luke to Mary, but other textual witnesses attribute it to Elizabeth. With the hindsight of almost a century, it is amusing to note that in 1912 that old ecclesiastical busybody, the Pontifical Biblical Commission, forbade Catholic scholars to adopt the interpretation which places the *Magnificat* on the lips of Elizabeth. Yet the reference to the low estate of the handmaid (Lk 1:48), corresponding to the lifting of reproach imposed by men on sterile women (Lk 1:25), fits better the circumstances of Elizabeth than those of Mary. Also, the *Magnificat* imitates in part the thanksgiving psalm of

Hannah in 1 Samuel 2:1–10 and Hannah is the model of Elizabeth, not that of Mary.

But looking at it objectively, the hymn contains a good many lines which have nothing to do with either Mary or Elizabeth. 'He has shown strength with his arm; he has scattered the proud in the thoughts of their hearts; he has put down the mighty from their thrones and exalted those of low degree' (Lk 1:51–52) is more applicable to a war situation than to the state of either of our two women. Half a century ago, Paul Winter pointed out that the *Magnificat* as well as the *Benedictus* could be identified as hymns composed during the war of the Maccabees against the Greeks of Syria and not very skilfully retouched for its new purpose by Luke. What has become the *Magnificat* was originally composed to celebrate victory over the enemies of the Jews and the *Benedictus* was a prayer before a battle. In fact, the most likely solution is that we are dealing here with pre-existent Jewish psalms similar to the hymns contained in the Dead Sea Scrolls. They consist of a cleverly combined anthology of poetic extracts from various parts of the Hebrew Bible. Recently, similarities have also been noted between the fragmentary Song of Miriam preserved in the Reworked Pentateuch from the Dead Sea Scrolls (4Q365) and some lines of the *Magnificat*.

In connection with the birth, circumcision and name-giving of John, Luke mixes traditional elements with some strange comments. At the beginning of the narrative, Zechariah is said to have lost his speech. Later he is also depicted as deaf so that the family is obliged to use sign language to communicate with him. The relatives apparently intended to give the father's name to the son, as though this was normal. But I am not aware of the existence of such a custom in ancient Judaism. Neither did

Palestinian Jews use writing tablets as Luke reports. Potsherds or bits of papyrus were their cheap writing material. Once Zechariah consented to call the boy John, he instantaneously regained the use of his tongue, a miracle that was seen as a good omen for the child's future.

The *Benedictus*, the thanksgiving hymn assigned to Zechariah, is as inappropriate in substance as the *Magnificat*. Its imagery is also bellicose and Messianic. It refers to the liberation of Israel, the lifting up of the Davidic horn of salvation against the enemies in remembrance of God's covenant with Abraham. Only verses 76 and 77, 'And you, child, will be called the prophet of the Most High; for you will go before the Lord to prepare his ways, to give knowledge of salvation to his people in the forgiveness of their sins', relate to John the Baptist and are obviously Luke's own composition. They are so formulated as to outline in advance John's future role in the Gospel (see Lk 3:3–5). The end of the section, Luke 1:80, also alludes to the prophetic destiny of the Baptist who will be 'strong in spirit' and to his ascetic-eremitic training in the desert prior to his appearance on the public scene.

The life of John in the desert, feeding on locusts and wild honey, can be envisaged as solitary, like that of the mid-first-century AD Jewish holy man Bannus whom the young Josephus chose as his guru. Bannus, he writes in his autobiography, 'dwelt in the wilderness, wearing only such clothing as trees provided, feeding on such things as grew of themselves, and using frequent ablutions of cold water, by day and night, for purity's sake' (*Life* 11). However, since the discovery of the Dead Sea Scrolls it has often been suggested that John joined a communal type of ascetic group like the community of the Essenes. Nevertheless, if he ever did so, one must presume that by the time he launched his movement of repentance in the Jordan valley, he was no longer a member of the Essene sect since it is known that the Essenes were forbidden to preach to outsiders.

It is a puzzle why Luke would couple his infancy narrative of Jesus with such a lengthy story of the Baptist. It has been advanced again and again that in fact he reused an extant birth narrative of the Baptist, originally handed down in the circles of John's disciples. There is no doubt that such circles existed; Josephus implies that John had many followers (*Antiquities* 18:116–117) and the New Testament explicitly testifies to it. John 3:25–26 alludes to jealous pupils of John who denounced Jesus to their master for baptizing on his own, amounting in their eyes to a unilateral declaration of independence. Moreover, the Acts of the Apostles records that the Alexandrian Apollos, Paul's associate, and some Ephesian disciples have joined the Church from John's baptismal circles (Acts 18:25; 19:3). They would have constituted the original audience for which the birth story of the Baptist was composed.

B. The young Jesus in the Temple

Lk 2:41–52

Now his parents went to Jerusalem every year at the feast of the Passover. And when he was twelve years old, they went up according to custom; and when the feast was ended, as they were returning, the boy Jesus stayed behind in Jerusalem. His parents did not know it, but supposing him to be in the company they went a day's journey, and they sought him among their kinsfolk and acquaintances; and when they did not find him, they returned to Jerusalem, seeking him.

After three days they found him in the temple, sitting among the teachers, listening to them and asking them questions; and all who heard him were amazed at his understanding and his answers. And when they saw him they were astonished; and his mother said to him, 'Son, why have you treated us so? Behold, your father and I have been looking for you anxiously.' And he said to them, 'How is it that you sought me? Did you not know that I must be in my Father's house?' And they did not understand the saying which he spoke to them. And he went down with them and came to Nazareth, and was obedient to them; and his mother kept all these things in her heart. And Jesus increased in wisdom and in stature, and in favour with God and man.

The anecdote appended by Luke to conclude his infancy narrative follows up his earlier statement about the infant Jesus in Nazareth: 'The child grew and became strong, filled with wisdom' (Lk 2:40). The present incident gives an example of the intellectual prowess of the twelve-year-old Jesus. The occasion is the pilgrimage to Jerusalem undertaken by the extended family – parents and kinsfolk – on the feast of Passover. This was one of the three festivals at which every adult male Jew was duty-bound to participate in Temple worship in Jerusalem. The moment of reaching adulthood was determined by sexual maturity for both men and women. Girls, as has been explained (pp. 64–65), came of age with the onset of menstruation, and young men with the appearance of pubic hair (Mishnah Niddah 6:11). From then on they were obliged to observe all the precepts of the Mosaic Law, including the thrice-yearly visit to the Temple. Later it was thought that a boy attained legal maturity or the status of *bar mitzvah* (son of the commandment) on his thirteenth birthday. Girls ceased to be minors a year earlier. It would seem that according to the tradition represented by Luke male majority also started at the age of twelve.

Luke narrates that in the chaotic city of Jerusalem, filled with Jewish pilgrims as Mecca is packed with Muslims during the season of hajj, Jesus lost contact with Mary and Joseph and his disappearance was not noticed until the end of the first day of the return journey to Galilee. The anxious parents looked for him for three days before finally finding the young man in what seems to be a school in the Temple. Jesus sat there among the teachers and took an active part in the discussion, showing in the process remarkable depth of sagacity and learning.

Precocious wisdom is part of the pattern of a famous man in Jewish legend and tradition. About the young Moses, Philo of Alexandria writes: 'Teachers . . . arrived from different parts, some unbidden from the neighbouring countries and the provinces of Egypt, others summoned from Greece . . . But in a short time he advanced beyond their capacities . . . indeed, he himself devised and propounded problems which they could not easily solve' (*Life of Moses* 1:21). Josephus, in turn, boastingly remarks about himself, 'While still a mere boy, about fourteen years old, I won universal applause for my love of letters; inasmuch that the chief priests and the leading men of the city used constantly to come to me for precise information about some particular in our ordinances' (*Life* 8).

In answer to the reproach of his worried and angry mother, 'Your father and I have been looking for you anxiously', Luke puts on the lips of Jesus the following haughty words which foreshadow the attitude to his family of the Jesus depicted in the Synoptic Gospels, 'How is it that you sought me? Did you not know that I must be in what is my Father's?' (Lk 2:49; see Mk 3:33–35; Mt 12:48–

50; Lk 8:21). No surprise that Mary and Joseph were dumfounded by the words of their provocative teenage son (see Lk 2:50).

Here ends Luke's Infancy Gospel with a reiterated assertion that the young Jesus continued to grow in wisdom and in favour with God and man. Accepting the pre-Lucan origin of the birth story of John, Luke's editorial retouches of the Baptist's infancy and the final anecdote concerning the young Jesus can best be understood as further preliminaries to the already fully formulated account of the Gospel drama in which Jesus of Nazareth is the star and John the Baptist plays only a supporting role.

Epilogue

The Infancy Gospels in retrospect

Having followed in the previous chapters step by step the unfolding of the Infancy Gospels, and completed a painstaking literary and historical analysis of their numerous particulars, we have now a clear idea of the individual details of the birth story of Jesus, but do we know what they all add up to? For what purpose were these narratives devised? Are they part of the original composition or were they affixed later to the Gospels of Matthew and Luke? Above all, where does history end and legend begin? To sum up our investigation and assess the significance of the two birth narratives we have to find answers to the following five questions:

1. What are the Infancy Gospels?
2. How do they relate to the main Gospels of Matthew and Luke?
3. When and why were they attached to them?
4. What can they reveal about their prehistory?
5. What is their historical value and theological significance?

1. What are the Infancy Gospels?

The Infancy Gospels are two parallel narratives, intended to recount the earliest period of the life of Jesus, starting with his conception and terminating with his arrival in Nazareth in the company of Joseph and Mary. The two accounts do not derive from one another. They have a few basic elements in common (extraordinary pregnancy, Bethlehem as birth place, Nazareth as permanent residence), but they display a much larger amount of divergent features.

Let us consider the differences between the two accounts. The original residence of Mary and Joseph is not stated in Matthew, but as the only travel involved prior to the journey to Galilee is the flight to Egypt, it must be Bethlehem. By contrast, in Luke Joseph and Mary had been living in Nazareth and made their way to Bethlehem only to comply with the obligation imposed on them by Augustus' order of a universal census. The newborn Jesus was welcomed in a stable by angels, local shepherds and town people according to Luke, while in Matthew he was worshipped in a house by the Magi. The interval between the birth of Jesus and his arrival in Nazareth entails in Matthew the escape to Egypt to avoid Herod's soldiers and a change of plan during the return trip demanding the migration from Judaea to Galilee, whereas in Luke Jesus, Mary and Joseph retrace their steps to the original home town of the parents in Nazareth after forty days spent peacefully in Bethlehem and Jerusalem.

2. How do the birth narratives relate to the main Gospels?

When considered against the principal account of the life of Jesus contained in Matthew chapters 3–28 and Luke chapters 3–24, the two infancy narratives stand apart and the bond linking them to the rest of the Gospel narratives appears extremely flimsy. If the first two chapters of Matthew and Luke had been lost, their disappearance would not be felt by the readers of the main story. The latter never refers back to events already recounted in the opening section; it simply has no awareness whatsoever of the infancy tales.

Let us change our point of view and look from the infancy accounts towards the main Gospels. None of the major items listed in the birth narratives is developed or even hinted at in the subsequent life of Jesus. In vain would you rummage through every line of Matthew or Luke to find a direct or even a veiled allusion to the miraculous conception of Jesus or his birth in Bethlehem, to the star and the wise men, to the immediate recognition of Jesus as the future Messiah by angels, shepherds, town folk, or by Simeon and Anna. Not even the apparently weighty matters of Joseph's intention to divorce Mary or the flight of the family to Egypt is ever remembered. If the main Gospel tradition had been aware of the wondrous features of the birth canvas, one would have expected to find here and there an innuendo to them, for instance when the people of Nazareth were discussing the origin of Jesus or on the occasion of debates about his messianic status.

On the other hand, the Infancy Gospels are acquainted

with the main accounts of Matthew and Luke and display a number of significant traits which are characteristic of the picture of Jesus in them. In particular, in both Matthew and Luke Jesus is portrayed as the Son of Abraham, the Son of David and the Son of God. In Matthew he appears also as the new Moses.

The Son of Abraham title underlines the Jewishness of Jesus, through his descent from the father of the Hebrew nation. It appears in both infancy narratives, but in Matthew the motif is given a salient position and figures already in the title of the Gospel: 'The book of the genealogy of Jesus ... the son of Abraham', and Abraham is, in addition, the absolute starting point of the Matthean genealogy. Jesus is also portrayed as the future saviour of his people by the angel addressing Joseph in his dream. This focus on Judaism is fully in line with the insistence in Matthew's main Gospel, or at least in the initial orientation of the main Gospel, on the exclusively Jewish direction of the ministry of Jesus and of his disciples, sent only to 'the lost sheep of the house of Israel' and not to the Gentiles or the Samaritans (Mt 10:5–6). But Matthew's infancy story also incorporates two elements which afford an opening towards the nations of the world. Non-Jewish women figure in the genealogical table of Jesus (see p. 30) and the Gentile Magi are the first to recognize and greet him (p. 110). This broadening of Matthew's outlook appears to reflect the evangelist's increasing disappointment with the Jewish response to the apostolic preaching and his later optimism regarding the mission to non-Jews which sees the Gospel more and more aimed towards the pagan world and depicts the messianic banquet as attended almost exclusively by Gentiles (Mt 8:11–12).

In Luke's list, Abraham is not brought into such a

pronounced relief. He is just one of the many ancestors of Jesus. On the other hand this non-Jewish evangelist includes in the birth story of Jesus the Mosaic customs of circumcision, the redemption of the firstborn and the purification of the mother forty days after giving birth to a male child; moreover he makes his devout elderly Simeon depict Jesus as 'the light ... for the glory of Israel' and inserts into his narrative the episode of Jesus' Passover pilgrimage to the Temple of Jerusalem, a Jewish custom par excellence. Nevertheless, this emphasis on Jewishness is balanced by a universalistic trend. Luke traces Jesus' family line not just to Abraham, but back to Adam, the father of all mankind, and in the hymn *Nunc dimittis* Simeon characterizes Jesus as 'a light for revelation to the Gentiles'. The same kind of universalism is present throughout in the Gospel of Luke, for instance in the mandate of Jesus to preach repentance and forgiveness to all the nations (Lk 24:47), and in the repeated omission of references to Jewish exclusiveness like the harsh words of Jesus addressed to the Syro-Phoenician woman (Mk 7:27; Mt 15:26) or his description of Gentiles as dogs or swine (Mt 7:6).

The second characteristic title of Jesus in the Infancy Gospels is that of Son of David, which indicates the messianic dignity attributed to him. In Matthew, Messiahship figures in the title of the Gospel: 'The book of the genealogy of Jesus Christ, the son of David' and king David stands at the head of the second group of fourteen generations, Abraham having opened the first. The Davidic descent is further stressed by Matthew when he adduces the biblical proof text of Micah, associating the birthplace of Jesus with the city of David, Bethlehem. Luke, even though he places no special emphasis on David in the genealogy of Jesus, similarly insists on his messianic future when the angel Gabriel promises to Mary that her child would inherit the royal throne and when the shepherds are informed about the birth of 'Christ the Lord' in 'the city of David'. The messianic theme that dominates the main Gospels of Matthew and Luke, as well as Mark and John, is thus firmly anticipated in the birth narratives.

The third title in the Infancy Gospels, 'Son of God', is a metaphor frequently encountered in the Hebrew Bible (see pp. 53–55), but Matthew and Luke and the rest of the New Testament have endowed the phrase with a meaning stronger than it usually carries in Jewish writings. Matthew applies to Jesus the name 'God with us', the Emmanuel of Isaiah 7:14, and claims that in him were fulfilled the divine words uttered by Hosea, 'Out of Egypt have I called my Son'. For Luke, too, the child borne by Mary is 'the Son of the Most High' and 'the Son of God'. This general elevation of Jesus, Son of David or Messiah, seemingly to a superhuman dignity, apparently starts from the extraordinary beginnings attributed to him in the Infancy Gospels. Early Christian legends progressively developing from the mid-second to the sixth centuries, for instance those recorded in the Greek Infancy Gospel of Thomas, portray the small child Jesus as healing the sick, raising the dead and even causing clay sparrows to take to the air, but occasionally also abusing his divine miracle-working power by striking dead a child who semi-accidentally had hit him with a stone.

The wonderful birth stories of the Hebrew Bible, as well as those of the literature representing Jewish religious thought in the age of Jesus, suggest that popular circles would have found it normal that the birth of the Messiah should display signs of special divine intervention. In this vein Luke, by propounding the wondrous pregnancy of the mother of John the Baptist, paves the way for the announcement of the even more marvellous beginnings of Jesus. Both infancy narratives identify the Holy Spirit as the arcane medium through which the virgin Mary conceives her son. This seems to have amounted in Matthew's final version of the story to a miraculous impregnation without the sperm of a human male, leading to the birth of the Son of God in fulfilment of the prophecy, 'A virgin (*qua* virgin) shall conceive and bear a son' – Emmanuel or 'God with us'. By contrast, the version underlying Luke's account may have to do with the extraordinary pregnancy, in a normal marital framework, of a girl not yet physically fit for motherhood. Essential elements of this mode of thinking are implicit in Luke's words, establishing an opposite parallelism between the way young Mary and the senescent Elizabeth became pregnant (Lk 1:34–37).

A fourth unformulated theological feature, prefiguring the notion of Jesus as another Moses, is contained in Matthew's story. It derives from the biblical and post-biblical portrayal of the origins of Moses on which Matthew's account of Herod's murder plot against Jesus and the latter's escape to Egypt are shaped. The Jewish Moses motif, typifying the future prophet, legislator and liberator of Israel, prefigures the picture embedded in the main Gospel of Matthew representing Jesus as the lawgiver and saviour of his people. In other words, the 'new Moses' feature of the Infancy Gospel supplies an advance insight into the future destiny of Jesus as perceived by the evangelist, especially in depicting Jesus' proclamation of the Sermon on the Mount as a re-enactment of the revelation of the Law by Moses at Mount Sinai (Mt 5:1–7:29).

In short the three principal aspects common to both

infancy narratives and the additional new Moses image in Matthew serve as connecting links which prepare and provide with a special perspective the full understanding of the Gospel message conveyed by the two evangelists. Luke's further supplements relating to the role of John the Baptist and the growth of Jesus in wisdom and grace reinforce the same conclusion.

3. When and why were the birth narratives attached to the Gospels?

The two principal properties of the infancy narratives, their anticipatory character in relation to the evolved message of Matthew and Luke and the fact that their peculiar feats are totally absent from the main body of the story of Jesus, demonstrate that they are later additions to the main Gospel account. Some of the elements, especially Matthew's various scriptural quotations and the idea of the virginal conception in direct conflict with the Judaeo-Christian tradition, make sense only if we envisage a second stage in the transmission of the Gospel message with the help of a Greek text and for the benefit of a Gentile Hellenic audience. The stress on universalism in Luke and even more so in Matthew is a further argument in favour of a relatively advanced date for the emergence of the infancy addenda. Finally, the ultimate proof that the birth story is not a natural introductory section of a biography is the absence of continuity between it and the rest of the Gospel. If we disregard the odd episode of the twelve-year-old Jesus' Passover pilgrimage to Jerusalem, none of the evangelists accounts for the three decades or so that separate the infancy of Jesus from his adulthood.

Observing them with the benefit of hindsight, the ultimate purpose of the Infancy Gospels seems to be the creation of a prologue, enveloping the newborn Jesus with an aura of marvel and enigma (mysterious conception, wonderful star, angelic messengers and revelatory dreams). This prologue forms the appropriate counterpart of the equally wondrous epilogue of the Gospels – also replete with angels, visions and apparitions – the resurrection of Jesus.

4. What can the Infancy Gospels reveal about their prehistory?

No doubt any attempt to venture into the obscure antecedents of the infancy narratives will carry with it even more speculation than we have been accustomed to so far. Nevertheless, let us proceed on the basis of as much evidence as can be mustered. Clearly, the two most fundamental points the birth narratives endeavour to make concern Jesus' messianic dignity (he is the Son of David) and his special relationship to the Deity (he is the Son of God). We must also take it for granted that the original elements of both these features sprang from a Galilean milieu and were expressed in the language and terminology of Palestinian Jews who spoke Aramaic or Hebrew or both.

It is clear that in Matthew as well as in Luke the first and foremost attribute of the infant Jesus is that he is the future saviour of Israel, the royal Messiah, Son of David. Two genealogies are produced to back up this claim. In Matthew, Joseph is addressed as 'son of David' and indirectly the Davidic connection of Jesus is argued from his being born in Bethlehem, the city of David and expected birthplace of the Messiah. Presuming that in the original Semitic infancy story the Hebrew version of Isaiah 7:14 was used, it announced the birth of the coming redeemer called 'God with us' or 'Son of God', understood as the equivalent of Christ-Messiah yet without implying a virginal conception which could enter the picture only on the secondary Greek level. The two terms, Messiah and Son of God, are interconnected and automatically follow one another as in 'You are the Christ, the Son of the living God' (Mt 16:16) or 'Tell us if you are the Christ, the Son of God' (Mt 26:63). So in this reconstructed original Semitic version of the Infancy Gospel, Jesus, the son of Joseph of the house of David, is proclaimed the Christ surnamed Emmanuel (God with us) or in usual parlance the Messiah, Son of God.

The Semitic layer of the tradition subjacent to Luke contains the same messianic concept. Jesus, the son of Joseph of the house of David is expected to inherit the royal throne and as Christ, the Lord, the Son of the Most High or the Son of God will reign over Israel for ever. A miraculous element is attached to the story of Mary's conception without the support of a biblical quotation and without actually denying Joseph's participation in the process. The model introduced to explain the extraordinary happening is the humanly incomprehensible, but biblically not unprecedented pregnancy of an aged woman, a 'virgin for the second time'. With Mary we seem to move in the opposite direction towards a pregnancy earlier than was thought possible and unparalleled in Scripture.

By the time the tradition reaches its Greek phase, thanks to the official Septuagint version of Isaiah 7 of the Greek-speaking Jews read with a Hellenistic mind set, the original imagery evolves into the divinely enacted mystery of the virginal conception. The child thus produced is more and more perceived not just figuratively but literally as divine, a son fathered not by Joseph of the house of David, but by God himself through his Holy Spirit.

5. What is the historical value and theological significance of the Infancy Gospels?

From the nature of the birth stories and the many fabulous features incorporated in them – angels, dreams, virginal conception, miraculous star – one is forced to repeat the conclusion of W. D. Davies and D. C. Allison, namely that the Infancy Gospels are 'not the stuff out of which history is made' (see p. 20). However, some elements of history may be buried beneath legendary wrappings. They are admittedly basic, but they enjoy a high degree of probability when seen against the main Jesus story recorded in the subsequent sections of the Gospels. They testify to the birth of a Jewish child by the name of Jesus (Yeshua in Hebrew) to a couple called Mary (Miriam) and Joseph. The birth occurred according to both Matthew and Luke while Herod was king of Judaea (in or before 4 BC), and most likely during the end period of his reign. The location of the birth in Bethlehem, though firmly asserted in both accounts on theological grounds, is directly contradicted in John and indirectly in the Synoptics where Galilee and Nazareth are designated as Jesus' home country and native town. On the other hand, both Matthew and Luke agree in pointing to Nazareth as the village where Jesus spent his youth. So if we were to reconstruct the birth certificate of Jesus, we could fill in the names and the place of residence of the child and the parents, but the date of birth could only be approximate, under Herod, and the locale controverted, Bethlehem according to tradition, but more likely Nazareth.

The doctrinal analysis of the Infancy Gospels shows that in their final stage of Greek development the central concepts of 'Messiah–Redeemer' and 'Son of God–God with us' are embedded in the miraculous atmosphere of the virginal conception and endowed with an enhanced theological content.

The essence of the joyful good tiding announced by the Nativity stories is that God has sent his Son, supernaturally born of a virgin mother, to save his people from their sins and bring peace to all men favoured by God. This is the happy message that the Christian world identifies with Christmas. To achieve this, we have to apply a selective reading to the Infancy Gospels. The glorious Nativity of Church tradition is built on the sweet and simple story of Luke with angels, shepherds and jolly neighbours. The merry Christmas that people wish to each other is purged from the spoiling effects of the Matthean drama with Joseph's psychological torture in face of the dilemma of what to do with the pregnant Mary and the fear, panic and tears caused by Herod's edict threatening with untimely extinction the budding life of the Son of God.

THE PASSION

Preface

The traditional version of the Passion of Jesus is coherent and straightforward, even simple. Whether it is preached from the pulpit or read in literature of piety, the story hardly varies. It may even be watched in the cinema: *The Passion of the Christ* by Mel Gibson, the international box-office hit of 2004, is still fresh in many people's minds. This is a story which is meant to be perceived with the eyes of faith. It recounts the sacrifice, the self-immolation of the Son of God who willingly offered his life, we are told, for the redemption of the sins of mankind. Without exception all the children of Adam have to accept their own responsibility for it if they are to reap the fruits of the atonement achieved for them all by Christ dying on the cross.

But the same story has also an historical (or I would say pseudo-historical) dimension. It emanates from a simplistic and selective reading of the Gospels without appropriate interpretation, indeed without any interpretation. According to this version the suffering and death of Jesus were the outcome of the hostility and hatred of his enemies, the Jewish priestly leaders and their council, who browbeat the weak but basically decent Roman governor, Pontius Pilate, forcing him to pronounce Jesus guilty, and successfully harangued the multitude of their compatriots to clamour for his crucifixion. Here the responsibility for *deicide*, the murder of the divine Christ, is placed squarely on the shoulders of the Jewish people.

This representation of the Passion, which will be shown to be biased and twisted, has influenced the Christian world over most of its history. Even today, when the official spokesmen of churches, chapels and denominations reject what the great French historian Jules Isaac once called the doctrine of contempt, *l'enseignement du mépris*, many Christians, clergy and laity, have instinctively applauded the Passion *à la* Mel Gibson. Even the Pope is reported to have approved the version of the movie seen by him with the Delphic words, 'It is as it was.'

It goes without saying that, like everything else we know about Jesus, the account of his last day derives from the New Testament, and more specifically from the discrete narratives of the four Gospels. Unlike the traditional story produced by the Church, they are neither simple nor coherent. On the contrary, as we shall see, they are filled with discrepancies. Without a deliberate and artificial harmonization, which was already attempted in the centuries when Christendom was young and has continued ever since, they seem disconcerting and confusing. They form a mystery within which real history lurks.

To penetrate this mystery, the reader must come to grips with the literary sources that are closest to the reality of the Passion and subject Mark, Matthew, Luke and John, our four principal witnesses, to a stringent critical scrutiny. I like to compare the historian-interpreter to a detective charged with preparing a report to a law court. Four documents lie on his desk. He must pore over them, seek to clarify obscurities, establish facts and point out contradictions. In reality, the process will be simpler than it first appears since three out of the four narratives of the Passion closely resemble one another. Two of them, Mark and Matthew, are nearly identical. In consequence, they can be surveyed together, grasped in a single glance, *synoptically*, while separate treatment is reserved for the occasional, but often momentous, divergences between the narratives, especially in the Gospel of Luke. Finally, the comparison of Mark, Matthew and Luke – the Synoptics – with the Fourth Gospel will make plain that the events of the last day of the life of Jesus have been transmitted in two fundamentally different traditions. To define, evaluate and interpret these differences with the help of expert knowledge peppered with common sense is the momentous task facing this inquiry.

Prologue

No attentive reader of the Gospels can fail to notice the striking contrast between the way the evangelists depict Jewish attitudes towards Jesus before the Passion and during the last few hours of his life.

Up until the fateful week in Jerusalem which ended with the crucifixion, Jesus appears as a charismatic healer and exorcist and a magnetic preacher, a greatly loved and much sought-after figure in the Galilean countryside around the Lake of Gennesaret. He attracted crowds. They avidly listened to him wherever he went, in synagogues, streets, public squares, on hillsides and on the lake shore. The rumour of his approach brought out the sick in droves. Those who were too weak to walk were carried to him on stretchers. Petty-minded synagogue presidents and quibbling village scribes envied him, and were overheard muttering words of disapproval. In their pedestrian thinking the blind, the lame and the lepers should have been cured, and the possessed delivered, on weekdays, not on the Sabbath. Insufficiently versed in Jewish theology, some Galilean scribes murmured 'blasphemy' when Jesus proclaimed that healing was the equivalent of forgiveness of sins, but even if they had dared to speak up, they would have been fighting a losing battle: the holy man from Nazareth enjoyed the trust and support of large segments of the local rural population. Both he and the crowd were familiar with the frame of mind of officialdom towards prophets of God. It did not bother them.

Not only in Galilee, but even on his arrival in Jerusalem, Jesus is portrayed as the hero of a joyful and welcoming crowd. He came to the holy city, according to the custom recorded by the Jewish historian Josephus, about a week before the feast (*Jewish War* 6:290). Mark, Matthew and John describe Jesus' approach to the capital as a triumphal entry universally acclaimed. Luke is less grandiose and ascribes the mood of festivity more specifically to the group of disciples who were the companions of Jesus. When observed more closely, the episode loses some of its intended radiance. Riding on a donkey was not that uncommon in the circumstances. We learn from rabbinic literature that ass drivers did lucrative business at the approach of festivals by hiring out their beasts to wealthy or important pilgrims. But the evangelists transform the incident into a royal messianic event, hailing the arrival of the Son of David. To make the messianic aspect more patent, Matthew cites the words of Zechariah, 'Behold your king is coming to you, humble and mounted on an ass, and on a colt, the foal of an ass.' 'On an ass' and 'on a colt, the foal of an ass' is of course the usual Hebrew poetic device of parallelism, the same idea being expressed in two similar expressions identical in meaning: they designate a single donkey. But in his zeal to equate prophecy and fulfilment, Matthew, unlike the other three evangelists, presents Jesus with two animals, a she-ass and her colt, and gives the impression that he was riding on both. The disciples put their garments 'on them', and Jesus sat 'on them'. To suggest that the first 'on them' refers to the animals and the second to the garments, smacks of special pleading. In fact, John corrects the misrepresentation by quoting, 'Behold your king is coming, sitting on an ass's colt.'

The Gospel account of Jesus' first two or three days in Jerusalem further attests indirectly that large groups were listening to his teaching in the Temple and that his patent popularity is given as the cause of why the priestly authorities abstained from immediately taking steps against him. In short, until his arrest Jesus seems to have been the darling of the Galilean country folk and even warmly welcomed by the Jewish crowd in Jerusalem.

Yet, if we are to believe the same evangelists, on the last day of the life of Jesus a sea-change suddenly occurred. Jesus became the object of hatred not only for the leaders of Judaism, the chief priests and the Sanhedrin, but also for the Jewish people at large. No one had a good word to say in his favour. Many witnesses testified against him, but none for him. The crowd abominated him. All the people, 'the Jews', asked for his death and egged on the Roman governor to crucify him. Luke, it is true, attempts to diminish the contrast by reporting that the previously hostile crowd present at the crucifixion beat their breasts after the death of Jesus, but this mitigating circumstance seems to be of the evangelist's own making, unsupported by Mark, Matthew or John.

What compelled the evangelists to present such an extraordinary contrast of pictures? How do the four Gospel accounts relate to one another and how do they tally with first-century AD Jewish and Roman reality as we know it from non-New Testament sources? What were the motives that influenced their chronicle of the Passion? These are the issues that the historian-exegete, or if you like the detective of the past, will have to investigate. He will assemble the evidence and inspect it through a magnifying glass before attempting to answer the final £1,000,000 question: What really happened on the day of the crucifixion of Jesus nearly 2,000 years ago?

I

Literary and historical preliminaries

A. The sources

The Passion of Jesus of Nazareth is part of history, but it is also the central core of Christian theology, the very nucleus of the Church's faith. The four evangelists who convey their doctrinal message in the form of a biography of Jesus are not detached story-tellers; they do not intend to record the final hours of the life and the death of their hero in an objective manner or, to use Tacitus' famous phrase, *sine ira et studio*, without fear or favour. They have a religious message to preach in a form adapted to the needs of their specific readership. So before we set out to examine what the evangelists want us to *believe* about the Passion, we must ask who they were, whom they addressed and what motivated their writings.

According to mainstream scholarship these four authors produced their works between *c.* AD 70 and 110. None of them identifies himself explicitly in his Gospel, but early Christian tradition yields some information about each of them. Mark is thought to be the earliest. The other two, Matthew and Luke, largely depend on the Gospel of Mark in the general gist of their narrative and often even display verbal similarities in their Greek text. If any of the Gospels ever existed in a written Aramaic (or Hebrew) version, no trace of it has come down to us in manuscript form.

Mark is usually identified with John Mark, a cousin of Barnabas, the colleague of St Paul. He later became a companion of Paul himself, but is also alluded to by the pseudonymous author of the First Letter of Peter (c. AD 100) as Peter's close associate. Outside the New Testament the earliest reference to Mark comes from a now lost work of Papias, an early second-century AD writer, quoted by the fourth-century Church historian Eusebius of Caesarea (c. 260–340). If Papias is to be believed, Mark was Peter's assistant, and wrote his Gospel at the instigation of the Roman Christians. Papias also states that Mark was not a direct witness of the Gospel events, but recorded the preaching of Peter. Christian tradition credits Mark with the establishment of the Church in Egypt. The large majority of modern scholars date Mark's account of the life and teaching of Jesus to the time of the first war between the Jews and the Romans (AD 66–74), more likely to the years following the destruction of Jerusalem in AD 70, that is, some forty years or so after the Passion.

Matthew is also mentioned by Papias. He is introduced as the compiler of the Sayings of Jesus written in the Hebrew dialect, i.e. in Aramaic, the common language of Palestinian Jews. Since no excerpts of these have been preserved, no one knows whether the Sayings are identical with the actual Gospel of Matthew or are only parts of it, and whether this Matthew is one of the twelve apostles of Jesus. Matthew's biblical quotations, which often make sense only on the basis of the Greek Old Testament, suggest that he was probably a Greek-speaking Jew. Most contemporary New Testament scholars place Matthew's work to c. AD 80–100.

Luke, the non-Jewish author of the Third Gospel, is believed to have been one of Paul's close associates. The earliest representation of Luke as an evangelist and the author of the Acts of the Apostles comes from the Muratorian Canon, the most ancient catalogue of the books of the New Testament, contained in an eighth-century Milanese manuscript and published in 1740 by L. A. Muratori. The original document is thought to date to *c.* AD 180.

The identity of the evangelist John is unascertainable. Apart from the title, 'according to John', the Gospel itself from chapter 1 to chapter 20 mentions no author. In chapter 21, someone distinct from the evangelist attempts to make him out to be 'the beloved disciple of Jesus'. This hint *tacitly* assumes that the Galilean fisherman John, the son of Zebedee and an eyewitness of the ministry of Jesus, was the fourth evangelist.

Now, the Church father Irenaeus, bishop of Lyons, reported *c.* AD 180 that the apostle John lived to a great age in the city of Ephesus in western Asia Minor, and produced the Fourth Gospel there. However, no New Testament evidence confirms this statement to connect John with Ephesus. The martyr bishop Ignatius of Antioch had a splendid opportunity to testify to John's presence in Ephesus, but failed to do so. In his letter to the members of the church of that city, written *c.* AD 110, he referred to the Ephesians as the people of Paul, and not as the children of John, who had lived among them only a few years earlier.

To envisage the author of the Fourth Gospel as an 'uneducated and common' Galilean fisherman (Acts 4:13), who was a centenarian, give or take a few years, yet was not only still creative but fully at home in Hellenistic mystical speculation, requires a leap of imagination which seems to be beyond the reasonable. In sum, the identity of the writer of the Fourth Gospel cannot be pinned down.

Regarding the date of this Gospel, the oldest known manuscript fragments of John belong to sometime between AD 125 and 150, and equally the oldest references to John's Gospel in early Christian literature come from the same period. So the work was completed before the mid-second century. On the other hand, the highly evolved doctrine of John demands that its composition should be placed after the redaction of the Synoptic Gospels, that is, after the last quarter of the first century AD. Likewise, the split reflected in John between Judaism and Christianity, with followers of Jesus being expelled from the synagogue, is hardly conceivable before the turn of the first century AD. The combined evidence suggests that the Fourth Gospel was published in the early second century, probably between the years AD 100 and 110. So the author of the Fourth Gospel is unlikely to have been a contemporary of the historical Jesus. None of the four authors seems to have been an eyewitness of the events chronicled in the Gospels. They completed their books forty to seventy years after the death of Jesus and relied on and transmitted traditions which they had inherited from various churches. The value of their testimony about the Passion will depend on the nature of the tradition transmitted by them.

The evangelists addressed their Gospels to those of their contemporaries whom they tried to persuade to embrace Christianity or to people who were already members of their churches. In other words, they either preached to convert or to the converted. Judging from their efforts to play down the Jewishness of Jesus, and the general anti-Jewish bent of the Passion stories, it is reasonable to deduce that the evangelization was no longer aimed at

Jews, but at the Gentile inhabitants of the Greek-speaking world. Indeed, the Jews are overwhelmingly depicted as the enemies of Jesus and his followers.

As far as the motivation is concerned, the story-tellers aim at presenting a Jewish Redeemer-Messiah crucified by Pontius Pilate so that he appears acceptable to the non-Jewish inhabitants of the Graeco-Roman world. The purpose of the evangelists is to prove implicitly that being a Christian is not incompatible with loyalty to Caesar and the Roman empire. Hence, as will be shown, they whitewash Pilate and Rome, and correspondingly denigrate the Jewish leaders and through them the Jewish people at large.

B. Jewish history and legal systems in force in Judaea in the age of Jesus

The historical background

The death of Jesus of Nazareth on the cross is an established fact, arguably the only established fact about him. It is attested not only by the four Gospels, the Acts of the Apostles and St Paul, but also outside the New Testament by Josephus ('Pilate ... condemned him to be crucified', *Jewish Antiquities* 18:64), Tacitus ('Christ ... had undergone the death penalty in the reign of Tiberius, by sentence of the procurator Pontius Pilate', *Annals* 15:44, 3) and, indirectly, by the Talmud ('On the eve of Passover they hanged Yeshu', Babylonian Talmud Sanhedrin 43a). The crucifixion is part of Jewish and Roman history of the first century AD. Therefore the historian must not treat it as an occurrence unique and *sui generis*, and any study of the Gospel accounts should be preceded by a survey of the chronological, cultural, religious and legal background of the Passion.

The life of Jesus began possibly in 6/5 BC, in the closing years of the reign of Herod the Great (37–4 BC), and ended during the governorship of Pontius Pilate (AD 26–36), probably in AD 30. His early childhood coincided with quarrels about the succession of Herod. Constant political turmoil was caused by a series of uprisings. The emperor Augustus divided the realm into three parts among the surviving sons of Herod. Archelaus was put in charge of Judaea, Idumaea and Samaria (4 BC–AD 6), Antipas of Galilee (4 BC–AD 39) and Philip of territories to the north and east of Galilee (4 BC–AD 33/34). None of them inherited the royal title.

Archelaus was dismissed by Augustus in AD 6. Judaea was then turned into a Roman province and the government of the country was transferred to a prefect, appointed by the emperor. The reorganization was effected by Quirinius, governor of Syria, who was also behind a new tax registration which led to an unsuccessful uprising fomented by Judas the Galilean, the founder of the Jewish revolutionary party of the Zealots. The extensive powers of Roman governors included the choice and dismissal of Jewish high priests. Unlike during the previous centuries, during the lifetime of Jesus most of these high priests installed by the Romans remained in office for only a short period, with the exception of Annas (AD 6–15) and Caiaphas (AD 18–36/7), to both of whom leading parts are assigned in the trial of Jesus. Under Roman surveillance, the Jewish high priest and his senate, the Sanhedrin, which acted as both council and tribunal, continued to play a significant role in the day-to-day government of Judaea and Jerusalem, whereas Galilee, the country of Jesus, enjoyed near complete independence under Herod Antipas as long as the taxes were duly delivered to Rome.

The public life of Jesus as a charismatic healer and teacher began in Galilee in the wake of the missionary activity of John the Baptist with whose message of repentance and proclamation of the approaching kingdom of God Jesus started his own preaching career. In the Gospel of Luke, John's mission is dated to the fifteenth year of the emperor Tiberius or AD 29. It was of short duration and ended with the beheading of the Baptist by order of Herod Antipas, ruler of Galilee, probably in the same year. The inauguration of Jesus' ministry must therefore also be placed in AD 29. The New Testament contains two views of the length of its duration. The Gospel of John, mentioning two or three Passovers, implies that it lasted at least three years. In the Synoptic Gospels, on the other hand, only one Passover and a single visit to Jerusalem are mentioned. This shorter chronology is historically the more likely. It is easier to explain why John, the most recent of the evangelists, felt the need to extend the period of the career of Jesus in order to accommodate his numerous and lengthy, almost certainly fictional speeches, rather than justifying its compression to less than twelve months, and possibly no more than six, by the three earlier evangelists. Before travelling to Jerusalem for the Passover pilgrimage, probably in AD 30, Jesus had been active in Galilee, in particular on the northern shore of the Lake of Gennesaret, with occasional short trips to the region of Tyre and Sidon in Lebanon and to the district of the Decapolis east of the Lake. Like most Galilean Passover pilgrims, he avoided the unfriendly land of the Samaritans and journeyed south along the Jordan valley passing through Jericho.

The Gospels differ on the circumstances of the execution of Jesus, but they unanimously assert that it happened at the end of a brief legal process or of two consecutive legal processes. Two types of law court functioned in first-century AD Palestine, whether under Roman or Herodian government. Jewish judges were always in charge of the administration of the law of Moses in conformity with the traditional regulations, but when Judaea came under direct Roman government, political matters were handled by the chief representative of the emperor, who, as a rule, was a high Roman civil servant. This governor bore the title of prefect between AD 6 and 41 and that of procurator from AD 44 to 66. In the intervening three years (AD 41–44) the Romans ceded all the governing powers to the Herodian-Jewish king Agrippa I.

Before investigating the two trial accounts contained in the Gospels, one before a Jewish court, as reported in the Synoptics, the other before Pilate's tribunal, it will be useful to outline the legal systems in force in Roman Judaea during the age of Jesus.

The Roman provincial system

Let us start with the Roman jurisdiction. The first-century Jewish historian Flavius Josephus (AD 37–c. 100) clearly states that at the moment of the introduction in AD 6 of direct Roman administration in Judaea, Coponius, the first prefect, arrived in Jerusalem, 'entrusted by Augustus with full powers, including the infliction of capital punishment' (*Jewish War* 2:117). This means that Pontius Pilate, who twenty years after Coponius came to occupy the office from AD 26 to 36, had absolute discretion regarding the fate of Jesus. Pilate had the authority to deal with him with all the severity of Roman law after Jesus had been charged with disloyalty to the emperor and the state. The normal penalty for the crime of sedition was crucifixion, reserved for foreigners, i.e. non-Roman citizens, as well as for bandits and slaves, and the governor personally had the right to inflict the appropriate punishment on such criminals. So the Roman side of the trial of Jesus, unlike that of Paul whose case was complicated by his claim of Roman citizenship, raises no legal or judicial problem of any kind. If Jesus was accused of revolutionary activity and was found guilty, Pilate had the right to crucify him. He was even duty-bound to do so.

The biblical legal system

The Jewish court proceedings and their relation to the legal competence of Rome are more complex. Hence in order to shed some light on the legal aspects of the Passion story it is necessary to glance at the juridical system directly inherited from Scripture by first-century Judaism.

On the lowest level, justice had been administered since biblical times by the elders of each locality, and the public venue of the hearings was the city gate. Punishment, including the death penalty, was imposed there and then after the examination of the cases in the presence of anyone wishing to attend (Dt 21:18–21; 22:13–21; 1 Kgs 21:11–13). But already during the time of the kings of Judah, before the first fall of Jerusalem in 586 BC, we encounter professional law officials, chosen by the Jewish kings to deal with offences. 'You shall appoint judges ... in all your towns and they shall judge the people with righteous judgement' (Dt 16:18). This new arrangement came into force as the result of the reform initiated by King Jehoshaphat in the middle of the ninth century BC. This king set up judges in all the major cities of the kingdom of Judah, as well as a special tribunal of priests in Jerusalem under the presidency of the high priest, to act as a kind of established appeal court, dealing with issues which exceeded the competence of provincial judges (2 Chron 19:4–11). Priestly supremacy in legal matters was codified in the legislation promulgated in the Book of Deuteronomy, which specifies that difficult legal matters, involving among other things assault and homicide, had to be dealt with by the supreme tribunal of 'the Levitical priests' in the capital city of Jerusalem (Dt 17:8–12).

In connection with the accounts of the trial of Jesus it must be remembered that according to biblical law, no court proceeding could take place unless trustworthy prosecution witnesses had proved that the accused had committed the offence or crime with which he was charged. Information about the stringent testing of witnesses is available in the apocryphal supplement attached to the Book of Daniel, dealing with Susannah and the wicked elders, and in the tractate of the Mishnah called Sanhedrin in rabbinic literature. In capital cases the testimony of two or three witnesses was required; no one could be convicted and put to death on the evidence of a single witness (Dt 17:6). When the execution was by stoning, the witnesses had to act also as executioners; they literally had to cast the first stones (Dt 17:7).

As far as capital sentences are concerned, the prohibition under pain of death of work on the Sabbath day (Ex 31:15) is illustrated in the Bible by the incident of a Jew caught gathering firewood in the wilderness on the day of sabbatical rest. The scriptural narrator reports that the unfortunate man was brought before Moses and Aaron, who ordered in

God's name that 'all the congregation [should] stone him with stones outside the camp' (Ex 31:32–6).

The Bible lists twelve categories of crime which carried the death penalty: (1) homicide (Ex 21:12; Lev 24:17; Num 35:16–21); (2) abduction of a man in order to sell him as a slave (Ex 21:16; Dt 24:7); (3) idolatry (Ex 22:19; Lev 20:1–5; Dt 13:2–19; 17:2–7); (4) blasphemy (Lev 24:15–16); (5) the breaking of the Sabbath (Ex 32:14–15; Num 15:32–6); (6) sorcery (Ex 22:17; Lev 20:27); (7) grave offences against parents (Ex 21:15, 17; Lev 20:8; Dt 21:18–21); (8) prostitution by a priest's daughter (Lev 21:9); (9) adultery (Lev 20:10; Dt 22:22); (10) incest (Lev 20:11–12, 14, 17); (11) male homosexual acts (Lev 20:13); and (12) bestiality (Lev 20:15–16). In the cases of the two gravest religious offences, idolatry and blasphemy, the prescribed form of execution was specifically by stoning.

Regarding the Jewish high court, which still functioned in Jerusalem in the first century AD, the Alexandrian Jewish philosopher Philo (*c.* 20 BC–*c.* AD 50) and the historian Flavius Josephus supply descriptions of great interest. Their accounts are very valuable for the understanding of the legal conditions which existed in the age of Jesus. Philo, interpreting Deuteronomy's depiction of the supreme court in Jerusalem, identifies the 'more discerning judges' with 'the priests and the head and leader of the priests', i.e. the Jewish high priest. In Philo's opinion, one of the commanding reasons for entrusting complicated cases to the high priest is that he was 'necessarily a prophet ... and to a prophet nothing is unknown' (*Special Laws* 4:190–92). Josephus also defines the high priest and his colleagues as the officials whose task is to 'safeguard the laws, adjudicate in cases of dispute and punish those convicted of crimes' (*Against Apion* 2:194). The supreme court in Jerusalem consisted, according to the same author, of 'the high priest and the prophet and the council of the elders' (*Jewish Antiquities* 4:218). While during the existence of the kingdom of Judah the participation of a court prophet, an appointed royal functionary, in the decision of law cases is conceivable, by the time of Philo and Josephus a different interpretation was needed and the high priest, no doubt on account of his wearing the biblical instruments of divination (*Urim* and *Thummim*, Ex 28:30) affixed to his breastplate, was held to be endowed with prophetic perspicacity. A striking phrase in the Gospel of John echoes this understanding. The evangelist declares that Caiaphas, because he was the high priest, 'prophesied' when he was speaking of Jesus (Jn 11:49–52).

Jewish law courts according to the Mishnah

The oldest rabbinic traditional law code, the Mishnah, has a special tractate called Sanhedrin, which contains a detailed account of the various Jewish tribunals and their procedural rules. The code itself was not written down before AD 200, by which time the great Sanhedrin of Jerusalem was no longer in existence. As a result, the acceptability and historical dependability of the information included in the Mishnah are hotly debated. Some features, like the attribution of the presidency of the court to the *Nasi* or chief rabbi instead of the high priest even before the destruction of the Temple, are patently incorrect. We know from the New Testament and Josephus that this was not so. The twist is due to the unwillingness of the rabbinic successors of the earlier Pharisees to accept that their opponents, the Sadducee chief priests, were *ex officio* in charge of the supreme tribunal. Nevertheless it is clear that apart from such 'religious-political' manipulations the tractate Sanhedrin preserves a number of legal traditions which are considerably older than AD 200. Some of these are likely to assist us when it comes to determining the reliability, or quite often the unreliability, of important particulars in the Gospel accounts of the Passion.

The Mishnah mentions three types of law court. At the lowest level stood the local tribunal competent to deal with run-of-the-mill civil cases (for example, who owes what to whom?). It consisted of three judges, or perhaps more exactly three arbitrators, and was probably not a standing body; each party designated his 'judge' for a given dispute and the two nominated judges coopted the third one.

The competence of the intermediate court, made up of twenty-three judges, covered criminal issues and even capital cases. This seems to have been a regional court. Originally these courts probably corresponded to the councils or synods established by the Roman governor of Syria, Gabinius, in the five districts into which he divided Palestine after it had been conquered by Pompey for Rome in 63 BC. Josephus lists Jerusalem and Jericho in Judaea, Sepphoris in Galilee, and Amathus in Transjordan as seats of such tribunals or Sanhedrins. The fifth place mentioned by him is Gadara, probably not a second city in Transjordan, but a third one in Judaea. Nevertheless it is possible that the name of the town, Gadara, is a mistake, in which case it should be corrected to read Adora, a place in Idumaea. If so, the southern region of the country would also be provided with its own tribunal (Josephus, *Jewish War* 1:169–70; *Jewish Antiquities* 14:91).

The Mishnah's supreme court, or the Great Sanhedrin of seventy-one judges, is located in Jerusalem. Its sessions were held in a special hall situated in the Temple area, the Hall of the Hewn Stone or *Lishkat ha-Gazit*. More than a tribunal, it was the senate of the Jewish people, its supreme judicial, legislative and administrative institution, three in one. In addition to dealing with major criminal cases, it was also empowered to declare war, change the boundaries of Jerusalem and the Temple, and above all to interpret the Law of Moses authoritatively. The Synoptic Gospels bring Jesus before this Sanhedrin, but at a meeting held not close to the Temple, but in the house of the high priest. The fact that the meeting entails the examination of witnesses and ends in Mark and Matthew by finding Jesus guilty of blasphemy, punishable by death, indicates that the evangelists envisage the 'council' (*synedrion*) as a tribunal, not simply as a consultative assembly.

As already established in connection with scriptural law, no accused person could be sentenced to death without the concurring testimony of at least two witnesses. It seems that in biblical times the witnesses could testify together, one being interrogated in the presence of the other, a condition which made the detection of false testimony more difficult. The apocryphal story of Susannah, mentioned earlier, represents a judicial innovation: the two elders, who jointly and mendaciously denounced Susannah as an adulteress, were separated and cross-examined singly by the wise judge Daniel. As a result, their testimony fell apart. One of them placed the sex incident under a mastic tree, whilst the other said that it happened under a yew tree. This discrepancy was sufficient to prove that the elders were liars. Consequently they, instead of Susannah, received the death penalty. The Mishnah sets out a list of circumstances on which the individually questioned witnesses had to agree. The absence of unanimous testimony is referred to in the account of the trial of Jesus by the Sanhedrin in the Gospels of Mark and Matthew. Only if the witnesses satisfied the court could the judges pursue the case further and reach a verdict. Each judge had to cast his vote, one after the other. Contrary to what we read in the Synoptics, no death sentence could be pronounced by common acclamation.

Every witness had to reassure the court about the due warning issued to the person who was on the point of committing a crime regarding the consequences of his action. The Bible enjoins that one should reprove one's neighbour in order to escape responsibility for shared guilt. The Mishnah expressly instructs judges specifically to inquire whether such a caution has been given. If not, the witnesses had to be disqualified. Was such a requirement in force in the age of Jesus? That it existed before the destruction of the Temple in AD 70 can be deduced from the Qumran Damascus Document, which makes formal warning a compulsory part of the legal procedure (9:2–9).

The need for the testimony of witnesses in capital cases is taken so literally that rabbinic law, codified in the Tosephta (third century AD), does not consider confession, that is, admission of guilt by the accused person, a sufficient ground for pronouncing a death sentence except in the specific case of secret propagation of idolatry, a crime which by nature was particularly difficult to prove. In all other cases conviction could follow only after the testimony of witnesses and after explicit warning (Tosephta Sanhedrin 11:1).

Another procedural rule of the Great Sanhedrin laid down that capital sentences could never be pronounced on the day of the court hearing itself; the decree of condemnation had to wait until the following day. 'Therefore trials involving death penalty may not be held *on the eve of sabbath or on the eve of a feast day*' (Mishnah Sanhedrin 4:1; Mishnah Betzah 5:2). That a court should not do business on a Sabbath is obvious. It is hardly surprising therefore that this is not expressly listed among the prohibited actions. In fact, since the proceedings had to be recorded by two court clerks, the Mishnah's prohibition to write as few as two letters on the Sabbath (Mishnah Shabbat 7:2) implicitly forbids the recording of minutes.

The issue is highly relevant to the assessment of the Passion account of the Synoptic Gospels. Some New Testament scholars are in principle unwilling to accept rabbinic literature as providing valid evidence for the age of Jesus. But if they object to the use of the Mishnah or the Tosephta because of the date of their redaction, they are not at liberty to reject first-century AD sources, such as Philo and the Dead Sea Scrolls. Philo writes: 'Let us not ... abrogate the laws laid down for its [the Sabbath's] observance and ... institute [on that day] proceedings in court' (*Migration of Abraham* 91). The Damascus Document from Qumran also firmly states that on the Sabbath day 'no one shall judge' (10:17–18).

Death penalties

The Hebrew Bible recognizes two forms of death penalty. The most commonly used mode of execution was by judicial stoning (to be distinguished from lynch justice, the on-the-spot killing of someone by an outraged crowd). Persons found guilty of blasphemy (Dt 24:15–16), idolatry (Dt 17:2–7), Sabbath-breaking (Num 15:32–6), adultery and rape (Dt 22:22–4), etc. were put to death by stoning. The other death penalty explicitly listed is burning, reserved for certain sexual offences such as an attempt to contract marriage simultaneously with a woman and her mother (Lev 20: 14) or prostitution committed by a priest's daughter (Lev 21:9). The Mishnah (Sanhedrin 7:1) further refers to beheading by the sword, practised by the secular power, and to strangling.

All four forms were in use in the age of Jesus. Various stoning episodes appear in the New Testament itself: John 10:31–3 and 2 Corinthians 11:25 allude to failed attempts to stone Jesus and Paul; Acts 7:58 describes the execution of Stephen; and John 8:7 recounts Jesus' intervention which stopped the stoning of a woman caught in adultery. According to Josephus, James the brother of Jesus was executed by stoning (*Jewish Antiquities* 20:200). The Mishnah alludes to an actual case of burning the harlot daughter of a priest (Mishnah Sanhedrin 7:2) and, in a different context, Josephus relates that on his deathbed Herod the Great ordered the execution by fire of two teachers of the law and some of their students responsible for the removal of the decorative eagle that Herod had installed in the Temple (*Jewish War* 1:655). The later Herodian rulers, Antipas, Tetrarch of Galilee, and King Agrippa I, ordered the decapitation respectively of John the Baptist and the apostle James son of Zebedee (Mk 6:27; Acts 12:1). Strangulation as a legal method of execution described in the Mishnah seems to be a rabbinic innovation, but it was certainly in use during the reign of Herod the Great. Two of Herod's sons, Alexander and Aristobulus, were strangled in prison by order of the king and with the consent of the emperor Augustus (Josephus, *Jewish War* 1:547; *Jewish Antiquities* 16:394).

As regards crucifixion, since pre-exilic biblical times the hanging of the corpse of a criminal put to death by stoning was part of the execution ritual (Dt 21:22–3). The purpose of this cruel custom was to deter people from breaking the law. Actual crucifixion, or 'hanging a man alive on the tree' according to the Hebrew metaphor used in the Dead Sea Scrolls, was no longer attested as part of Jewish legal practice in the Herodian age, that is, from 37 BC onwards. Before Herod, however, the Maccabaean-Hasmonaean Jewish priest-king Alexander Jannaeus (103–76 BC) chose crucifixion for the punishment of 800 Pharisees who had rebelled against him and helped the invading Syrian Greek king Demetrius III. This is gruesomely described by Josephus (*Jewish War* 1:96–8; *Jewish Antiquities* 13:380–91) and is hinted at in the Qumran Nahum Commentary (4Q169 Nahum Commentary on Nahum 2:13). The utopian legislation contained in the Dead Sea Temple Scroll (64: 6–13) also threatens traitors of the Jewish people with crucifixion.

Nevertheless, from the death of Herod the Great up to the fall of Jerusalem and Masada (from 4 BC to AD 73/74) the cross was the visible and tangible sign, indeed the hallmark, of the cruel presence of Rome in the Jewish lands. Having suppressed the rebellion which broke out after the death of Herod, Varus, the Roman governor of Syria, ordered the mass crucifixion of 2,000 Jewish revolutionaries in the Jerusalem area. The most dreadful cases occurred during the siege of Jerusalem (AD 70) when at one time up to 500 captured Jews were crucified by the Romans *every day*. We are told that there was not enough space in Jerusalem for the crosses and not enough crosses for the victims. Cruel Roman legionaries enjoyed beating and torturing the prisoners before crucifixion. In 1968 the bones of a first-century crucified Jew by the name of Yehohanan were discovered in Jerusalem. The nail is still fixed in the heel bones and the shinbones are broken.

For Christians the cross of Jesus is a unique phenomenon. For a first-century Jew it was a tragic everyday spectacle, but in Roman eyes it was insignificant, an unavoidable, if horrible, necessity. Crucifixion was a Roman speciality and Rome alone bore the responsibility for the crucified multitudes. Yet Cicero is fully justified when he calls it *crudelissimum teterrimumque supplicium*, the most cruel and abominable form of execution.

C. The Temple authorities and Jesus

According to the Synoptic evangelists, Jesus provoked the hostility of the priestly authorities of the Temple almost immediately on his arrival in Jerusalem. Who were these authorities?

It goes without saying that the high priest occupied a leading position in Temple worship. Certain cult acts, such as entering the Holy of Holies of the sanctuary once a year on the Day of Atonement, was his exclusive privilege. He was also *ex officio* the president of the Great Sanhedrin or supreme court and principal doctrinal institution of Judaism. Moreover, the Romans treated him also as the civic and political chief of the Palestinian Jews. Josephus remarks: 'After the death of [Herod and the dismissal of Archelaus] the constitution became an aristocracy, and the high priests were entrusted with the leadership of the nation' (*Jewish Antiquities* 20:251). The high priest and his council were invested by the Roman governors of Judaea with the duty of safeguarding peace in the province and maintaining law and order, especially in the Temple, the most important meeting place in the city.

It would seem that because of his potential and often

very real influence, the Herodian and the Roman secular authority felt obliged to keep an eye on the high priest. This was done in a curious fashion. The pontifical office was surrounded by formalities, including the duty to wear the prescribed garments for the performance of certain functions. Therefore Herod the Great (37–4BC) and his successors, Agrippa I (AD 41–44) and Agrippa II (AD 50–c. 100), as well as the Roman governors during the intervening years, removed the ceremonial vestments of the high priest from the Temple and kept them under their own custody. It is hardly likely that they wished to interfere with the religious functions of the pontiff. The purpose of the move was political; the secular rulers intended to make it obvious to whom the ultimate authority belonged. The Roman governors of Judaea also desired to have prior knowledge of the high priest's plans (for example, his intention to convoke the Sanhedrin) for which, it must be surmised, the wearing of solemn robes was demanded by custom. On the occasion of religious feasts the vestments were delivered to the Temple seven days in advance. Meanwhile they were kept under lock and triple seal in the Antonia Fortress, next door to the Temple of Jerusalem (see Josephus, *Jewish Antiquities* 15:403–8; 18:93–4; 20:6–7).

The high priests were expected to collaborate with the secular power, and if they failed to do so, they were unceremoniously sacked. Herod the Great deposed the high priest Matthias son of Theophilus (5/4 BC) because of his involvement in the removal of the golden eagle from the Temple. The successor of Matthias, Joazar son of Boethus, was dismissed by Herod the Great's son, Archelaus, for supporting the popular revolt which broke out in 4 BC after the death of his father. Joazar was reinstated and first supported the census, which the Roman governor of Syria Quirinius implemented in Judaea in AD 6. Joazar then switched allegiance and toed the nationalist line, obliging Quirinius to depose him in favour of Annas (AD 6–15) of Gospel notoriety. Finally, when in AD 66 it became obvious that the war against Rome was unavoidable, the chief priests and the leading citizens of Jerusalem, representatives of the aristocratic peace party, wishing to prove their loyalty to the Romans, informed the procurator Florus of the failure of their efforts to pacify the people (Josephus, *Jewish War* 2:417–18).

Threats against the life of Jesus are occasionally recorded in the Gospels before the Passion, but they stand on flimsy ground or are based in John on much later Christian concepts anachronistically traced back to the lifetime of Jesus. Luke can hardly be believed when he asserts that the inhabitants of Nazareth attempted to murder Jesus for choosing Capernaum rather than his home town for the venue of his healing activity (Lk 4:23–30). The charges of Sabbath-breaking through charismatic healing or of blasphemy by Jesus calling God his Father are far-fetched, and in no circumstances can either of them be built up into a capital offence (Mk 3:6; Mt 12:14; Jn 5:18).

The real conflict between Jesus and the authorities stems in Mark, Matthew and Luke from the fateful incident which goes under the title of the cleansing of the Temple. In John the episode is placed in the beginning of the ministry of Jesus (Jn 2:13–21) and not in the last week of his life, and consequently has no impact on the Passion story. The Synoptic chronology, nevertheless, makes much better sense.

Mark, Matthew and Luke record that after his arrival in Jerusalem Jesus entered the Temple. There, we must deduce from what follows, he witnessed the goings-on in the busy merchants' quarter. Jesus, the rural holy man, was shocked by the hurly-burly of business in the Temple courtyard where sacrificial animals were sold, and by the noisy bargaining between money-changers and their clients, who had to convert ordinary currency into valuable silver drachms minted in Tyre, the only coins deemed suitable for sacred donations. Jesus decided there and then to put an end to these unholy dealings; he overturned the pigeon-vendors' stalls and the tables of the bankers and stopped all the wanderings in the holy place that buying and selling necessitated. The evangelists placed a combined quotation from the Bible in the mouth of Jesus: 'My house shall be called a house of prayer [Isa 56:7], but you have made it a den of robbers' (Jer 7:1), but this fits better with the need for biblical proof in the early Church than with the spontaneity of the style of teaching of Jesus (Mk 11:11–17; Mt 21:10–13; Lk 19:45–6).

A number of interpreters argue that this act of 'cleansing' was in fact a rebellion against the ritual worship in the sanctuary; that in fact Jesus was opposed to the Temple. There is a much simpler and more cogent interpretation, however. The holy northern provincial from Nazareth found intolerable what for the local people of Jerusalem and the officials was routine business required for the day-to-day and feast-to-feast running of the Temple. As had been pointed out earlier, this was Jesus' first visit to Jerusalem since he had become a public figure, and on the spur of the moment, the rural prophet allowed his hot Galilean blood to boil over. Naturally a noisy and tumultuous mayhem followed and the priestly guardians of law and order were bound to take notice. Not only did they resent the fact that their supremacy was spurned by a provincial upstart, they were also concerned that the creation of disorder in the Temple, with enormous crowds assembled there in Passover week, might bring about the violent intervention of the Romans. Jesus was a potential threat to peace in the same way as John the Baptist's eloquence was seen, according to Josephus, as a revolutionary threat, causing the powers that be to step in. According to Josephus this brought about the decapitation of John by the ruler of Galilee, Herod Antipas (*Jewish Antiquities* 18:118). Nevertheless, the chief priests did not intervene immediately because they apparently feared that any action against Jesus, held in high esteem by the people on account of his healing charisma, might seriously backfire against them and provoke a dangerous riot (Mk 11:18–19; Lk 19:47–8).

A second episode that testifies to the growing worry about Jesus on the part of the authorities is recorded by the Synoptic evangelists as occurring the following day. They relate that the day after the fracas in the Temple the chief priests, scribes and elders sent a deputation to Jesus. The envoys approached him when he was walking in the Temple, and sought to find out who had authorized him to 'do these things'. The phrase 'these things' can only refer to the brawl in the merchants' quarter. One can guess at the chief priests' line of thought: We did not commission you; who did? Jesus' purported reply was bound further to exasperate the already tense situation. He would answer the authorities only if they would tell him in public what they thought of John the Baptist. This was a clever trap in which the chief priests were bound to be caught. If they admitted that the Baptist was a messenger of God, Jesus would ask: Why did you not follow him then? On the other hand, if they denied that John was a prophet, the people, sympathetic to John, would be infuriated and might stone them. Their cowardly 'We do not know' elicited a triumphant 'If you don't know, I won't tell!' The Gospels make Jesus look very threatening (Mk 11:27–33; Mt 21:23–7; Lk 20:1–8).

The next move described in the Synoptics is the natural sequel to Jesus' challenge. The priestly guardians of order conceived an actual plot against him. The Synoptics date it two days before Passover, occurring in the palace of the high priest Caiaphas (Mt 26:3). The chief priests and the scribes met there and resolved to get rid of Jesus. However, they still lacked the courage to do so openly and face the music as they were afraid of widespread indignation because of the popularity of Jesus: 'Not during the feast, lest there be a tumult in the people.' The chief priests looked instead for an opportunity to arrest him by stealth on a later date (Mk 14:1–2; Mt 26:3–5; Lk 22:2).

In the Gospel of John, with its extended time-scale of the public life of Jesus, the enmity between him and the chief priests is depicted as of longer duration. It is attributed to the resentment felt by the representatives of officialdom at the sight of the charismatic activity of Jesus, which had recently culminated in the raising from the dead of his friend Lazarus (a person unknown to the Synoptics), an event described as having had wide repercussions in Jerusalem. Religious authority always looked with suspicious eyes on prophets performing miracles whose control was beyond their power. Without giving a precise date, John places the high-priestly plot against Jesus in the week before Passover. Alarmed by the enthusiasm surrounding Jesus, the chief priests, we are told, convoked the council. Jesus' success was seen as the likely cause of great popular excitement which the nervous, sword- and spear-brandishing Romans might have mistaken for the signs of an imminent rebellion. Military intervention of terrible consequences might follow. In the words attributed to the high priest, the Romans might come and 'destroy both our place (the Temple) and our nation'.

It was on that same occasion that the high priest Caiaphas is said to have proclaimed, 'It is expedient for you that one man should die for the people, and that the whole nation should not perish' (Jn 11:45−52). As the official in charge of the safeguard of the community, the pontiff had to take precautionary measures. John makes Caiaphas enunciate here an important Jewish legal principle, namely, that the welfare of the community overrides the life of an individual. The issue was repeatedly discussed by the later rabbis. They had to determine what to do when the Romans demanded the extradition of a Jewish revolutionary under the threat of indiscriminate reprisal against the population of the town or village which was harbouring the fugitive. The rabbis were generally unwilling directly to hand over a Jew to Gentiles. However, in order to protect the larger community, they attempted to persuade the fugitive to give himself up of his own accord.

So from that moment on Jesus lived on borrowed time although he still did not seem in imminent danger. For even when the council met, the day before the eve of Passover, the intervention of the authorities was planned to take place only after the festival. No reason is given in the Gospels for the sudden change of strategy. It must have been the surprise treachery of Judas that struck the chief priests as a godsend. Being experienced statesmen, they grasped the opportunity without hesitation and sent in their troops in the dead of night.

II

The evangelists' accounts of the Passion

In the pages that follow I intend to sketch, interpret and, if necessary, query the way the evangelists present to their readers the thirteen episodes of events that occurred during the final day of the life of Jesus of Nazareth, starting with the Last Supper and ending with his death and burial.

1. The Last Supper

Mk 14:17, 22–5

And when it was evening he came with the twelve. And as they were eating, he took bread, and blessed and broke it, and gave it to them and said, 'Take; this is my body.' And he took the cup, and when he had given thanks he gave it to them, and they all drank of it. And he said to them, 'This is my blood of the covenant, which is poured out for many. Truly I say to you, I shall not drink again the fruit of the vine until the day when I drink it new in the kingdom of God.'

Mt 26:20, 26–9

When it was evening, he sat at table with the twelve disciples. Now as they were eating, Jesus took bread, and blessed and broke it, and gave it to the disciples and said, 'Take, eat, this is my body.' And he took the cup, and when he had given thanks he gave it to

them, saying, 'Drink of it, all of you; for this is my blood of the
covenant, which is poured out for many for the forgiveness of sins.
I tell you I shall not drink again this fruit of the vine until the
day when I drink it new with you in my Father's kingdom.'

Lk 22:14–20
*And when the hour came, he sat at table, and the apostles with him.
And he said to them, 'I have earnestly desired to eat this Passover
with you before I suffer; for I tell you I shall not eat it until it is
fulfilled in the kingdom of God.' And he took a cup, and when he had
given thanks he said, 'Take this, and divide it among yourselves; for
I tell you that from now on I shall not drink the fruit of the vine
until the kingdom of God comes.' And he took bread, and when he
had given thanks he broke it and gave it to them, saying, 'This is
my body which is given for you. Do this in remembrance of me.'
And likewise the cup after the supper, saying, 'This cup which is
poured out for you is the new covenant in my blood.'*

Jn 13:1–2, 27–9
*Now before the feast of Passover ... during supper, the devil had
already put it into the heart of Judas Iscariot, Simon's son, to
betray him. ... Then after the morsel [given to Judas by Jesus],
Satan entered him. Jesus said to him, 'What you are going to do,
do quickly.' ... Some thought that, because Judas had the money
box, Jesus was telling him, 'Buy what we need for the feast' ...*

According to the time reckoning of the Jews the day begins
at dusk when the first stars become visible in the sky. So
the last day of the life of Jesus started in the evening of
what we would consider the previous day with his Last
Supper. A last dinner shared with the twelve apostles is
reported in all four Gospels, but the picture given by the
Synoptics differs greatly from John's version.

In the Fourth Gospel Jesus' Last Supper is given an extensive treatment. According to his habit, John inserts long speeches into his narrative on the '*new* commandment', which was not really new, of loving one another; on Jesus as the 'way' to the Father; on the Holy Spirit, and similar subjects. Jesus' humility is demonstrated in washing his apostles' feet, and the dinner ends with a magnificent prayer by Jesus for his followers (Jn 13–17). The event is not given a precise date beyond being placed '*before* the feast of Passover', but the subsequent narrative suggests that it happened at the start of 14 Nisan, the day before Jews celebrated the Passover, implying that this Last Supper was not a Passover meal. John's account contains no allusion to the institution of the Eucharist, but it makes clear that in the course of that supper Judas Iscariot, identified as 'Simon's son', made up his mind and left the company to betray Jesus. Some of the apostles apparently thought that Judas was sent by Jesus to purchase what was needed for the feast the following day (Jn 13:1–2, 21–31).

By contrast, the occasion is presented by the Synoptic evangelists as definitely a Passover dinner. It should be noted in passing that Passover could fall on any day of the week. In the morning of that day, the fourteenth day of the Jewish month of Nisan, the *eve* of the great feast, which was a Thursday, Jesus is reported as instructing his disciples to obtain and prepare the foodstuffs required by Jewish religious tradition for the celebration of the important ritual meal prescribed by the Bible. This included above all the Passover lamb, which was to be taken to the Temple where it would be ceremonially slaughtered by the priests. After sunset, at the start of 15 Nisan, Jesus reclined at table with his apostles and celebrated what is known in contemporary Judaism as the *Seder* meal. As the main dish, Jesus and his contemporaries ate roast lamb. In the course of this meal, during which unleavened bread was eaten and according to tradition four cups of wine were ritually blessed and drunk, the Synoptic evangelists report what is usually understood to be the institution of the Eucharist, the sacrament commemorating the Last Supper (Mk 14:12–21; Mt 26:17–25; Lk 22:7–14, 21–3). Thus the Eucharist is implicitly linked to the Passover in Mark and Matthew, and explicitly in Luke, where Jesus declares, 'I have earnestly desired to eat *this Passover* with you' (Lk 22:15). The three Gospels do not agree on the details of the ceremony. In particular, whereas neither Mark nor Matthew actually asserts that Jesus ordered the reiteration of the ritual, Luke adds, 'Do this in remembrance of me' (Lk 22:19). In this he is followed by, or more likely he follows, St Paul who, in his first letter to the Corinthians written in the mid-fifties AD, expressly claims that Jesus ordered the repetition of the ceremonial after both the bread and the cup (1 Cor 11:24–5). It is important to emphasize that all three evangelists refer to Jesus' vow of abstention from wine until the coming of the kingdom of God (Mk 14:25; Mt 26:29; Lk 22:18), with the implied meaning that he was not foreseeing his imminent death but was looking forward to the forthcoming completion of his divinely entrusted mission, the ushering in of God's everlasting reign.

At some stage during the supper, or immediately after it, Judas disappeared to do his deed, while Jesus and the eleven completed the ceremony by singing a hymn (Mk 14:26; Mt 26:30), no doubt the last of the Halleluiah Psalms (Pss 113–18) prescribed for that occasion. Having finished, the whole company headed out of the city towards a nearby orchard, known as Gethsemane (meaning oil press or valley of oil), on the Mount of Olives.

2. The arrest of Jesus

Mk 14:32, 43–50

And they went to a place which was called Gethsemane ... And immediately, while he was still speaking, Judas came, one of the twelve, and with him a crowd with swords and clubs, from the chief priests and the scribes and the elders. ... And they laid hands on him and seized him. But one of those who stood by drew his sword, and struck the slave of the high priest and cut off his ear. And Jesus said to them, 'Have you come out as against a robber, with swords and clubs to capture me? Day after day I was with you in the temple teaching, and you did not seize me. But let the Scriptures be fulfilled.' And they all forsook him and fled.

Mt 26:47–56

Then Jesus went with them to a place called Gethsemane ... While he was still speaking, Judas came, and with him a great crowd with swords and clubs, from the chief priests and the elders of the people. ... Then they came up and laid hands on Jesus and seized him. And behold one of those who were with Jesus stretched out his hand and drew his sword, and struck the slave of the high priest, and cut off his ear. Then Jesus said to him, 'Put your sword back into its place; for all who take the sword will perish by the sword'. ... At that hour Jesus said to the crowds, 'Have you come out as against a robber, with swords and clubs to capture me? Day after day I sat in the temple teaching, and you did not seize me. But all this has taken place, that the Scriptures of the prophets might be fulfilled.' Then all the disciples forsook him and fled.

Lk 22:47–53

*And when he came to the place.... While he was still speaking,
there came a crowd, and the man called Judas, one of the twelve,
was leading them.... And when one of those who were about him
saw what would follow, they said, 'Lord, shall we strike with the
sword?' And one of them struck the slave of the high priest and cut
off his right ear. But Jesus said, 'No more of this!' and he touched
his ear and healed him. Then Jesus said to the chief priests and
officers of the temple and elders, who had come out against him,
'Have you come out as against a robber, with swords and clubs?
When I was with you day after day in the temple, you did not lay
hands on me. But this is your hour, and the power of darkness.'*

Jn 18:1–12

*When Jesus had spoken these words, he went forth with his
disciples across the Kidron valley, where there was a garden which
he and his disciples entered. Now Judas, who betrayed him, also
knew the place; for Jesus often met there with his disciples. So
Judas, procuring a band of soldiers and some officers from the chief
priests and the Pharisees, went there with lanterns and torches
and weapons.... Then Simon Peter, having a sword, drew it and
struck the high priest's slave and cut off his right ear. The slave's
name was Malchus. Jesus said to Peter, 'Put your sword into its
sheath; shall I not drink the cup which the Father has given me?'
So the band of soldiers and their captain and the officers of the
Jews seized Jesus and bound him.*

John, who has abandoned the company of the Synoptics
in the account of the Last Supper, rejoins them in the
episode of the arrest of Jesus. He designates the venue
as a garden across the Kidron valley, without calling it
Gethsemane. But since for John this was not Jesus' first
visit to Jerusalem, he can remark that the place had been

regularly frequented by Jesus on previous occasions, and in consequence was known to Judas.

Jesus prayed there in the solitude, invoking God as '*Abba*', 'Father' or 'My Father'. The word is given in Aramaic in Mark and in Greek in Matthew and Luke. *Abba* is a familiar but also respectful expression. It is not the equivalent of 'Daddy', as some New Testament scholars have unwisely ventured to propose. It is one of the few words which have been preserved and transmitted by the evangelists in Jesus' mother tongue. While he was lost in prayer, his exhausted disciples could no longer keep their eyes open and fell asleep (Mk 14:26–42; Mt 26:30–46; Lk 22:39–46).

In the concise dramatic orchestration of the story the quiet rest is disturbed by the arrival of Judas and a group of armed men. The Synoptics and John are not wholly in agreement here. According to the former, the men were the law enforcers controlled by the chief priests and the elders who dispatched them to place Jesus under arrest. Luke, probably mistakenly as it is against all verisimilitude, reports that the chief priests, the officers of the Temple and their lay supporters, the elders, also accompanied Judas (Lk 22:52). There is a tendency in the Synoptics to assert the presence of these 'enemies' everywhere from the arrest of Jesus until his crucifixion. But nothing in the later story would support Luke's allegation.

John in turn speaks of the arrival of a contingent of soldiers, commanded by a fairly high-ranking officer as well as 'the officers of the Jews' (Jn 18:12). Is this a hint at Roman participation in the arrest of Jesus with the moral support of Jewish liaison officers? The matter will be given further consideration at a later stage. In John the super-natural superiority of Jesus is manifested through the soldiers falling to the ground when Jesus tells them that he is the man they are looking for.

The arrival of the police or soldiers triggered off a token armed resistance by one of the apostles, in the course of which a slave or servant of the high priest was wounded. In John, the anonymous disciple of the Synoptics becomes Simon Peter, the leader of the apostles, and the injured slave/servant is named Malchus. The wounded man was miraculously healed by Jesus in Luke, but not in the other two Synoptics or John. With the exception of Mark, who remains silent on the matter, the other evangelists present Jesus as opposed to violence. Surprisingly, the attacker was not held by the forces of order. At the end, only Jesus was detained against his verbal protest. John, but not the Synoptics, makes the policemen bind him before he is led away. His pusillanimous disciples, with one exception, abandoned him and ran (Mk 14:43–52; Mt 26:47–56; Lk 22:47–53).

The exception was Peter, the leader of the apostles, who inconspicuously followed Jesus to the courtyard of the high priest. But forgetting his loud protest that he would never betray his master, he showed himself to be a coward. He repeatedly denied that he was a follower of Jesus. And when his dialectal Aramaic revealed to the Judaeans that he was Galilean – the 'stupid' Galilean with a funny accent was a proverbial object of mockery in Jerusalem according to the rabbis – he still insisted that he did not even know him (Mk 14:53–4, 66–72; Mt 26:57–8, 69–75; Lk 22:54–62).

In sum, the four evangelists have handed down basically identical traditions apart from three instances. They differ on the date when the event was supposed to occur: before Passover in John, on the festival of Passover in the Synoptics. They also leave slightly ajar the door leading to the question of the identity of the members of the arresting party guided by Judas. Did legionaries take part in the raid or was it a purely Jewish affair? The third discrepancy concerns the next stage of the story: Jesus was taken in one direction according to John and in another according to the Synoptics.

3. The interrogation of Jesus according to John

Jn 18:13–14, 19–24

First they led him to Annas; for he was the father-in-law of Caiaphas, who was high priest that year. It was Caiaphas who had given counsel to the Jews that it was expedient that one man should die for the people. . . . The high priest then questioned Jesus about his disciples and his teaching. Jesus answered him, 'I have spoken openly to the world; I have always taught in synagogues and in the temple, where all Jews come together; I have said nothing secretly. Why do you ask me? Ask those who have heard me, what I said to them; they know what I said.' When he had said this, one of the officers standing by struck Jesus with his hand, saying, 'Is that how you answer the high priest?' Jesus answered him, 'If I have spoken wrongly, bear witness to the wrong; but if I have spoken rightly, why do you strike me?' Annas then sent him bound to Caiaphas, the high priest.

In John's narrative, the detachment of soldiers (*speira* or cohort) under the command of a tribune (a *chiliarchos*), together with 'the officers of the Jews', took Jesus to Annas, described as the high priest (Jn 18:19). Who was this Annas? John and Luke muddle the issue of the Jewish high priesthood, although Luke's mistake occurs in an earlier section of his Gospel and is not repeated in the Passion account.

According to John, the high priest Annas was the father-in-law of Caiaphas, the high priest 'of that year'. In Luke's Gospel at the start of the public activity of John the Baptist, Annas and Caiaphas jointly hold the high priesthood (Lk 3:2). However, in virtue of the unanimous testimony of the Bible, Josephus, Philo and the rabbis, the pontifical office could be occupied only by a single incumbent. Also, there was no annual rotation in the high-priestly succession. The error of the evangelists stems from two likely sources. In the first century AD, and more precisely between the creation of the Roman province of Judaea in AD 6 and the outbreak of the first Jewish war against Rome sixty years later, there were eighteen holders of the high-priestly office. Of these Annas sat on the pontifical throne for nine years, Caiaphas for eighteen years and Ananias son of Nedebaeus for twelve years. This adds up to thirty-nine years. In other words, the remaining fifteen high priests lasted twenty-one years all told, which means that few of them held the post for as long as two years and some of them for less than one year.

The inquiry by Annas is presented as informal, without the presence of a council or the calling of witnesses. He was interested in Jesus' Galilean disciples and in his private teaching. While nothing is stated in plain words, the high priest seems to have angled for politically compromising words on the part of Jesus. Galileans had the reputation of being revolutionaries. But according to John, Jesus' main defence was that he had nothing to hide; he had been teaching openly in the Temple and had no secret agenda. In this account Jesus, instead of remaining silent, stands up for himself, and when an overzealous Jewish officer strikes him for being disrespectful to Annas, instead of offering the other cheek, he objects with dignity (Jn 18:23).

No other detail of the interrogation is given in John. All we learn is that Annas sent the prisoner, still bound, to the high priest Caiaphas. Since the Fourth Gospel contains no further proceedings against Jesus by the Jewish authorities, we must conclude that the subsequent decision by Caiaphas to deliver Jesus to the Romans was based on the report of the preliminary inquiry conducted by Annas.

4. The night trial of Jesus before the Sanhedrin

Mk 14:53, 55–65

And they led Jesus to the high priest; and all the chief priests and the elders and the scribes were assembled. . . . Now the chief priests and the whole council sought testimony against Jesus to put him to death; but they found none. For many bore false witness against him, and their witness did not agree. And some stood up and bore false witness against him, saying, 'We heard him say, I will destroy this temple that is made with hands, and in three days I will build another, not made with hands.' Yet not even so did their testimony agree. And the high priest stood up in the midst, and asked Jesus, 'Have you no answer to make? What is it that these men testify against you?' But he was silent and made no answer. Again the high priest asked him, 'Are you the Christ, the Son of the Blessed?' And Jesus said, 'I am; and you will see the Son of man seated at the right hand of Power, and coming with the clouds of heaven.' And the high priest tore his garments, and said, 'Why do we still need witnesses? You have heard his blasphemy. What is your decision?' And they all condemned him as deserving death. And some began to spit on him, and to cover his face, and to strike him, saying to him, 'Prophesy!' And the guards received him with blows.

Mt 26:57, 59–68

Then those who had seized Jesus led him to Caiaphas the high priest, where the scribes and the elders had gathered. . . . Now the chief priests and the whole council sought false testimony against Jesus that they might put him to death, but they found none, though many false witnesses came forward. At last two came forward and said, 'This fellow said, I am able to destroy the temple of God, and to build it in three days.' And the high priest stood up and said, 'Have you no answer to make? What is it that these men testify against you?' But Jesus was silent. And the high priest said to him, 'I adjure you by the living God, tell us if you are the Christ, the Son of God.' Jesus said to him, 'You have said so. But I tell you, hereafter you will see the Son of man seated at the right hand of Power, and coming on the clouds of heaven.' Then the high priest tore his robes, and said, 'He has uttered blasphemy. Why do we still need witnesses? You have now heard his blasphemy. What is your judgement?' They answered, 'He deserves death.' They then spat in his face, and struck him; and some slapped him, saying, 'Prophesy to us, you Christ! Who is it that struck you?'

Lk 22:54, 63–5

And then they seized him and led him away, bringing him into the high priest's house. . . . Now the men who were holding Jesus mocked him and beat him; they also blindfolded him and asked him, 'Prophesy! Who is it that struck you?' And they spoke many other words against him, reviling him.

Whilst in the Gospel of John Jesus is examined by Annas, in the Synoptic accounts the Jewish policemen take him directly to the house of the high priest, nameless in Mark and Luke, but identified as Caiaphas in Matthew, as in John too.

From the start, the story teems with difficulties.

Although the arrest of Jesus was sudden and unprepared, the evangelists declare that the whole august body of the Sanhedrin – consisting of seventy-one members according to the Mishnah – was already assembled in the high priest's palace at night, and on Passover night of all nights. Not only were the councillors present, but there was also a whole bunch of witnesses ready to testify against Jesus. Was all this carefully organized when it was still uncertain whether Jesus would actually be found let alone detained?

The harmony between the Synoptics immediately breaks down. Luke makes no mention of a nocturnal session of the Sanhedrin. If we now turn to Mark and Matthew, another oddity emerges. Although we are told that the authorities had decided in advance that Jesus must be eliminated (Mk 14:1; Mt 26:4; Lk 22:2), they carefully maintain the outward appearances of a due legal process. No one should be condemned without witnesses; so we are presented with witnesses for the prosecution. They are already there, waiting. They come forward and make their depositions, but although the judges seem to be interested only in conviction – Matthew even claims that the court was looking for *pseudomartyria* or *false* testimony (Mt 26:59) – the accusations are all rejected because, to quote Mark's sober comment, they 'did not agree'. When finally two witnesses stand up and proffer an identical charge, namely, that Jesus had issued threats against the Temple, the tribunal, abiding by the law governing testimony in capital cases, is still unsatisfied (Mk 14:55–9; Mt 26:59–61). This quibbling about minutiae is surprising and perhaps explains why Luke prefers to keep altogether silent about the witnesses.

After this punctilious adherence to the rules, one would have expected the dismissal of the case, but the evangelists suddenly change direction. First the high priest invites Jesus to respond to the charges, although they have already been dismissed. Not surprisingly, Jesus refuses to answer them. Next, Mark and Matthew assert that Caiaphas adopted the tactic of direct challenge and confronted Jesus with 'Are you the Christ, the Son of the Blessed?' – the 'Blessed' being a substitute name for God. The words can be paraphrased, 'Are you the Messiah, the promised royal deliverer of Israel?' In Jewish religious thought, before and after the age of Jesus, a king of the House of David, and above all the King-Messiah, was considered the 'Son of God' on the basis of Psalm 2:7, where on the occasion of the enthronement of the Israelite monarch, God declares: 'You are my son, today I have begotten you.' Elsewhere he also makes a promise to King Solomon: 'I will be his father, and he shall be my son' (2 Sam 7:14). Indeed, in the commonly used metaphorical terminology of Judaism 'Messiah' and 'Son of God' were interchangeable; they were synonyms.

Jesus' answer to the high priest's question varies in the Gospels. In Mark we are faced with a straight 'I am', but with a less direct 'You say that I am' in several important Mark manuscripts. Luke employs the same formula and Matthew has 'You have said so.' The indirect style, which seems to have been Jesus' favourite way of speaking about himself, is equivocal; theoretically it can be understood as either yes or no. However, the expression is found with a definitely negative connotation in rabbinic literature: 'You have said it' is tacitly paraphrased 'You, not I', meaning 'I would disagree, or at least I would not put it that way.'

Nevertheless Jesus' answer was taken by the high priest and the judges as a plain admission not only in Mark, but also in Matthew and Luke who use ambiguous formulas.

Combined with Jesus' further comment about the 'Son of man [being] seated on the right hand of the Power and coming with the clouds of heaven', a description of the triumphal revelation of the Messiah at the end of time, his words without any further inquiry were judged by the high priest as blasphemous. Caiaphas then suddenly reverted to ceremonial orthodoxy. We are told that he rent his garments, as required by rabbinic law. Then he and all the members of the Sanhedrin pronounced a unanimous verdict of guilty. Jesus had committed blasphemy and therefore deserved the death penalty. But the fundamental question is whether Jesus' words, supposing that he actually uttered them, can be construed as amounting to the capital crime of blasphemy.

Strangely, the Sanhedrin breathes no word about execution. Biblical law, as we have seen, prescribes stoning as the punishment for blasphemy, and the New Testament itself and Josephus report that it was in practice in the age of Jesus. Instead, the case is transferred without any explanation to a different jurisdiction, that of the Roman governor of Judaea.

The pronouncement of the capital sentence was accompanied by abuse and mocking of the prisoner Jesus. Mark and Matthew insinuate that the perpetrators were the judges themselves: 'And they all condemned him as deserving death. And some began to spit on him', etc. They were playing the prophet game in which the blindfolded Jesus was beaten and asked to 'prophesy' who had hit him (Mk 14:60–65; Mt 26:62–7). According to Mark, the policemen also joined the magistrates and the dignified courtroom was transformed into a scene of pandemonium. Luke also reports the mockery and ill-treatment of Jesus, but attributes them with greater verisimilitude to the guards who were holding him during the night, prior to his arraignment before the court the following morning (Lk 22:63–5). Luke elsewhere notes that Herod Antipas' soldiers also poked fun at Jesus (Lk 23:11). Finally, a scene of scoffing by Roman legionaries follows the scourging of Jesus (Mk 15:16–20; Mt 27:27–31). Some of these incidents could well be duplicates.

In sum, the reliability of the account of Jesus' appearance before the Sanhedrin and his condemnation to death is seriously undermined by the repeated contradictions and historical and legal improbabilities of Mark's account, which has been copied in substance by Matthew. Luke and John further muddy the waters. John ignores any trial of Jesus by a Jewish court and Luke omits the night session of the Sanhedrin. However, the four evangelists are once more reunited in their report of the events which occurred the following morning.

5. The morning meeting of the Sanhedrin

Mk 15:1
And as soon as it was morning the chief priests with the elders and the scribes, and the whole council held a consultation; and they bound Jesus and led him away and delivered him to Pilate.

Mt 27:1–2
When morning came, all the chief priests and the elders of the people took counsel against Jesus to put him to death; and they bound him and led him away and delivered him to Pilate, the governor.

Lk 22:66–23:1

When day came, the assembly of the elders of the people gathered together, both chief priests and scribes; and they led him away to their council, and they said, 'If you are the Christ, tell us.' But he said to them, 'If I tell you, you will not believe; and if I ask you, you will not answer. But from now on the Son of man shall be seated at the right hand of the Power of God.' And they all said, 'Are you the Son of God then?' And he said to them, 'You say that I am.' And they said, 'What further testimony do we need? We have heard it ourselves from his lips.' Then the whole company of them arose, and brought him before Pilate.

Jn 18:28

Then they led Jesus from the house of Caiaphas to the praetorium. It was early. They themselves did not enter the praetorium so that they might not be defiled, but might eat the Passover.

John, let it be repeated, mentions no meeting of the chief priests and their council. Jesus is simply dispatched from the house of the high priest to the *praetorium*, Pilate's Jerusalem residence in the palace of Herod. The time is defined: it happened early in the morning of the eve of Passover, 14 Nisan, definitely *before* the Passover supper.

The three Synoptic evangelists describe a gathering of the members of the Sanhedrin in the morning of Passover day. This meeting, the second in Mark and Matthew and the only one in Luke, is called a consultation. We are not told whether Jesus was present and absolutely no detail of the discussion is given. Only the final resolution of the court is revealed, namely, that the prisoner Jesus should be bound and transferred to the tribunal of Pontius Pilate (Mk 15:1; Mt 27:1–2; Lk 22:66–23:1). Although it is not explicitly admitted, it becomes clear from what follows that the Sanhedrin suddenly changed tack. During the night the alleged messianic claim of Jesus was treated as a religious offence; in the morning, like a chameleon, blasphemy changed its colours and was conveniently metamorphosed into a political offence, anti-Roman revolutionary activity. However, none of the evangelists specifies in advance the indictment that the chief priests are to present to Pilate. The unformulated charge will come into the open through the question addressed by the governor to Jesus. By any standard this sweeping change of tactics would require some explanation, for instance that a new political accusation acceptable to Pilate was necessary because the Sanhedrin lacked the power to sentence and execute Jesus for blasphemy. However, no such justification is given.

Luke, who follows a tradition in which there is no night trial of Jesus, having acquainted himself with the version of Mark and/or of Matthew, attempts here to combine their account with his own morning-only Sanhedrin meeting. He ascribes the question about the Messiahship of Jesus not to the high priest, as do Mark and Matthew, but to the judges ('they said'), and follows it up with an evasive reply from Jesus: It is not worth answering as the court will not believe anything he may say. Then Luke reproduces from Mark and Matthew the abridged version of Jesus' statement about the Son of man sitting on the right hand of God. Significantly, while in Luke the Sanhedrin declares the saying of Jesus to be a confession of guilt, it pronounces no sentence of condemnation, nor does it refer to the death penalty (Lk 22:63–5, 67–71).

In short, in Luke's tradition there is only a morning meeting of the council without witnesses: Jesus' words are declared as evidence of his guilt but are not qualified as blasphemous and the court passes no judgement. What is common to all four Gospels is the decision to deliver Jesus to the Roman authority.

6. The suicide of Judas

Mt 27:3–10

When Judas, his [Jesus'] betrayer, saw that he was condemned, he repented and brought back the thirty pieces of silver to the chief priests and the elders, saying, 'I have sinned in betraying innocent blood.' They said, 'What is that to us? See to it yourself.' And throwing down the pieces of silver in the Temple, he departed and he went and hanged himself. But the chief priests, taking the pieces of silver, said, 'It is not lawful to put them into the treasury, since they are blood money.' So they took counsel, and bought with them the potter's field, to bury strangers in. Therefore that field has been called the Field of Blood to this day. Then was fulfilled what had been spoken by the prophet Jeremiah, saying, 'And they took the thirty pieces of silver, the price of him on whom a price had been set by some of the sons of Israel, and they gave them for the potter's field, as the Lord directed.'

Matthew inserts a brief interlude about Judas between the trial of Jesus by the Sanhedrin and the transfer of the case to Pilate. He makes the traitor repent and return the bribe. The evangelists are innocent of modern speculations about Judas' higher motives such as his wish to catapult Jesus into revealing his concealed Messiahship. No clear time of the event is given. According to Matthew the trial of Jesus took place in the house of Caiaphas, but Judas' meeting with the chief priests and elders is located in the Temple, a different venue no doubt on a different occasion.

As the priestly authorities refused to take back the money, Judas threw it away and in despair hanged himself. The rest of the story has all the appearances of a folk tale artificially combined with a scriptural citation to turn the event into the fulfilment of a prophecy. Left with an unpleasant dilemma – what to do with the returned blood money unfit for the Temple treasure – the chief priests decided to buy with it a field for the burial of strangers. There was a plot of land in Jerusalem known as the 'Field of Blood', and early Christian tradition associated it with the misadventure of Judas. The prophetic aspect of the incident is largely manufactured by Matthew. The quotation is said to be of Jeremiah, but it is invented or is more exactly a garbled mixture of Zechariah 11:12–13 and Jeremiah 18:2–3, 36:6–15. It is impossible to discern in the biblical excerpts even a remote connection with the Judas episode. Here, as in many other places, Matthew endeavours to portray the Passion story, disturbing for believers and unattractive for would-be converts, as a sequence of prophetically foretold and therefore providentially predestined events.

7. Jesus before Pilate

Mk 15:2–5
And Pilate asked him, 'Are you the King of the Jews?' And he answered him, 'You have said so.' And the chief priests accused him of many things. And Pilate again asked him, 'Have you no answer to make? See how many charges they bring against you.' But Jesus made no further answer so that Pilate wondered.

Mt 27:11–14

Now Jesus stood before the governor; and the governor asked him, 'Are you the King of the Jews?' Jesus said, 'You have said so.' But when he was accused by the chief priests and elders, he made no answer. Then Pilate said to him, 'Do you not hear how many things they testify against you?' But he gave them no answer, not even to a single charge; so that the governor wondered greatly.

Lk 23:2–5

And they began to accuse him saying, 'We found this man perverting our nation, and forbidding us to give tribute to Caesar, and saying that he himself is Christ a king.' And Pilate asked him, 'Are you the King of the Jews?' And he answered him, 'You have said so.' And Pilate said to the chief priests and the multitudes; 'I find no crime in this man.' But they were urgent, saying, 'He stirs up the people, teaching throughout all Judea, from Galilee even to this place.'

Jn 18:29–38

So Pilate went out to them and said, 'What accusation do you bring against this man?' They answered him, 'If this man were not an evildoer, we would not have handed him over.' Pilate said to them, 'Take him yourselves and judge him by your own law.' The Jews said to him, 'It is not lawful for us to put any man to death.' This was to fulfil the word which Jesus had spoken to show by what death he was to die. Pilate entered the praetorium again and called Jesus, and said to him, 'Are you the King of the Jews?' Jesus answered, 'Do you say this of your own accord, or did others say it to you about me?' Pilate answered, 'Am I a Jew? Your own nation and the chief priests have handed you over to me; what have you done?' Jesus answered, 'My kingship is not of this world; if my kingship were of this world, my servants would fight that I might not be handed over to the Jews; but my kingship is not of the world.' Pilate said to him, 'So you are a king?' Jesus answered, 'You say that I am a king. For this I was born, and for this I have come into the world, to bear witness to the truth. Every one who is of the truth hears my voice.' Pilate said to him, 'What is truth?' After he had said this, he went out to the Jews again, and told them, 'I find no crime in him.'

As has been noted, in the morning session of the Sanhedrin, no mention is made by Mark and Matthew of the charge to be levelled against Jesus. We must conclude, however, in the light of the governor's question, 'Are you the King of the Jews?' that the indictment concerned Jesus' royal and messianic claim, namely, that he pretended to be the King-Messiah (Mk 14:2–5; Mt 27:11–14). Luke is more specific. He makes the Jewish representatives explicitly accuse Jesus of sedition: he assumes the royal title of the Christ, perverts the nation, and, worst of all from the Roman point of view, forbids the payment of taxes to the emperor. The latter accusation is, of course, diametrically opposed to the words earlier attributed to Jesus by all the Synoptics, including Luke. His saying about the tax money, 'Render to Caesar the things that are Caesar's', is the characteristic utterance not of a revolutionary, but of an apolitical teacher (Mk 12:17; Mt 22:21; Lk 20:25).

To Pilate's straight question whether he was the King of the Jews Jesus gives his customary noncommittal answer: 'You have said so.' And if the testimony of the Synoptics is accepted, he simply refused to reply to the many further accusations heaped on him by the chief priests.

In John the main lines of the account of Jesus' encounter with Pilate are the same, but there are also some notable variants. John depicts Pilate, to whom Jesus was probably presented at short notice, as obliging and cooperative.

He receives the chief priests early in the morning and, respectful of their purity concerns, meets them outside his residence. He politely inquires about the reason of their coming: 'What accusation do you bring against this man?' The Jewish delegation is described as cagey and in a hurry. No doubt they had many pressing matters to attend to in preparation for Passover. On that same afternoon the Temple was to become a giant slaughterhouse where priestly butchers would kill the thousands of Passover lambs for the *Seder* supper. And there were the preparations for the solemn ritual of the fifteenth day of Nisan, which the chief priests had to conduct. It consisted, Josephus tells us, of the sacrifice of two bulls, a ram and seven lambs to serve as burnt offerings, and a kid for sin offering (*Jewish Antiquities* 3:249). So when Pilate asks about the charges against Jesus, he is curtly told that the accused is a wrongdoer; otherwise they would not have brought him here. To this Pilate sensibly retorts – and John's Pilate is even more sensible than the Pilate of the Synoptics – that if the chief priests have nothing against him that concerns Rome, they should try him themselves according to Jewish law. This reply gives rise to a totally unexpected riposte, which grotesquely amounts to a tutorial on Roman law given by the Jewish delegation to the Roman prefect. He should know that the Romans have deprived the Sanhedrin of the right to pronounce and execute capital sentences: 'It is not lawful for us to put any man to death.' This extraordinary statement will be examined later. John's Pilate takes the reproof in his stride and meekly agrees to handle the case. So Jesus is ordered inside the palace, and the governor focuses his inquiry on Jesus' kingship. Pilate is told that it is spiritual, not of this world, John informs us. Pilate then concludes that the priestly leaders are trying to involve him in a theological dispute about something he would have called their *superstitio*, and impresses on them that religious matters are outside his sphere of competence and that he can find no crime in Jesus in the political domain.

At this juncture the evangelists, like virtuoso wizards, present their readers with a surprise, the unforeseen legal custom (or fiction) of the *privilegium paschale*, or Passover amnesty.

8. Jesus sent to Herod Antipas and back to Pilate

Lk 23:6–11
When Pilate heard this, he asked whether the man was Galilean. And when he learned that he belonged to Herod's jurisdiction, he sent him over to Herod, who was himself in Jerusalem at that time. When Herod saw Jesus he was very glad, for he had long desired to see him, because he had heard about him, and he was hoping to see some sign done by him. So he questioned him at some length; but he made no answer. The chief priests and the scribes stood by, vehemently accusing him. And Herod with his soldiers treated him with contempt and mocked him; then, arraying him in gorgeous apparel, he sent him back to Pilate. Pilate then called together the chief priests and the rulers of the people and said to them, 'You brought me this man as one who was perverting the people; and after examining him before you, behold, I did not find this man guilty of any of your charges against him; neither did Herod, for he sent him back to us. Behold, nothing deserving death has been done by him; I will therefore chastise him and release him.'

In Luke's special version of the dialogue between Pontius Pilate and the chief priests, two passing references deserve further attention. First, the chief priests are said to be accompanied by 'the multitudes'. No such large crowd has been mentioned before; who are they and where have they come from? John's account implicitly echoes Luke's and even enlarges on it. The delators of Jesus are no longer just the chief priests, but the chief priests and the whole nation, or simply 'the Jews'.

Second, Jesus is portrayed by his accusers as a mischief-maker who has been fomenting trouble 'from Galilee' to Jerusalem. The reminder that Jesus is Galilean provides Pilate with an opportunity to hand over a case which he does not fancy to the ruler of Galilee. Herod would understand everything so much better. In similar circumstances, we find another Roman governor, Festus, seeking King Agrippa II's help for formulating the charges against St Paul which would then be transmitted to the emperor Nero (Acts 25:24–7). Very conveniently Herod Antipas, no doubt trying to please the Jewish citizens of his realm, travelled to Jerusalem to attend, or to be seen to attend, the celebration of the Passover. Apparently he welcomed the chance given him by Pilate to make the acquaintance of Jesus. However, Jesus remained silent throughout the whole episode, as he was silent before Pilate, despite the many questions of the Herodian prince. He also refused to answer the renewed accusations of the chief priests and scribes, who followed him to the residence of Antipas. Herod's patience ran out with the tiresome prophet, and after allowing his soldiers to make fun of him and clothe him in royal garments, he politely returned Jesus to Pilate (Lk 23:2–12).

Luke's episode makes the already tight time schedule even tighter. The chief priests left the *praetorium* when Pilate had decided to hand the case over to Antipas and followed Jesus. They were then summoned again by the governor to resume the proceedings. In Luke all this is supposed to happen on Passover day. On returning to the governor's palace, the priests are told that having been found innocent by both Pilate and Herod, Jesus was going to be released, but not without a good beating to remind him of the advisability of staying on the straight and narrow path. As we shall see, flogging could be a preliminary to crucifixion, but it could also be inflicted on its own as a warning. The gesture seems to be intended to appease the chief priests; they would not be sent away without the feeling of having achieved at least something.

9. The Passover amnesty and Barabbas

Mk 15:6–11
Now at the feast he used to release for them one prisoner for whom they asked. And among the rebels in prison, who had committed murder in the insurrection, there was a man called Barabbas. And the crowd came up and began to ask Pilate to do as he was wont to do for them. And he answered them, 'Do you want me to release for you the King of the Jews?' For he perceived that it was out of envy that the chief priests had delivered him up. But the chief priests stirred up the crowd to have him release for them Barabbas instead.

Mt 27:15–20
Now at the feast the governor was accustomed to release for the crowd one prisoner whom they wanted. And they had then a notorious prisoner called Barabbas. So when they had gathered, Pilate said to them, 'Whom do you want me to release for you, [Jesus] Barabbas or Jesus who is called Christ?' For he knew that

it was out of envy that the chief priests had delivered him up. Besides, while he was sitting on the judgement seat, his wife sent word to him, 'Have nothing to do with that righteous man, for I have suffered much over him today in a dream.' Now the chief priests and the elders persuaded the people to ask for Barabbas and destroy Jesus.

Lk 23:17–19
Now he was obliged to release one man to them at the festival. But they all cried out together, 'Away with this man and release to us Barabbas' – a man who had been thrown into prison for an insurrection started in the city, and for murder.

Jn 18:39–40
'But you have a custom that I should release one man for you at the Passover; will you have me that I release for you the King of the Jews?' They cried out again, 'Not this man, but Barabbas!' Now Barabbas was a robber.

The surprise slant introduced into the Passion narrative by all the evangelists is the *Paschal privilege*, which entails the granting of reprieve to a Jewish prisoner held by the governor on the occasion of the feast of Passover. It is unheard of outside the Gospels and the Gospels themselves offer substantially different versions of the usage.

Some important manuscripts of Luke and the Gospel of John assert that the proclamation of amnesty at the festival was the Roman governor's duty. Mark and Matthew, in their turn, describe the amnesty as the governor's custom, but add a most unlikely detail: the reprieve was to be open-ended and the Jewish crowd could choose any detainee they desired. We are also faced with compromise solutions. Pontius Pilate himself proposes a choice between two named individuals, Jesus or Barabbas (Matthew), or he selects his preferred beneficiary, but the people attempt to bargain for another: 'I will let the King of the Jews go,' proposes the governor; 'No, we want Barabbas,' shout the crowds (Luke).

The manner of offering the alternatives may be confused, but the outcome is invariably the same. When invited to choose between a certain Barabbas, or Jesus Barabbas according to some manuscripts, and Jesus surnamed the Christ, the Jewish populace, persuaded by the chief priests (Mark and Matthew), not only demands the release of Barabbas, but also preposterously clamours for the crucifixion of Jesus. It is hard, indeed almost impossible, to imagine a nationalist Jewish crowd encouraging the Romans to kill one of their countrymen. Of Barabbas nothing is known outside the New Testament. John calls him a robber, a *lêstês* in Greek, a word regularly applied to Jewish revolutionaries or Zealots in Josephus. The Gospels imply that he was held in prison for his participation in a failed insurrection in Jerusalem in the course of which someone was murdered, no doubt by Barabbas (Lk 23:25). An odd candidate for prefectorial clemency, one would say. Some New Testament scholars, desirous to maintain the historicity of the Barabbas episode, point out that another governor, Albinus (AD 62–4), released Jewish prisoners on his arrival in Jerusalem. But from a closer reading of Josephus it appears that the pardon was selective. Criminals who deserved to be put to death were executed, and amnesty was extended only to people gaoled for petty offences (*Jewish Antiquities* 20:215). Barabbas was not the kind of person a Roman administrator would have felt at liberty in ordinary circumstances to let loose in a turbulent country. But maybe the circumstances were not normal on that particular Passover?

10. The death sentence

Mk 15:12–20

And Pilate again said to them, 'Then what shall I do with the man whom you call the King of the Jews?' And they cried out again, 'Crucify him.' And Pilate said to them, 'Why, what evil has he done?' But they shouted all the more, 'Crucify him.' So Pilate wishing to satisfy the crowd, released for them Barabbas; and having scourged Jesus, he delivered him to be crucified. And the soldiers led him away inside the palace (that is, the praetorium); and they called together the whole battalion. And they clothed him in a purple cloak, and plaiting a crown of thorns they put it on him. And they began to salute him, 'Hail, King of the Jews!' And they struck his head with a reed, and spat upon him, and they knelt down in homage to him. And when they had mocked him, they stripped him of the purple cloak, and put his own clothes on him. And they led him out to crucify him.

Mt 27:21–31

The governor again said to them, 'Which of the two do you want me to release for you?' And they said, 'Barabbas.' Pilate said to them, 'Then what shall I do with Jesus who is called the Christ?' They all said, 'Let him be crucified.' And he said, 'Why, what evil has he done?' But they shouted all the more, 'Let him be crucified.' So when Pilate saw that he was gaining nothing, but rather that riot was beginning, he took water and washed his hands before the crowd, saying, 'I am innocent of this man's blood, see to it yourselves.' And all the people answered, 'His blood be on us and on our children!' Then he released Barabbas, and having scourged

Jesus, he delivered him to be crucified. Then the soldiers of the governor took Jesus into the praetorium, and they gathered the whole battalion before him. And they stripped him and put a scarlet robe upon him, and plaiting a crown of thorns they put it on his head, and put a reed in his right hand. And kneeling before him they mocked him, saying, 'Hail, King of the Jews!' And they spat upon him, and took the reed and struck him on the head. And when they had mocked him, they stripped him of the robe, and put his own clothes on him, and led him away to crucify him.

Lk 23:20–24
Pilate addressed them once more, desiring to release Jesus, but they shouted out, 'Crucify, crucify him!' A third time he said to them, 'Why, what evil has he done? I have found in him no crime deserving death; I will therefore chastise him and release him.' But they were urgent, demanding with loud cries that he should be crucified. And their voice prevailed. So Pilate gave sentence that their demand should be granted. He released the man who had been thrown into prison for insurrection and murder, whom they asked for; but Jesus he delivered up to their will.

Jn 19:1–16
Then Pilate took Jesus and scourged him. And the soldiers plaited a crown of thorns, and put it on his head, and arrayed him in a purple robe; they came up to him, saying, 'Hail, King of the Jews!' and struck him with their hands. Pilate went out again, and said to them, 'See, I am bringing him out to you, that you may know that I find no crime in him.' So Jesus came out, wearing the crown of thorns and the purple robe. Pilate said to them, 'Behold the man!' When the chief priests and officers saw him, they cried out, 'Crucify him, crucify him!' Pilate said to them, 'Take him yourselves and crucify him, for I find no crime in him.' The Jews answered him, 'We have a law, and by that law he ought to die, because he has

made himself the Son of God.' When Pilate heard these words, he was the more afraid; he entered the praetorium again and said to Jesus, 'Where are you from?' But Jesus gave no answer. Pilate therefore said to him, 'You will not speak to me? Do you not know that I have power to release you, and power to crucify you?' Jesus answered him, 'You would have no power over me unless it had been given you from above; therefore he who delivered me to you has the greater sin.' Upon this Pilate sought to release him, but the Jews cried out, 'If you release this man, you are not Caesar's friend; everyone who makes himself a king sets himself against Caesar.' When Pilate heard these words, he brought Jesus out and sat down on the judgement seat at a place called The Pavement, and in Hebrew, Gabbatha. Now it was the Day of Preparation of the Passover; it was about the sixth hour. He said to the Jews, 'Behold your King!' They cried out, 'Away with him, away with him, crucify him!' Pilate said to them, 'Shall I crucify your King?' The chief priests answered, 'We have no king but Caesar.' Then he handed him over to them to be crucified.

After all the efforts deployed by the evangelists to exonerate Pilate, he is finally allowed to bring the proceedings to an unhappy conclusion by giving in, against his better judgement, to the repeated and increasingly furious Jewish demands. Barabbas was freed and Jesus was sentenced to be crucified. Pilate further instructed the soldiers to administer the scourging customary prior to execution (Mk 15:6–15; Mt 27:15–26). In Luke the flogging is only a bargaining ploy suggested by Pilate to the Jews – I will chastise him before releasing him – but nowhere does this evangelist say that his offer was accepted, let alone implemented (Lk 23:13–25).

In John the flogging appears to be Pilate's final stratagem to save Jesus. He hoped that the sight of the tortured man would make his accusers relent. But the Jewish crowd is becoming more furious and threatening. They would denounce Pilate as someone neglecting his duty to protect the interest of the emperor. Pilate, who could have put them to flight by a discreet hand-signal to his legionaries, is portrayed as frightened, and lets the Jews have their way. He sat on the judgement seat and handed Jesus over to them to be crucified. 'To them' is equivocal: it no doubt means the soldiers, but in the spirit of the Gospel it applies also and very particularly to the Jews.

Mark and Matthew insert here another scene of mockery of the prisoner, this time by the Roman soldiers (Mk 15:16–20; Mt 27:27–31), similar to the episode attributed by Luke to the Jewish policemen during the night after his arrest, and to Herod Antipas and his soldiers (Lk 22:63–6; 23:11), or to the insults and beatings of Jesus by the judges and the guards following his night trial and condemnation by the Sanhedrin for blasphemy (Mk 14:63–5; Mt 26:67–8). Again the derision of Jesus by the Roman soldiers after the death sentence pronounced by Pilate, recounted by Mark and faithfully repeated by Matthew (Mk 15:16–20; Mt 27:27–31), is omitted by Luke. Or perhaps more exactly Luke moved it to the scene of crucifixion, with the executioners jibing at Jesus and inviting the King of the Jews to save himself (Lk 23:35).

It may be of interest to recall here the yobbish horseplay described by Philo which took place in Alexandria on the occasion of the visit to the city by the Jewish Herodian king Agrippa I (*Flaccus* 36–40). The Greek crowd, intent on ridiculing the Jewish king, dressed a lunatic called Carabas in mock royal garments with a papyrus crown and a sceptre, provided him with a bodyguard, and gave him comic salute before beating him up. An attempt to link

Carabas to Barabbas has been advanced by some scholars, but it seems far-fetched.

Matthew appends three special supplements to Mark's account. First, Pilate is warned by his wife, who having had a nightmarish dream about Jesus urges her husband to have nothing to do with 'that righteous man' (Mt 27:19). Second, before sentencing Jesus to die on the cross, the governor protests his own, and symbolically the Romans' innocence, by washing his hands in public of the blood guilt of Jesus. Third, in addition to exculpating Rome, Matthew wishes to put the responsibility for the murder of Jesus fair and square on the whole Jewish race, present and future, by making 'all the people' cry out 'His blood be on us and on our children!' (Mt 27:24–5).

11. The crucifixion

Mk 15:21–32

And they compelled a passer-by, Simon of Cyrene, who was coming in from the country, the father of Alexander and Rufus, to carry his cross. And they brought him to a place called Golgotha (which means the place of a skull). And they offered him wine mingled with myrrh; but he did not take it. And they crucified him, and divided his garments among them, casting lots for them, to decide what each should take. And it was the third hour, when they crucified him. And the inscription of the charge against him read, 'The King of the Jews'. And with him they crucified two robbers, one on his right and one on his left. And those who passed by derided him, wagging their heads, and saying, 'Aha! You who would destroy the temple, and build it in three days, save yourself, and come down from the cross!' So also the chief priests mocked him to one another with the scribes, saying, 'He saved others; he cannot save himself. Let the Christ, the King of Israel, come down from the cross, that we may see and believe.' Those who were crucified with him also reviled him.

Mt 27:32–44
As they went out, they came upon a man of Cyrene, Simon by name; this man they compelled to carry his cross. And when they came to a place called Golgotha (which means the place of a skull), they offered him wine to drink, mingled with gall; but when he tasted it, he could not drink it. And when they had crucified him, they divided his garments among them by casting lots; then they sat down and kept watch over him there. And over his head they put the charge against him: 'This is Jesus the King of the Jews.' Then two robbers were crucified with him, one on the right and one on the left. And those who passed by derided him, wagging their heads, and saying, 'You who would destroy the temple, and build it in three days, save yourself! If you are the Son of God, come down from the cross.' So also the chief priests, with the scribes and elders, mocked him, saying, 'He saved others; he cannot save himself. He is the King of Israel; let him come down from the cross, and we will believe in him. He trusts in God; let God deliver him now, if he desires him; for he said, "I am the Son of God."' And the robbers who were crucified with him also reviled him in the same way.

Lk 23:23–49
And as they led him away, they seized one Simon of Cyrene, who was coming in from the country, and laid on him his cross, to carry it behind Jesus. And there followed him a great multitude of people, and of women who bewailed and lamented him. But Jesus turning to them said, 'Daughters of Jerusalem, do not weep for me, but weep for yourselves and for your children. For behold, the days are coming when they will say, "Blessed are the barren, and the wombs that never bore, and the breasts that never gave suck!" Then

they will begin to say to the mountains, "Fall on us"; and to the hills, "Cover us." For if they do this when the wood is green, what will happen when it is dry?' Two others also, who were criminals, were led away to be put to death with him. And when they came to the place which is called the skull, there they crucified him, and the criminals, one on the right and one on the left. And Jesus said, 'Father, forgive them; for they know not what they do.' And they cast lots to divide his garments. And the people stood by, watching; but the rulers scoffed at him saying, 'He saved others; let him save himself, if he is the Christ of God, his Chosen One!' The soldiers also mocked him, coming up and offering him vinegar, and saying, 'If you are the King of the Jews, save yourself!' There was also an inscription over him, 'This is the King of the Jews.' One of the criminals who were hanged railed at him, saying, 'Are you not the Christ? Save yourself and us!' But the other rebuked him, saying, 'Do you not fear God, since you are under the same sentence of condemnation? And we indeed justly; for we are receiving the due reward of our deeds; but this man has done nothing wrong.' And he said, 'Jesus, remember me when you come into your kingdom.' And he said to him, 'Truly, I say to you, today you will be with me in Paradise.'

Jn 19: 17–27

So they took Jesus, and he went out, bearing his own cross, to the place called the place of a skull, which is called in Hebrew Golgotha. There they crucified him, and with him two others, one on either side, and Jesus between them. Pilate also wrote a title and put it on the cross; it read, 'Jesus of Nazareth, the King of the Jews.' Many of the Jews read this title, for the place where Jesus was crucified was near the city; and it was written in Hebrew, in Latin, and in Greek. The chief priests of the Jews then said to Pilate, 'Do not write, "The King of the Jews", but, "This man said, I am the King of the Jews."' Pilate answered, 'What I have written,

I have written.' When the soldiers had crucified Jesus they took his garments and made four parts, one for each soldier; also his tunic. But the tunic was without seam, woven from top to bottom; so they said to one another, 'Let us not tear it, but cast lots for it to see whose it shall be.' This was to fulfil the Scripture, 'They parted my garments among them, and for my clothing they cast lots.' So the soldiers did this. But standing by the cross of Jesus were his mother, and his mother's sister, Mary the wife of Clopas, and Mary Magdalene. When Jesus saw his mother, and the disciple whom he loved standing near, he said to his mother, 'Woman, behold your son!' Then he said to the disciple, 'Behold your mother!' And from that hour the disciple took her to his own home.

Only one incident is recorded by all the Synoptic Gospels concerning Jesus' journey from the residence of Pilate to Calvary; the forced recruitment by the soldiers of a passer-by, Simon from Cyrene, to help Jesus to carry the cross. He has never been heard of before nor is he mentioned again. The help that Simon gave to Jesus is commemorated at one of the Stations of the Cross. Several additional incidents are listed at the Stations of the Cross: the three falls of Jesus under the weight of the gibbet, his meeting with Mary, his mother, and with Veronica on whose scarf the image of Jesus is believed to have imprinted itself, but these purported happenings are all without New Testament foundation. The encounter of Jesus with the lamenting women of Jerusalem is mentioned in the Gospel of Luke, but there alone (Lk 23:27–31).

The Synoptic evangelists report that Jesus was crucified at the third hour of the day, i.e. nine o'clock in the morning, together with two other condemned Jews on a hill called 'the skull', or Golgotha in Aramaic. According to John, the crucifixion happened three hours later, at midday, the sixth hour. (The Jewish night ran from 6 p.m. to 6 a.m., and the day from 6 a.m. to 6 p.m.) The reference to a drink of wine mixed with myrrh or vinegar (Mk 15:23; Mt 27:34; Jn 19:29) is more likely to stem from the evangelists' wish to see another fulfilment of Scripture (Ps 69:21) than from the hardened Roman executioners' sympathy for a crucified Jew. It is true that in Mark 15:36 and Matthew 27:48 some Jews offer Jesus a drink, but they give him vinegar in straight fulfilment of the words of the Psalm. Their purpose was not to diminish consciousness, as some kind-hearted later rabbis proposed that one should assist people to be executed (Babylonian Talmud Sanhedrin 43a), but to prolong the life of the crucified out of curiosity: they wanted to see whether Elijah would come to the rescue of the dying Jesus.

Jesus' cross bore an inscription or title (*titulus*), composed by Pilate himself if we believe John, giving the reason for his execution. Not one of the four Gospels fully agrees with any other in recording the short text. The briefest is Mark's with 'The King of the Jews', and the longest is the version of the Fourth Gospel, 'Jesus of Nazareth, the King of the Jews', with John's added note that the inscription was in Hebrew (Aramaic), Latin and Greek (Jn 19:19–20). John further remarks that the Jewish chief priests tried to quibble and petitioned Pilate to correct the text to read: 'This man said, I am King of the Jews.' However, they were given short shrift by the governor: 'What I have written, I have written' – *Ho gegrapha, gegrapha* – *Quod scripsi, scripsi* (Jn 19:21–2). With this, the Jewish delegation disappears from John's story. No doubt they rushed to the Temple to perform their other duties. Contrary to the Synoptics, the author of the Fourth Gospel does not bring the chief priests to the cross.

The evangelists find not a single Jew to say a kind word about Jesus. Not only the chief priests, the scribes and the elders, who pursued him to Calvary, but also all the passers-by, and even the two other crucified criminals, according to Mark and Matthew, mocked and railed him. In Luke only one of them did so, while the other begged for the intercession of Jesus and received from him a promise of reassurance: 'Today you will be with me in Paradise' (Lk 23:39–43).

The compassionate Luke, endeavouring to improve Mark's version, introduces elements of pity which are no doubt of his own creation. Note among his retouches, in addition to the repentant robber, Jesus' healing of the wounded slave of the high priest in Gethsemane (Lk 22:51), the lament of the sympathetic women of Jerusalem (Lk 23:27), the multitude of onlookers beating their breasts after the death of Jesus, and the mention of *all* his acquaintances standing at some distance from the cross (Lk 48–9).

In the crucifixion story itself Luke departs from Mark on an important point. He introduces a saying of the dying Jesus immediately after the mention, 'there they crucified him'. His words run: 'Father, forgive them; for they know not what they do' (Lk 23:34). Attentive readers are bound to be puzzled by the absence of this verse, so typical of the thought of Jesus, from half of the ancient codices of Luke and from all the other Gospels. Has Jesus' prayer of forgiveness been deliberately deleted? Also, for whom does Jesus beg God's pardon? The context suggests that the pronoun 'they' most probably points to the Roman soldiers, the executioners who attached him to the cross: 'there *they* crucified him'. The same Roman soldiers remain the subjects of the next sentence: 'and *they* cast lots' (Lk 23:34). But according to the main New Testament tradition the Romans were not the real guilty party in the story of the Passion. They had already been exonerated when Pilate was whitewashed; so Jesus did not need to pray for them to be forgiven. The remaining alternative is that 'they' refers to the Jews. Attributing their action against Jesus to ignorance, 'they know not what they do', would be in harmony with the thought of the primitive Jerusalem church. The Jewish leaders acted in ignorance, the author of the Acts of the Apostles makes Peter say (Acts 3:17). But reference to mitigating circumstances in favour of the Jews would not tally with the story-line adopted by Mark, and especially by Matthew with his cry, 'His blood be on us and on our children' (Mt 27:25). Hence the editors of the first two Gospels ignored the saying, 'Father, forgive them', and in the course of time many copyists even excised the verse from the manuscripts of the gentle Luke, thus revealing the basic anti-Jewish tendency of early Christianity.

12. The death of Jesus

Mk 15:33–41

And when the sixth hour had come, there was darkness over the whole land until the ninth hour. And at the ninth hour Jesus cried with a loud voice, 'Eloi, Eloi lama sabachthani?' which means, 'My God, my God, why hast thou forsaken me?' And some of the bystanders hearing it said, 'Behold, he is calling Elijah.' And one ran and, filling a sponge full of vinegar, put it on a reed and gave it to him to drink, saying, 'Wait, let us see whether Elijah will come and take him down.' And Jesus uttered a loud cry, and breathed his last. And the curtain of the temple was torn in two, from top to bottom. And when the centurion, who stood facing him, saw that he thus breathed his last, he said, 'Truly this man is a son of God!' There were also women looking on from afar, among whom were Mary Magdalene and Mary mother of James the younger and Joses, and Salome, who, when he was in Galilee, followed him, and ministered to him; and also many other women who came up with him to Jerusalem.

Mt 27:46–56
Now from the sixth hour there was darkness over the whole land until the ninth hour. And about the ninth hour Jesus cried with a loud voice, 'Eli, Eli, lama sabachthani?', that is, 'My God, my God, why hast thou forsaken me?' And some of the bystanders hearing it said, 'This man is calling Elijah.' And one of them at once ran and took a sponge, filled it with vinegar, and put it on a reed, and gave it to him to drink. But the others said, 'Wait, let us see whether Elijah will come to save him.' And Jesus cried again with a loud voice and yielded up his spirit. And behold the curtain of the temple was torn in two, from top to bottom; and the earth shook and the rocks were split; the tombs were also opened, and many bodies of the saints who had fallen asleep were raised, and coming out of the tombs after his resurrection they went into the holy city and appeared to many. When the centurion and those who were with him, keeping watch over Jesus, saw the earthquake and what took place, they were filled with awe, and said, 'Truly this was a son of God!' There were also many women there, looking on from afar, who had followed Jesus from Galilee, ministering to him; among them were Mary Magdalene, and Mary the mother of James and Joseph, and the mother of the sons of Zebedee.

Lk 23:44–9
It was now about the sixth hour, and there was darkness over the whole land until the ninth hour, while the sun's light failed; and the curtain of the temple was torn in two. Then Jesus, crying with

a loud voice, said, 'Father, into thy hands I commit my spirit!' And having said this he breathed his last. Now when the centurion saw what had taken place, he praised God, and said, 'Certainly this man was innocent!' And all the multitudes who assembled to see the sight, when they saw what had taken place, returned home beating their breasts. And all his acquaintances and the women who had followed him from Galilee stood at a distance and saw these things.

Jn 19:28–37
After this Jesus, knowing that all was now finished, said (to fulfil the Scripture), 'I thirst.' A bowl full of vinegar stood there; so they put a sponge full of the vinegar on hyssop and held it to his mouth. When Jesus had received the vinegar, he said, 'It is finished'; and he bowed his head and gave up his spirit. Since it was the Day of Preparation, in order to prevent the bodies from remaining on the cross on the Sabbath (for that Sabbath was a high day), the Jews asked Pilate that their legs might be broken, and that they might be taken away. So the soldiers came and broke the legs of the first, and of the other who had been crucified with him, and when they came to Jesus and saw that he was already dead, they did not break his legs. But one of the soldiers pierced his side with a spear, and at once there came out blood and water. . . . For these things took place that the Scripture might be fulfilled, 'Not a bone of him shall be broken.' And again another Scripture says, 'They shall look on him whom they have pierced.'

The end of Jesus, Mark and Matthew tell their readers, came soon at the ninth hour (three o'clock in the afternoon) after six hours of agony on the cross. In John the time between crucifixion and death is reduced to three hours, from noon till 3 p.m. The first two evangelists record a cry of Jesus, *Eloi, Eloi, lama sabachthani?* (My God, my

God, why hast thou forsaken me?). The words are the Aramaic equivalent of the opening line of the Hebrew Psalm 22 (*Eli, Eli, lama 'azabtani*), and since two other verses of the same Psalm are cited in the crucifixion narrative, one apropos of the railing of Jesus by the passers-by and the other about the division of his clothes with the help of a die (Ps 22:8, 19), the quotations are thought by many to constitute a literary and theological device employed by Mark and Matthew. The events are presented as the fulfilment of Scripture. However, it must be observed that the words attributed to Jesus, *Eloi, Eloi, lama sabachthani?*, are given in Mark in Aramaic and not in the original Hebrew, the language in which the Psalms were normally recited by most Jews in the Temple and the synagogue. I think the best explanation for this unexpected use is that the phrase had become in the vernacular of the time of Jesus a kind of proverbial saying, expressing religious incomprehension and bewilderment. It is fascinating to note that Mark and Matthew claim that the bystanders misheard and misunderstood the cry. They believed that Jesus was calling, not on God, but on the miracle-working prophet Elijah, and excitedly commented: 'Wait. Let us see whether Elijah will come to take him down' (Mk 15:36; Mt 27:49).

John emphasizes that Jesus had truly expired; hence there was no need to break his legs, as was done to the two other crucified to precipitate the end before the start of the Sabbath and of Passover. However, just to make sure, one of the soldiers pierced Jesus' side with a spear and was satisfied that he was no longer alive (Jn 19:31–7).

Mark and Matthew refer also to another scream without recording the words. Luke's tradition identifies it as a peaceful parting prayer: 'Father, into thy hands I commit my spirit!' With this last cry Jesus gave up the ghost (Mk 15:33–7; Mt 27:45–50; Lk 23:44–6).

According to the Synoptic Gospels, Jesus died abandoned by his family and his male friends. The only sympathetic witnesses of his last moments were a few women who faithfully followed him from Galilee to Jerusalem. Frightened of approaching the crucified, they watched him die from afar. Those named are Mary Magdalene, Mary mother of James and Joses, and Salome, the wife of Zebedee and mother of the apostles James and John (Mk 15:40–41; Mt 27:55–6). Among the absentees figure all the apostles and disciples, and Mary, mother of Jesus and the rest of his family. Luke is vague, but slightly more generous; he brings to the proximity of the cross all the acquaintances of Jesus and the women who had followed him from Galilee (Lk 23:49).

In the Fourth Gospel there are no jeering spectators, no chief priests or passers-by. The small group of sympathizers who stood at the foot of the cross is not quite the same as in the Synoptics. The ever-faithful Mary Magdalene is there, as is also the other Mary, here identified as the wife of Clopas. But the chief difference consists in the presence of the mother of Jesus and the apostle whom he especially loved (identified as John son of Zebedee by Christian tradition). John records that Jesus entrusted his mother and his favourite disciple to each other's care. 'It is finished', or perhaps better 'It [the whole prophetic destiny of Christ] is fulfilled' constitutes Jesus' last theological statement in the Fourth Gospel (Jn 19:23–30).

The three Synoptic Gospels describe various miraculous events preceding and following the death of Jesus. They allude to sudden darkness at noon lasting until 3 p.m., a common element of apocalyptic imagery (Mk 25:33; Mt 27:45;

Lk 23:44). They also mention the rending of the curtain of the Temple (Mk 15:38; Mt 27:51; Lk 23:45), an event in which Christianity has seen the symbolical end of Judaism. Matthew speaks also of an earthquake, another apocalyptic feature, which opened tombs and allowed many bodies contained in them to rise from the dead (Mt 27:52–3).

All three Synoptic Gospels record the proclamation of the centurion, head of the execution squad, that Jesus was a son of God (Mark and Matthew) or an innocent man (Luke). The privilege of being the first to confess the greatness of Jesus after his death is granted by Mark to a Gentile and, perhaps most significantly, to a Roman.

13. The burial of Jesus

Mk 15:42–7
And when evening had come, since it was the Day of Preparation, that is, the day before the Sabbath, Joseph of Arimathea, a respected member of the council, who was also himself looking for the kingdom of God, took courage and went to Pilate, and asked for the body of Jesus. And Pilate wondered if he were already dead; and summoning the centurion, he asked him whether he was already dead. And when he learned from the centurion that he was dead, he granted the body to Joseph. And he bought a linen shroud, and taking him down, wrapped him in the linen shroud, and laid him in a tomb which had been hewn out of the rock; and he rolled a stone against the door of the tomb. Mary Magdalene and Mary the mother of Joses saw where he was laid.

Mt 27:57–66
When it was evening, there came a rich man from Arimathea, named Joseph, who also was a disciple of Jesus. He went to Pilate

and asked for the body of Jesus. Then Pilate ordered it to be given to him. And Joseph took the body, and wrapped it in a clean linen shroud, and laid it in his own new tomb, which he had hewn in the rock; and he rolled a great stone to the door of the tomb, and departed. Mary Magdalene and the other Mary were there, sitting opposite the sepulchre. Next day, that is, after the Day of Preparation, the chief priests and the Pharisees gathered before Pilate and said, 'Sir, we remember how that impostor said, while he was still alive, "After three days I will rise again." Therefore order the sepulchre to be made secure until the third day, lest his disciples go and steal him away, and tell the people, "He has risen from the dead," and the last fraud will be worse than the first.' Pilate said to them, 'You have a guard of soldiers; go, make it as secure as you can.' So they went and made the sepulchre secure by sealing the stone and setting a guard.

Lk 23:50–56
Now there was a man named Joseph of the Jewish town of Arimathea. He was a member of the council, a good and righteous man, who had not consented to their purpose and deed, and he was looking for the kingdom of God. This man went to Pilate and asked for the body of Jesus. Then he took it down and wrapped it in a linen shroud, and laid it in a rock-hewn tomb, where no one had ever yet been laid. It was the Day of Preparation, and the Sabbath was beginning. The women who had come with him from Galilee followed, and saw the tomb, and how his body was laid; then they returned, and prepared spices and ointments. On the Sabbath they rested according to the commandment.

Jn 19:38–42
After this Joseph of Arimathea, who was a disciple of Jesus, but secretly, for fear of the Jews, asked Pilate that he might take away the body of Jesus, and Pilate gave him leave. So he came and took

away his body. Nicodemus also, who had at first come to him by night, came bringing a mixture of myrrh and aloes, about a hundred pounds' weight. They took the body of Jesus, and bound it in linen cloths with the spices, as is the burial custom of the Jews. Now in the place where he was crucified, there was a garden, and in the garden a new tomb, where no one had ever been laid. So because of the Jewish Day of Preparation, as the tomb was close at hand, they laid Jesus there.

The three Synoptic evangelists report that at the approach of nightfall on Friday, shortly before Sabbath began, Joseph of Arimathea, a member of the Sanhedrin and a crypto-sympathizer, obtained permission from Pilate to take down the body from the cross. Luke specifies that Joseph had disagreed with his fellow councillors regarding Jesus, but no one mentions this in the context of the trial of Jesus by the Sanhedrin. The centurion in command of the executioners testified before the governor that Jesus had already died, and Joseph was granted permission to proceed with a hasty burial. Without the use of the customary spices, he wrapped the body in a linen shroud which he had purchased. He then laid the body in a freshly hewn rock tomb, the entrance of which was protected from wild animals and thieves by a large and heavy rolling stone. The Jewish custom was to leave the body in the tomb cave until the flesh disintegrated. At some later date the bones were collected and placed into a box made of wood, plaster or stone. These boxes or ossuaries were then kept in family burial tombs. In the Synoptics Mary Magdalene and another woman, also named Mary (so Mark and Matthew) or Galilean women (Luke), are said to have watched Joseph of Arimathea at the tomb (Mk 15:42–7; Mt 27:57–61; Lk 23:50–56).

The tradition transmitted by John is in partial agreement with the Synoptics. Joseph of Arimathea, a clandestine follower of Jesus 'for fear of the Jews', is the protagonist, but in John he is joined by a second secret disciple, Nicodemus (Jn 3:2). Joseph does not buy the linen shroud; it is brought along by Nicodemus together with a mixture of spices weighing about 100 pounds. (How he put his hands on all this at a moment's notice and carried it outside the city remains unexplained.) Be this as it may, as the start of Passover was close, the two Jewish dignitaries hurriedly buried Jesus in a new tomb in a nearby garden without being observed by any female witness (Jn 19:38–42).

Matthew further notes, no doubt with the hindsight of later Christian polemical considerations, that the Jewish leaders, fearful that the disciples of Jesus might steal his body and stage a fake fulfilment of his predicted resurrection from the dead, asked Pilate to keep the tomb under military observation. 'Do it yourselves' seems to have been the governor's sharp reply. So the chief priests sealed the entrance of the cave and sentries were posted there to keep away intruders.

The account of the burial of Jesus closes the Gospel story of the Passion. As has been made obvious in the running commentary, the evangelists are not altogether logical in themselves, nor is the tradition underlying the Synoptic Gospels compatible with that of the Fourth Gospel. Our next task therefore is to state the problems as clearly as possible both in their New Testament dimension and in comparison with all the relevant data arising from Jewish and Roman history and culture of the age of Jesus.

III

The Passion accounts compared with one another and with sources from outside the New Testament

Having completed the survey of the Passion story in the separate Gospels, the moment has arrived for the detective-historian to cast a comprehensive glance at the evidence and investigate how the accounts of the four evangelists relate to one another. A list of the main common features appearing in the Gospels followed by another consisting of the obvious differences will facilitate the overall comparison.

There is general *agreement* among the evangelists on seven incidents of the Passion story.

1. They all place the arrest of Jesus in a garden outside Jerusalem late in the evening, after supper. John expressly mentions that the soldiers sent to look for Jesus were carrying lanterns and torches (Jn 18:3).

2. The following morning Jesus was transferred from the palace of the high priest (Caiaphas) to the residence of the Roman governor to be tried by Pontius Pilate on a political charge.

3. During the hearing the question of the Passover amnesty was brought up by Pilate.

4. Pilate condemned Jesus to death and an inscription affixed to the cross stated that Jesus was crucified as 'The King of the Jews'.

5. Jesus' garments were divided among the members of the execution squad, four Roman soldiers according to John (Jn 19:23).

6. Jesus died on the cross.

7. He was immediately buried in a rock tomb, the entrance of which was closed by a large rolling stone.

The five *disagreements* neatly fall between the Synoptic Gospels and John.

1. The date of the Last Supper, arrest and cruxifixion of Jesus: Thursday evening/Friday, 15 Nisan = Passover (Synoptics); *or* Thursday evening/Friday, *14* Nisan = *eve* of Passover (John). In John 15 Nisan = Passover falls on Friday evening/Saturday (Jn 19:14, 31).

2. The reason why the apostles left Jesus: they fled (Synoptics) *or* were allowed to go (John).

3. The venue and character of the proceedings during the night following the arrest: Jesus was taken to Caiaphas and tried and sentenced on the religious charge of blasphemy (Mark and Matthew with a revised scenario in Luke) *or* he was first interrogated by the former high priest Annas and then sent to Caiaphas without religious trial or sentence (John). The issue of the competence of a Jewish court to execute a capital sentence (John) is also relevant here.

4. The identity of the persons at the cross: Galilean women (Synoptics) *or* the mother of Jesus and his beloved disciple as well as Galilean women (John).

5. The identity of the men who buried Jesus: Joseph of Arimathea (Synoptics) *or* Joseph of Arimathea and Nicodemus (John).

Nothing is more revealing in the comparative study of texts than a parallel presentation of agreements and disagreements. Therefore in order to assist the reader to perceive at a simple glance identities and discrepancies among the Gospels, the contents of the Passion narratives are printed in four parallel columns. Mark's Gospel, being the ultimate source of the Jesus story in the Synoptics, appears in the first column and thus serves as pattern. Peculiarities in the diverse Gospels are set in bold print; identical reports are marked by –"–, and missing items by [----].

MARK	MATTHEW

Last Supper (Eucharist)   14:22–5
[Passover meal 14:12]

Last Supper (–"–)   26:26–9
[–"–26:17]

Arrest   14:26, 43–52
Judas + chief priest's men
Arrest
Disciple draws sword [----]
Jesus protests innocence
Disciples flee

Arrest   26:30, 47–56
–"–
–"–
–"–Jesus stops disciple
–"–
–"–

Jesus in the high priest's house
                    14:53–65
Night trial by Sanhedrin
Witnesses rejected by court
High priest: Are you Christ?
Jesus: **Yes.** Seated on right of
   God
High priest: Blasphemy – death
Assault on Jesus by judges and
   guards

Jesus in Caiaphas' house   26:57–68

–"–
–"–
–"–
You say so

–"–
–"–
[----]

LUKE		JOHN	
Last Supper (–"–)	22:15–20	*Last Supper* **[No Euch.]**	13:1–2, 29
[–"–22:7–8, 15]		**Before** Passover	
		Judas to buy things for Passover	
Arrest	22:39, 47–53	*Arrest*	18:2–11
–"–		Judas+**cohort of soldiers**	
–"–		From chief priests. **Fall to ground**	
		Jesus: Let disciples go	
–"–Jesus stops disciple, **heals** slave		**Peter** resists. Jesus stops him	
[----]		[----]	
Jesus in high priest's house	22:54	*Jesus in **Annas'** house*	18:12–14
		[No Jewish trial]	
[No night trial]		**Cohort+tribune+Jewish officers**	
[----]		**Jesus interrogated** by Annas	
[----]		**Jesus claims innocence**	
[----]		**Annas sends him to Pilate**	
[----]			
[----]			
Mockery by guard	22:63–5		

MARK		MATTHEW	
Morning meeting	15:1	*Morning meeting*	27:1–2
Case sent to Pilate		–"–	
		Judas' suicide	27:3–10

Jesus before Pilate	15:2–5	*Jesus before Pilate*	27:11–14
Pilate: Are you King of Jews?		–"–	
Jesus: You say so		–"–	
Accused by chief priests		–"–	
No answer by Jesus		–"–	
Pilate astonished		–"– **greatly**	

Morning council   22:66–71
Judges: Are you Christ?
You say so.–"–
Are you Son of God?
Judges: We heard him
[No sentence]

Jesus before Pilate   23:2–5   *Jesus before Pilate*   18:28–38
                                        Early on eve of Passover
Chief priests charge Jesus   **Pilate: What is the charge?**
–"–   **Pilate: You judge him**
–"–   **Jews: We cannot execute**
–"–   **Pilate: Are you King of Jews?**
–"–   **Jesus: Kingdom not of the**
–"–   **world**
Pilate: I find no crime   **–"–**
Chief priests: Troublemaker
   from Galilee to Jerusalem

Jesus before Herod   23:6–12
Jesus questioned, mocked,
   returned to Pilate
Pilate: No guilt.
Pilate: Will flog and release
   Jesus?

MARK		MATTHEW	
Passover amnesty	15:6–14	*Passover amnesty*	27:15–25
Pilate: Release King of Jews?		Pilate: **Barabbas or Jesus?**	
		Pilate's wife's nightmare	
Chief priests urge for Barabbas		–"–	
Pilate: What to do with Jesus?		–"–	
Chief priests: Crucify him!		–"–	
		Pilate washes hands	
		Jews: His blood be on us	

MARK		MATTHEW	
Sentence of death	15:15–20	*Sentence of death*	27:26–31
Barabbas released		–"–	
Jesus flogged		–"–	
Delivered to be crucified		–"–	
Mocked by soldiers		–"–	

LUKE		JOHN	

Passover amnesty	23:17–23	*Passover amnesty*	19:38–40
Jews: Crucify Jesus, free Barabbas			
_"_		_"_	
_"_		_"_	
_"_		_"_	

Sentence of death	23:24–5	*Sentence of death*	19:1–15
_"_		[----]	
[----]		_"_	
_"_		Mocked by soldiers	
[----]		**Pilate: No crime**	
		Behold the man	
		Pilate: You crucify him	
		Jews: Son of God	
		Jesus: Jews more guilty	
		Pilate: Will release him	
		Chief priests: No friend of Caesar	
		Jesus delivered to them	

MARK		MATTHEW	
Crucifixion	15:21–32	*Crucifixion*	27:32–44
Simon of Cyrene		–"–	
His sons		[----]	
Golgotha		–"–	
Wine+myrrh		–"–	
Crucifixion+2		–"–	
Garments		–"–	
Inscription		–"–	
Passers-by		–"–	
Chief priests		–"–	
Robbers		–"–	

MARK		MATTHEW	
Death	15:33–41	*Death*	27:45–56
Darkness from 6 to 9		–"–	
Eloi		Eli	
Calling Elijah		–"–	
Sponge		–"–	
Last cry		–"–	
Curtain split		–"–+**tombs–saints**	
Centurion: son of God		–"–	
Women: M. Magdalene, Mary,		–"–	
Salome		Wife of Zebedee	

LUKE		JOHN	
Crucifixion	23:26–43	*Crucifixion*	19:16–27
–"–		[----]	
[----]		[----]	
Multitude+Jerusalem women		Golgotha	
Crucifixion+2		–"–	
Father, forgive		Crucifixion+2	
Garments		Inscription **by Pilate**	
Rulers (chief priests)		**Chief priests quibble**	
Mocked by soldiers		Garments	
Inscription		**At cross mother of Jesus+**	
Robber reviling		**Disciple**+two Marys	
One robber praying			
Promise by Jesus			

LUKE		JOHN	
Death	23:44–9	*Death*	19:28–37
–"–+ curtain split		[----]	
[----]		[----]	
[----]		[----]	
[----]		**I thirst+** wine	
Father, into thy hands		**It is finished**	
		[----]	
Centurion		[----]	
Repentant multitude		**Legs broken**	
All acquaintances+women		**Side pierced**	

MARK		MATTHEW	
Burial	15:42–7	*Burial*	27:57–61
Joseph of Arimathea – Pilate		–"–	
Member of council		**Rich man**	
Centurion reporting		[----]	
Body wrapped in shroud		–"–	
Rock tomb+stone		–"–	
M. Magdalene+Mary		–"–	
		Guard posted	

LUKE		JOHN	
Burial	23:50–56	*Burial*	19:38–42
_"_		_"_	
_"_		Disciple	
[----]		[----]	
_"_		**Nicodemus+spices**	
_"_		_"_	
		Tomb **in garden**	
		[----]	

1. Comments on the general agreements

Most of the agreements require no further comment, nevertheless four issues deriving from them may benefit from some additional explanation.

1. Although this is not explicitly formulated, it would seem that substantial disparity is concealed in the terminological variations attested in John and the Synoptics concerning the composition of the party which arrested Jesus in the garden of Gethsemane. In the Synoptics the priestly authorities dispatch armed men led by 'the officers of the Jews'. They appear to represent the Jewish Temple police. John, by contrast, refers to members of what seems to be a military unit, *speira* in Greek, under the command of a high-ranking *chiliarchos* (major or colonel). These soldiers were accompanied by 'the officers of the Jews' (Jn 18:12). A *speira* corresponds to the Roman cohort, and its commander is a *tribunus* or tribune, the Latin equivalent of the Greek *chiliarchos*. The words occur elsewhere in the military vocabulary of the New Testament. The Roman centurion Cornelius, who was to become a Christian, belonged to the 'Italian cohort' stationed in Caesarea, and Paul was arrested in the Temple by the Roman tribune Claudius Lysias (Acts 10:1; 21:31; 23:26). Does this suggest that Jesus was apprehended by a unit of *Roman* soldiers assisted by Jewish liaison officers and not by Jewish Temple policemen? This would put a different complexion on the whole Passion story.

The theory that Jesus was taken into custody by Roman legionaries has been advanced among others by Paul Winter (*On the Trial of Jesus*, 1974, pp. 61–9), Fergus Millar ('Reflections on the Trials of Jesus', in *A Tribute to Geza*

Vermes, 1990, p. 370) and Paula Fredriksen (*Jesus of Nazareth, the King of the Jews*, 1999, p. 258). The interpretation of the military vocabulary as alluding to the Roman army has, however, been challenged in the light of Josephus' use of the same expressions in a Jewish context (*Jewish Antiquities* 17:215; *Jewish War* 2:578). Nevertheless Josephus definitely alludes to armies, either to those of the Herodian ruler Archelaus or to the revolutionary forces of John of Gischala during the first war against Rome. These forces were explicitly organized on the model of the Roman legions. It is however debatable whether the nomenclature appropriate for an army can simply be transferred to the Temple police.

2. The next query regards the Passover amnesty. As has been noted, such an amnesty is nowhere mentioned outside the Gospels, not even in Josephus, who was so well informed about first-century AD matters, and the evangelists themselves fail to agree on its precise nature. Was it a Roman practice (Lk 23:17) or a Jewish usage (Jn 18:39), or was the person to benefit from the free pardon chosen by the governor or by the people (though the latter alternative is intrinsically unlikely)? Hence the historicity of the amnesty is questionable. On the other hand, the imminently expected announcement of the release of a prisoner could account for the foregathering at the palace of Pilate of a multitude of Jews (Mk 16:6–11; Mt 27:15–18; Lk 23:4).

3. The division of the garments of Jesus among the legionaries is conceivable, though it may be asked whether the soldiers would be interested in the scourged Jesus' bloodstained clothes. On the other hand, the account may be due to the evangelists' wish to draw attention to another fulfilment of Scripture: 'They divide my garments among them, and for my raiment they cast lots' (Ps 22:18).

4. That Jesus actually died on the cross is firmly stated in every Gospel. The emphasis, especially in John, is probably meant to refute in advance doubts about the reality of the resurrection: the disappearance of the body of Jesus was not due to the revival of a comatose man. The recovery of crucified men was not unheard of. After Josephus' intercession, three of his crucified Jewish friends were taken down from the cross on Titus' order and were looked after by physicians, with the consequent return to health of one of the three (*Life* 420). The Islamic teaching that the death of Jesus on the cross was merely apparent may have derived from such early rumours.

2. Comments on disagreements between the Synoptics and John

Some of the discrepancies in the story of the Passion between the Synoptics and John present the interpreter with serious dilemmas. The ultimate question is: Are these contradictions reconcilable or must one choose one of the alternatives and reject the other?

1. Chronology stands at the top of the list of disagreements. The time difference between John and the Synoptics is admittedly only twenty-four hours, but the possible repercussions are enormous.

The Last Supper in the Synoptic Gospels is a Passover meal. This is clearly indicated in the run-up to the event, with disciples dispatched to make the necessary preparations for the Passover dinner that same evening. It is also expressly declared by Jesus in Luke: 'I have earnestly desired to eat this Passover with you' (Lk 22:15). Yet if the Passover supper was eaten on the prescribed date and at the prescribed time, i.e. around 6 p.m. at the start of 15 Nisan, the further stages of the Passion story are affected by major consequential problems: events that are not supposed to happen during a feast day (e.g. the trial of a capital case) are said to have occurred on this occasion. By contrast, if the chronology of the Fourth Gospel is followed – i.e. the meal eaten on 14 Nisan was not a Passover meal – there would be no legal difficulties, but the link of the Last Supper with the Passover dinner would disappear. Yet these paschal roots of the Eucharist are taken for granted not only by the Synoptics, but also by St Paul writing fifteen to forty-five years before them. Paul states that the Lord's supper was celebrated on the night of his betrayal (1 Cor 11:23) shortly before his immolation as 'our Passover lamb' (1 Cor 5:7).

It is possible to circumnavigate these danger points by surmising that Jesus' religious calendar differed from that of mainstream Judaism. This hypothesis has been advanced in the wake of the discovery of the sectarian calendar of the Dead Sea Scrolls. The Qumran-Essene year of 364 days is so arranged that the first day of the first month (Nisan) always falls on a Wednesday, and so too does Passover two weeks later on 15 Nisan. If Jesus had embraced the Essene time reckoning, he could have had his Passover dinner on an earlier evening than the Temple priests and their coreligionists. In fact, however, this theory creates more difficulties than it resolves. In the first instance, there is no valid evidence in the Scrolls of any influence of sectarian (Essene) religious practice on the Galilean Jesus. Moreover, if Jesus ate his Passover meal on Tuesday evening, as the Essenes would have done, and was tried and executed the following day, we are left with the insoluble riddle stemming from the repeated assertion in the

Gospels that the day following the crucifixion was a Sabbath. The Qumran-inspired solution is therefore a red herring.

2. The next difference is connected with the flight of the disciples of Jesus in the garden of Gethsemane after the arrest of their master. According to Mark and Matthew (Luke is silent on the incident), all the apostles abandoned Jesus and ran away (Mk 14:27–8; Mt 26:31–2). This shocking incident is explained away in both Gospels by a citation of the prophet Zechariah 13:7, 'I will strike the shepherd and the sheep will be scattered.' The justification of the apostles' desertion of Jesus by the necessity of the fulfilment of Scripture looks like an editorial manoeuvre, however, for, contrary to the evangelists' habit, no mention of the realization of prophecy is made when the escape of the disciples is reported. John, on the other hand, attributes to the intervention of Jesus the granting of free passage to the disciples by the soldiers. This smacks of typical Christian apologetics.

3. The real crux in the Passion story centres on the venue and nature of the night proceedings against Jesus and the identity of the priestly leader conducting them. In John, Jesus was taken to, and interrogated by, Annas, who then sent him to Caiaphas, and Caiaphas in turn delivered him to Pilate. In the Synoptics, Jesus is tried by the Sanhedrin under the presidency of Caiaphas.

Annas (Hanan) or Ananus son of Sethi was the most influential high priest in the first century AD. Appointed in AD 6 by Quirinius, governor of Syria, he held his job until a newly arrived Roman prefect of Judaea, Valerius Gratus, removed him from office in AD 15. The same Annas is also not only associated with the case of Jesus, but is mentioned again together with Caiaphas at the later inquiry into the apostles Peter and John by the Sanhedrin in Jerusalem (Acts 4:6). Annas' powerful influence with the Romans resulted in the elevation to the pontifical office not only of his son-in-law Caiaphas, but also, one after another, of five of his sons and one grandson.

There is nothing extraordinary in Jesus' appearance before Annas as we know from Josephus that former high priests often continued to play an important role in Jewish life in the first century AD. Indeed, if the case of Jesus was thought to be a complicated or delicate one, Annas was the obvious official to deal with it. His report to Caiaphas must have been that the easiest way of getting rid of Jesus was to hand over to Pilate this would-be Messiah as someone who claimed to be the King of the Jews, dirty words in Roman ears.

It is of primary importance to stress that in the Fourth Gospel *there is no Jewish trial*, there are no witnesses, and no sentence is pronounced by Jewish judges on religious or any other grounds. The only tribunal before which Jesus appeared in John was that of the Roman governor of Judaea. That the arrest and the questioning took place the day *before* Passover are also positively confirmed in John's account of the indictment of Jesus before Pontius Pilate. The versions of John and the Synoptics flatly contradict one another.

The Synoptic version of the trial of Jesus occurring at Passover night (or in the morning of Passover according to Luke) seems to be intrinsically vitiated. Both the timing of the hearing and the charge of blasphemy create apparently insoluble legal difficulties. According to the Mishnah, no capital sentence could be pronounced by the Sanhedrin on the day of the court hearing itself; it had to wait until the following day, allowing the judges to reflect on their verdict during the night. 'Therefore trials involving death penalty may not be held *on the eve of sabbath or on the eve of a feast day*' (Mishnah Sanhedrin 4:1; Betzah 5:2). That a court should not do business on a Sabbath is obvious. Apart from all other considerations, since the proceedings had to be recorded by two court clerks, the Mishnah's prohibition to write as few as two letters on the Sabbath (Shabbat 7:2) would exclude the recording of minutes and thereby render court proceedings impossible.

But many New Testament scholars object to the use of the Mishnah as a term of comparison for the study of the Gospels because of its date of redaction (*c*. AD 200). Be this as it may, the Mishnah passage is not the only relevant evidence. First-century AD sources, such as Philo and the Dead Sea Scrolls, also testify to the illegality of court business on Sabbaths/feast days. Thus Philo writes: 'Let us not . . . abrogate the laws laid down for its [the Sabbath's] observance and . . . institute [on that day] proceedings in court' (*Migration of Abraham* 91), and the Damascus Document from Qumran states just as firmly that 'no one shall judge' on the Sabbath day (10:17–18).

Caiaphas' attempt, reported in the Synoptics, to induce Jesus to incriminate himself would also have been illegal if the relevant rabbinic law decreeing invalid the admission of guilt by the accused without confirmation by witnesses was in force in the age of Jesus.

As for the crime of blasphemy with which Jesus was charged, its definition must next be examined. In the language of the Bible, in Philo and Josephus, as well as in secular Greek and in the Septuagint, the meaning of the concept of blasphemy lacks precision. In the Old Testament one can blaspheme the deity, but one can also blaspheme the king (Ex 22:28). Similarly in Josephus (and in the Acts of the Apostles) the verb is successively used with reference to disparaging God, the Jews, the ancestral laws of the Jews and their Law-giver Moses (*Against Apion* 1:143, 223, 279; Acts 6:11). Blasphemy, in other words, signifies any kind of disrespectful speech, but clearly not every disrespectful speech is punishable by death.

It may be argued that in the age of Jesus the attribution to a man of actions which are normally associated with God could also be considered blasphemous. For example, some Galilean scribes wondered whether Jesus was blaspheming when he promised forgiveness of sins to a paralysed man in Capernaum (Mk 2:7), yet none of them clamoured for Jesus' life. Indeed, in the terminology of charismatics healing and exorcism were the equivalent of forgiveness of sin, but since such charismatic acts were believed to be performed with the help of God, they did not entail anything religiously improper.

To establish the precise meaning of blasphemy, we must recall that from biblical times onwards the *legal language* used by Jews saw a special link between blasphemy and the divine *name* (Lev 24:11–16). Originally the prohibition concerned any irreverent speech about God, but by the start of the first century AD blasphemy came to be specifically linked to the pronunciation of the Tetragram. The four-lettered divine name, YHWH, was unutterable and had to be replaced even in prayer by substitutes such as Lord, Heaven or Temple. The protection of the name of the God of Israel went so far that both Philo (*Special Laws* 1:53) and Josephus (*Jewish Antiquities* 4:207; *Against Apion* 2:279) condemn abusive references to pagan deities lest Gentiles are impelled to retaliate and blaspheme the God of the Jews.

The Community Rule of Qumran seems to point in the

same direction when it strictly prohibits the enunciation of the sacrosanct divine Name in any circumstance. 'If any man has uttered the [Most] Venerable Name even frivolously, or as a result of shock or any other reason whatever, when reading the Book [the Bible] or blessing [reciting a prayer], he shall be dismissed, and shall return to the Council of the community no more' (6:27–7:2). The punishment at Qumran was irrevocable excommunication, the spiritual equivalent among the Essenes of the death penalty (Josephus, *Jewish War* 2:144).

Rabbinic literature lays down that the utterance of the sacrosanct Tetragram was an absolute requisite for someone to be charged with blasphemy: 'The blasphemer is not guilty unless he pronounces the Name' (Mishnah Sanhedrin 7:5). Reviling a substitute name was disapproved of, but did not carry the death penalty. It is apposite therefore to underline that in all three Synoptic Gospels Jesus is presented as employing a substitute name for God in his answer to the high priest and speaks not of the right hand of God, but of 'the right hand of the *Power*' (Mk 14:62; Mt 26:64; Lk 22:69). The alleged judgement of the Sanhedrin, 'You have heard his blasphemy' (Mk 14:64) appears therefore precipitate.

To recapitulate, no Jewish law of any age suggests that messianic claim amounted to the crime of blasphemy. Josephus refers to many an individual who prior to the outbreak of the first rebellion against Rome pretended to be the Messiah, and in the early second century AD Simeon Bar Kokhba was spoken of in the same terms, but none of them was accused of, or tried for, blasphemy.

It would therefore seem that the Synoptic tale of the night proceedings against Jesus lacks real foundation. To what, then, does it owe its existence? One may ask whether

Jesus' Jewish religious trial was built by Mark and his followers on a linguistic anachronism. The Synoptics take the Semitic metaphor 'Son of God', designating in the age of Jesus someone especially favoured by heaven (for instance, the royal Messiah), as the equivalent of their theological notion in the final decades of the first century AD, when it had already become among the Gentile Christians addressed by the Gospels the title of a person believed to share the nature of God in some way. In brief, Mark, Matthew and Luke appear to ascribe to Caiaphas their own understanding of Messiah=Son of God. As Rudolf Bultmann pertinently remarked, 'For the later Christian tradition Jesus' messianic claim, which was the chief issue between the Church and Judaism, could very well appear to be the ground of his condemnation' (*History of the Synoptic Tradition*, 1963, p. 270).

To put the matter into proper perspective, it is worth reflecting on a famous saying of Rabbi Abbahu, a third-century AD teacher from Caesarea, which is without any doubt a veiled criticism of Jesus. But observe the difference of attitude revealed in his words.

'If a man says to you, "I am God", he lies. "I am the Son of man" [a human being], he will be sorry at the end [as he will die]. "I will go up to heaven", he says so, but will not fulfil it' (Jerusalem Talmud Taanit 65b).

4. Another important issue is raised only in John, although it would have been useful for the Synoptics: Did Jewish courts have capital jurisdiction in the age of Jesus? In John Pilate suggests that Jesus should be dealt with by the chief priests' tribunal, but is reminded by them that the Sanhedrin had no power to order the execution of a Jewish criminal convicted by Jewish law: 'It is not lawful for us to put any man to death' (Jn 18:31).

Already in Christian antiquity some perspicacious Church fathers, wrestling with exegetical issues, interpreted the saying as alluding to the feast of Passover during which no execution could lawfully take place. 'They were not allowed to put any man to death because of the sanctity of the feast day,' writes St Augustine (*On the Gospel of John*, Tractate 114:4). St John Chrysostom makes a similar remark (*Homily on John* 83:4), echoing the Mishnah's prohibition of trying a capital case on the eve of Sabbath or of a festival (see p. 100).

In Old Testament times, during the existence of the independent Jewish kingdoms, biblical law did not distinguish between religious and civil issues, and secular and priestly judges dealt jointly with the administration of justice. The same combined legal authority functioned also under the Maccabaean-Hasmonaean high-priestly rulers (140–40BC). The most notorious affair was the summoning of the young Herod, governor of Galilee, before the supreme court in Jerusalem, made up of priests and lay Pharisees, under the presidency of the high priest Hyrcanus II. Herod was accused of putting a group of Jewish rebels to death without the due process of the law, but with Roman help and the complicity of Hyrcanus he escaped punishment (Josephus, *Jewish Antiquities*, 14:168–79).

A new situation arose with the establishment of direct Roman government in Judaea after the deposition of Herod's son Archelaus in AD 6 when the first Roman governor arrived with the power to convict and execute criminals (see p. 16). But did the granting of capital jurisdiction to the chief representative of Rome automatically abolish that of the Jewish high court in regard to offenders against the Mosaic Law? A number of New Testament scholars – by no means all of them dyed-in-the-wool fundamentalists – maintain with John that in the first century AD the Sanhedrin was forbidden to carry out executions. According to them, the order had to be issued by the Roman prefect or procurator. In support of this view there is a relatively late and somewhat vague talmudic statement implying that forty years before the destruction of the Temple the Sanhedrin lost its right to try capital cases (Jerusalem Talmud Sanhedrin 18a). However, apart from John, no historical source records such a change, datable to about AD 30. Should one none the less adopt the view of the Sanhedrin's incapacity to execute convicted criminals, the need to hand Jesus over to Pilate – on a new political charge – after his condemnation for blasphemy would become intelligible. But oddly, the Synoptics remain silent on the matter.

However, the opposite opinion, namely that the Sanhedrin continued to possess capital jurisdiction, can also marshal strong arguments. In the first place, common sense dictates that Roman governors would not interfere in religious or social matters lacking political dimension. For instance, adultery and rape carried the death penalty in Jewish law. Is it conceivable that each case had to be presented to the prefect? Above all, would any representative of Rome involve himself in purely religious matters such as blasphemy or idolatry?

Common sense is backed by literary and epigraphic evidence from the first century AD. It indicates that Jews were entitled to put to death both Jews and foreigners, even Roman citizens, if they caught them in the forbidden area of the Temple of Jerusalem. Philo of Alexandria explains that any Jewish intruder, even a priest, faced '*death without appeal*' if found in the innermost Holy of Holies of the sanctuary. Only the high priest could enter once a year, on the Day of Atonement. Philo further adds that the same prohibition applied not only to Jews, but also to 'other races' (*Embassy to Gaius* 212, 306–7). Josephus, in turn, explicitly mentions a warning engraved on slabs in Greek and Latin and displayed at regular intervals along the Temple boundaries, forbidding foreigners to cross the line on pain of death (*Jewish War* 5:194; *Jewish Antiquities* 15:417). An inscription found in Jerusalem and published by Charles Clermont-Ganneau in 1872 confirms Josephus. It reads: 'No foreigner is to enter within the balustrade and the embankment around the sanctuary. Whoever is caught will have *himself to blame for his ensuing death.*' The need for Roman approval before execution is nowhere mentioned in these sources. What is more, Josephus reports that Titus, the general of the besieging Roman forces and future emperor, reminded the Jews fighting in the Temple of the warnings in question and commented, 'And did we not permit you to put to death any who passed [the boundary wall], even were he Roman?' (*Jewish Antiquities* 6:125–6).

Actual examples point in the direction of the competence of the Sanhedrin to deal with capital cases. Even if we were to discount the stoning of the proto-martyr Stephen as possibly an act of mob violence rather than the execution of a judicial sentence, we still have to reflect on the two-year-long dispute (AD 58–60) between the Sanhedrin and the Roman procurators as to whether Jews or Romans should try Paul. It is clear from this that the members of the council, headed by the high priests Ananias son of Nedebaeus and Ishmael son of Phiabi, considered themselves competent to deal on their own with Paul, arrested in the Temple on the apparently erroneous charge of complicity in bringing a Gentile, the Ephesian Trophimus, into the prohibited area (Acts 21:29), which they considered as a capital crime (Acts: 23–5). Likewise, when in AD 62 the high priest Ananus son of Ananus arraigned James the brother of Jesus before the supreme council and sent him to his death by stoning, he was taken to task by the Roman governor Albinus, not for pronouncing and executing a capital sentence, but for convening a meeting of the Sanhedrin during the vacancy of the procuratorial office. He was accused of an administrative offence and not of the criminal charge of murder.

A further indirect confirmation of the Jewish high court's capital jurisdiction exercised even after the fall of Jerusalem in AD 70 comes from the early third century AD. The great Alexandrian Bible expert Origen, who lived in Caesarea between *c.* AD 230 and 250, in his letter to a learned Christian, Julius Africanus, describes the *Nasi* or chief rabbi as an official exercising with the emperor's consent as much power among the Jews as did the kings of the other nations. Origen continues: 'Trials are held secretly according to the Law and *some are condemned to death.* This is done neither in complete openness, nor without the knowledge of the [Roman] ruler' (Letter to Julius Africanus 20 [14]).

The hint at the quasi-secret character of the proceedings in capital cases may open a new perspective on the introduction of strangling as a non-biblical form of execution after the cessation of the Sanhedrin as a state institution in AD 70. The most common forms of execution, stoning and burning, had to be performed in the open in full public view. Strangling could be done quietly indoors.

In fact, it is most likely that during the procuratorial period the Roman and the Jewish legal systems were again and again in competition with each other. The authority which was the quickest to act tried and, when appropriate, executed the culprit. So, all things considered, one can make out a good case either for or against the Jewish high court's ability to try, sentence and execute Jesus. But if the view that the Sanhedrin had the power to impose and carry out the death sentence prevails, the fact that it referred the case of Jesus to Pilate would mean that it *chose* not to exercise its prerogative.

5. A less significant difference between John and the Synoptics relates to the presence of the mother of Jesus and 'the disciple whom he loved' at the foot of the cross. This is perfectly in line with the Fourth Gospel's devout attitude towards Mary, and is in sharp contrast with the Synoptics' outlook in which after their clash with Jesus in Galilee the family completely disappears from sight until and including the Passion (Mk 3:31–5; Mt 12:46–50; Lk 8:19–21).

6. A further difference between John and the Synoptics centres on Nicodemus' association with Joseph of Arimathea in the burial of Jesus. The mention in John's account of Nicodemus bringing with him a large quantity of spices pre-empts the need stated in the Synoptics for the Galilean women friends of Jesus to visit the tomb, after the Sabbath rest, on (Easter) Sunday morning to complete the unfinished burial rites (Mk 16:1; Mt 28:1; Lk 23:55–24:1).

7. Finally, some minor points on which John and the Synoptics differ relate to the sudden darkness that fell on Jerusalem during the last three hours of the life of Jesus (Mk 15:33; Mt 27:45; Lk 23:44). It is not presented as the realization of prophecy, but it is part of the Jewish eschatological imagery of the day of the Lord. It is to be treated as a literary rather than historical phenomenon notwithstanding naive scientists and over-eager television docu-

mentary makers, tempted to interpret the account as a datable eclipse of the sun. They would be barking up the wrong tree. The rending of the curtain of the Temple from top to bottom is another apocalyptic-eschatological symbol. Rabbinic literature lists various odd happenings forty years before the destruction of the Temple and speaks of Titus cutting the curtain of the sanctuary into two (Babylonian Talmud Gittin 56b). If, as is generally thought, the recording of the Synoptic Gospels took place after the fall of Jerusalem, these Jewish folk tales surrounding the great catastrophe of AD 70 may have cast their shadow on the evangelists' portrayal of the death of Jesus.

3. Comments on some peculiarities in Luke

Special material preserved in Luke alone and some of Luke's distinctive adjustments of Mark's narrative call for further exploration. The only additional story of historical relevance in Luke is the examination of Jesus by the ruler of Galilee, Herod Antipas (Lk 23:6–12). In its favour one can cite diplomatic courtesy, which is in fact a convenient attempt to 'pass the buck' first from Pilate to Herod and then from Herod back to Pilate. A similar, though one-sided, ploy between the Jewish authorities and the Roman governor is reported by Josephus in connection with Jesus son of Ananias, the charismatic who was making a nuisance of himself in Jerusalem during the feast of Tabernacles in AD 62 (*Jewish War* 6: 300–309). The Temple leaders, unable to silence the turbulent prophet by means of corporal punishment and a little worried by the possibility that this Jesus was a spokesman of God, handed him over to the Roman procurator Albinus to sort out the matter. He did, and after administering a severe beating to Jesus son of Ananias, he let him go.

Against the historicity of the Herod episode speaks the silence of the other three evangelists, and the fact that a visit to Antipas entailing a lengthy questioning by him and no doubt equally lengthy accusations by the chief priests are difficult to fit into the tight timetable of the Synoptics who place the crucifixion at nine o'clock in the morning. John's scenario with the crucifixion at noon could better accommodate the Herod excursus, but John knows nothing of it.

A number of other small variations also appear in Luke. Whilst in Mark and Matthew both crucified 'brigands' scoff at Jesus, Luke turns one of them into a decent human being who rebukes his fellow and begs for Jesus' help. Again Jesus' disturbing last cry, 'My God, my God, why hast thou forsaken me?' (Mark, Matthew) is replaced in Luke by the pious 'Father, into thy hands I commit my spirit.' At an earlier stage, Luke not only stops one of the sword-waving apostles in the garden of Gethsemane, but also miraculously heals the injured servant of the high priest. Finally, the harsh account of Mark that the only sympathizers watching the dying Jesus from a distance were a few women is replaced in Luke by the presence of all Jesus' acquaintances in addition to the women who had followed him from Galilee (Mk 15:40; Mt 27:55; Lk 23:49). Whether these extras correspond to reality or rather reflect Luke's compassionate temperament remains to be decided.

By now the full evidence has been laid out before the reader and all the arguments, pro and con, have been stated. All that remains is to propose a reconstruction of the real story of the Passion of Jesus and sketch the portraits of the protagonists of the drama.

IV

The dénouement

Readers expecting a dramatic unravelling of the plot as is customary in detective novels will be disappointed. Historical reality seems to be less unpredictable than fiction. In fact, most of the clues concealed in the Passion story have been fully or partially disclosed in the course of our earlier examination of the evidence. All we need to do now is to state the findings.

The most significant dilemma, which arises from the conflicting chronologies, is relatively easy to solve. The timing of the events in the Synoptic Gospels is quasi impossible. The sequence proposed by Mark and Matthew, and in a slightly more confused and hesitant way by Luke, is hindered at every inch of the way. It is hard to imagine in a Jewish setting of the first century AD that a capital case would be tried at night, and in particular on the feast of Passover. It is equally unlikely that the leaders of the Jewish religion, neglecting their Temple duties, would act as accusers in a hearing held by the Roman governor on the morning of the fifteenth day of Nisan and spend the rest of Passover in following Jesus to Golgotha and watching him die on the cross. I omit rehearsing the embarrassing and ill-conceived scenario of a Jewish religious trial in which the testimony of all the witnesses is thrown out, yet the accused is condemned to death on more than dubious grounds as a blasphemer and afterwards subjected to abuse by the judges themselves. Without explaining why, these same judges then manufacture a new charge and agree to transfer the case to a different jurisdiction.

The scheme presented by John avoids all these pitfalls. If Jesus is taken into custody during the evening of the fourteenth day of Nisan and tried by Pilate in the early morning of the eve of Passover, a hurried appearance of the chief priests before the governor and their disappearance after sentencing can be envisaged without difficulty. In conformity with their obligations towards their Roman masters, they act as prosecutors against a suspected Jewish revolutionary who, in their judgement, is a threat to the peace and well-being of the community. They have done their duty; their conscience is clear; let the Romans do the dirty work. In John there is no illegal night trial, indeed there is no Jewish religious trial at all: Jesus is only interrogated by the most experienced and wiliest of judges, the former high priest Annas. The main problem one has to face if John's version is preferred comes from the late date of the Fourth Gospel (*c.* 100–110); as a rule the Synoptics represent the more primitive version of the Jesus story. Nevertheless, the generally greater historical reliability of Mark does not necessarily exclude the possibility of John occasionally inheriting a more authentic tradition. In the case of the chronology of the Passion John is clearly independent of the Synoptics. His timing makes sense; that of the Synoptics does not.

The Johannine version of the trial of Jesus is partially supported by Luke, who like the author of the Fourth Gospel has no knowledge of a night session of the Sanhedrin. His transposition of a garbled compact version of the alleged night proceedings to the morning meeting of the court is attributable to his desire to stay as close as possible to his model, Mark.

Did Roman soldiers participate in the arrest of Jesus as John may insinuate? All things considered, I doubt it. There is no clue anywhere in the Gospels hinting at Roman suspicion in regard to Jesus. Also, the military notions used are inappropriate. A cohort comprising 600 men was too large a force, and a tribune too senior an officer, for the job. The Temple police led by Jews sufficed. They were able to implement the orders of the chief priests, official guardians of peace, during the dangerous pilgrimage period when Pilate himself came to Jerusalem and was keeping an eye on them.

The trial of Jesus before Pilate, once we disregard the evangelists' determination to exculpate the governor, raises no real problems, and the death sentence after an indictment for sedition is exactly what one would expect. The only uncertainty concerns the Passover amnesty. The four evangelists unanimously attest it; Roman sources, Josephus, Philo and the rabbis are equally unanimously silent on the matter. Barabbas, the lucky winner, is a totally unknown entity. According to the normal rules of historical research one should query both the custom of amnesty and the existence of Barabbas. Yet the episode has all the appearances of being real. It is not important enough for the main story to need to be invented. Nothing essential hinges on it. No doubt the Jews' choice of Barabbas rather than Jesus makes them look extremely prejudiced, but they are portrayed in the darkest colours even without that choice. The fact that the incident has no specific purpose is in its favour. Moreover, public knowledge of the forthcoming amnesty would account for the presence of a crowd at the praetorium. Supposing the people present were mostly supporters of Barabbas and that popular clamour influenced Pilate's decision about whom he would pardon, Jesus, deserted by his Galilean followers, was bound to be the loser. Hence I hesitantly cast my vote for the authenticity of the Barabbas episode.

Of the repeated scenes of insult, violence and mockery the one involving the Roman soldiers, between the flogging and the crucifixion, appears to be the most likely (see Josephus, *Jewish War* 5:449).

Again, the absence of purpose for inventing it is the strongest argument in favour of the historicity of the Simon of Cyrene episode.

Among the three verbalized final cries of Jesus, *Eloi, Eloi, lama sabachthani?* – My God, my God, why hast thou forsaken me? (Mark, Matthew); 'Father, into thy hands I commit my spirit' (Luke); and 'It is finished' (John), the last two are theologically correct and reassuring formulations, whereas the first, preserved in Aramaic, is unexpected, disquieting and in consequence more probable. It is noteworthy that this is the only prayer of Jesus in which God is not addressed as Father.

As for the identity of the sympathizers who followed Jesus to the cross, Mark's version of some women including Mary Magdalene, another Mary and Salome proves best how abandoned Jesus was in his hour of need. Matthew speaks of *many* women in addition to the three named ones, and Luke brings along all Jesus' acquaintances (male and female?) as well as the Galilean women. John cuts down the number of attendants but raises their standing. They comprise the mother of Jesus, his maternal aunt and Mary Magdalene as well as his beloved disciple. The clear impression one gathers is that Luke, Matthew and John deliberately try to smooth the picture. Mark's terseness is preferable.

This leaves us with the final dilemma: was Jesus buried by Joseph of Arimathea alone (Synoptics) or by Joseph and Nicodemus (John)? As there are no special arguments in favour of either, the question may be left unanswered. Indeed, both alternatives are organically integrated into the story. The hasty burial of the body by Joseph explains the need for a completion of the funeral rites in the Synoptics with the subsequent visit of three women to the tomb after the end of the Sabbath. In John, on the other hand, Nicodemus brings spices, so that nothing remains undone regarding the ritual, and if Mary Magdalene returns to the grave, it is out of piety rather than to attend to unfinished business.

In the Prologue I have asked the question: What really did happen on the day of the crucifixion of Jesus nearly 2,000 years ago?

Here now is the answer.

1. On Thursday evening, when the *eve* of Passover (14 Nisan) began, Jesus held a common meal with his apostles which turned out to be his last. It was not a Passover supper, nor did it contain the institution of the Eucharist.

2. He was arrested by an armed unit of the Jewish Temple police sent by the chief priests and led by Judas.

3. He was taken to the former high priest Annas for interrogation and sent by him to the house of the high priest Caiaphas where he was kept during the night.

4. On Friday morning (14 Nisan) the Sanhedrin held a consultation and decided to arraign Jesus before the tribunal of the Roman governor and charge him with sedition.

5. Pilate heard the charges of sedition arising from Jesus' alleged (political) claim that he was the King of the Jews,

but proposed to handle the case in the framework of the supposedly customary Passover amnesty. The assembled Jewish crowd hoping to obtain the release of another prisoner voted for Barabbas who was subsequently set free.

6. Jesus was condemned to crucifixion by Pilate and his priestly accusers left the scene.

7. As a preliminary to his crucifixion, Jesus was scourged. He was also subjected to mockery and beating by the Roman soldiers.

8. Simon of Cyrene was forced to help Jesus to carry the cross to Golgotha.

9. Jesus was crucified at noon on the eve of Passover (14 Nisan).

10. He was heard crying in Aramaic, '*Eloi, Eloi lama sabachthani?*,' and died at 3 p.m. on the same day, watched by a small group of Galilean women. Neither his apostles nor his family attended.

11. With Pilate's permission Joseph of Arimathea, or Joseph and Nicodemus, laid the body of Jesus in a new rock tomb shortly before the onset of the feast of Passover and the Sabbath on Saturday, 15 Nisan.

Finally, on the basis of astronomical calculation it can be argued that in AD 30, the year of the Passion, Passover celebrated at the full moon on 15 Nisan fell on Saturday, 8 April, and that consequently Jesus, crucified on the eve of Passover (14 Nisan), died on Friday, 7 April AD 30.

Thus ends the story of the Passion. The Resurrection narratives open a new chapter in the biography of Jesus and cannot be discussed here.

Epilogue
The leading actors of the Passion story

So far the examination of the Passion accounts has been mostly analytical. It is advisable therefore to end it on a constructive note and sketch the protagonists of the drama, the Jewish people, Caiaphas, Pontius Pilate and Jesus himself in four vignettes. The evangelists, above all Matthew and John, paint a deeply antipathetic picture of the first two. They all put Pontius Pilate in the best possible light. As for Jesus, patently the central figure, he plays a subdued role, quite often even refusing to answer questions.

The Jews

General Jewish hostility to Jesus is not manifest everywhere in the Gospel story. The Prologue has underlined the difference between the antipathy verging on viciousness encountered by Jesus in Jerusalem during the last day of his life and the warmth of the Galilean population towards the charismatic healer and teacher from Nazareth. His sympathetic reception in his home country was apparently also matched by a cordial acclaim given him on his entry into the holy city. But from the moment of his arrest not only all the Jewish leaders, but also the entire Jewish crowd, both at the palace of Pilate and on Golgotha, are said to have displayed a profound hatred towards him.

This negative unanimity is astounding as it contradicts the evidence expressed elsewhere in the New Testament. Prior to the arrest, the chief priests hesitated to make an immediate move against Jesus because they feared massive popular outrage. Later in the Acts of the Apostles the Jewish leaders of Jerusalem are not depicted as blindly inimical to the followers of Jesus. Peter attributed ignorance or lack of understanding rather than ill will to the chief priests (Acts 3:17). The famous Pharisee rabbi Gamaliel pleaded for fairness towards the apostles before the high court (Acts 5:34–9) and even during a stormy meeting of the Sanhedrin dealing with Paul, accused of preaching against the Law, the Pharisee members of the council openly supported him: 'We find nothing wrong with this man. What if a spirit or an angel spoke to him?' (Acts 23:9). The only rational explanation consists in assigning the hostile tendency of the Gospels to the increasingly powerful anti-Judaism of the early Gentile Church. In fact the Jews as such cannot be held guilty for their leaders' action resulting in the tragedy of Jesus.

Caiaphas

Caiaphas, the high priest, and the chief priests are the villains of the Passion story. Does this portrait reflect historical reality or is it also the product of the theological and apologetic speculation of the evangelists? Their thorough-going antagonism to Jews seems to suggest that they had given up hope of any further successful mission among the Jews. Also, by the time of the redaction of the Passion narratives the synagogue and the Church had already split. Late first-century AD (Gentile) Christians perceived the Jews as *the* enemies. The 'they against us' situation prevailing by then could easily be retrojected to the time of the

Passion itself and lead to the de-Judaization of Jesus and his followers. Since Jesus was seen as persecuted by *the Jews*, he ceased to be apprehended as belonging to the Jewish people and was simply turned into a Christian.

To judge his real role in the Passion, Caiaphas' likely motivation needs to be investigated. It may be argued that if he saw, in his capacity of high priest, any potential political danger in Jesus, he would react out of fear of Roman criticism for failing to maintain order in Jerusalem combined with a sentiment of duty to protect the Jewish community against foreseeable Roman excesses. His ultimate purpose, summed up in the principle that the whole nation is more important than a single individual, was no doubt based on a misjudgement of Jesus, but it cannot be qualified as wholly dishonourable. Arguably he did what a man in his position had to do, and this could occasionally entail the unpalatable duty of sacrificing an individual for the common good. Besides, the fact that he managed to keep his job for eighteen years when most of his predecessors and successors were sacked in their first or second year in office proves that Joseph Caiaphas was a shrewd operator. He was not a satanic figure, however, just an efficient quisling, responsible for handing over Jesus to the Romans in full awareness of the likely outcome. Nevertheless, the ultimate *legal responsibility* for the crucifixion lies with Pilate and the Roman empire. In all probability it was a major miscarriage of justice as Jesus does not seem to have been motivated by political ambitions.

Pilate

Pilate's portrait by the evangelists is that of a sensible if irresolute judge. He no doubt took with a pinch of salt the accusations levelled against Jesus by the chief priests, suspecting intra-Jewish jealousies, and Jesus' unco-operative behaviour baffled him. He was prepared to let him go – maybe after a good beating – or make him candidate for the Passover amnesty. Pilate's almost abject pleading with the priestly leaders and the Jewish crowd, and his fear of a riot seem to be baseless and out of character. An order to his legionaries would have made all the vociferous Jews run for their lives. On the whole, the Roman governor of the Gospels is pictured as a man who believed Jesus to be innocent but allowed himself to be manipulated by the Jews and ended by sending their king to the cross.

However, the Pilate of the New Testament has little in common with the Pilate of history. Indeed, Philo of Alexandria and Flavius Josephus, the two outstanding Jewish writers of that age, have a great deal to report about the prefect of Judaea, and what they have to say is far from flattering. Philo (*Embassy to Gaius* 299–305) quotes the opinion of the Jewish king Herod Agrippa I who, writing to the emperor Gaius Caligula, portrays Pilate as a stubborn, irascible, vindictive, naturally inflexible, self-willed and obdurate man who committed insults, robberies, outrages and wanton injuries. He also became notorious for venality and many acts of grievous cruelty as well as for numerous executions without trial.

The Pilate of Josephus is also a harsh, inconsiderate and ruthless official. Soon after his arrival in Judaea, he broke with the custom of his predecessors and tactlessly offended the religious sensibilities of the Jews of Jerusalem by commanding his soldiers to carry into the city Roman standards bearing the image of the emperor. He is known to have ordered the massacre of unarmed Jews who protested against his unlawful appropriation of the *Corban* (offering) from the Temple treasury. Among the calamities caused by Pilate, Josephus lists the crucifixion of Jesus. A further criminal act, a murderous attack on a group of Samaritans, finally forced Vitellius, Roman legate of Syria, to relieve Pilate of his governorship and send him to Rome to account to the emperor for his misdeeds (*Jewish War* 2:169–77; *Jewish Antiquities* 18:35–89). These negative representations by first-century Jewish writers, who were by no means anti-Roman, find a surprising echo even in the New Testament. The Gospel of Luke once mentions a massacre of Galilean pilgrims 'whose blood Pilate had mixed with their sacrifices' (Lk 13:1).

The only argument that can be quoted in favour of the Gospel portrayal of Pilate is the apparent general unwillingness of Roman magistrates to touch Jewish matters with religious ramifications. It is sufficient to cite the refusal of Gallio, proconsul of Achaia, to adjudicate in the quarrel between Paul and the Jewish leaders of Corinth (Acts 18:14–15).

All told, the Pilate picture of the Passion story is best held to be fiction, devised by the evangelists with a view to currying favour with Rome, in whose empire the nascent Church was developing. Christianity being generally unpopular in Roman eyes – Tacitus calls it a 'pernicious superstition' (*Annals* 15:44) – it was in the interest of the Gospel writers to placate the authorities. Also, by the time of the recording of the Passion narratives the Jewish rebellion had been put down by the armies of Vespasian and Titus. It was therefore politically doubly correct to blame the Jews for the murder of Christ and to absolve the Roman Pontius Pilate. In some corners of the Christian world he was treated as a crypto-believer and ended up as a saint in the Coptic Church of Egypt. The spin doctors of antiquity were no less inventive than their modern successors.

Jesus

The Passion accounts on their own are unsuitable for drawing a true picture of Jesus. In the course of his arrest in the Synoptics and in his answer to Annas in John Jesus pleaded innocence in politics: he had no secret agenda and always taught in public. The otherworldly superiority of the Johannine Christ figure mirrors the highly evolved theology of the Fourth Gospel, which was far in advance on the historical Jesus. The mighty soldiers fell to the ground when he told them that he was the man they were looking for, and Pilate, the representative of the greatest world power, was frightened by his mysterious silence.

Nevertheless, there are two incidents in the Passion which may convey a deep perception of the real Jesus. Even during his Last Supper, he is drawn by the Synoptics as hopeful and looking forward to completing his mission. He made a vow not to touch wine again until the coming of the kingdom of God (see p. 37). If he had been aware of his impending demise, such a vow of abstemiousness would have been empty of meaning. Finally, the Aramaic words *Eloi, Eloi lama sabachthani?* bear all the appearances of a genuine cry. Representing the consternation of a man of faith at the sudden realization that God would not come to his rescue, the exclamation is a piously inspired prayer of disbelief. But 'Why hast thou forsaken me?' is followed in Mark and Matthew by another loud clamour, the words of which, perhaps in order to enhance the dramatic effect, remain untold. Did they repeat the quintessential prayer of Jesus, 'Thy will be done'?

THE RESURRECTION

Foreword

Each of the main topics of the New Testament focused on Jesus – the Nativity, the Passion and the Resurrection – confronts the historian with its own special problem. Complicated though its source material may seem, Good Friday, the culmination of the last few days of the life of Jesus, is in reality the simplest. Let me state plainly that I accept that Jesus was a real historical person. In my opinion, the difficulties arising from the denial of his existence, still vociferously maintained in small circles of rationalist 'dogmatists', far exceed those deriving from its acceptance. In my opinion, the scholar's task is simply to sort out and assess the evidence and determine the reasons why, when and by whom Jesus was arrested, tried and crucified. It is even possible to propose, with the help of known astronomical data, the most likely date for the event – Friday, 7 April AD 30 – corresponding to the eve of the Passover full moon.[1] Other scholars may disagree and advance a different date or shift the blame more on to the Jewish authorities than on the Roman governor, Pontius Pilate, but the debate will remain firmly set in the real world of history and law, Jewish and Roman.

The story of the birth of Jesus is surrounded by thicker haze and is less solidly grounded in fact. The information relating to time and space is more dubious and the legendary elements abound (virgin birth, miraculous star, angels and dreams). Nonetheless it is hardly questionable that shortly before the death of Herod the Great, a Jewish boy was born in Bethlehem or Nazareth, who, about thirty years later, following a brief public career, died on a cross and was buried not long after the fifteenth year (AD 29) of the reign of the Roman emperor Tiberius.[2]

The resurrection of Jesus 'on the third day' after his burial, followed by his ascension to heaven on the same day or after forty days, is of a quite different nature. Unlike the crucifixion, it is an unparalleled phenomenon in history. Two types of extreme reactions are possible: faith,[3] or disbelief.[4]

My own standpoint will differ from both of these as I intend to act as a detective seeking, as I did in my previous studies, to investigate what the authors of the New Testament actually say in their writings, and not what interpretative Church tradition attributes to them. The purpose of this volume is to unravel the true meaning conveyed by the evangelists, Paul and the other authors of the Christian scriptures and illuminate it with what we know from the Old Testament and all the relevant Jewish and Graeco-Roman literary and archaeological sources. Its aim is the construction of a tenable hypothesis, but ultimately it will be up to the readers to make up their minds. The dilemma to be confronted and resolved is how to reconcile the extreme importance ascribed to the resurrection by Christianity with the very limited amount of discernible interest in the subject in the authentic teaching of Jesus.

Not long ago an eminent Anglican churchman asked me what I was busying myself with and when he heard that after *The Passion* and *The Nativity* I was writing a book on the resurrection, he sagaciously observed, 'That seems to be the end of the story, except perhaps for the judgement.'

Prologue

The Christian notion of resurrection and its historical antecedents

Resurrection is unquestionably one of the most important and intriguing concepts of the Christian faith. Saint Paul, to whom this religion owes more than to anyone else, leaves his readers in no doubt in this respect:

If there is no resurrection of the dead, then Christ has not been raised; if Christ has not been raised, then our preaching is in vain and your faith is in vain . . . If Christ has not been raised, your faith is futile (1 Cor 15:13–14, 17).

It is true to say that the emphasis laid on the notion of resurrection, and the centrality it is accorded in the Church's teaching, are unparalleled in the religions of antiquity. In the Judaism of the Old Testament resurrection made only a few, late and foggy appearances, probably not before the end of the third century BC. It was not asserted definitely before the time of the Maccabaean revolution in the 160s BC and from then on its acceptance grew slowly and remained far from universal. In its strict meaning, i.e. the revival of a corpse, it struck non-Jews in the Graeco-Roman world as at best a nice dream, but more generally as folly (*dementia*), according to Pliny the Elder's sharp remark.[1] Even in the Acts of the Apostles of the New Testament, when Paul preached 'the resurrection' in the

Areopagus of Athens, most of his philosophically educated listeners, Stoics and Epicureans, simply poked fun at his 'babbling' (Acts 17:18, 32).

Resurrection, or more precisely bodily resurrection, is definitely a Jewish idea. It entails the corporeal revival of the dead, the reunification of the spiritual soul and the material body of a deceased person. In the Hebrew Bible, resurrection first appears as a metaphor, symbolizing the rebirth of the nation. According to the mystical vision of the prophet Ezekiel, it depicts the figurative clothing with flesh of the dry bones of the people of Israel, and the blowing by God of the breath of life into the skeletal remains of a defeated, dispersed and exiled nation. The resurrection of the dry bones indicates something different from spiritual survival. It is not to be confused with the Greek (Platonic) concept of the escape of the soul from the prison of the body to proceed towards the Elysian Field of Heaven. It is not identical with the eternal life of the spirit. This idea of liberation is a familiar feature of the writings of Hellenized Jews of the Diaspora and the notion of eternal life without specifically implying a renewed presence of the body is also commonly attested in the Greek New Testament. These are ill-defined notions which must be handled with great care if confusion is to be avoided.

Another setting for the resurrection of the dead is provided by the awesome and majestic image of the final judgement when, at the end of the age known to man, Jewish and Christian religious visionaries imagine a universal roll-call of humanity by a blazing angelic trumpet. The dead will then be restored to their former bodies and face God or his representative, variously called the Messiah, the Chosen One or the Son of Man. The task of the final Judge will be to separate the resurrected into righteous sheep and wicked goats, and assign them eternal reward or eternal punishment. The righteous will be granted ever-lasting joy in the celestial abode and the wicked will be cast into the endless torment of a fiery hell. This universal settlement of accounts is the final stage of the doctrinal development in Judaism. An earlier version of the resurrection of the dead envisages only the revivification of the just, first and foremost the martyrs who in the course of a religious persecution have sacrificed their lives for the sake of Heaven. As the later Jewish rabbis would put it, they accepted agony and violent death for 'the sanctification of God's name'. In sum, resurrection preliminary to the great judgement pertains to eschatology, to the events of the end of times. This is tantamount to stating the obvious, namely that rising from the dead is alien to man's normal, historical experience.

While the Christian Church continues to proclaim belief in a universal resurrection and a new life in the age to come, it also firmly maintains that Jesus was raised from the dead in time past, on the third day after he had expired on the cross. In other words, the phenomenon of the dead Christ regaining life is claimed to have actually occurred in this world, before daybreak on a Sunday, probably on 9 April AD 30, if the dating of the crucifixion to the afternoon of Friday 7 April of that year is accepted. This belief turns resurrection – previously envisaged as either a metaphor or a future eschatological event – into a reality that occurred in a given place at a specific time. The basis of this innovative perception and the arguments supporting the resurrection belief will be scrutinized in the pages that follow, but in the meantime some further preliminary clarifications are needed.

In one sense, the resurrection of Jesus is presented by

the New Testament and the Church as a unique happening that can be dated and located. However, it is also linked to the eschatological raising of the dead of which, in St Paul's terminology, Christ's resurrection constituted the 'first fruits'. At the same time, according to the Old and New Testament sources, Jesus was not the only human being to rise from the dead. The scriptures refer to the resurrection of other individuals. The Old Testament prophets Elijah and Elisha resuscitated two children, and Jesus himself is reported to have brought back to life two others in the Synoptic Gospels (pp. 87–9) and a third one, Lazarus, in John (p. 90), not to mention two further miraculous stories connected with St Peter and St Paul (p. 91). The revival of a young bride in Rome, credited to the first-century AD neo-Pythagorean holy man Apollonius of Tyana, belongs to the same category.[2]

These stories about resurrection in general and the reviving of the dead by Jesus in particular will be examined in detail in Part II of this book, together with the doctrinal and theological considerations which fill the pages of the New Testament and especially the letters of St Paul. To give one example, words dealing with resurrection figure no less than nineteen times in 1 Corinthians, chapter 15. The opinion of the Jewish population of the late Second Temple period was more divided on the subject. The Pharisees were the only wholehearted champions of belief in bodily resurgence. When the ancient rabbis took over the Pharisaic legacy after the destruction of the Temple of Jerusalem in AD 70, they provided a niche for the doctrine of the resurrection in the Mishnah, Talmud, Midrash and Targum, but their interest in the faith in resurrection was not as prominent and exuberant as that of their Christian contemporaries.

The present study is essentially devoted to the evidence relating to the doctrine of the resurrection developed in the New Testament. However, it is impossible to understand the Christian scriptures without first inspecting their sources and models, the Hebrew Bible and early post-biblical Jewish literature not only as far as the resurrection imagery itself is concerned, but also in a broader sense regarding the ideas of life and death and even the underworld where, according to the Christian Creed, the dead Jesus descended before rising again on the third day.

I

Afterlife in the Jewish world
before Jesus

I

A bird's-eye view of human destiny in the Bible: From lost immortality to resurrection

Resurrection, the reversal of death, is presented by Christianity as the apogee of divine benevolence obtained for mankind by Jesus. Yet it is no more than second best among the possible options. Immortality, or escape from death, would have been the apex of all the possibilities, the dream of every human being ever since time began. The 'myth' of the creation, a sacred epic narrative included in chapters 2 and 3 of the biblical Book of Genesis, was meant to explain the fundamental phenomena affecting humanity. It is an attempt to account, in moral terms, for death or the loss of immortality, while ancient pagan epics attribute it to the caprice or jealousy of the gods.

The divine Potter of the Hebrews fashioned out of the dust of the ground the first creature, Adam, and shaped for him a female partner to keep him happy. The Creator installed both Adam and Eve in the glorious Garden of Eden and freely supplied them with all their needs. Their life was an endless holiday, with no obligation to work. They might, as it were, have lived happily for ever in Paradise, miraculously nourished by the fruits of the trees, among which stood the Tree of Life and the Tree of Knowledge. Death does not seem to have played a part in the original divine plan. But the first couple spoiled their blessed destiny of a joyful and immortal future when they allowed the Devil, or Serpent, to lead them astray, and transgressed the single restrictive rule that God had imposed on them: the prohibition to eat the fruit of the Tree of Knowledge.

The price they had to pay for what became in the theological jargon of the Church the 'original sin' was not only the forfeiture of an endless insouciance, but also the inevitability of death. The divine sentence proclaimed: 'In the sweat of your face you shall eat bread till you return to the ground, for out of it you were taken; you are dust and to dust you shall return' (Gen 3:19).

Later Jewish tradition and Pauline Christianity sought to apportion the blame for this loss of immortality between the three protagonists: the Devil, Adam and Eve. The male-chauvinist author of Genesis and the similarly inspired Jewish sage of the early second-century BC Jesus Ben Sira pointed the finger at Eve: she was the first to taste the forbidden fruit and enticed Adam to do the same. 'From a woman sin had its beginning and because of her we all die', lamented Ben Sira two centuries before Jesus (Ecclus 24:25). A little later, the author of the Greek Book of Wisdom philosophically assigned the primary guilt for the mortal fate borne by mankind to Satan, the source of all evil: 'Through the devil's envy death entered the world' (Wis 2:24). But in the eyes of St Paul, Adam, the forefather of the human race, bore full responsibility for the misery inflicted on his children: 'Sin came into the world through one man and death through sin' (Rom 5:12). Nevertheless, the first man was seen by Paul as the prototype of Christ, the last Adam, who remedied through his resurrection from the dead the lethal harm caused by the first Adam's foolishness.

Unlike the Jews of the Old Testament period, the inhabitants of ancient Mesopotamia seem to have simply refused to accept their mortal destiny. In the famous epic of Gilgamesh, the age-old creation myth of the peoples living in the lands between the Tigris and the Euphrates, the hero Gilgamesh, first faced with death when he lost his friend Enkidu, set out at once in search of the secret of immortality. But Utnapishtim – the Noah of the Babylonian flood legend – whom the gods spared from death as a reward for his saving from drowning the world and its inhabitants, declined to divulge the precious mystery. So Gilgamesh and the people after him had to acquiesce in their mortal condition. The traffic into the Mesopotamian underworld was one-way only – it was a 'land of no return' – and the same is true of the infernal region of the Bible and the Hades of the Greeks. 'Those who go down to Sheol do not come up', scripture tells us (Job 7:9).

For a long period, the biblical Israelites accepted that the common lot of mankind consisted in a gloomy, sleepy, semi-conscious and chilly endless existence in the abode of the dead. Apart from one allusion in the New Testament to Christ's preaching to the spirits gaoled in the netherworld, and unlike the Mesopotamian and Greek myths of the descent of various deities and heroes to Hades, Jewish tradition never describes any visit to the subterranean land of Sheol. The First Book of Enoch, where the antediluvian patriarch is shown the country of the dead, is a strange exception (see pp. 45–5). In mainstream Jewish thought, through the Old Testament period down to the beginning of the second century BC, all the humans of past ages were viewed as inheriting a diminished, joyless subsistence in a land of darkness into which they entered through the grave. God was consigned to oblivion in this 'land of forgetfulness' (Ps 88:12). He was unreachable among the shades; they neither worshipped him, nor could count on his helping hand. The various pagan religions honoured underworld deities, rulers of the realm of the dead: Nergal, Tammuz and Ereshkigal in Mesopotamia, Hades and Persephone among the Greeks and Pluto and Proserpina among the Romans. Jewish monotheism excluded this possibility and Sheol was in consequence a religionless, even Godless place: 'From the dead, as from one who does not exist, thanksgiving has ceased' (Ecclus 17:28).

This gloomy outlook on the destiny of the deceased – stoically accepted with blind resignation as the will of God – had a fortunate positive sequel; a renewed appreciation of this world with the recognition of the priceless religious potential of time. The true Creator was the God of the living and in the healthy realism of the ancient Hebrews religiousness could find expression only on this side of the grave. Hence the dream of the biblical Israelites – especially in the pre-exilic age, before the sixth century BC – was to enjoy a God-fearing, long and happy life amid their families and expect at the end, having reached the fullness of years, to join peacefully their predecessors in the ancestral tomb. According to the standard formula of the Old Testament, the Jewish kings 'went to sleep with their fathers' and were buried in the royal mausoleum. Prior to this pious reunion only those who were 'alive and well', rich or poor, kings or servants, had a chance to 'sing the Lord's praises' (Ecclus 17:28).

During the years of the Babylonian exile the idea of renewed existence suddenly sprung up at the national level following the loss of Jewish independence in 587 BC. The prophet Ezekiel's mystical vision of the revival of dry bones symbolized the resurrection from the dead of the people of Israel, really or figuratively slain by the armies of Nebuchadnezzar, king of Babel. But as well as this aspiration for collective renaissance we can find signs in post-exilic writings which show that individuals too yearned for escape from Sheol. In addition to man's innate dread of death and its consequences, the urge for flight from the underworld derived from the religious person's desire to go on praising, worshipping and giving thanks to the Lord. The Psalmist personified the devout Jew imagining himself in Sheol, and proclaiming there his wish to love God and confess his faith even beyond the grave. Did he just dream of a prolonged new life after death? No doubt, many of these exclamations can be explained as prayers uttered by the sick for deliverance from *premature* death, but occasionally the poet's eyes appear to transcend the perspective of the present life:

Nevertheless I am *continually* with Thee;
Thou dost hold my right hand.
Thou dost guide me with thy counsel
and afterwards thou wilt receive me to glory . . .
My flesh and my heart may fail,
but God is the rock of my heart and my portion *for ever*
(Ps 73:23–24, 26).

Moreover the traditional view, that in the hereafter all will be treated as equals, is replaced by a new vision with a distinction between the righteous and the wicked prevailing even in the land of the dead. Sheol is the home of the fools; only they are there to stay. But for the devout a ray of hope will shine: 'God will ransom my soul . . . for he will receive me' (Ps 49:14–15). By contrast, the Jews who have lived a devout life will reside with the Patriarchs. They will be brought to Abraham's bosom, to use a rabbinic phrase (*behiqqo shel Abraham*), the antiquity of which is guaranteed by its appearance in the New Testament (Lk 16:22). In short, during the centuries following the Babylonian exile an image different from death's dreamless sleep flickers over the Jewish religious horizon.

The new outlook developed along two separate paths in the post-exilic period (after 539 BC). It found its first formulation during the latter part of the third century, and gained strength in the course of the second and first centuries BC. It is attested on the one hand in the Hebrew Bible in the little Apocalypse inserted into the Book of Isaiah (chapters 23–27) and in chapter 12 of Daniel, and in the Book of Wisdom of Solomon among the Greek Apocrypha in the Septuagint on the other hand.

In Hebrew thought, victory over Sheol was revealed in the reanimation of the dead bodies of the righteous. The author of the Apocalypse of Isaiah rejoices: 'Thy dead shall live, their corpses shall rise, O dwellers in the dust, awake and sing for joy' (Isa 26:19). The wicked rulers of past ages would reap destruction as their just deserts, and their memory be blotted out for ever (Isa 26:13–14). In this vision, resurrection is envisaged as the reward reserved for the just. At the next stage, in the Book of Daniel, it becomes universal and was followed by divine judgement remunerating the good and annihilating the godless: 'And many of those who sleep in the dust of the earth shall awake, some to everlasting life, and some to shame and everlasting contempt' (Dan 12:2).

However, beside the Palestinian Jewish concept of the restored unity of body and soul, the reawakening of the 'sleepers in the dust', Hellenized Jews, such as the author of the Greek Wisdom of Solomon, shun the idea of a renewed bond between the soul and the body and prefer to envisage the immortality of afterlife as the liberation of the spirit from the prison or the 'earthly tent' of the flesh (Wis 9:15).

The idea of an afterlife victorious over Sheol, be it through the resurrection of the body or the deliverance of the immortal soul, was not universally embraced by the Jews at the turn of the era. As we shall see, it was a belief characteristic of the Pharisees in the age of Jesus, but the Sadducees, the conservative priestly aristocracy of the late Second Temple period, firmly adhered to the traditional concept of the finality of death. 'Do not forget, there is no coming back', declared Jesus Ben Sira, who also testified to a quasi-fatalistic outlook: 'This is the end for all flesh decreed by the Lord' (Ecclus 38:21; 41:4).

It is in this context of contradictions that we will have to confront the New Testament statements of Jesus and of his followers regarding the resurrection from the dead. However, before envisaging these lofty ideas, we will need a deeper grasp of ancient Judaism's perception of death with its sequels, the grave, Sheol and afterlife, as reflected in the literary legacy of the Jewish inhabitants of the Graeco-Roman world.

2

Death and its sequels in ancient Judaism: Paving the way for resurrection

Sometimes one can be forgiven for stating the obvious: no one can be resurrected unless he has died first. Consequently, before reflecting on the meaning of resurrection we must grasp what cessation of life signified to Jews two thousand years ago. With this in mind, let us focus on the blurred and sketchy pictures of death, the grave and the underworld of Sheol. In fact, without a full understanding of these concepts we cannot even begin to perceive what the early Christian writers tried to convey when they told their readers about Christ's rising from the dead. Here are the details transmitted by the New Testament. Jesus *died* on the cross. His body was immediately *buried* in a *tomb*. Some forty hours later, several women friends came to complete the *funeral rites*; the anointing of his body had had to be postponed because of the onset of the Sabbath. Between death and resurrection, Jesus in spirit descended to the *underworld* to preach to the spirits imprisoned there. On the third day after his death, his *resurrected body* appeared to his apostles, although they first believed it was a *ghost*.

For the religious Jew of the biblical age life originated with the spirit breathed by God into the first human shape that, according to Genesis, he had made of dust or clay. As a result, Adam became a *nephesh hayah*, a 'living soul', an animated being. When this breath of life departs, the living being turns into a 'dead soul', a *nephesh met*. The person remains identifiably the same, but starts a different, diminished, inferior state of existence.

Out of respect for the deceased person his relatives washed, clothed and buried the body. In earlier times no coffins were used. Embalming, an Egyptian custom, is not attested in the Jewish Bible except for the patriarchs Jacob and Joseph who died in Egypt (Gen 50:2, 26). By New Testament times, in connection with Jesus, reference is made of the application of spices to the body (Mk 16:1; Lk 24:1) and more specifically a large quantity of myrrh mixed with aloes is mentioned (Jn 19:39).

An unburied corpse left as prey for birds and scavenging dogs was seen as the worst fate that could await a man. It is alluded to in the curse of Deuteronomy (28:26), pronounced on those unfaithful to the covenant: 'Your dead body shall be food for all the birds of the air, and for the beasts of the earth, and there shall be none to frighten them away.' The duty of the living, in the first instance the sons of the dead person, was to lay the body to rest. They buried it in the ground or deposited it in a natural or manmade rock cavity, the opening of which was protected against intruders by a heavy stone. Persons of means were placed in family tombs, like the Hebrew patriarchs in the cave of Macpelah, near Hebron. Sarah was buried there by Abraham, Abraham by his sons Isaac and Ishmael, Isaac by Esau and Jacob, and Jacob by Joseph, who repatriated the remains of his father from Egypt to Canaan.

About the end of the Old Testament period and in the age of Jesus, wealthy Jews constructed elaborate funerary monuments, often decorated and bearing commemorative inscriptions of the dead. Some of the rock tombs contained an antechamber where the body remained until the flesh had decomposed. Then the bones were collected and placed in containers, mostly made of limestone and known as ossuaries or bone boxes. The name of the deceased was often scratched or engraved on them and they were kept in rock chambers inside the tomb. The entrance of the tomb, as is also attested in the case of Jesus, was closed with a large round stone. According to the Gospel of Mark (Mk 16:3), the women who visited Jesus' grave at dawn on the Sunday after the crucifixion anxiously asked themselves whether they would be strong enough to roll the stone away.

In ancient Judaism's cultic dichotomy of the ritually pure and impure, dead bodies and everything associated with them belonged to the domain of the unclean, and had to be kept at a definite distance from anything or anybody associated with the holiness of the divine. Since a corpse was, as it were, 'contagious', those entrusted with worship had to avoid contact with it. Hence Jewish Temple personnel (Lev 21:1–4), like the priest and the Levite in the parable of the Good Samaritan (Lk 10:30–36), as well as the Nazirite votaries committed to the strictest adherence to purity rules (Num 6:6–7), were forbidden to touch a dead body and even to attend funerals except when the dead was a very near kin (father or mother, a son or a daughter, a brother or an unmarried sister). The effect of uncleanness was temporary; it lasted one week, and could be removed by means of two ritual purificatory baths, one on the third and the other on the seventh day. The Bible orders that a person condemned to death by a court should be buried on the day of his execution before sunset (Dt 21:22–23), as happened to Jesus, too. It may be taken for granted that the same rule applied in cases of natural death as well. All the regulations relating to dealings with dead bodies derive from the demands of primitive hygiene in a country with a hot climate.

For most Jews of the Old Testament period – the exceptions belong to the last two hundred years of the pre-Christian era and to the first century AD – the grave marked the final end of a man's story. Death was seen as inescapable and universal, or almost; the two biblical exceptions being the antediluvian patriarch Enoch and the prophet Elijah. Death is portrayed as the shepherd of all humans, whose flock is destined to the underworld (Ps 49:14). Death is 'the way of all the earth'; it cuts down the greatest like King David (1 Kings 2:1), just as it does the humble poor man. They all share the unending 'sleep of death' (Ps 13:3). Before the idea of resurrection was first mooted, the poetic author of the Book of Job wrote:

> But man dies and is laid low;
> man breathes his last, and where is he? . . .
> Man lies down and rises not again,
> till the heavens are no more he will not awake,
> or be roused out of his sleep (Job 14:10–12).

For the down-to-earth Jew of the biblical era, death was simply the common heritage of all the living. Christians brought up on the idea of resurrection and heavenly (or infernal) afterlife may be shocked to the core by the casualness of the biblical sage:

For the fate of the sons of men and the fate of the beasts is the same; one dies, so dies the other. They all have the same breath; and man has no advantage over the beasts . . . All go to one place; all are from the dust, and all turn to dust again (Eccl 3:19–20).

Being laid to rest in the grave, the 'dead soul' begins a new, transformed and final stage of existence in the underworld, the Sheol of the Bible, identical with the Hades of the Greeks. Sheol was imagined to be in the depth of the earth, the opposite of high heaven (Isa 7:11),[1] a land of doom, chaos and deep darkness, from where there is no return (Job 10:21–22). Sheol is compared to a fortified city whose gates are locked and reinforced with iron bars.

Two great poets, the prophets Isaiah and Ezekiel, offer highly colourful and picturesque descriptions of the entry of dead persons to this underworld. The all-powerful sovereign of Babylon is taunted on his arrival in Sheol by the vanquished kings whose remains lie in peace in their tombs, while the body of the Babylonian tyrant is cast away and trodden underfoot.

Sheol beneath is stirred up to meet you when you come,
it rouses the shades, to greet you . . .
all who were kings of the nations.
All of them will speak and say to you:
'You have become as weak as we!
You have become like us!'
Your pomp is brought down to Sheol,
the sound of your harps;
maggots are the bed beneath you,
and worms are your covering (Isa 14:9–11).

On earth, even the trees exult: 'The cypresses rejoice at you, the cedars of Lebanon, saying, "Since you were laid low, no hewer comes up against us"' (Isa 14:8). Sheol is the great equalizer, Ezekiel tells us. Even the proud Pharaoh of Egypt is finally cut down by the Lord God and brought low there in the midst of all the fallen peoples (Ez 32:19–32).

In biblical Jewish thought the dead do not vanish and turn into nothingness. They become emptied and weakened shades (the *rephaim*) who, incapable of producing normal sounds, communicate with hushed squeaks: 'Your voice shall come from the ground like the voice of a ghost, and your speech shall whisper out of the ground' (Isa 29:4).

Ancient Jewish magic and superstition offered a means to communicate with the inhabitants of Sheol. Ghosts were thought to possess knowledge potentially useful to the living, as long as the latter found a way to contact them by means of necromancy, entailing the use of a medium or a wizard. Necromancy is prohibited by the Mosaic Law under pain of death by stoning (Lev 20:27). Yet the Torah notwithstanding, the practice survived, and a fascinating account about King Saul summoning up the recently deceased prophet Samuel with the help of a medium illustrates both necromancy and the ancient Jewish ideas about a shade, or ghost (*'ov*).

Necromancy is a subdivision of the art of obtaining secret information that exceeds ordinary human faculties. The first Israelite ruler, Saul, intent on reading the future when he had to engage in combat with the Philistines, found that the permitted media (dreams, divination by the priestly Urim and prophecy) were useless. So he got hold of one of the rare clandestine necromancers still in the country after his earlier royal decree of expulsion of all the mediums and wizards. This woman, from the village of Endor, obeyed the king's order to bring up Samuel from Sheol. She saw his spirit, referred to as 'a god' (*'elohim*), rising out of the earth, looking like an old man wrapped in a robe. Saul recognized him as the prophet Samuel. The shade complained about being 'disturbed', woken up from his sleep, and in his bad-tempered mood shattered the king's last hope by announcing that next day Saul himself, together with his sons and the whole army of Israel, would join Samuel in the kingdom of the dead (1 Sam 28:8–19). The two main points that emerge from this story are that the shade summoned from Sheol was believed to have kept his recognizable shape, that of 'an old man', his individuality and to some extent his ability to think and to communicate with others. Outwardly, he appeared just as he was prior to his death and Saul had no doubt about whom he was seeing. The apparitions of the risen Jesus differ from that of Saul. Neither his disciples, nor Mary Magdalene, are said to have recognized him until he identified himself to them. Nevertheless, notwithstanding their surviving intellectual ability, the shades prefer to remain undisturbed and enjoy the deep sleep of death.

How did the idea of Sheol affect the outlook on life of the pious Jew? Absence of a second chance invested life on earth with a unique value. All good things happen to man between his birth and his death and the practice of religion is restricted to the here and now. Since only the living thank God (Isa 38:19), the days of this life are priceless. As reward for piety was expected before death, a kind of religious hedonism, consisting of eating, drinking and taking pleasure, was preached by the wise men of the Old Testament (Eccl 3:13). In lieu of mortification and asceticism, the Bible fully encourages the Jew to take delight in his days.

Go, eat your bread with enjoyment,
and drink your wine with a merry heart;
for God has already approved what you do.

Let your garments be always white;
let not oil be lacking on your head.
Enjoy life with the wife you love,
all the days of your vain life,
which he has given you under the sun.
Whatever your hand finds to do, do it with your might;
for there is no work or thought or knowledge
or wisdom in Sheol, to which you are going (Eccl 9:7–10).

Ecclesiastes, anticipating Horace's *carpe diem*,[2] preached a kind of Epicurean philosophy approved and blessed by God. Yet while having such an exclusive value placed on everyday existence strengthened practical religion, through emphasis on the service of God by the sanctification of every single act of life, it necessarily contained also a seed of discontent. A man with eyes to see could not help noticing that the principle underlying biblical Judaism would not withstand scrutiny. After all, the devout observer of all the precepts of the God-given Torah was not invariably rewarded, nor was the constant lawbreaker always chastised. Contrary to the assertion of Proverbs 3:33, the Lord's curse was not perpetually on the house of the wicked, and he did not continuously bless the abode of the righteous. Could one really believe in the splendid divine proclamation of Deuteronomy?

If you obey the commandments of the Lord, . . . you shall live and multiply and the Lord God will bless you . . . But if your heart turns away, . . . you shall perish . . . I have set before you life and death, blessing and curse; therefore choose life, that you and your descendants may live, loving the Lord your God, . . . for that means life to you and length of days, that you may dwell in the land which the Lord swore to your fathers . . . to give them (Dt 30:16–20).

319

The wise man knew from experience that real life did not mirror the ideals sketched by the lawgiver. Good health, peace and divine protection were not necessarily the wages of the law-abiding Jew. We need only read the sapiential and prophetic books of the Bible to discover that the devout were frequently sick, penniless and abused while the godless led a carefree and luxurious existence. The Psalmist's complaint, 'How long shall the wicked exult?' (Ps 94:3), was echoed by Jeremiah's indignation, 'Why does the way of the wicked prosper? Why do all who are treacherous thrive?' (Jer 12:1).

Ecclesiastes and Job went further and attacked head-on the official preaching of Deuteronomy about the mandatory prosperity of the virtuous and the inescapable comeuppance of the sinners. The sage Ecclesiastes phlegmatically remarked: 'In my vain life I have seen everything; there is a righteous man who perishes in his righteousness, and there is a wicked man who prolongs his life in evil-doing' (Eccl 7:15). Job, on the other hand, the prototype of the traditional idea of the religious man, rebelled with dramatic acuity. He was blessed by God, had seven sons and three daughters, seven thousand sheep, three thousand camels, five hundred yoke of oxen, five hundred she-asses and innumerable servants. Then all of a sudden he lost everything, possessions and children, and on top of it all, he was inflicted with a horrible and painful skin disease. Yet despite his misery, he continued to praise and worship God. His friends tried to demonstrate that he must have done something wrong, but Job tenaciously went on protesting his innocence. Even though at the end of the story, an editor of the book endeavoured to defend the status quo by restoring Job to his former condition, giving him another seven sons and three daughters, and doubling his original wealth, he could not remove the large question mark placed by the poetic author against the accepted formulation of the traditional religious wisdom.

The weakness of this formulation was further stressed when in the exilic age the idea of the vicarious punishment of sins was attacked by the prophets Jeremiah and Ezekiel. They both cited the proverb, 'The fathers have eaten sour grapes, and the children's teeth are set on edge' (Jer 31:29; Ezek 18:2), implying that innocent later generations could be chastised for the wrongdoings of their elders. They declared it untenable and insisted on personal responsibility: 'Behold, all souls are mine; the soul of the father as well as the soul of the son is mine: *the soul that sins shall die*' (Ezek 18:4; see Jer 31:30).

Contradictory attitudes stood side by side until an unprecedented historical phenomenon – martyrdom – reinforced the doubts of thinking Jews. Jews of the Maccabaean period showed a willingness to sacrifice their lives rather than deny their faith. Their death was not a punishment for betrayal of the Law; on the contrary, they died because of their attachment to it, and this revolutionary novelty opened the door to a fresh representation of afterlife, envisaged henceforth either as the survival of the immortal soul or as the resurrection of the body.

However, before turning the searchlights on the question of the resurrection expected at the end of times, we ought to cast an eye on the exceptions listed in the Bible and post-biblical Jewish literature concerning the revivification of the dead or escape from the underworld by means of divinely engineered assumption or ascension to heaven.

Biblical and post-biblical antecedents of the resurrection and ascension of Jesus

While the Hebrew Bible maintains that death and Sheol are the unavoidable destiny of mankind, it nevertheless records a few exceptions to the rule, and post-biblical Jewish literature slightly lengthens the list by adding two further cases. One escape route from the perpetual sleep of the underworld was through recall to life soon after man's last breath, before, as it were, he had time to reach Sheol and settle in.[1]

Assumption or ascension with the help of God was another means to escape Sheol. Both the concepts of revivification and rising above the human sphere are significant for the student of the New Testament. The former exemplifies the reanimations recorded in the New Testament, and the latter serves as the prototype of Jesus' ascent to heaven depicted by Luke in his Gospel and the Acts of the Apostles and also stated in the longer ending of Mark.

The resuscitation of a recently deceased person may be classified as the highest achievement of religious healing. The Books of the Kings recount how the wonderworking prophets, Elijah and Elisha, brought back to life two young boys, the children of the widow from Zarephath and of a wealthy woman of Shunem, both generous benefactresses of the prophets. The method of raising the dead is similar in both cases and consists not just in words of command or bodily contact, but in a kind of total identification with them in order to reintroduce breath into their corpses by means of a shamanistic kiss of life.

In the case of the son of the widow from Zarephath, Elijah laid the boy on his bed and stretched himself on him three times; as a result, the child was revived (1 Kings 17:17–22). According to the Greek version of the passage, instead of stretching himself on the boy, the prophet breathed thrice on him. The Aramaic translation is equivocal, as the verb employed can mean either to stretch himself or to sneeze. The resuscitation of the son of the Shunemite woman by Elisha is more colourfully sketched. First Gehazi, Elisha's servant, was dispatched to revive him by waving above the boy the prophet's staff, but this was of no avail. Next, Elisha lowered himself on the child and touched with his mouth, eyes and hands the mouth, eyes and hands of the boy, seeking to warm up his body. Then he stretched himself on him once more and the child returned to life after sneezing seven times (2 Kings 4:18–37).[2]

In both episodes, the narrators purport to convey stories of real revivals that occurred in time and space. The boys were dead, but thanks to the intervention of the prophets began to live again. The author of Ecclesiasticus, singing the Praises of Famous Men, expressly notes that Elijah 'raised a corpse' and brought it back from Hades (Ecclus 48:5).[3] One would expect the heroes of such events to become notorious, but no detail relating to their later life has been preserved either in the Bible or in post-biblical sources. They, like the individuals resuscitated by Jesus in the Synoptic Gospels and St Paul in the Acts of the Apostles, promptly disappear from the scene.

Elisha's name is linked to another case of miraculous resurrection, but it is attributed not to the living prophet, but to his relics – his bones – which were buried in a cave. According to the biblical account of the story, members of a funeral procession, while trying to escape a band of marauders, cast into Elisha's tomb the body they were carrying to the burial place. But as soon as it touched the prophet's remains, it miraculously revived and walked away (2 Kings 13:20–21). In his *Jewish Antiquities* Flavius Josephus (AD 37–*c.* 100) recounts essentially the same tale, except that in his version the man was murdered by the robbers and his body was thrown by them into the prophet's grave (*Ant* 9:183).[4] In his vignette dedicated to Elisha, Ben Sira also puts into relief the prophet's wonderworking powers: 'Nothing was too hard for him, and when he was dead, his body prophesied. As in his life he did wonders, so in death his deeds were marvellous' (Ecclus 48:13–14).

In sum, it should be stated that in the framework of popular prophetic Judaism, in which the curing of the sick occupied an important place, the phenomenon of resurrection, the restoration to life of a person recently deceased, in no way appeared to be out of place.

Besides resurrection, ascension or assumption, a miraculous transfer of the deceased to the supraterrestrial world provides another way to be exempted from the common fate of humankind. A person may be translated bypassing death completely, or after a quasi-instantaneous revival that followed departure from among the living. Prior to Jesus, the Hebrew Bible lists two cases of direct transfer, Enoch and Elijah, and Jewish tradition adds a further two, Moses and Isaiah, with the difference that their elevation happens after death.

The assumption of the antediluvian patriarch Enoch is alluded to in mysterious, elliptic style in Genesis 5:24: 'And

Enoch walked with God; and he was not, for God took him.' In the earliest comment on the verse we are told that it was on account of his righteous behaviour that God took Enoch to himself. Ben Sira stresses the patriarch's piety: 'Enoch pleased the Lord' (Ecclus 44:16) and so do the Septuagint and the Targums of Genesis 5:24: 'Enoch was well pleasing to God' (LXX); 'Enoch walked in the fear of the Lord' (Onkelos); 'Enoch served before God in truth' (Fragmentary Tg, Ps.-Jonathan and Neofiti). However, a later rabbinic view contests this positive assessment and asserts that the name of Enoch was inscribed in the scroll of the wicked and that this was why God had taken him, or that he was sometimes good and sometimes bad so God decided to snatch him while he was righteous (GenR 25:1).

The second half of the biblical verse, 'and he was not, for God took him', is explained by some as the transfer of the living Enoch from among 'the sons of men' (Jub. 4:23) or from 'the inhabitants of the earth' (Ps.-Jon. on Gen. 5:24) to a far distant place, 'beyond the land of Parwaim' (1QGen. Ap. 2:23), or to 'the ends of the earth' (1 En 106:8), where his son Methuselah was able to visit him. However, according to Jubilees 4:23 he was carried by angels to the 'garden of Eden', a place of ill-defined location, possibly lying somewhere between heaven and earth. A second interpretation firmly sets Enoch in the celestial realm. The Slavonic Enoch or the Second Book of Enoch makes its hero visit the seven heavens and Targum Ps.-Jonathan (Gen 5:24) portrays him as elevated to the firmament to act as God's secretary and given the name Metatron, 'great scribe'.[5] Irrespective of the explanation one adopts, Jewish Bible exegesis and folklore identify Enoch as the first human to be spared from a descent to the underworld. He needed no resurrection as he was transferred alive to paradise or heaven.

The biblical narrator also describes the elevation to the celestial sphere of the living prophet Elijah, witnessed by his disciple Elisha, who had inherited his spirit and his miracle-working mantle. Elijah rose upwards in a chariot of fire drawn by fiery horses in the midst of a whirlwind. Josephus, generally inclined to play down the miraculous in scripture, prefers to speak of the disappearance of Elijah and Enoch rather than their ascension to heaven (*Ant* 9:28), and even the Greek Bible puts an 'as it were' before stating that Elijah was lifted on high.

Biblical and post-biblical Jewish tradition maintains the reality of Elijah's elevation as it attributes to the *returning* prophet an important eschatological function, the preparation of the day of the Lord by reconciling fathers and children (Mal. 4:5; Ecclus 48:10). Indeed, Jesus himself was associated by some of his contemporaries with the new Elijah (Mk 8:27; Mt 16:14; Lk 9:19), and the evangelists themselves acknowledged John the Baptist as Elijah *redivivus* (Mk 1:2; Mt 11:10; Lk 7:27).

Further biblical figures credited with assumption or ascension in post-biblical Judaism are Moses and Isaiah. In the case of Moses, Deuteronomy 34:5 expressly asserts that he actually died after he had been permitted to view the promised land from the top of Mount Nebo in Transjordan. According to the Bible no human eyes witnessed the end of Moses, and it was God who buried the Lawgiver in a secret place known only to himself. Without specifying their identity, the Greek Bible attributes the laying to rest of Moses not to God alone, but to an anonymous plurality: 'and *they* buried him'. Later tradition suggests that angels performed part of the ceremony. The New Testament, in turn, alludes to a fight between Satan and the archangel Michael for the body of Moses (Jude 9) and the Pseudo-Jonathan Targum (Dt 34:6) colourfully depicts the funeral rites of the Lawgiver. The chief angels Michael and Gabriel prepared the bed, which was decorated with diamonds and precious stones; Metatron, Yophiel, Uriel and Yephiphiah placed the body of Moses on it and God carried the bed to its resting place in the valley four miles away, opposite Beth-peor. However, according to the Church Father Origen, a Jewish writer dating to the first century AD followed up the burial with Moses' transfer to heaven. The proof derives from the title of the work, The Assumption of Moses, for unfortunately the end of the story is missing from the single Latin manuscript which has preserved this apocryphon. The implication is that after it had been laid to rest by the angels and God, the body of Moses was revived and lifted up to heaven.

There is no biblical evidence describing the death and the afterlife of the prophet Isaiah, but rabbinic tradition knows about his murder. Fleeing from Manasseh, the wicked king of Israel, Isaiah concealed himself in a hole within a cedar tree, but the king ordered the tree, together with the prophet inside it, to be sawn into two (ySanh 28c; bYeb 49b). An apocryphon, the Ascension of Isaiah, written by a Jewish author in the first century AD and re-worked by a Christian editor, recounts that after his execution the prophet journeyed upward, as Enoch did before him, and was led by an angel through the seven heavens (chapters 7–9).

In sum, pre-Christian Judaism was aware of some peculiar cases where death was not the end of the story for certain important individuals. We are not told what happened to the two children resurrected by Elijah and Elisha, but if their revival was seen as temporary they would have the unique quality of having experienced death twice. Moses and Isaiah, like Jesus, are portrayed as passing through death, resurrection and ascension, whereas Enoch and Elijah are depicted as bypassing death and experiencing only ascension without resurrection.

4

Martyrdom and resurrection in late Second Temple Judaism

In 168 BC, Antiochus IV Epiphanes, the Hellenistic king of the Seleucid dynasty who ruled over Syria and Judaea, set out to invade the rival Hellenistic Kingdom of the Ptolemies in Egypt. His plans were frustrated by the intervention of the Roman fleet, dispatched by the Senate to put an end to the expansionist plans of the Seleucids. Humiliated and compelled to retreat from Alexandria, Antiochus turned his fury on the unsympathetic Jews and after massacring the population of Jerusalem and pillaging the city, he decided to blot out the Jewish religion altogether. The Temple of Jerusalem was transformed into a sanctuary of Zeus. Every act of Jewish cult was abolished and the observance of the Law, including the commandments relating to the Sabbath and to the circumcision of boys, was prohibited (1 Mac 1:41–51; 2 Mac 6:1–2). Those Jews who refused to comply were subjected to torture, and if they resisted, they were put to death. The Second Book of the Maccabees portrays the heroic self-sacrifice of the ninety-year-old Jew Eleazar, and of seven brothers who together with their mother preferred to surrender their lives rather than transgress the Torah by eating swine flesh. Thus Jewish teachers found themselves for the first time faced with the idea of martyrdom. The new circumstances resulting from religious persecution affected the accepted attitudes concerning life and death. Commonly held wisdom maintained that the pious could expect a long and happy life. How then was one to interpret its denial by God to the eminently devout, those who went so far as to sacrifice their existence in order to remain faithful to the commandments of the Law of Moses?

The records of Jewish history of the Second Temple period testify to a twofold attempt made during the last couple of centuries of the pre-Christian era to resolve this painful dilemma, and discover a way to recompense the righteous whose life had been unjustly cut short by God. Palestinian Jews came up with the idea of bodily resurrection, while their brethren in the Greek-speaking Diaspora opted along Platonic lines for immortality of the liberated soul, enjoying divine bliss after escaping from the ephemeral and corruptible body.

The revival of individuals after their death had figurative antecedents. In the family, children succeeded parents and made life continue. On the national level the defeat and oppression inflicted on the Jewish people by their enemies and the eventual exile of Israel from their ancestral land are compared in the poetic and metaphorical language of the Old Testament prophets to striking, wounding and killing, and the divine help that followed as healing, binding and resurrection. An anticipatory example goes back to the prophet Hosea in the eighth century BC. In the shadow of the threat from Assyria, he wrote some memorable lines whose echoes continued to reverberate down to the age of the New Testament:

Come, let us return to the Lord;
For he has torn, that he may heal us;
He has stricken, and he will bind us up.

After two days, he will revive us;
On the third day he will raise us up,
That we may live before him (Hos 6:1–2).

However, the most impressive resurrection imagery comes from Ezekiel's vision of a large amount of dispersed dry bones, symbolically representing the defeated and exiled Israel, lying unburied on a plain. On God's command these bones all come together amid much rattling and are lifted up to form an enormous army:

Behold, I will cause breath to enter you,
and you shall live.
And I will lay sinews upon you,
and will cause flesh to come upon you,
and cover you with skin,
and put breath in you, and you shall live (Ezek 37:5–6).

Together with the reawakened victims of the battles, their deported compatriots who died in captivity would also be raised from their graves, and led back to the land of Israel (Ezek 37:12). The metaphor of the army of walking skeletons, shaking off the stupor of the sleep of death, offered a powerful image to the creators of the new concept of bodily resurrection. The vivified dry bones symbolized the granting of a second chance to those devout Jews who had been denied the fullness of days and the living out of their lives in peace, security and happiness.

The first attempt to apply to single individuals the symbol of collective national renaissance appears in a brief eschatological supplement inserted into the work of the eighth-century prophet Isaiah. The somewhat hazy message of chapters 24–27 probably dates to the latter part of the Persian era in the third century BC. The segment, known as the Isaiah Apocalypse, anticipates Daniel and the Second Book of the Maccabees. The author foresees that the wicked, personified by the oppressors of the Jews, are destined for perpetual annihilation:

O Lord, . . . other lords besides thee have ruled over us . . .
They are dead, they will not live; they are shades, and will not
  arise;
to that end thou hast visited them with destruction,
and wiped out all remembrance of them (Isa 26:13–14).

In contrast to the annihilation of the persecutors, corporal resurrection awaits God's dead. The persons designated as the 'dwellers in the dust' are ordered to 'awake and sing for joy' (Isa 26:19). The passage may allude to a renewed life after death awaiting the righteous. However, since the Isaiah Apocalypse represents poetry, it is possible that it speaks figuratively and refers to living people portrayed by anticipation as corpses.

The biblical Book of Daniel, which was given its final formulation in the 160s BC and is attested in manuscript fragments from Qumran dating to the end of that same century, yields the first definite expression of belief in the resurrection of the dead. The context is that of the end of times, the aftermath of the great battle between the heathen forces and the Jewish nation assisted by the angelic army of Michael, the great heavenly prince. All the chosen Jews, those whose names are inscribed in God's book, will be on the winning side. The wise and righteous teachers, resplendent in their glory like the stars of the firmament, will head the risen multitude, some of whom will inherit eternal life, while the hostile pagans and the unfaithful

Jews will be destined to everlasting shame (Dan 12:1–2). The text is usually taken as conveying the idea of corporeal resurrection, even though it does not formally assert the reunification of body and soul.

Universal resurrection, granted both to the righteous and to the wicked, foreshadows in Daniel the image of the eschatological scene adopted later by Judaism (and Christianity), in which the resuscitated dead await God's last judgement. But there is an alternative in which revival is reserved only for the just and is denied to the ungodly. This second type of scenario may be found in the Psalms of Solomon, Greek poems dating to the first century BC:

The sinner . . . fell . . . and he shall not rise up.
But they that fear the Lord shall rise to life eternal
and their life . . . shall come to an end no more (Pss of Sol.
    3:9–12)

The same concept continued to be voiced at the end of the first century AD in the Syriac Apocalypse of Baruch:

When the Messiah will return in glory to the heavens, then all who have died and set their hopes on him will rise again (2 Bar 30:1).

The idea is emphatically stressed, however, in the Second Book of the Maccabees (c. 100 BC), in the story of the seven brothers tortured and put to death by Antiochus Epiphanes. The brothers and their mother, who was the last to die after encouraging and witnessing the martyrdom of her sons, all professed the belief that God would recompense them with an 'everlasting renewal of life' for their sufferings and death, while the tyrant and his henchmen would be condemned to eternal destruction (2 Mac

7:1–41). The author of 2 Maccabees renders explicit the generally implicit assertion of bodily resurrection when he makes the third brother declare regarding his tongue and hands, 'I got these from Heaven, and because of [God's] laws I disdain them, and from him I hope to get them back again' (2 Mac 7:11).

These texts indicate that collective self-sacrifice in a battle fought for the sake of heaven and individual martyrdom, inflicted by the ungodly on the just as a punishment for their attachment to the Jewish religion, gave birth to the teaching of the resurrection of the dead. The doctrine, succinctly set out in the Testament of Judah – 'those who have been put to death for the Lord's sake will awake to life' (Test. of Judah 25:4) – continued to develop during the Hellenistic and Roman period, and reached its climax during the persecution of observant Jews in the course of the second war against Rome under Hadrian in AD 132–135. The rabbis of the Talmudic age went so far as to specify that a man's risen body would be exactly the same as the one he had possessed when he died: the lame would be raised lame and the blind blind, but they would be healed if found among the righteous (Eccl.R 1:4; GenR 95:1).

In addition to the idea of bodily resurrection, which was the main eschatological concept of Palestinian Judaism and of New Testament Christianity of the Pauline variety, we encounter in the Apocrypha and the rest of post-biblical Jewish literature the notion of a purely spiritual survival, usually designated as the immortality of the soul. It is important to observe that the expression 'eternal life', commonly used in the New Testament too, can equally apply to either form of survival.

The principal source of the notion of spiritual survival

is the Wisdom of Solomon, a work composed by a Jew in Greek and approximately dated between 50 BC and AD 50. Its main message is that the incorruptible souls of the righteous will enjoy eternal immortality:

God created man for incorruption
and made him in the image of his own eternity,
but through the devil's envy death entered the world,
and those who belong to his party experience it.
But the souls of the righteous are in the hand of God,
and no torment will ever touch them.
In the eyes of the foolish they seemed to have died,
and their departure was thought to be an affliction,
and their going from us to be their destruction;
but they are at peace.
For though in the sight of men they were punished,
their hope is full of immortality (Wis 2:23–3:4).

The same escape of the soul from Hades to live on for ever with God is also testified to in the wisdom sayings attributed to Pseudo-Phocylides, a Hellenized Jew writing in the first century BC:

All alike are corpses, but God rules over the souls.
Hades is our common eternal home and fatherland,
a common place for all, poor and kings.
We humans live not for a long time, but for a season.
But our soul is immortal and lives ageless for ever
(Ps.-Phoc. 111–115).

Another Hellenistic work, the Fourth Book of the Maccabees, also underlines that the righteous martyrs, who have given their lives for the Torah, share the destiny of

Abraham, Isaac, Jacob and all the Patriarchs. They join the choir of their fathers, having received from God 'pure and deathless souls' in exchange for their mortal coil (4 Mac 16:25; 18:23). Josephus attributes a similar view to the martyr-teachers Judas and Matthias, who were put to death by Herod for exhorting their pupils to pull down the golden eagle from the Temple. They argued that self-sacrifice for the laws of one's country was rewarded by 'immortality and an abiding sense of felicity' (*War* 1:650).

Likewise the Essene martyrs, who preferred torture and death by the hands of the Romans to the denial of their religion by cursing Moses or eating forbidden food, 'resigned their souls, confident that they would receive them back again' (*War* 2:152–153). Also Eleazar ben Yair, the captain of Masada, encouraging his men not to be taken alive by the Romans, portrays death as the act 'that gives liberty to the soul and permits it to depart to its own pure abode' (*War* 7:343).

Spiritual survival is bestowed for all eternity not only on martyrs, but also on those who have died in righteousness, according to the Book of Admonitions of the Ethiopic Enoch (chapters 91–105). The spirits of the just will live and rejoice and their memory will remain with God (1 En 103:4), and in the Parables of Enoch (chapters 37–72), the risen righteous will be 'like angels in heaven' (1 En 51:4), reminiscent of Jesus' similar saying in the New Testament (Mk 12:25; Mt 22:30; Lk 20:36).

These excerpts will give the reader a useful insight into the Jewish representation of afterlife, but the picture can be completed by the account of Enoch's visit to the realm of the dead and to Paradise, described in the First Book of Enoch, chapters 22, 25–27. The imagery differs from the common biblical idea of a subterranean underworld and locates Sheol in the western extremity of the world. Led by the angel Raphael, Enoch climbs a high mountain with huge caves where the souls of the deceased reside, separated according to their conduct in the past. A spring with bright waters refreshes the righteous while the wicked suffer. After the final judgement the ungodly, who have already received their punishment on earth, will be annihilated without trace. Those among the wicked who have escaped chastisement in their lifetime will be raised and transferred to the Valley of Hinnom (*Ge' Hinnom* = Gehenna) to suffer everlasting torment, while the righteous will inhabit the mountain of God at the summit of which stands the divine throne.

The surveyed literary evidence makes it unquestionable that the ideas of resurrection and incorporeal immortality were not unknown in Palestinian and Diaspora Jewry during the final centuries of the Second Temple. Nevertheless, before directly confronting the Gospels and Paul, three further questions need to be answered:

1. How widely and deeply did the concept of resurrection affect first-century AD Jewish society?

2. Did the Jews in the age of Jesus envisage resurrection in individual historical terms as distinct from the great eschatological event outlined in the literature of the period?

3. Is there any indication that they expected the Messiah to die and rise from the dead?

5

Jewish attitudes to afterlife in the age of Jesus

There is no doubt that the ideas of resurrection and immortality were sporadically attested in the latest layers of biblical literature as well as in the early post-biblical writings of Judaism, but does this mean that they had widely penetrated the religious consciousness of the Jews of the period? In the absence of direct reports, the best we can do is to examine the contemporaneous historical sources that describe the beliefs prevalent in that age among diverse Jewish groups. Thanks to Philo, Josephus, the Dead Sea Scrolls and the oldest strata of rabbinic literature, it is possible to arrive at an approximate assessment of the religious attitudes of the society in which Jesus ministered and to which the earliest Christian message, anchored on the notion of his resurrection, was first preached.

Let us begin with the Egyptian philosopher and religious teacher Philo of Alexandria (c. 20/10 BC–AD 40/50), the quintessential representative, indeed the personification, of a fully Hellenized Jew. He professed a Greek-type doctrine of immortality. For him, the soul was incarcerated in the body during a man's life. It was 'like a prisoner in the gaol', but on death it retrieved its freedom. 'When it has gone out of this city', Philo remarks, 'its thought and reflections are at liberty, like the hands and feet of the unbound prisoner' (*On Drunkenness* 101). Even more strikingly, echoing Plato's pun, Philo equates the body (*sôma*) with a tomb (*sêma*), out of which the soul arises for true life.

When we are living, the soul is dead and has been entombed in the body as a sepulchre; whereas should we die, the soul lives forthwith its own proper life, and is released from the body, the baneful corpse to which it was tied (Allegory 108).

It should surprise no one that the notion of the resurrection of the body never appears in his vast work. For educated Hellenists, reunion of the noble and liberated soul with the vile body was a denial of the highest philosophical principles, as St Paul had to find out for himself when he engaged in debate with learned Hellenes at 'speakers' corner' in Athens (Acts 17:16–33). It would seem, therefore, that the Christian preaching focused on the cross and resurrection of Christ appealed only to uncultured Greeks. Indeed, among Paul's habitual Greek clientele 'not many . . . were wise according to worldly standards' (1 Cor 1:26).

In a similar fashion, the upper echelons of Palestinian Jewish society also appear to have been hostile to the idea of resurrection. The leading classes of the Jerusalem priesthood and their wealthy and well-schooled aristocratic allies, who together formed the party of the Sadducees, were basically traditionalists. They did not speculate over-much about afterlife and stuck to the conventional biblical wisdom emphatically and fatalistically defined in the Apocrypha by the author of the Book of Ecclesiasticus, Jesus Ben Sira, himself probably a priest from Jerusalem:

Do not fear the sentence of death;
Remember your former days and the end of life;

This is the decree from the Lord for all flesh,
And how can you reject the good pleasure of the Most High?
Whether life is for ten, or a hundred or a thousand years,
There is no inquiry about it in Hades (Ecclus 41:3–4).

According to Josephus, himself of chief-priestly origin (although at the age of nineteen he decided to switch his allegiance to the Pharisees (*Life* 1–12)), the Sadducees rejected the idea of survival after death and did not believe in future retribution. In Josephus' own words, 'The Sadducees hold that the soul perishes along with the body' (*Ant* 18:16), that is to say, at death life is extinguished for good. He further declares, 'As for the persistence of the soul after death, penalties in the underworld, and rewards, they [the Sadducees] will have none of them' (*War* 2:165). In the Gospels the Sadducee creed proclaims, 'There is no resurrection' (Mk 12:18; Mt 22:23; Lk 20:27). In a polemical episode, to be examined later (pp. 69–72), the Sadducees ridicule the notion of rising from the dead (Mk 12:18–27; Mt 22:23–32; Lk 20:27–38).

The Acts of the Apostles goes even further than Josephus and the Gospels when it turns the Sadducees into complete materialists who denied not only the resurrection of the dead, but also the existence of angels and spirits (Acts 23:8). However, this exaggeration should probably be blamed more on the Gentile Luke's unfamiliarity with Palestinian Jewish thought than on the Sadducees, for angels are commonly mentioned in the Bible and the Sadducees were sticklers for the letter of scripture.

The stand taken by the Essenes on resurrection is more difficult to establish. Josephus, who claims to have experienced the life of this sect and studied their philosophy (*Life* 10), reports that the kind of afterlife they envisaged was different from resurrection. His final word on the subject in *Jewish Antiquities* (end of the first century AD) was that the Essenes believed in spiritual survival, the immortality of the soul (*Ant* 18:18). In the earlier account of the *Jewish War*, Josephus, like Philo and Hellenistic Judaism, paints a detailed Platonic canvas that after death incorruptible souls receive eternal reward or punishment.

For it is a fixed belief of theirs that the body is corruptible and its constituent matter impermanent, but that the soul is immortal and imperishable. Emanating from the finest ether, these souls become entangled, as it were, in the prison-house of the body, to which they are dragged down by a sort of natural spell; but when once they are released from the bonds of the flesh, then, as though liberated from a long servitude, they rejoice and are borne aloft. Sharing the belief of the sons of Greece, they maintain that for the virtuous souls there is reserved an abode beyond the ocean, a place which is not oppressed by rain or snow or heat, but is refreshed by the ever gentle breath of the west wind coming in from the ocean; while they relegate base souls to a murky and tempestuous dungeon, big with never-ending punishment ... Their aim was first to establish the doctrine of the immortality of the soul, and secondly to promote virtue and to deter from vice; for the good are made better in their lifetime by the hope of a reward after death, and the passions of the wicked are restrained by the fear that, even though they escape detection while alive, they will undergo neverending punishment after their decease (War 2:154–157).

If this was a true picture of the Essene representation of afterlife, a message centred on a risen Messiah (like the Jesus preached by Christians) would not have had much hope of success among them. However, for whatever it's worth, the Church father Hippolytus has left us a second version, purported to be Josephus' account, in which a very different picture is sketched:

The doctrine of the resurrection also is firmly held among them. For they confess that the flesh also will rise and be immortal as the soul is already immortal, which they now say, when separated from the body, enters a place of fragrant air and light, to rest until the judgement . . . (Refutation of All the Heresies 9:27).

Is the difference due to the pen of Hippolytus, wishing to portray the Essenes as proto-Christians, or was Josephus guilty of twisting the evidence in order to make the Essene teaching palatable to his Greek readers? While the first view is more commonly held, there are defenders of the second, too. Clarification of the problem may be sought by means of the Dead Sea Scrolls.

However, the outcome of the study of the Qumran texts both on the subject of afterlife in general, and on resurrection in particular, is rather disappointing. The Scrolls contain a surprisingly small amount of relevant information. There are some general allusions to afterlife which may coincide with Josephus' idea of spiritual immortality. For example, the Sons of Light are promised 'eternal joy in life without end, a crown of glory and a garment of majesty in light without end' (1QS 4:7–8). They are also said to share their future destiny with angels called the Holy Ones and the Sons of Heaven (1QS 11:5–9). A couple of poetic passages may be interpreted as referring to bodily resurrection. Thus people who 'lie in the dust' and 'bodies gnawed by worms' are commanded to hoist a banner or rise from the dust to the counsel of God's truth (1QH 14:34–35; 19:12). Nevertheless, it is equally possible that the language is allegorical and no actual bodily revival is envisaged. The only text among the hundreds of manuscripts found at Qumran which clearly refers to resurrection is the so-called Messianic Apocalypse, a verse composition that includes a line from Isaiah (61:1), to which is added a reference to the resurrection of the dead, namely that God will 'heal the wounded and revive the dead and bring good news to the poor' (4Q521, frag. 2 ii, line 12). The statement could possibly signify that the Qumran community believed in the rising of the dead, but since the manuscript exhibits no sectarian features, it may not belong to the Essenes and could represent a work akin to late biblical poetry such as Isaiah 24–27.

All in all, the available evidence does not permit us to conclude that either the Essenes, as portrayed by Josephus, or the Qumran sectaries of the Scrolls, were champions of the belief in bodily resurrection, although there is evidence that both of them contemplated an afterlife in the form of the immortality of the soul. As for Philo's notices on the Essenes, they have nothing to say on the subject.

This leaves us only with the Pharisees, who were the renowned protagonists of the doctrine of the resurrection. Josephus reports their teaching in each of his three works, the *War*, *Against Apion* and the *Antiquities*, and on a further occasion in the *War* he expresses in a speech his own Pharisaic convictions about afterlife.

His doctrine on the resurrection is not entirely homogeneous, nor does it clearly convey the teaching of mainstream Pharisaism. In his earliest summary, he brings into relief the incorruptibility of the spirit of man, but his description of the spirit's reunion with the body sounds more like metempsychosis or transmigration of the soul than bodily resurrection. He also appears to restrict corporeal revival to the righteous, as did 2 Maccabees and the

Psalms of Solomon before him (see p. 333). The pious alone are to enjoy eternal corporeal bliss, while the wicked souls, seemingly without new bodies, are to suffer everlasting torment: 'Every soul, they maintain, is imperishable, but the soul of the good alone passes into another body, while the souls of the wicked suffer eternal punishment' (*War* 2:163).

In the same *Jewish War*, in an effort to dissuade his fellow rebels from committing suicide, Josephus assures them that taking their own lives will deprive them of new bodies in God's realm:

*Know you not that they who depart this life in accordance with the law of nature and repay the loan which they received from God, when He who lent is pleased to reclaim it, win eternal renown; that their houses and families are secure; that their souls, remaining spotless and obedient, are allotted the most holy place in heaven, whence, in the revolution of the ages, they return to find in chaste bodies a new habitation? But as for those who have laid mad hands upon themselves, the darker regions of the nether world receive their souls . . . (*War* 3:374–375).*

Even in his two later works, *Against Apion* and *Jewish Antiquities*, written in the AD 90s, he seems to grant the privilege of resurrection only to the good; the ungodly are condemned to remain eternally imprisoned in Sheol:

*They believe that the souls have power to survive death and that there are rewards and punishments under the earth for those who have led lives of virtue or vice: eternal imprisonment is the lot of evil souls, while the good souls receive an easy passage to a new life (*Ant* 18:14).*

In *Against Apion* Josephus insists that only the strict observers of the Law, and especially those who are ready to die rather than disobey the commandments, will reap the reward of the resurrection:

For those ... who live in accordance with our laws the prize is not silver and gold, no crown of wild olive or of parsley with any such public mark of distinction. No; each individual, relying on the witness of his own conscience, and the lawgiver's prophecy, confirmed by the sure testimony of God, is firmly persuaded that to those who observe the laws, and, if they must needs die for them, willingly meet death, God has granted a renewed existence and in the revolution of the ages the gift of a better life (c. Ap. 2:217–18).

Shortly after the time of Josephus, around the turn of the first century AD, the rabbinic heirs of the Pharisees continued to propound, without distinguishing between the good and the bad, the doctrine of resurrection as one of the two pivotal teachings of Judaism, the other being the divine origin of the Torah. Thus the tractate Sanhedrin of the Mishnah, the oldest rabbinic code of law, declares:

All Israelites have a share in the world to come ... And these are they who have no share in the world to come: he that says that there is no resurrection of the dead [prescribed in the Law], and that the Law is not from Heaven (mSanh 10:1).[1]

At about the same time (c. AD 100) was formulated also the second benediction of the *Tephillah* (the Prayer par excellence), also bearing the title of the *Eighteen Benedictions*, recited in standing position three times a day, morning, afternoon and evening, as specific thanksgiving to God for raising the dead. It has been preserved in two versions, the

Babylonian and the Palestinian, but on this point both convey the same message:

Lord, Thou art almighty for ever, who makest the dead alive . . . Thou makest the dead alive out of great mercy . . . Thou keepest thy word faithfully to them who sleep in the dust . . . Thou art faithful to make the dead alive. Blessed art Thou, Lord, who makest the dead alive (Babylonian version).

Thou art mighty . . . Thou livest for ever and raisest the dead . . . Thou providest for the living and makest the dead alive . . . Blessed art Thou, Lord, who makest the dead alive (Palestinian version).

It would seem, therefore, that by the second century AD, faith in bodily resurrection was an essential constituent of the Pharisaic-rabbinic religion. But at first sight there is no positive evidence to indicate that this was the case during the lifetime of Jesus, the ministry of Paul or the early decades of Christianity. Yet for the evaluation of how prepared the audiences of Jesus and of the apostolic preachers were for the idea of the resurrection, it would be useful to have the means to grasp the extent of the spread of this notion in the various layers of Jewish and Graeco-Roman society in the first century AD.

To begin with, the three groups, Sadducees, Essenes and Pharisees, about whose attitude towards resurrection we know something, represent only a small fraction of the Jewish population of Palestine in the age of Jesus.

No source supplies direct information about the number of the Sadducees, who comprised the upper layers of the priesthood and their aristocratic lay supporters, but attempts have been made to estimate the size of the Temple personnel, priests and Levites. Already about four hundred years before the age of Jesus the Book of Nehemiah refers to 1,192 priests in Jerusalem (Neh 11:10–19). Closer to New Testament times, towards the end of the second century BC, the author of the Letter of Aristeas asserted that seven hundred priests were on duty every day in the Temple, not counting those in charge of sacrifices (Aristeas 95). Since the service in the sanctuary was performed by one of the 24 weekly units, or 'courses', each of which was on duty twice a year, 24 × say 750 would give a total for the Jewish clergy (priests and Levites) of eighteen thousand. In the late first century AD Josephus suggests a similar figure when he speaks of four priestly tribes, each comprising upwards of five thousand men, amounting to over twenty thousand (c. AP. 21:108). While it is known that by that time some of the priests adhered to the teaching of the Pharisees, one can still suppose that a fair proportion of them held to the party doctrine laid down by the upper clergy, and were opposed to the idea of resurrection.

As for the membership of the Pharisee associations, we know from Josephus that, as a body, over six thousand of them refused to swear the oath of allegiance to Herod the Great (*Ant* 17:42). The number of the Essenes was put both by Philo (*Omnis probus* 75) and by Josephus (*Ant* 18:20) at above four thousand.

What do these figures tell us? Among those who did not believe in the resurrection of the dead we may count more than four thousand Essenes and probably a good proportion of the 15,000–20,000-strong Temple staff, together no doubt with their families and their upper-class lay allies. Against these stood some six thousand Pharisees, their families and followers. Taken together, both the opponents and the supporters of the doctrine of the resurrection formed only a small portion of the Jewish population of

Palestine in the first century AD, estimated at between 500,000 and 1,000,000, but more likely to have amounted to between 500,000 and 600,000.[2] It is widely maintained, however, that the Pharisees controlled most of the Jewish population of Roman Palestine, and that consequently the majority of the Jews of the Holy Land believed in the resurrection of the dead. It has even been proposed that the fairly widespread, though far from universally adopted custom of secondary burial, *viz.* the collecting of the bones of the deceased and placing them in ossuaries, was a Pharisee innovation inspired by faith in individual revival. But this is a misunderstanding that must be dispelled.

In truth, the thesis of an all-pervasive Pharisaic impact on the whole Jewish population has no evidential support. According to Josephus, the Pharisees were influential, not across the board of society, but mostly among the 'townsfolk' or the 'inhabitants of the cities' (*Ant* 18:15), that is to say, their followers were recruited among the moderately well-to-do urban artisan classes. Also, territorially, their main constituency was Jerusalem and the towns of Judaea.

But Judaea differed from Galilee, and in this connection one should recall that in the age of Jesus, Pharisee presence in Galilee was scarce, if it existed at all. It became dominant only after the resettlement of the defeated Judaeans in the northern province following the first rebellion against Rome (AD 66–70). A careful reader of the New Testament will observe that various Pharisees and scribes, mentioned in the Gospels, are explicitly said to have been visitors from Jerusalem and not Galilean citizens (Mk 3:22; 7:1; Mt 12:24; 15:1). The impression given by Mark and Matthew of a Pharisee-free Galilee is further reinforced by Josephus. He refers to the presence of only three Pharisees during his tenure as revolutionary military commander of the province, and names them as Jonathan, Ananias and Jozar. But they were not local people. They were sent to the northern province by the chief Pharisee of the capital, Simeon ben Gamaliel, to engineer the downfall of Josephus (*Life* 197).

As far as the general influence of Pharisaic ideas was concerned, one should further remember that in both Judaea and Galilee the bulk of the population did not reside in cities, the Pharisees' strongholds, but lived in the country. They were the village farmers and agricultural workers, the 'people of the land' (*'am ha-arets*), who ploughed the fields and cultivated the orchards, olive groves and vineyards, as appears so clearly in the rural parables of Jesus. So it would seem that we simply do not know how generally accepted the doctrinal leadership of the Pharisees was in first-century AD Palestine, and consequently how widespread the belief in bodily resurrection was at that time.[3]

If literature provides no further assistance for an assessment of the impact of the Pharisaic belief in resurrection in wider Jewish society, can archaeology and funeral inscriptions help? Some experts have voiced a firmly negative opinion. In his monumental study of the Essene doctrine on life after death, Émile Puech declares that funerary art on tombstones and ossuaries displays no clear hint at eschatological expectations.[4] The author of the latest monograph on funeral epigraphy, P. W. van der Horst, also complains of the 'disappointingly little information' the inscriptions yield about life after death.[5] Such pessimistic forecasts must not, however, prevent us from re-examining the evidence.

The most common decorative figure on Jewish ossuaries

and tombstones is the *menorah*, the seven-branched lamp-stand. Modelled on the candelabrum of the Jerusalem Temple, taken to Rome by Titus after the fall of Jerusalem, and represented on his triumphal arch constructed in the Roman Forum in AD 81, it had become the principal symbol of Judaism. Sometimes accompanied by other decorative motives, the citron (*ethrog*), the palm-branch (*lulab*) and the scroll of the Law, it appears fairly frequently on Jewish tombs and bone boxes. There is no unanimity regarding its meaning. It can merely denote the Jewishness of the person or possibly his priestly connections. E. R. Goodenough, the leading expert on the subject, remarks however that the *menorah* was of the greatest importance for Jews to have on their tombstones and symbolized yearning for light in the darkness of the grave.[6] It appears fairly often in the Jewish catacombs of Rome and in Beth Shearim, dating to the third and fourth centuries AD, but there are also a few earlier attestations. The oldest is on what is known as Jason's tomb in Jerusalem, but what in fact is the tomb of the priestly family of the Sons of Hezir (second or first century BC). Two more figure on Palestinian ossuaries,[7] probably belonging to the first or second century AD. A few representations of the *menorah* may be found on Egyptian Jewish tombs, probably from the second century AD. Nothing directly connects the candelabrum with the resurrection of the dead, but there is a legitimate surmise that this symbol of illumination is meant to remind the onlooker of a bright and hopeful hereafter of some sort.

Only a small proportion of the funeral inscriptions allude to the beliefs of the deceased or of those who ordered the epitaphs. On one ossuary the idea of resurrection is firmly rejected in the Sadducee manner: 'No man goes up [from the grave]; not Eleazar or Sapphira' (Rahmani, no. 455). Unparalleled is the invitation tainted with irony that the Roman Jew, Leo Leontius, has issued to his associates: 'Friends, I am waiting for you here' (*Amici ego vos hic exspecto*) (CIJ *32).[8] Another inscription from Beth Shearim, 'Good luck with your resurrection', may be either cynical or a serious affirmation of belief in the reawakening of the dead (BS II, 194). As for the often repeated 'No one is immortal', a phrase that is found on pagan epitaphs as well, it expresses the outlook of the Old Testament and the Sadducees, although some detect a hopeful overtone in the exhortation, 'Be of good courage!' (BS II, 59, 127, 136, etc.) placed before it. 'May your sleep be peaceful!', frequently read on Roman epitaphs, can also be interpreted as a wish for undisturbed rest in the tomb and a protection against grave robbers on whom God's judgement accompanied by a curse is again and again invoked. However, the word 'peace', sometimes written as *shalom* in Hebrew, is capable of deeper meaning, implying fullness and religious perfection.

A small number of Greek inscriptions from Leontopolis in Egypt and Beth Shearim seem to allude to the idea of immortality. The soul of Arsinoe, a young Jewess who died in labour when she was producing her first child, 'has gone to the holy ones', we read on an inscription dating to the twenty-fifth year of Augustus or 5 BC (CIJ 1510). Rachel, aged about thirty years, entertains a good hope in God's mercy, which implies expectation of some form of future life (CIJ 1513), and in a Hebrew inscription from Antinoopolis a Jew called Lazar expects his soul to find rest in the 'bundle of the living' (CIJ 1534). In a similar Greek epitaph from Beth Shearim someone wishes that the souls of his or her parents 'be bound in the bundle of immortal life' (BS II, 130), while a certain Hesechios, also from Beth Shearim, threatens with the loss of 'a portion in eternal life' anyone daring to open his and his wife's grave (BS II, 129). Karteria and Zenobia, her daughter who arranged her funeral, long to 'enjoy again new indestructible riches' (BS II, 183). In these inscriptions the spiritual survival of Hellenistic Judaism is voiced without any hint at the doctrine characteristic of the Pharisees.

The very common wish at Beth Shearim that the deceased should 'possess a good portion' (*eumoirei, eumoros*), a Greek phrase reminiscent of the Hebrew Pharisaic-rabbinic 'portion' (*heleq*) in the world to come, may insinuate the idea of resurrection, but it could also refer only to the survival of the soul. Indeed, a clear confession of belief in bodily revivification is exceptional among the epitaphs. I have counted two or possibly three occurrences in the Corpus of Jewish Inscriptions, the Palestinian ossuaries and the Beth Shearim material. The uncertain case, already referred to, is 'Good luck with your resurrection' (BS II, 194). If it is taken at its face value with no undertone of cynicism, it has a positive religious significance. By the way, this is the only case where the term *anastasis* (rising, resurrection) is used. Of the other two, the first comes from Beth Shearim, and employs the verb 'to revive', while issuing a warning against interference with the contents of the grave. 'Anyone who changes this lady's place, He who promised to revive (ζôποiêsê) the dead will Himself judge [him]' (BS II, 162). The second, a direct proclamation of faith in the resurrection of the dead, is the versified Latin epitaph of the Roman Jewess, Regina. It was set up in the second century AD by her husband, with whom she lived twenty-one years, four months and eight days:

Hic Regina sita est tali contecta sepulcro
Quod coniunx statuit respondens eius amori . . .
Rursum victura reditura ad lumina rursum
Nam sperare potest ideo quod surgat in aevum
Promissum quae vera fides dignisque piisque
Quae meruit sedem venerandi ruris habere
(CIJ 476).

Here lies Regina, concealed in such a sepulcher
That her husband has set up responding to her love . . .
She will live again and will again return to the light
For she can hope to rise for eternity
As is promised by true faith to the worthy and the pious.
She has deserved to have a place in the venerable land.

The expression *surgere in aevum* (to rise for eternity) definitely refers to corporeal resurrection and if the phrase 'venerable land' denotes the Holy Land, the writer of the poem seems to allude to the rabbinic idea that the resurrection of the dead will take place, or at least will begin, in Jerusalem.

In conclusion, let us revert to the first question posed at the end of the previous chapter: How widely and deeply did the concept of resurrection affect first-century AD Jewish society? The long and the short of the answer is that the notion of bodily resurrection propagated by the Pharisees was alien to first-century Hellenistic Jews, and was on the whole unfamiliar in most layers of Palestinian Jewry. Our study of the New Testament will have to keep this remark firmly in mind.

II

Resurrection and eternal life in the New Testament

6

Introductory note

Our survey of the Hebrew Bible, post-biblical Second Temple literature and archaeology has shown that the idea of the resurrection of the dead was a latecomer in Jewish religious thought. Moreover, it turned out to be only one of the possibilities of man's survival after death. Since the individuality of the deceased was thought to continue even beyond the grave, as the story of the reappearance of the prophet Samuel in the Bible indicates, the just and the wicked, originally thought to share the same address in the underworld, ended up being moved to different domains. The righteous Jews kept company with the holy Patriarchs, while the ungodly were to suffer the torments of hell.

With the emergence of the idea of an eschatological divine judgement inaugurating the kingdom of God, the ultimate reward of the good and chastisement of the wicked were substituted for the unilateral notion of recompense, whether resurrection or immortality, awarded only to the pious. This type of resurrection, as distinguished from resuscitation shortly after death, like the acts performed by Elijah and Elisha, was conceived as a peculiar occurrence marking the end of times. Finally, however significant resurrection appeared to be to the eschatologically motivated, it occupied only a small area of the broad religious canvas of late Second Temple Judaism.

The New Testament completely altered the vista and changed the perspective. In it the individual resurrection of one Jew, Jesus of Nazareth, predominates. It is set in time and space and integrated into history, and is anticipated by other resurrections achieved by or connected with him. The rising of Jesus is claimed to account for the religious movement, later designated as Christianity, that two thousand years on is still flourishing and numbers among its adherents a substantial portion of mankind. According to the Gospels, Jesus had repeatedly prepared his intimates for his return from the tomb yet it hit them suddenly like a bolt out of the blue.

The situation is profoundly perplexing and the historian must come to grips with this puzzle. In the first instance, he has to re-examine the written evidence. What do the accounts of the burial and resurrection of Jesus actually say? How do the four Gospel narratives relate to one another? How do they fit into the eschatological teaching of Jesus about eternal life and resurrection? How should one judge Jesus' predictions of his rising from the dead and the claim made by him and/or his immediate followers that the resurrection was the fulfilment of biblical prophecies? Finally, since the chapters relative to the resurrection form only a small part of the Gospels – eight verses in Mark, twenty in Matthew, fifty-three in Luke and fifty-six in John – how did they manage to take on such an overall importance?

To approach all these questions in the right order, we shall first examine the teaching of Jesus on resurrection and eternal life (chapter 7). This will be followed by a survey of the passages in the New Testament where Jesus predicts his rising from the dead, or claims that the event has been foretold by the biblical prophets (chapter 8). The next step will take us to the resurrection narratives, first the accounts of Jesus raising other people from the dead (chapter 9) and above all, the records of his own resurrection (chapter 10) which will then be fully analyzed and initially evaluated (chapter 11). The discussion of the resurrection of Jesus will be followed by its interpretation in the Acts of the Apostles (chapter 12), St Paul (chapter 13) and the remaining writings of the New Testament (chapter 14). The full survey will permit us to investigate the meaning of the resurrection in its Jewish and Graeco-Roman context (chapter 15) with a glance at its overall significance in antiquity and in the twenty-first century.

7

The teaching of Jesus on resurrection and eternal life

1. Resurrection

Ever since St Paul wrote his letters in the fifties AD, the resurrection of Jesus and resurrection in general have stood at the centre of New Testament thought and Christian theology. Paul is adamant on the subject: without belief in resurrection, primarily in the resurrection of Christ, his preaching is baseless, the Christians are misled by him and their faith is futile (1 Cor 15:12–17). In these circumstances one would justifiably expect to find in the teaching of Jesus, as handed down in the Gospels, numerous references to the raising of the dead and to his own resurrection. Those who labour under such an illusion must brace themselves for a big surprise. General pronouncements by Jesus on resurrection are few and far between. Allusions to his rising can be counted on the fingers of one hand, and when scrutinized with critical eyes, they turn out to be inauthentic. Let us investigate these passages, leaving to chapters 9 and 10 the examination of the narrative accounts: the 'resurrection miracles' performed by Jesus and the Gospel stories of his own resurrection.

There are two passages in the Synoptic Gospels dealing with resurrection in which Jesus is neither the resuscitator nor the raised (see chapter 9), and four predictions are recorded concerning his own rising (see chapter 8). Out of the two general resurrection references, one is merely cursory and simply dates another event; the other is substantive, and is embedded in a controversy story. The former occurs in a parable dealing with the guests summoned to a banquet which is preserved only in Luke (Lk 14:7–14). In it, Jesus advises the host to show disinterested benevolence by inviting not friends, members of his family and *rich* neighbours, but 'the poor, the maimed, the lame and the blind'; those who are unable to reciprocate his generosity. So, instead of hoping for immediate repayment in the form of similar invitations to festivities, he postpones his reward until the end, until 'the resurrection of the just' (Lk 14:14).

There is only one relatively extensive Synoptic treatment of the problem of the resurrection ascribed to Jesus. It appears in a debate with the Sadducees in a collection of controversies situated in Jerusalem. However, while the other polemics on divorce, the authority of Jesus, the legitimacy of the payment of taxes to Rome and the precise identity of the Son of David fit well into the context of Jesus' arrival in the Holy City during the week of the fateful Passover, the meeting with the Sadducees is haphazard. It is no doubt put in its present place because it is a doctrinal argument which must have taken place in the Holy City, and in the Synoptic Gospels Jesus only once visits the capital of Judaea.

And Sadducees came to him, who say that there is no resurrection;
and they asked him a question, saying, 'Teacher, Moses wrote for us
that if a man's brother dies and leaves a wife, but leaves no child,
the man must take the wife, and raise up children for his brother.
There were seven brothers; the first took a wife, and when he died
left no children; and the second took her, and died, leaving no children;
and the third likewise; and the seven left no children. Last of all the
woman also died. In the resurrection whose wife will she be? For the
seven had her as wife' (Mk, Mt, Lk). *Jesus said to them, Is not this*
why you are wrong, that you know neither the scriptures nor the
power of God?

For when they rise from the dead, they neither marry nor are given
in marriage, but are **like the angels in heaven** (Mk, Mt).

[The sons of this age marry and are given in marriage;
but those who are worthy to attain to that age and to the
resurrection from the dead neither marry, nor are given in
marriage, for they cannot die any more, because they are
**equal to angels, and are sons of God, being sons of
the resurrection** (Lk).]

The anecdote, which carries the message on resurrection, recounts the curious adventure of a Jewish woman,
told against the background of the biblical law regulating
leviratic marriage (Deut 25:5–6). The Mosaic legislation
obliged a childless widow to marry her deceased husband's
brother if he was willing to take her as his wife. The purpose of the rule was to provide the former husband with
an heir: the first male child born of the new union was
indeed legally recognized as the deceased brother's son.

In the story quoted by the Sadducees, the woman went
through successive marriages with her six brothers-in-law,

burying them all one after the other, without producing a child. Finally she also joined the seven dead husbands in Sheol. The tantalizing question put to Jesus concerned the eschatological future of the widow of seven spouses: 'In the resurrection whose wife will she be?'

Most critical commentators rightly assume that the conflict is inauthentic and probably reflects by anticipation arguments opposing the haughty Sadducees and the representatives of the apostolic Church in the latter part of the first century, but there is no reason to doubt that the ideas expressed here correspond to the eschatological thought of Jesus.

The tale itself smacks of fiction. From what we learn from other Gospel accounts about Jesus as polemist – for instance his proud refusal to declare to the envoys of the chief priests the source of his authority (see Mk 11:27–33; Mt 21:23–27; Lk 20:1–8) – it is hard to imagine him naively putting up with what seems to be a cynical leg pull by the Sadducees. The Gospel story has all the appearances of an upper-class Jews' joke, addressed not to Jesus whom the chief priests feared, but to the apostles who for them counted as uncouth boors from Galilee (see Acts 4:13).

The reply placed on Jesus' lips provides an insight into how some first-century AD Jews, and possibly Jesus himself, conceived of the state of a person raised from the dead. The 'sons of the resurrection' were thought to be *bodiless* and resembled the 'angels of God' or the 'sons of God'. The picture is paralleled in contemporaneous Jewish literature such as the First Book of Enoch (in the section of the Parables, datable to the last quarter of the first century AD), whose author, like Jesus of the Synoptics, compared the resurrected righteous to the 'angels in heaven' (1 En 51:4). The Second Book of Baruch (equally from the late first century AD) also speaks of the glory of the risen just that is similar to, and even surpasses, the splendour of the angels (2 Bar 51:5, 10, 12). So for Jesus, or at least for his later disciples, the sons of the resurrection had an angelic, non-corporeal, quality. If so, the idea of marriage, with its bodily implications, was inapplicable to them.

Consequently, in the eyes of Jesus, resurrected persons, or more precisely the raised just, the people he seems to have most of the time envisaged as worthy of resurrection, were purely bodiless beings without the needs and functions of flesh and blood.[1] This would imply that in Jesus' mind the distinction between resurrection and mere spiritual survival was minimal. Study of his concept of 'life' or 'eternal life' will confirm this conclusion (see pp. 75–8). The only sustainable conclusion is that corporeal resurrection played no significant part in the thinking of Jesus although he was undoubtedly aware of the idea. If so, the concept must have gained popularity at a later stage.

i. Resurrection in the Gospel of John

By contrast, due to the peculiar perspective of the evangelist, a totally different picture emerges from the Gospel of John. John's Jesus pre-existed in heaven. He descended to earth for a short duration and he had long since reascended to heaven to be with the Father by the time the Gospel was written at the turn of the first century AD. Some of his followers were already dead and others were expected to die before the D-day of the final resurrection. In John's eyes, the principal task Jesus, the glorified Son of God, received from the Father was the raising of the dead, or more specifically the raising of his deceased disciples on the last day, as is obvious from the words placed by the evangelist on Jesus' lips:

*For I have come down from heaven, not to do my own will, but the will of him who sent me; and this is the will of him who sent me, that I should lose nothing of all that he has given me, but **raise** it up at the last day. For this is the will of my Father, that everyone who sees the Son and believes in him should have **eternal life**; and I will **raise** him up on the last day* (Jn 6:38–40).

*No one can come to me unless the Father who sent me draws him; and I will **raise** him up at the last day* (Jn 6:44).

The means by which the faithful are to be revived for ever is the symbolical body and blood of Jesus that they must sacramentally consume.

*He who eats my flesh and drinks my blood has **eternal life**, and I will **raise** him up on the last day* (Jn 6:54).

This cannibalistic allegory is hardly attributable to Jesus speaking to his Galilean listeners. Most first-century AD Palestinian Jews, hearing these words, would have been overcome by nausea. The eating of blood was a deeply ingrained biblical taboo, since the Mosaic law identified blood with life and life belongs to God alone (Lev 17:10–11). It follows, therefore, that John's words are those of a possibly Gentile Christian preacher addressed to a non-Jewish audience. Let it be recalled that even some twenty years after the death of Jesus, the council of the apostles in Jerusalem compelled non-Jews wishing to join the Church to abstain from blood (Acts 15:20), that is to say, to eat only the meat of animals slaughtered according to Jewish ritual law.

John's Jesus metaphorically presents himself to the sister of his deceased friend Lazarus as the embodiment of resurrection as far as the dead are concerned, and as the source of life for the living: 'I am the **resurrection** and the **life**; he who believes in me, though he die, yet shall he live, and whoever lives and believes in me, shall never die' (Jn 11:25).

Following the model adopted with a single exception by the Synoptics (see p. 155, n. 1, to chapter 7), in John, too, as a rule resurrection is promised to the just alone; the fate of the wicked is left out of consideration. Universal renascence of the dead – both good and evil, preceding judgement – is first mooted in the Book of Daniel before becoming common doctrine professed by rabbinic Judaism, and is heard only on a single occasion in John.

*For as the Father has life in himself, so he has granted the Son to have life in himself, and has given him authority to execute judgement, because he is the Son of man. Do not marvel at this; for the hour is coming when all who are in the tombs will hear his voice and come forth, those who have done good, to the **resurrection of life**, and those who have done evil, to the **resurrection of judgement*** (Jn 5:26–29).

Here ends our extremely meagre harvest of sayings on resurrection, using the actual words 'to rise' and 'resurrection', attributed to Jesus by the Gospels. However, it is possible to cast the net wider and hunt also for references to 'life' or 'eternal life', not necessarily including the concept of corporeal reawakening, in an attempt to establish whether it alters the picture.

2. Eternal life

Here again the first fact that strikes the observer is the paucity of attestation in the Synoptics; four units if parallel passages are not counted separately, as against three for resurrection.

i. The Synoptic Gospels

Although the concepts of eternal life and resurrection are interconnected, curiously they do not figure together in the Synoptic Gospels as they do in the later work of John. Nevertheless, there is one example in the Synoptics in which the idea (though not the actual term) of bodily resurrection is presumed.

*And if your hand causes you to sin, cut it off; it is better for you to enter **life** maimed than with two hands to go to hell, to the unquench-able fire. And if your foot causes you to sin, cut it off; it is better for you to enter life lame than with two feet to be thrown into hell. And if your eye causes you to sin, pluck it out; it is better for you to enter the **kingdom of God** [Mt: **life**] with one eye than with two eyes to be thrown into hell, where their worm does not die, and the fire is not quenched* (Mk 9:43–48; Mt 18:8–9).

According to Jesus, it is worth sacrificing a limb or an eye if it opens the gate to life, that is to say to eternal blessedness. Elsewhere he hyperbolically recommends self-castration if it is required for access to the kingdom of heaven (Mt 19:12).

In the other Synoptic passages, eternal life is used as the equivalent of 'kingdom of God', the central topic of the preaching of Jesus in Mark, Matthew and Luke, that plays practically no part in the Fourth Gospel. Neither formula is ever properly defined, but both indicate in general terms the transformation of the conditions of existence from those that prevail in the present era to the state of affairs in the world to come. By contrast, damnation is depicted with the help of the biblical imagery of worms and hell-fire.[2] Jesus seems less interested in the details of the future life than in the overall qualifications which authorize entry to the kingdom of God. The best illustration is yielded by the story recounting a conversation between Jesus and a pious wealthy man:

And as he was setting out on his journey, a man ran up and knelt before him, and asked him, 'Good Teacher, what must I do to inherit **eternal life***?' . . . You know the commandments . . .' And he said to [Jesus]: 'Teacher, all these I have observed from my youth.' And Jesus . . . said to him, '. . . [S]ell what you have, and give it to the poor . . .' And Jesus . . . said to his disciples, 'How hard it will be for those who have riches to enter the* **kingdom of God***! . . . It is easier for a camel to go through the eye of a needle than for a rich man to enter the* **kingdom of God***'* (Mk 10:17–25; Mt 19:16–24; Lk 18:18–25).

'Truly, I say to you, there is no one who has left their house Lk: or wife] *or brothers or sisters or mother or father or children or lands, for my sake and for* **the gospel** [Mt: **for my name's sake**; Lk: **for the sake of the kingdom of God**]*, who will not receive a hundredfold now in this time, houses and brothers and sisters and mothers and children and lands, . . . and* **in the age to come** **eternal life***'* (Mk 10:29–30; Mt 19:29; Lk 18:29–30).

In his answer to the question of how to be saved, Jesus declared that obedience to God's commandments, especially as they are expressed in the Decalogue, is the way to 'eternal life', but renunciation of worldly goods, too, constitutes a simple and safe access. Indeed, approach to the kingdom of God or eternal life is hindered by wealth, and to attain it is just as impossible for a rich man as it is for a camel to pass through the eye of a needle.[3] In short, the accent is laid not on the ultimate target, but existentially, as is often the case with Jesus, on the means enabling one to reach the goal.

The typical exaggeration of abandoning parents, siblings, spouses and children for the sake of Jesus[4] simply means that preference is due to what is the most important, namely the ultimate life which can be reached only in the footsteps of the Master. Once again, the emphasis is not on the target but on the action leading towards it.

A further rather particular mention of 'eternal life' may be found in the Gospel of Matthew; it figures at the end of the parable of the last judgement: 'And they will go away into eternal punishment, but the righteous into eternal life' (Mt 25:31–46). The scene recalls the Similitudes of Enoch, a book probably contemporaneous with and possibly influencing Matthew, where the Son of Man or the Elect condemns the sinners to destruction. Though not expressly stated, it presupposes the resurrection both of the righteous and of the wicked, followed by divine retribution to all.

It is to be borne in mind that with the possible exception of the last example, 'life' and 'eternal life' are never actually associated with resurrection or even necessarily imply the idea of it. So when, on rare occasions, Jesus spoke of eternal life, it is possible that he meant immortality. Also those Jews who thought they belonged to the final period (and Jesus was definitely one of them), believed that the reign of God was on the point of bursting into this world. Consequently they imagined that they could pass into the 'age to come' without experiencing death and therefore needed no resurrection (Mk 9:1; Mt 16:28; Lk 9:27). Indeed we know that according to the teaching of Jesus, the kingdom of God was 'at hand' (Mk 1:15; Mt 4:17) and was already in the midst of his generation (Lk 17:20–21), as revealed by the charismatic exorcisms and healings performed by him and his envoys (Mt 11:4–5; Lk 7:22; Mt 10:7–8).

These few quotations from the first three Gospels obviously lead to the conclusion that the subject did not play a major role in Jesus' teaching as reflected in the Synoptics. It was only in the context of the eschatological end of time (which after the death of Jesus was developed by St Paul and the early Church to encourage belief in resurrection) that the topic acquired a climactic position in the thought of early Christianity. An examination of the part played by the concept of eternal life in the Fourth Gospel will help us to grasp its rising momentum.

ii. The Gospel of John

Compared to the four passages in the Synoptics, John's Gospel counts twenty-five occurrences of 'life' or 'eternal life' in the sayings ascribed to Jesus. The acts which in John are thus rewarded in most cases differ from those in the Synoptics. It is true there is one passage where 'life' is said to be earned by a hard-working harvester through his devotion to duty: 'He who reaps receives wages, and gathers fruit for **eternal life**' (Jn 4:36). And on another occasion 'eternal life' is the prize granted to a man who, inspired by outstanding moral heroism, sacrifices all his worldly values (Jn 11:25). However, most of the time, 'life', a kind of continued and renewed existence with God, is ultimately the reward of faith in Jesus, and/or in God the Father, who has sent Jesus: 'For God so loved the world that he gave his only Son, that whoever believes in him should not perish but have **eternal life**' (Jn 3:16). The same theme is repeated again and again in John: 'He who believes in the Son has **eternal life**; he who does not obey the Son shall not see **life**, but the wrath of God rests upon him' (Jn 3:36). Finally, presenting both Christ and God as the source of the gift, 'eternal life' is promised to those who hear the word of Jesus and believe in the Father who sent him (Jn 5:24).

In addition to the passages where belief in Jesus is the recipe for gaining eternal life, John includes a whole series of symbolical images where Jesus is depicted as the **fountain of life**. He is 'the spring of water welling up to eternal life' (Jn 4:14); 'the food which endures to eternal life' (Jn 6:27); 'the bread of life' (Jn 6:35, 48) his 'flesh' and 'blood' give 'eternal life' (Jn 6:53–54) and he is the 'light of life' (Jn 8:12). It will come in useful later on to remember that belief not only in Jesus, present among the faithful, but also in the name of Jesus, no longer in tangible contact with his disciples, was considered to give them life: 'These are written that you may believe that Jesus is the Christ, the Son of God, and that believing you may have **life in his name**' (Jn 20:31).

In John, as in the Synoptic Gospels, with the possible exception of Matthew's account of the last judgement (Mt 25:46), only the Jewish followers of Jesus are promised eternal life. We have to wait first until the charismatic conversion of the Roman centurion Cornelius and ultimately until the acceptance of the apostolic mission of

Paul in the Graeco-Roman world before encountering for the first time the possibility of non-Jews being judged worthy of eternal life without being compelled to pass through Judaism.

Whereas in the Synoptics Jesus is painted as the guiding light to the kingdom of God and in it to eternal life, in John we witness a more advanced stage of doctrinal development. Eternal life can be inherited by those who believe, not just in the words of Jesus the teacher, but in his heavenly power deriving from his special relationship with God the Father.

In conclusion, it must be recalled that Jesus' eschatological imagery in Mark, Matthew and Luke is centred not on resurrection,[5] but on the idea of the 'kingdom of God' or 'kingdom of heaven'. This is revealed by the frequency of the two formulae in the Synoptic Gospels where they appear more than eighty times as against two occurrences in a single passage of the Gospel of John (Jn 3:3, 5). Resurrection is an uncommon concept in the authentic message of Jesus revealed by the Synoptics, and the source of its central significance in Christian ideology must be sought elsewhere (see chapter 13). As for 'eternal life', while only sporadically used in the Synoptics, it gains increasing momentum and import in the Gospel of John.

8

Predictions of the resurrection of Jesus

All three Synoptic evangelists emphatically state that during the final period of his life Jesus repeatedly announced to his closest disciples his death and his resurrection. The Gospel of John contains nothing comparable. In it only an obscure forewarning is given, not to the apostles, but privately to Nicodemus, in the form of a symbolical reinterpretation of an Old Testament image, the brazen serpent which was set up by Moses in the wilderness as a talisman to protect against snake bites (Num 21:6–9). As it saved the Jews who looked at it with trust, so will the 'uplifted' (crucified, risen and glorified) Jesus give eternal life to the believers (Jn 3:14). We find another cryptic reference in Matthew's treatment of the sign of Jonah, alluding to the duration of Jesus' stay in the tomb before his resurrection: 'For as Jonah was three days and three nights in the belly of the whale, so will the Son of man be three days and three nights in the heart of the earth' (Mt 12:40).

Elsewhere Mark, Matthew and Luke are less mysterious. With greater or smaller detail they make Jesus foretell the events of the end of his life. The first occasion is Peter's confession at Caesarea Philippi of the Messiahship of Jesus acknowledged by all the apostles:

*And he began to teach them that the Son of man must suffer many things, and be rejected by the elders and the chief priests and the scribes, and be killed, and **after three days rise again** (Mk 8:30–31).*

Jesus forbade Peter to proclaim that he was the Christ and in the form of a tacit denial of the confession, he emphatically foretold the tragedy of his end and his rising from the dead.

In one or possibly two of the six occurrences, the last of them dated to two days before Passover, the forewarning is restricted to the arrest and the cross with no mention of the resurrection (Lk 9:44; Mt 26:2). Luke 9:22 repeats almost word for word the statement of Mark as quoted above (Mk 8:30–31) and so does Matthew too (Mt 16:21). Peter's reaction is at odds with the story which includes the resurrection. He 'rebukes' Jesus: 'God forbid, Lord! This shall never happen to you', a reproach that in turn provokes Jesus' angry ripòste and disapproval of Peter: 'Get behind me, Satan!' (Mt 16:22–23; Mk 8:32–33).

The second, indirect prediction is associated with Jesus' order to the three leading apostles, Peter, James and John, who have accompanied him to the Galilean mountain of the Transfiguration, not to divulge their experience until he has risen from the dead (Mk 9:9; Mt 17:9). The extraordinary clarity of the announcement is offset by Mark's remark that the apostles had no idea what rising from the dead meant which, in turn, confirms our finding that resurrection had had no prominent part in Jesus' previous teaching.

The third premonition is also situated in Galilee. It is couched in generic terms – Jesus will be delivered into the hands of unspecified 'men' – and as in the previous case, the apostles did not know what he was talking about, but contrary to their habit, they were afraid to inquire (Mk 9:30–32; Mt 17:22–23; Lk 9:43–45).

The fourth episode is set during Jesus' last trip to Jerusalem, just a few days before Good Friday. In Mark's version it has all the appearances of a prophecy after the fact, mirroring in detail all the stages of the Passion, the arrest by the chief priests, the condemnation to death, the handing over to the Gentiles (the Romans), the mocking, spitting on and scourging, the execution and the rising from the dead on the third day.

In Luke, instead of adhering to the customary style of a direct prediction by Jesus, we encounter for the first time a reference to the fulfilment of prophecies: 'Behold, we are going up to Jerusalem, and everything that is written of the Son of man by the prophets will be accomplished' (Lk 18:31). The same formula is repeated later in Luke, first in the conversation of the risen Jesus with the disciples on the way to Emmaus:

O foolish men, and slow to believe all that the prophets have spoken! Was it not necessary that the Christ should suffer these things and enter into his glory? (Lk 24:25).

And later in Jesus' address to the apostles in Jerusalem:

These are my words which I spoke to you, while I was still with you, that everything written about me in the law of Moses and the prophets and the psalms must be fulfilled (Lk 24:44).

In the last, straightforward prediction, a couple of days before the crucifixion, Jesus foretells in Jerusalem his impending arrest and death: 'You know that after two days the Passover is coming, and the Son of man will be delivered up to be crucified' (Mt 26:2).

If we leave aside the examples of the brazen serpent and the sign of Jonah, all the predictions are couched in clear and simple language that no one could possibly misunderstand. It is hardly possible that they did not hear the message. Indeed, on one occasion Jesus is said to have explicitly drawn the apostles' attention to what he was going to tell them: 'Let these words sink into your ears; for the Son of man is to be delivered into the hands of men' (Lk 9:44).

In the circumstances, it is remarkable that the evangelists time and again assert, as we have shown above, that the disciples found the announcements of Jesus incomprehensible:

They kept the matter to themselves, questioning what the rising from the dead meant (Mk 9:10).

They did not understand the saying, and they were afraid to ask him (Mk 9:32; Lk 9:44).

But they understood none of these things; this saying was hid from them, and they did not grasp what was said (Lk 18:34).

Later we learn something even more bizarre. The women friends of Jesus had actually forgotten what appears to have been their Master's most momentous statement until two angels in human appearance refreshed their memory (Lk 24:8).

One detail of the prediction is reiterated several times: the resurrection was expected to take place either 'on the third day' or 'after three days'. The typology of Jonah involves three days and three nights, corresponding to the time spent by the fugitive prophet in the belly of the big fish (Mt 12:40). Mark, on the other hand, speaks of 'after three days' (8:31; 9:31; 10:34) and Matthew and Luke refer to 'the third day' (Mt 16:21; 17:22; 20:19; Lk 9:22; 18:33; 24:46).

According to our way of counting, three days mean three 24-hour periods, but Jesus did not remain that long in his grave, as he was buried late afternoon on Friday and the resurrection is placed by the evangelists before dawn on Sunday. The phrase of Matthew and Luke, 'on the third day', would suit this reckoning, but it is more likely that the expression was chosen because it was a typical Old Testament formula marking seven significant biblical events occurring 'on the third day'. Among these are Abraham's discovery of the site of the sacrifice of Isaac: 'On the third day Abraham lifted up his eyes and saw the place afar off' (Gen 22:4) and Hosea's prophecy of the resurrection, 'After two days, he will revive us, on the third day he will raise us up' (Hos 6:2). One should also take into account that according to rabbinic reckoning part of a day or night counted as a full day or night (yShabbath 2a; bPesahim 4a).

There may have been another reason in favour of the choice of the third day. According to an ancient Jewish belief, after death the departed soul did not wish to abandon the body and was keen to rejoin it. Hence for three days it continued to hover over the body or kept on revisiting the grave (Genesis Rabba 100:7; yYebamoth 15c).

The predictions of the resurrection of Jesus and the reactions ascribed to the disciples are filled with oddities. Contrary to what we have found in connection with the surviving sayings of Jesus about afterlife, they suddenly turn resurrection into an issue of central importance, one that was forecast not only by Jesus, but also foreseen and foretold by the prophets of the Old Testament. In other words, the execution and subsequent resurrection of Jesus were part of his foreknowledge and on account of the relevant 'prophecies', belonged to traditional Jewish messianic expectation. If so, the arrest, crucifixion and resurrection of Jesus could not have come out of the blue. On the contrary, they must have been dead certainties for his apostles and disciples.

Yet all the four Gospels prove the contrary. The cross and the resurrection were unexpected, perplexing, indeed incomprehensible for the apostles. When Jesus was captured in the garden of Gethsemane, his apostles abandoned him and fled, at least according to the testimony of the Synoptic evangelists.[1] Peter even denied that he had known Jesus. As for the resurrection, no one was awaiting it, nor were the apostles willing to believe the good news brought to them by the women who had visited the tomb of Jesus.

In fact, we have two sets of evidence which contradict one another with no possibility for reconciliation, since it is hardly likely that the dishonourable behaviour of the apostles does not correspond to reality and is a mere invention. One must conclude that the predictions by Jesus of his death and resurrection and his reference to biblical prophecies about his suffering and glorification are inauthentic. They appear to represent the tracing back to Jesus of some of the weapons of the apologetical-polemical arsenal of the Jewish-Christian Church: Jesus informed his confidants about the cross and the resurrection, which could also be guessed by enlightened readers of the Bible. The realization of the predictions proved to the apostles and to the members of the nascent Church that however astonishing the two events appeared, they were willed, foreordained and engineered by God.

9

Resurrection accounts in the New Testament regarding persons other than Jesus

The resurrection of Jesus is by no means the one and only revival story in the New Testament. In addition to rumours of a risen John the Baptist, the Gospels and the Acts of the Apostles mention five particular resuscitations: three are attributed to Jesus and one each to St Peter and St Paul.

When Jesus inquired from his apostles about who people thought he was, they referred to rumours according to which he was the reborn Elijah, Jeremiah or another biblical prophet. He was also held to be John the Baptist (Mk 8:28; Mt 16:14; Lk 9:19). A similar story circulated in Galilee in the court of Herod Antipas, purporting that Jesus was the reincarnation of John the Baptist, whom Antipas had executed (Mk 6:14–16; Mt 14:1–2; Lk 9:7–9). The expectation of the return of Elijah was part of Old Testament tradition: the prophet Malachi spoke of God dispatching again his messenger, Elijah (Mal 3:1; 4:5), and the New Testament also associates John the Baptist with the risen Elijah (Mk 1:2).

The first of the resuscitations reported in the Synoptics, that of the daughter of a certain Jairus, is placed at the beginning of the Galilean career of Jesus. There is uncertainty among the evangelists about the identity of the father, who approached Jesus (Mk 5:21–43; Mt 9:18–26; Lk 40–56). While all agree that he was called Jairus, or Yair in Hebrew, Mark and Luke describe him as the president of a local synagogue, whereas in Matthew he is a nameless 'ruler', an important figure, no doubt belonging to the local council of elders. In Matthew the girl is already dead and the father invites Jesus to come to his house and raise her. In the other two Gospels she is on the point of dying and the news of her death reaches the father during his conversation with Jesus. Although Jesus tries to disguise the miraculous quality of his intervention and equivocally refers to her condition as sleep, a designation that serves also as a metaphor for death, the sarcastic reaction of the attendants makes clear that by the time of the arrival of the miracle-worker, the twelve-year-old young woman was no longer among the living (Lk 8:53).

According to Mark and Luke, the performance of Jesus' miracle is witnessed by three apostles and the parents of the girl. Like healings and exorcisms, the resuscitation too was brought about by a command, *Talitha cum*,[1] reproduced in Aramaic in Mark and followed by a slightly expanded Greek translation, 'Little girl, I say to you, arise!' In Luke it appears only in straight literal Greek, 'Child, arise!' In Matthew, the revivification was preceded by bodily contact. Meeting Jesus, the father asked him to lay his hands on the dead girl and on their arrival in the house Jesus grasped her hand and raised her up. Luke expressly states that the spirit returned to her, implying thereby that she rose from the dead rather than just woke up from a coma. In conformity with his habit, Jesus forbade the divulgation of the miracle, but predictably the rumour of it spread in the neighbouring districts.

The second raising of the dead, transmitted only by Luke, is said to have happened in full publicity in Nain, an otherwise unknown Galilean village situated not far from

Capernaum. It was observed by Jesus' disciples and a great crowd. At the gate of the locality, Jesus and his followers met a funeral cortège carrying a young man, the only son of a widowed mother. Once more, the raising of the dead is performed by touch and speech. Jesus put his hand on the bier and issued the order, 'Young man, I say to you, arise!', probably '*Talya qum*' in Aramaic. When the dead youth sat up and started to speak, the onlookers proclaimed Jesus a great prophet and, as one would expect, the news was broadcast far and wide in the country (Lk 7:11–17).

These resuscitations recall the Old Testament stories of Elijah and Elisha (see pp. 30–32). While the reviving of the son of the widow from Zarephath and the son of the Shunamite woman increased the fame of the ancient prophets as miracle-workers, nothing is said about the further life of the two young men. Likewise, in the Galilee of the first century AD, the reputation of Jesus continued to grow after his raising of a girl and a young man, but neither the daughter of Jairus nor the resuscitated youth from Nain is mentioned thereafter. Similarly, no recipient of Jesus' charismatic healing and exorcistic activity is referred to again, with the exception of Mary Magdalene, out of whom Jesus is said to have expelled seven demons (Lk 8:2; Mk 16:9).

In the Synoptic Gospels, as well as in the Acts of the Apostles, raising the dead differs from the stories of Elijah and Elisha in so far as it is connected with the final period preceding the establishment of the kingdom of God. Thus in a message sent to the imprisoned John the Baptist, Jesus implied that his ministry was accompanied by the rising of the dead and foreshadowed the onset of the messianic age: 'The blind receive their sight and the lame walk, lepers are cleansed and **the dead are raised up** (Mt 11:4–5; Lk 7:22).

However, by the time of the Fourth Gospel, the outlook had changed and a clear distinction was made between 'the resurrection at the last day' (Jn 11:24) and the resuscitation of a person in what counted as the present time, as can be seen in the account of Lazarus. According to the story told by John (Jn 11:1–46), Lazarus had fallen ill, died and had already been buried for four days before Jesus arrived in Bethany, the home town of Lazarus and his sisters. By then the decomposition of the corpse had already started. Yet when Jesus cried out with a loud voice, 'Lazarus, come out!', the dead man, with his hands and feet bound, and his face wrapped with a cloth, rose and emerged from the tomb. The attendants had to unbind him before he could properly walk.

The principal discrepancy between John's report and the Synoptics relates to the aftermath of this resurrection. In the Synoptics the resurrected persons are assumed to live on, yet they disappear over the horizon. They are simply the beneficiaries of the miracle-working activity of the holy man. By contrast, we learn from the fourth evangelist that many Jews, friends and neighbours who came to comfort the bereaved sisters of Lazarus, saw what happened and made the story public, thus turning not only Jesus, but even Lazarus, into a celebrity. So when the raised Lazarus was sitting at the table at a dinner party in the company of Jesus, a great local crowd surrounded the house, eager to see the former dead man enjoying a meal next to the prophet who had restored him to life. According to John, the impact of the sight had led many Jews to believe in Jesus, and this nearly brought a premature second death to Lazarus. We are told that the chief priests, in order to stop the growing popularity of Jesus, were plotting the assassination of Lazarus (Jn 12:9–11).[2]

As has been noted, according to the Synoptic Gospels, charismatic power was not the exclusive privilege of Jesus. He is reported as sharing it with his disciples right from the beginning of his Galilean activity. When the twelve apostles were sent on their first missionary tour, they were commanded to preach, heal the sick, cleanse lepers, expel evil spirits and **raise the dead** (Mt 10:7–8). In fact, a case of resuscitation is attributed on a later occasion to Peter, who restored to life a charitable woman disciple from Joppa, called 'Deer' – Tabitha in Aramaic and Dorcas in Greek (Acts 9:36–41). Paul matched Peter's performance and apparently revived Eutychus, a young man from the Mysenian coastal city of Troas in Asia Minor. The unfortunate youth fell to his death from a third-storey window after dozing off during Paul's overlong after-dinner speech (Acts 20:7–10). We do not hear of either of them again, but their stories serve to illustrate the continuing charisma in the early Jesus movement which enveloped the ministry of Jesus and of his apostles and disciples with a splendid messianic aura.

How were such resurrection stories received by first-century AD Palestinian Jews? Josephus may help to answer this question. His depiction of the extraordinary miracles of the prophet Elisha, which many of Josephus' co-religionists have accepted as established facts, gives a valuable insight into the mentality of the age. No doubt the sophisticated Josephus preferred to sit on the fence, especially as he was addressing a Roman readership:

Now I have written about these matters as I have found them in my readings; if anyone wishes to judge otherwise of them, I shall not object to his holding a different opinion (Ant 10:281).

However, popular Jewish circles in the age of Jesus were without such scruples. They happily accepted miracles and some of them joined the Jesus movement and believed in the resurrection of Christ despite the problematic character of the Gospel evidence as we shall outline in the next chapter.

Appendix

A token resurrection after the death of Jesus

A unique and otherwise unclassifiable incident is reported by Matthew as coinciding with the death of Jesus on the cross. According to his Gospel, the tragic event was marked by an earthquake, a common feature together with thunder, tornado and fire, of the eschatological crescendo in scripture (Isa 29:6; Ps 18:7; Mk 13:8; Mt 24:7; Lk 21:11). Following this earthquake, rocks were split and tombs were opened. Out of them emerged the risen bodies of many saints who were seen by numerous inhabitants of Jerusalem following the resurrection of Jesus (Mt 27:51–53). Needless to say, nothing is heard of them afterwards.

Matthew's account is best understood as symbolical and suggests that an anticipatory resurrection, the disgorging of the raised 'saints' (i.e. righteous) by the gaping tombs, happened immediately after Jesus had expired. Yet the saints are said to have appeared to 'many', not on Friday, but early on Sunday. Therefore the religious message hints at a link between the death and consequent resurrection of Jesus and the general raising of the dead. This idea points to St Paul's definition of the rising of Jesus as the 'first fruits' of the general resurrection. It is to be observed that Matthew speaks again of an earthquake at the moment of the resurrection of Jesus (Mt 28:2). There is no further reference to the story in New Testament tradition.

10

The Gospel accounts of the resurrection of Jesus

Preliminary: The burial of Jesus[1]

The three Synoptics, Mark, Matthew and Luke, report that at the approach of nightfall on Friday, 15 Nisan, Joseph of Arimathea, a member of the Sanhedrin and a crypto-sympathizer of Jesus, obtained permission from the Roman governor to take down the body from the cross. The centurion in command of the execution squad testified before Pontius Pilate that Jesus had already died, and Joseph was granted permission to proceed with a hasty burial. Without the use of the customary spices, he wrapped the body in a linen shroud. He then laid it in a freshly hewn rock tomb, the entrance of which was protected by a large and heavy rollable stone. Mary Magdalene and another woman, also named Mary, and one more or several further Galilean women are said to have watched Joseph of Arimathea burying Jesus (Mk 15:42–47; Mt 27:57–61; Lk 23:50–56).

The tradition transmitted by John partly disagrees with the Synoptics. The crucifixion takes place on 14, not 15, Nisan. Joseph of Arimathea is helped by a second secret disciple of Jesus, Nicodemus, to lay Jesus in the tomb (Jn 3:2). Nicodemus brings a linen shroud, together with a large quantity of spices, and the two hurriedly place Jesus in a new tomb in the midst of a garden, without being observed by any woman witness (Jn 19:38–42). In John's account there is no need for the women's services as Jesus' body has already been anointed by the two men.

Matthew, unlike the other evangelists, further notes that the Jewish leaders, fearing that the disciples of Jesus might steal his body to fake the fulfilment of his predicted resurrection, ask Pilate to keep the tomb under military guard. The governor leaves the matter in their hands and the chief priests post sentries at the tomb after sealing the entrance of the grave.

Thus the scene is set for the story of the resurrection. The evidence will be considered in reverse chronological order, starting with John, the latest of the Gospels, and finishing with Mark, the earliest.

1. The resurrection in John

Chapters 20 and 21 of the Fourth Gospel recount the resurrection of Jesus and the appearances that followed it. With chapter 20 ends John's original account, stating:

Now Jesus did many other signs in the presence of the disciples, which are not written in this book; but these are written that you may believe that Jesus is the Christ, the Son of God, and that believing you may have life in his name (Jn 20:30–31).

Chapter 21 has its own particular conclusion, which reveals its supplementary nature:

But there are also many other things which Jesus did; were every one of them to be written, I suppose that the world itself could not contain the books that would be written (Jn 21:25).

John offers the most detailed picture of the purported apparitions of the risen Jesus. His narrative consists of eight stages:

1. Early on Sunday morning, 'while it was still dark', Mary Magdalene, without being accompanied by other Galilean women, went to the burial place and found it open, with the stone rolled away (Jn 20:1).

2. At once she reported to Peter and the anonymous 'beloved disciple' that the body of Jesus had been moved by unknown people. 'They have taken the Lord out of the tomb, and we do not know where they have laid him' (Jn 20:2).

3. The two men ran to the sepulchre and Peter, who entered first, noticed only the linen cloths and the napkin separately folded, but saw no body. The 'beloved disciple' is said to have at once 'believed', although at that moment neither he nor Peter knew that Christ's resurrection had been predicted either by Jesus or by the scriptures. Thereupon, according to John, both left the place and went home without saying a word or expressing any surprise or emotion (Jn 20:3–10).

4. By contrast, Mary Magdalene, who had followed Peter and his companion to the garden, remained there weeping. Peering into the tomb, she saw two angels, and when they asked her why she was crying, she told them that someone had removed the body of Jesus and transferred it to an unknown location. The angels made no comment (Jn 20:11–13).

5. Next, Mary became aware of the presence of a man standing behind her, whom she took for the gardener in charge of the burial ground. Presuming that it was he who had displaced the body, she inquired where he had put it, so that she could take it away. When the presumed gardener addressed her as 'Mary', she identified him as Jesus and called him in Aramaic 'Rabbuni', my Master. She was ordered by the visually unrecognizable Jesus not to cling to him as he had not yet gone to the Father and he told her to inform the apostles about his impending ascent on high (Jn 20:20:17). So Mary Magdalene hastened to the disciples and reported to them all that she had seen and heard (Jn 20:14–18).

6. Mary Magdalene's vision was followed by the appearance of Jesus to the disciples on the same evening. Although the doors were shut, he entered the house and breathed on them the Holy Spirit, thus granting them power to pardon or retain sins in the course of their apostolic mission (Jn 20:19–23).

7. Thomas the Twin, who was not present, did not trust his colleagues' testimony:

But he said to them, 'Unless I see in his hands the print of the nails, and place my finger in the mark of the nails, and place my hand in his side, I will not believe' (Jn 20:19–25).

8. Eight days later, the figure of Jesus was seen re-entering the house despite the shut doors, and he invited Thomas to touch his wounds. He did so and believed (Jn 20:26–29).

John's account of the resurrection is followed by an additional episode, in which a third apparition to some disciples takes place not in Jerusalem, but in Galilee, by the Sea of Tiberias. Seven apostles spent the whole night fishing without catching anything. At dawn they saw a man on the beach, but like Mary Magdalene, they did not recognize him as Jesus until the 'beloved disciple' told them that he was the Lord (Jn 21:1–7).

The rest of the chapter is not directly relevant to the resurrection story. It goes without saying that John is substantially at variance with the Synoptics.

2. The resurrection in Luke

Luke's resurrection narrative, nearly as long as John's, is made up of five parts:

1. Mary Magdalene, Joanna and Mary the mother of James, together with other Galilean women disciples, arrived at the tomb early on Sunday to anoint the body. They knew the place, having kept Joseph of Arimathea under observation two days earlier. They found the stone rolled away and the tomb empty. Two men in glittering clothes suddenly appeared and reminded them of Jesus' earlier predictions:

Remember how he told you, while he was still in Galilee, that the Son of man must be delivered into the hands of sinful men, and be crucified, and on the third day rise (Lk 24:6).

Mary Magdalene and her friends informed the eleven apostles, but they haughtily shrugged off their words as women's silly tales (Lk 24:1–12).

2. On the same Sunday, Cleopas and another disciple travelled from Jerusalem to the village of Emmaus and were discussing the tragedy of Jesus. They met a stranger on the road, who did not seem to know anything about the events that had shaken up Jerusalem during the previous days. The disciples put him in the picture, told him of the empty tomb and about the women hearing from angels that Jesus was alive, and that some of their male colleagues had confirmed the disappearance of the body. At that juncture, the stranger proceeded to demonstrate to them from the scriptures that the Messiah had first to suffer and then be glorified. They invited him to stay with them in Emmaus and during the meal they were sharing, at the sight of some unspecified idiosyncrasy in the stranger's benediction ritual, it dawned on them that their travelling companion was Jesus. But by then he had vanished.

The two disciples at once rejoined the apostles and their associates in Jerusalem, but even before they could report what they had seen, they were told that Jesus had appeared to Peter (Lk 24:13–35).

3. At that moment the apostles and disciples saw a ghost: 'They were startled and frightened, and supposed that they saw a spirit' (Lk 24:37).

This ghost turned out to be Jesus, whose wounded hands and feet could be touched. To prove his real humanity, he asked for food and ate some fish before their eyes (Lk 24:36–43).

4. The risen Jesus then explained to them all the scriptural predictions that related to him in the Law, the Prophets and the Psalms, and ordered the apostles to evangelize in his name across the whole world (Lk 24:46). To make the story consistent with the Acts of the Apostles, where the Ascension takes place forty days after Easter,

the apostles are also commanded not to leave Jerusalem until they have received the Holy Spirit (Lk 24:49).

5. Yet apparently on the same day, the Sunday of the resurrection, Jesus took them out of Jerusalem to Bethany, where they saw him rising to heaven (Lk 24:50–53).

3. The resurrection in Matthew

The account of Matthew, consisting of seven sections, is considerably shorter than those of John and Luke:

1. Two women, Mary Magdalene and 'the other Mary' (no doubt the mother of James, as in Luke 24:10), went to the tomb on Sunday towards dawn. As they are not said to be carrying spices, we must surmise that their visit was motivated by piety (Mt 28:1).

2. In the course of an earthquake, an angel, wearing shiny white garments, rolled back the stone from the opening of the rock cavity and sat on it. The guards posted there by the chief priests 'trembled and became like dead men' (Mt 28:2–4).

3. The angel reassured the frightened women and announced that Jesus had risen, hence the empty tomb, and ordered them to report the news to the disciples and instruct them to meet Jesus in Galilee (Mt 28:5–7).

4. Frightened as well as delighted, the women immediately set out to do as they were told, and on the way they had a vision of Jesus, who repeated to them the angel's instructions (Mt 28:8–10).

5. When the guards recovered their senses, they went to tell the chief priests about the disappearance of the body of Jesus. The priests bribed them to pretend that

the apostles had stolen the corpse during the night. This rumour continued to circulate among the Jews even in Matthew's day (Mt 28:11–15).

6. Jesus was not seen in Jerusalem. The only vision the eleven apostles experienced was on a Galilean mountain. On that occasion, some of them believed, but others did not (Mt 28:16–17).

7. The resurrection narrative and the Gospel end with the risen Jesus commissioning his disciples to baptize all the nations (Mt 28:18–20).

4. The resurrection in Mark

The oldest codices of Mark's Gospel, the Sinaiticus and the Vaticanus (fourth century AD), as well as the old Sinaitic Syriac translation (fourth/fifth century), abruptly terminate chapter 16 at verse 8. This is the so-called shorter ending of Mark. The longer ending (Mk 16:9–19), a later revision of the account, will follow in section b.

(a) The shorter ending

This compact finale of Mark constitutes by far the briefest account of Jesus' rising from the dead. In fact, the generally agreed chronological sequence of the four Gospels, Mark, Matthew, Luke, John, presents a progressively developing description of the resurrection. Three stages can be distinguished in the chain of events as recorded in Mark 16:1–8.

1. Three women, Mary Magdalene, Mary the mother of James and Salome,[2] went to the tomb of Jesus before sunrise on Sunday with spices to anoint his body, wondering

how they would be able to remove the heavy stone from the entrance (Mk 16:1–3).

2. They found the stone rolled back and saw inside the tomb a young man seated and robed in a white garment, from whom they learned that Jesus was no longer in his grave. The women were commanded to announce his resurrection to the apostles and tell them to meet him in Galilee (Mk 16:4–7).

3. Terrified, they did not follow the order and kept the story to themselves:

They went out and fled from the tomb; for trembling and astonishment had come upon them; and they said nothing to any one, for they were afraid (Mk 16:8).

The Gospel dramatically breaks off on this note of suspense. Mark abstains altogether from mentioning any resurrection appearance. However, a later editor or editors of the chapter who appended the longer ending felt it necessary to smooth down the ruggedness of Mark's story and fill in the gaps under the influence of the Gospels of Luke and John.

(b) The longer ending
The longer ending completes the main gap and inserts into Mark's narrative several apparitions of the risen Jesus:

1. Early on Sunday, Jesus revealed himself in a vision to Mary Magdalene, out of whom he had previously expelled seven demons (see Lk 8:2). Mary reported the matter to the grieving apostles, but they refused to believe her (Mk 16:9–11).

2. The longer ending makes Jesus appear in the country

to two travelling disciples, as he did in Luke's Emmaus episode. Without delay, they acquainted the apostles with their experience, but their report, like that of Mary Magdalene, fell on deaf ears (Mk 16:12–13).

3. Next, Jesus appeared in a vision to the eleven apostles and rebuked them for their lack of faith in the testimony of Mary Magdalene and the two travellers (Mk 16:14).

4. The vision ends with the risen Jesus ordering the apostles to proclaim the message of the Gospel to the whole world and promising to them the gift of charismatic powers to be exercised in his name (Mk 16:15–18).

5. Then, seemingly on the same day, Jesus was lifted up to heaven to sit at God's right hand (see also Lk 24:51). The disciples, in turn, departed to preach the Gospel and confirmed their message by the charismatic miracles guaranteed to them by Jesus (Mk 16:19–20).

Appendix

The Ascension

Since the longer ending of Mark's resurrection story and that of Luke contain a description of Jesus' ascent to heaven, it is appropriate to include here some comments on the account of the Ascension given by Luke in the opening chapter of the Acts of the Apostles. The three sources yield conflicting data.

1. In the dedication of the Acts of the Apostles to his patron, Theophilus (see also Lk 1:3), Luke refers to his 'first book' – the Gospel – dealing with Jesus' life and teaching up to the moment of his elevation to heaven, seemingly on Easter Sunday. According to this second

book, Jesus stayed with his disciples for forty days after his resurrection, instructing them about the kingdom of God, during which period they remained in Jerusalem and waited for the Holy Spirit (Acts 1:1–5).[3]

2. While refusing to reveal to the apostles the moment of the restoration of the kingdom of Israel, no doubt identical with the inauguration of God's kingdom, Jesus promised them the charismatic gift of the Holy Spirit in order to make them his witnesses among Jews and Gentiles (Acts 1:6–8).

3. From the Mount of Olives (Acts 1:12), he was then borne heavenwards by a cloud until he disappeared from the sight of the apostles. At once two white-robed men (angelic beings?) materialized and announced that he would return: 'This Jesus, who was taken up from you into heaven, will come in the same way as you saw him go into heaven' (Acts 1:11).

The sketches assembled in this chapter constitute the sum total of the New Testament's 'documentary' evidence concerning the resurrection of Jesus.

All that remains now is to assess the reports included in the Gospels and supplement them with the relevant extracts from the Acts, Paul and the rest of the New Testament material.[4] The existing interpretations represent the full scale of the spectrum. To quote the two extremes, N. T. Wright, the learned twenty-first-century Bishop of Durham, author of a disquisition of over 800 pages, concludes that the resurrection of Jesus was a historical event.[5] By contrast, the more succinct David Friedrich Strauss, one of the creators of the historico-critical approach to the Gospels in the nineteenth century, declares that 'rarely has an incredible fact been worse attested, and never has a badly attested fact been intrinsically less credible'.[6]

11

Initial evaluation of the accounts of the resurrection of Jesus

While a full appraisal of the New Testament evidence concerning the meaning of Jesus' resurrection will have to wait until chapter 15 and the Epilogue, our preliminary task here is to clarify the confused and often contradictory data contained in the Gospels and in chapter 1 of the Acts of the Apostles.

The uncertainties concern the sequence of the events, the identity of the informants and witnesses, the number and location of the apparitions of Jesus, the presentation of prophecies relating to the resurrection and finally the date of Jesus' purported departure from earth. The discrepancies among the various accounts regarding both details and substance cannot have escaped the eyes of attentive readers.

The most significant peculiarity of the resurrection stories is that they nowhere suggest that the rising of Jesus from the dead was expected by anyone. In Matthew, Mark and John the resurrection complex is presented as falling straight out of the blue, a complete surprise. Luke mentions Jesus' earlier announcement of his rising that was either misunderstood or forgotten (!?!) by his disciples.

The most irreconcilable versions are yielded by John on the one hand, and by Mark's shorter ending – or Mark A – on the other.

In John's narrative the removal of the stone from the grave is not linked to the idea of resurrection, but is attributed by Mary Magdalene to some unknown person who had entered it and had taken away the body of Jesus. The idea of resurrection does not arise at all in her report to two apostles. Neither is there any hint at resurrection in the conversation between Mary Magdalene and the two angels.

At the other extreme, Mark A offers as the sole source of the story of the resurrection the words of an unknown young man clad in white (an angel?). The women are told that the tomb is empty because Jesus has risen. Mary Magdalene and her two friends communicate their experience to no one. There is no reference to any vision of Jesus in Mark A, just as there is no allusion to the empty tomb in Paul's account in 1 Corinthians 15.

Characteristically, Jesus was never identified in any of his appearances. Mary Magdalene took him for the gardener and the disciples travelling to Emmaus, and the apostles by the Sea of Tiberias, thought he was a stranger. In Jerusalem the apostles believed they were seeing a ghost. The risen Christ did not display the familiar features of Jesus of Nazareth.

Going through the stories, stage by stage, each of them contains unique elements missing from the other Gospels. Some of them lack parallels, others attest details that are irreconcilable:

1. In John, Mary Magdalene ventures alone to the tomb and conveys her discovery of the disappearance of Jesus' body to Peter and the 'beloved disciple'. Peter and his companion do not trust Mary and go to check her report. The 'beloved disciple' *believes*, but we are not told exactly

what he believes. By implication, this means that Peter does not share his belief. Still in John, Mary Magdalene announces to the apostles that Jesus is going to the Father, apparently excluding the possibility of a further stay with them, let alone of a visit to Galilee. However, this statement is contradicted in John's additional account in chapter 21, where Jesus meets some of his apostles by the Sea of Tiberias. In Matthew, a Galilean mountain is the only place where Jesus appears to the apostles. In Mark A a visit to Galilee is announced by the young man in the tomb, but the matter is dropped there and then. Unparalleled are the confirmation of Peter's leading position among the apostles, and the two episodes relating to Thomas as recorded in John.

2. Luke's particular contribution consists in his emphasis on the prophecies announcing the resurrection. The two men (angels?) seen by the women at the tomb recall Jesus' prediction of his suffering and rising and in both his conversation with the disciples on the road to Emmaus and during his appearance to the apostles in Jerusalem Jesus expounds the biblical prophecies foretelling his resurrection. Peter's prominence is indicated by a special vision of Jesus, exclusive to him, prior to the return of the disciples from Emmaus and the apostles' vision of Christ in Jerusalem. Is this the apparition to Peter mentioned later by Paul (1 Cor 15:5)?

3. In his resurrection account Matthew speaks of the guards fainting when the angel opens the tomb in the midst of an earthquake and of their later report of the event to the chief priests. Also peculiar to Matthew is the claim, attributed to the priests, that the apostles have stolen the corpse, and the reference to the continued circulation of the rumour among hostile Jews at the time of Matthew's

writing his Gospel. A further detail attested only by Matthew concerns the appearance of Jesus to the two women who were bringing to the apostles the news of Jesus' resurrection. This is the only apparition of Jesus mentioned by Matthew as occurring in Jerusalem. Finally, only Matthew describes the meeting of Jesus with his apostles on a mountain in Galilee, and notes that several of them continued to harbour doubts, a detail left unresolved unlike John's story of Thomas, first doubting but later believing.

4. The unparalleled characteristics in the shorter ending of Mark are the evangelist's assertion that the frightened female witnesses of the empty tomb kept the story to themselves, and the complete absence of apparitions. In the longer ending of Mark, the unmatched remarks relate to the unwillingness of the apostles to believe the testimony of either Mary Magdalene or the disciples returning from Emmaus about their vision of Jesus, and to the detailed list of charismatic phenomena promised to the believers in the risen Christ.

Finally, there are flat contradictions between the sources:

1. The accounts differ regarding the number and identity of the women who visited the tomb: one, Mary Magdalene, in John and Mark B; two, Mary Magdalene and the other Mary, in Matthew; three, Mary Magdalene, Mary the mother of James and Salome, in Mark A; and several, Mary Magdalene, Joanna, Mary the mother of James and other women from Galilee, in Luke. Such variations would have rendered the testimony unacceptable in a Jewish law court.

2. The number of persons seen by the women at or in the tomb and the message they have received from them vary too. In John two angels appear to Mary Magdalene,

but they do not ask her to do anything. In Luke the two men remind the women of Christ's prophecy about his resurrection. In Matthew and in Mark A, the one angel entrusts Mary Magdalene and her friends with the duty to convey to the apostles the news of the resurrection of Jesus and an invitation to meet him in Galilee. However, in Mark the women do not obey this command; nor do we find there, not even in the longer ending, a reference to a trip to Galilee.

3. The number and the location of the apparitions of Jesus also greatly differ in the various Gospels. In Mark A there is none. In John, prior to his apparition to the apostles, Jesus shows himself to Mary Magdalene; in Matthew, to the women on their way to the apostles; in Luke to the two disciples in Emmaus and to Peter alone in Jerusalem, while Mark's longer ending speaks of apparitions of Jesus both to Mary Magdalene in Jerusalem and to the travelling disciples away from the capital. A vision by all the apostles occurring in Jerusalem is reported by Luke and Mark B (the longer version of Mark). The same is referred to in John, except that on the first occasion Thomas is absent and eight days later he is present. By contrast, according to Matthew, a Galilean mountain is the setting of the only apparition of Jesus to the apostles, while in John's supplementary evidence the Sea of Tiberias is the site of a final vision of Jesus by seven apostles. Luke, by contrast, expressly excludes any departure from Jerusalem, so for him no visionary encounter with Jesus can be situated in Galilee.

4. The apostolic mission is conferred on the disciples by the risen Jesus in Jerusalem according to John, Luke and the longer ending of Mark. According to Matthew this happens in Galilee. No actual meeting is stated in Mark A,

although a confusing mention of a promised encounter in Galilee figures in the instruction given by Mark's young man to the three women at the tomb.

5. Jesus' ascension to heaven takes place in Jerusalem in Mark B and by implication in John; in Bethany according to Luke; and on the Mount of Olives (in the area of Bethany) in the Acts of the Apostles. The sources are, however, at variance as regards the date of the event. Mark B puts it as Easter Sunday, but in the Acts it happens forty days later. Luke is equivocal. 'He led them out as far as Bethany' could be understood as immediately following Jesus' address to the apostles on the day of the resurrection, but the previous mention of staying in Jerusalem until they are 'clothed with power from on high' (an allusion to Pentecost) might suggest that Luke both in his Gospel and in the Acts allows nearly six weeks to elapse between Easter and the Ascension. In John, Jesus' journey to the Father is implied as happening on Easter Sunday, too.

In sum, a double argument is offered by the evangelists to prove the resurrection of Jesus. The first is the Synoptic version, based on the discovery of the empty tomb, and interpreted by one or two mysterious messengers as the proof that Jesus has risen. The legal value of this attestation is weakened by the fact that the witnesses are women. Female testimony, flippantly called nonsense (*lêros*) by the apostles in Luke, did not count in Jewish male society. Besides, the number and identity of the women witnesses remain in doubt. John and Luke try to improve the evidence by introducing two, or several, male witnesses (Peter and the 'beloved disciple' in John; 'some of those who were with us' in Luke) to confirm the women's report in so far as the disappearance of the body of Jesus is concerned. But, as will be shown in chapter 15, resurrection is not the only possible explanation of an empty tomb.

The second line of argument relies on visions and apparitions, which amount for those who accept them as first-hand evidence. But quite apart from the wide variations in the accounts regarding the time and place of the appearances and the identity of the visionaries, there are no *independent* witnesses from outside the circle of the followers of Jesus to corroborate them.[1] In fact, here and there we find hints indicating that even some of the insiders remained unconvinced. The risen Lazarus is said to have been seen moving, eating and drinking by all and sundry, friend and foe, so that the chief priests were thinking of eliminating him. Nothing similar is voiced about Jesus.

This glance at the evidence relative to the resurrection of Jesus ends on a perplexing note. We will return to it and to the theories it has generated after the investigation of the remainder of the material in the Acts of the Apostles, the letters of Saint Paul and the rest of the New Testament has been completed.

Synopsis of Parallels

MM = Mary Magdalene
BD = Beloved Disciple

ACTS	JOHN	LUKE	MATTHEW	MARK A	MARK B
	MM at tomb.	MM, Joanna & M mother of James.	MM + other Mary.	MM, Mary mother of James, Salome.	
	No spices.	Spices.	No spices.	Spices.	
			[Earthquake.]		
	Stone taken away.	Stone moved. 2 men seen. Reminded women of prophecies.	Stone moved by 1 angel. Tells women J gone. Apostles to meet him in Galilee.	Stone moved. 1 young man. J gone. Apostles to meet him in Galilee.	
			[Guards faint.]		
	[MM reports to Peter & Beloved Disciple that J's body removed.]				
		Women report to apostles. Disbelief.	Women frightened and joyful – run to apostles and report.	[Terrified women fled, not saying anything to anyone.]	
			[Vision of J on the way.]		[MM vision of J. Reports to apostles. Disbelief.]
		[Road to Emmaus. J explains prophecies. J seen by Peter.]			[Appearance to 2 disciples. They report. Disbelief.]
	[Peter & BD go to tomb. BD believes. Both go home.]				
			Women report to apostles.		
	MM sees 2 angels.				

405

ACTS	JOHN	LUKE	MATTHEW	MARK A	MARK B
			[Guards tell priests: body stolen.]		
	[MM sees gardener = J. Tell apostles J going to Father.]				
	Appearance to apostles in Jerusalem.	Appearance to apostles in Jerusalem. Touch and eating. J explains prophecies.			Appearance to apostles in Jerusalem. Rebuke.
	Mission + Holy Spirit in Jerusalem.	Mission + Holy Spirit. Stay in Jerusalem.			Mission [& promise of charisma] in Jerusalem.
	[Thomas absent.]				
	[Thomas present.]				
	Sea of Galilee. J unrecognized. Peter confirmed.		Appearance to apostles in Galilee: belief and disbelief. Mission.		
Ascension from Mt of Olives 40 days on.		Ascension from Bethany.			Ascension from Jerusalem.

12

The resurrection of Jesus in the Acts of the Apostles

Our examination of the sayings relating to the resurrection and to the topic of eternal life attributed to Jesus in the Gospels without necessarily implying bodily revival has turned up a surprisingly small amount of material. Afterlife did not seem to have occupied a central position in the thought of Jesus. Perhaps the most likely explanation for this absence is that during his ministry Jesus' eyes were so galvanized on the imminent arrival of the kingdom of God that both he and his followers assumed the transition between their era and the age of the kingdom of God to entail no passing through death. It was only during the brief period separating the cross from the almost instantly expected glorious return of Christ, a period during which some believers would inevitably pass away (1 Thess 4:13–17), that the problem of their resurrection would arise (see pp. 123–5).

The subject of the resurrection gains importance through the treatment of two aspects of the life of Jesus in the Gospels. To serve the apologetical needs of the Church in explaining the cross and the subsequent rising of the Messiah, the evangelists felt obliged to insert into their account of the final phase of the life of Jesus repeated predictions of his coming death and resurrection (see chapter 8). These prophecies apparently aimed at preparing

Jesus' closest associates for his unanticipated downfall and exaltation at the end of his career. It is obvious that in attempting to report the resurrection of Jesus, the evangelists faced an uphill task. Their accounts display numerous inconsistencies. Yet the seven or eight decades – the years between AD 30 and AD 100–110 that separate the death of Jesus from the completion of John's Gospel – witnessed a steadily increasing certainty in the early Church regarding the resurrection of Jesus and his spiritual presence among his followers.

Chronologically, the earliest comments are those of St Paul, whose literary activity extended over the fifties and possibly the early sixties of the first century. Nevertheless, the ideas attributed to the beginnings of the Jesus movement in Jerusalem and Judaea, chronicled in the Acts of the Apostles, have every probability of mirroring in substance the earliest thoughts of the first Jewish-Christian communities of Palestine. The Book of the Acts represents an ideology which still reflects the freshness and the lack of sophistication of the original Jewish followers of Jesus before Paul conquered the intellectual high ground in the Church and exported his ideology to the non-Jewish world of Syria, Asia Minor, Greece and Italy.

The contribution of the Acts to the development of the doctrine on the resurrection is significant, both in the section centred on the activity of Peter (chapters 1–12) and on that of Paul (chapters 13–28). Attention is focused on two main subjects: the fulfilment of prophecies regarding the ultimate fate of the Messiah, and the witnessing role assigned to the apostles, whose principal task was to prove to their compatriots the reality of the resurrection of Jesus.

If we hold the view that Luke is the author of both

the Third Gospel and the Acts we will not be surprised to discover that the prophetic argument in favour of the resurrection of Jesus is attested in both works. Already in Luke's Gospel, as against Mark, Matthew and John, the prediction of the cross and the resurrection is more emphatically assigned to the prophets of the Old Testament than to Jesus.

In the first speech, placed by Luke on the lips of Peter addressing the assembled Jewish multitude in Jerusalem at the feast of Pentecost, the leader of the apostles was determined to prove from the Psalms that the resurrection had been predestined by God and foretold by 'the prophet' David.[1] Luke uses Psalm 16:10, 'For Thou wilt not abandon my soul to Hades, nor let Thy Holy One see corruption', as one of his main proof texts for the resurrection. Pointing out that these words could not refer to David, who lay buried in his tomb in Jerusalem, Peter asserted that the Psalmist must have foretold the triumph over death of the future Messiah, Jesus Christ.[2] It is worth noting that the resurrection of Jesus was inseparably connected with his exaltation and his sitting at the right hand of the Father (Acts 2:22–36). It was further corroborated by the statement that in Jesus came to fulfilment David's prophecy in Psalm 110:1, 'The Lord [God] said to my Lord [the Messiah], Sit at my right hand' (Acts 2:34). With the resurrection and the glorification of Jesus is coupled the charismatic miracle of the reception of the Holy Spirit from God the Father and its transmission to the apostles by Christ (Acts 2:32).

In Jesus was also realized Psalm 118:22, which metaphorically announced the transformation of the stone rejected by the builders into the essential corner stone of a new edifice, the Church (Acts 4:8–11). Finally, speaking in general terms in the house of the Roman centurion Cornelius, Peter declared that according to the testimony of all the prophets Jesus, empowered by the Holy Spirit, mastered diseases and the Devil not only during his life, but also after being raised by God from the dead (Acts 10:34–43).

The second characteristic concerning the passages under consideration relates to the apostles' role in propagating faith in Christ, 'the Author of life' whom God has raised from the dead (Acts 3:15). 'Witness' and 'to witness' are words that turn up again and again in the first ten chapters of the Acts, and the testimony in question is regularly allied to the manifestation of charismatic power.

Already in Acts 1, the purpose of the election of Matthias to the college of the apostles, replacing the traitor Judas, was to make him (together with the other eleven close associates of Jesus) a *witness* of the resurrection. The choice of the new apostle by casting lots contains the suggestion that the winner was selected by God (Acts 1:26), but the most spectacular example of charisma was revealed at Pentecost when Peter and his companions proclaimed to the crowd: 'This Jesus God raised up, and of that we are all witnesses' (Acts 2:32). Their testimony was prompted, we are given to believe, by the glorified risen Jesus who, sitting at God's right hand, completely transformed his hitherto spineless disciples through the gift of the Holy Spirit (Acts 2:33).

The healing of a lame man in the Temple by Peter and John 'in the name of Jesus of Nazareth' (Acts 3:1–16) was another form of witnessing that Christ had been raised from the dead and was active through Peter and his associates. Even when no details are listed, the way of life of the Jerusalem Church under the guidance of the apostles is depicted as a powerful testimony to the resurrection of Jesus (Acts 4:33). Later, when ordered by the high priest to stop creating trouble through preaching about Christ, Peter and his colleagues affirmed it to be their God-given and Spirit-inspired duty to announce the resurrection and exaltation of Jesus and testify to it by word and deed: 'We are witnesses to these things, and so is the Holy Spirit whom God has given to those who obey him' (Acts 5:32).

Finally, in Caesarea, in the house of the Roman centurion Cornelius, Peter's pronouncement concerning the apparition of the resurrected Jesus to him and his companions and the obligation imposed on them to act as his witnesses, was immediately followed by a major charismatic event, the pouring out of the Holy Spirit over the whole Gentile family of Cornelius that made its members speak in tongues and praise God (Acts 10:34–47).

The writer of Acts was not preoccupied by the resurrection of Jesus as such. A risen Messiah, no longer visibly active in society, would not have made much impact on the audience of the apostles. So they presented the resurrection in context. It was a first step conducive to the exaltation and glorification of Jesus and his enthronement in heaven next to God from where he was to dispense the Holy Spirit through his earthly representatives to the world at large. This is an essentially new portrayal of the resurrection of Jesus in the framework of the charismatic activity of the nascent Church.

No presentation of the resurrection in the Acts can be considered complete without touching on three passages expressing the opinion ascribed to Paul on the matter. They foreshadow the point of view encountered in the Pauline letters. Belief in the dying and rising Christ is the most fundamental tenet of the teaching of Paul. Indeed, he asserted before the Jewish high court that all his troubles with the Temple authorities, dominated by the anti-resurrection Sadducees, arose from his belief in the rising of the dead. As a clever rhetorician, he used to his polemical advantage the disagreement on the subject of the resurrection that he knew existed between the Sadducee and Pharisee members of the Sanhedrin. 'Brethren, I am a Pharisee, a son of Pharisees', he cried out in the council, 'with respect to the hope and the resurrection of the dead I am on trial' (Acts 23:6). Thus all of a sudden the Pharisee councillors turned pro-Paul, apparently declaring, 'We find nothing wrong in this man' and even willing to accept that Paul had a supernatural experience: 'What if a spirit or an angel spoke to him?' (Acts 23:9). Paul later reiterated before Felix, the Roman procurator of Judaea, that his preaching of the resurrection was the main reason for the conflict opposing him to the Jewish leadership (Acts 24:15). Lastly, in the presence of the Jewish king, Agrippa II, Paul once again maintained that the chief accusation levelled against him concerned his hope in the resurrection (Acts 26:8) and his teaching that Christ's rising from the dead was the anticipation of the general resurrection (Acts 26:23).

Such is the new perspective opened by the Acts of the Apostles on the resurrection of Jesus. It was the inward motor that propelled the budding Church to preach the Gospel to Jews and Gentiles. This idea now needs to be followed up by the more personal testimony relating to the resurrection contained in the letters of St Paul. It conveys not the tradition handed down by the companions of Jesus during his lifetime, as the Book of the Acts purports to do, but the insights of the great visionary at the gate of Damascus, whose perceptions were to lay the foundations of fully-fledged Christianity.

13

The resurrection of Jesus in Saint Paul

The difference between the approaches to the resurrection in the Gospels and the rest of the New Testament is principally due to the varying stances taken by their writers. As we have seen, the purpose of the evangelists was three-fold. They sought to present the teaching of Jesus about the resurrection and eternal life; to list the predictions made by himself or by the ancient prophets of his death and rising; and to outline the events that happened before dawn on the first Easter Sunday. The other New Testament authors endeavoured to derive from the resurrection story doctrines concerning Jesus and his followers. Put differently, Luke in the Acts, Paul and the rest of the letter writers of the New Testament, took the rising of Christ for granted and endeavoured to describe the impact of the resurrection on the theological understanding of Jesus, or on the apostles and the first Christians.

Saint Paul played a crucial role in establishing resurrection as the kernel of the Christian message. We have already seen that in the Acts Paul's perception of the death and resurrection was the focus of the religion preached by him. More than once he identified his doctrinal outlook as hope founded on the resurrection. He comments only once on the events surrounding the resurrection of Jesus when he passes on to his flock in Corinth a tradition he has inherited from his seniors in the faith concerning the death, burial and resurrection of Jesus:

For I delivered to you as of first importance what I also received, that Christ died for our sins in accordance with the scriptures, that he was buried, that he was raised on the third day in accordance with the scriptures, and that he appeared to Cephas, then to the twelve. Then he appeared to more than five hundred brethren at one time, most of whom are still alive, though some have fallen asleep. Then he appeared to James, then to all the apostles. Last of all ... he appeared also to me (1 Cor 15:3–8).

The tradition received by Paul includes features which are absent from the other resurrection accounts of the New Testament. In his detailed list, there are several otherwise unattested apparitions, such as the vision of the risen Jesus at some unspecified place and time by more than five hundred followers, most of whom were still alive in AD 53 or thereabouts, when Paul wrote his first letter to the Corinthians. He refers to subsequent appearances of Christ to Cephas-Peter and James, the two dominant figures of the primitive Church and the only two apostles whom Paul decided to meet on his first visit to the Jewish-Christian community in Jerusalem. He adds also his own vision of Jesus, no doubt his mystical experience outside Damascus (Acts 9:3–4).[1] It is noteworthy that, although Paul refers to the burial of Jesus, he does not know or wish to mention the discovery of the empty tomb and the disappearance of the body of Christ.

While his report, written in the fifties of the first century, predates Mark, Matthew and Luke by some fifteen to forty-five years, it could well reflect a revised and edited version of events influenced by Paul's 'political' considerations. By asserting that he, too, was granted an appearance of the risen Jesus, Paul intended to insinuate his equality to Peter and James. Also, by omitting to mention the legally worthless female testimony about the empty tomb and the first apparitions of the resurrected Christ to women, he meant to strengthen the evidence coming from reliable male witnesses – Peter, James, Paul himself and a large group of men – many of whom could still be interviewed by any Corinthian pilgrim to the Holy Land keen enough to seek out the survivors. It would seem, however, that when Paul wrote the epistle, the debate was not about the validity of the tradition concerning the resurrection of Jesus, but about the idea prevalent in the Hellenistic world that the return from Hades was meaningless. 'How can some of you say', Paul indignantly inquired, 'that there is no resurrection of the dead?' (1 Cor 15:12).

1. Paul's teaching on the resurrection in 1 Thessalonians

A careful look at Paul's texts reveals that the issue of the resurrection of Jesus did not arise from either historical consideration or from philosophical reflection, but from lively debates in the Pauline communities about the practical sequels of the faith in resurrection. It was connected with the conviction that the dead would rise at the impending *Parousia*, or return of Christ.

Resurrection linked to the *Parousia* arose in the early stages of Paul's literary activity as it is attested in the first letter to the Thessalonians between AD 50 and 52. The eyes of the faithful in the Church of Thessalonica were focussed on the imminent coming from heaven of Christ, the Son of God, risen from the dead and deliverer of the faithful from judgement (1 Thess 1:9–10; see also 2 Cor 4:14; 5:14–15).

The eschatological enthusiasm generated by the expectation of the *Parousia* produced, Paul tells us, extravagant ideas among the Thessalonians. Some of them went so far as to proclaim that the Lord had already arrived and his return had been announced in a letter by Paul himself (2 Thess 2:1–2).[2]

The Thessalonians were eagerly awaiting the great event, but some of them expressed concern about the fate of those Church members who had died before the day of Christ's return. Paul reassured them: as God raised Christ, he would also revive the dead who had believed in the risen Jesus. His resurrection holds the key to salvation. Paul then presented the following scenario of the *Parousia*: The Lord Jesus would descend from heaven and order an archangel to sound the trumpet for resurrection. Then 'the dead in Christ' would return to life and be lifted up by clouds, vehicles of heavenly transport, to meet Jesus in the air, while the living Christians, including Paul himself, without passing through death would be caught up with them and join Jesus and remain with him for ever. In short, Paul and his early followers envisaged the resurrection of Jesus first and foremost as the prototype and cause of the rising of the dead and as the source and guarantee of the eternal salvation of all the chosen.

But we would not have you ignorant, brethren, concerning those who are asleep . . . For since we believe that Jesus died and rose again, even so, through Jesus, God will bring him to those who have fallen asleep. For this we declare to you by the word of the Lord, that we who are alive, who are left until the coming of the Lord, shall not precede those who have fallen asleep. For the Lord himself will descend from heaven, with a cry of command, with the archangel's call, and with the sound of the trumpet of God. And the dead in Christ will rise first; then we who are alive, who are left, shall be caught up together with them in the clouds to meet the Lord in the air; and so we shall always be with the Lord (1 Thess 4:13–17).

While on this occasion the beneficial effects of Christ's resurrection were seen as affecting only deceased Church members, a few years later in the mid-AD 50s the perspective broadened. After a short while, in his first correspondence with the Corinthians, Paul mentions the curious custom of Christians undergoing baptism on behalf of the dead. The vicarious rite was intended to ensure that deceased pagans close to Church members might draw some benefit from the resurrection of Jesus.

Since for Paul the resurrection of Jesus was the token of the future resurrection of the baptized, his theory applied only to a tiny portion of the dwellers in Sheol, a handful of dead Christians and a few pagans redeemed through the baptism for the dead. Paul's perspective did not include all the righteous who had died before Christ, let alone the resurrection of all the just and the wicked since Adam.

2. Paul's teaching on the resurrection in 1 Corinthians

Paul's preoccupation with the problem of the resurrection did not come to an end with the first letter to the Thessalonians, but revealed itself to be especially lively in the first letter to the Corinthians. Indeed, chapter 15 of that letter provides the most detailed record of Paul's understanding of the impact of the resurrection of Jesus on Christian believers. Here again Paul confronts a theological problem from a practical point of view. He condemned Christian men frequenting prostitutes because he perceived a mystical union between the human body and the body of Christ. In his view, the bodies of the faithful belonged to the Lord. Having died with the crucified Christ when they were dipped into the baptismal pool, their flesh was symbolically raised with the risen Christ when they emerged from the water. Hence Paul's negative answer to the question, 'Shall I take the members of Christ and make them members of a prostitute? Never' (1 Cor 6:15).

The same letter speaks of members of the Church querying the possibility of the resurrection of the dead. For Paul, this was tantamount to a denial of the resurrection of Christ and of the faith he had preached. If the dead cannot be raised, he argues, then Jesus was not raised. Consequently, sins are still unredeemed, hope in the resurrection is futile, and all the deceased Christians are lost (1 Cor 15:12–18). However, he continues, the resurrection of Jesus was not for his own sake alone, but being 'the first fruits' of all those to be raised, it marked the beginning of a multitude of reawakenings. As the first Adam inflicted death on all his posterity, the risen Christ mystically enabled those who were to believe in him to have a share in life through his resurrection (1 Cor 15:20–23).

As a Jew, Paul could not conceive of resurrection without envisaging some kind of a body, but, combining his Jewish legacy with the Hellenistic ideas of his readers, he insisted that this body would be totally different from the one that had died. The risen body would be imperishable, glorious and powerful, bearing the image not of the mortal

Adam, but that of the glorified Christ. The raised dead would be granted a spiritual body, and the just, alive at the *Parousia*, would have their earthly bodies transformed into spiritual ones:

We shall not all sleep, but we shall all be changed, in a moment, in the twinkling of an eye, at the last trumpet. For the trumpet will sound, and the dead will be raised imperishable, and we shall be changed. For this perishable nature must put on the imperishable, and the mortal nature must put on immortality (1 Cor 15:51–54).

In sum, in his address to the Corinthians, Paul did not seek to clarify the meaning of Jesus' resurrection, but its effects on his followers. The resolution of the significance of the resurrection as far as Jesus himself was concerned had to wait until Paul's later correspondence, especially until the epistle to the Romans.

3. Paul's teaching on the resurrection in the letter to the Romans

Writing to the Romans in the mid or late AD 50s, Paul reflected on the resurrection considered from the angle of Christ's relation to God and to the community of believers. Unlike John, who in the Prologue of his Gospel identified Jesus as the eternal divine Word become human for a short time, Paul, moving in the opposite direction, solemnly declared that the man Jesus, born of a Jewish woman as a descendant of King David, rose to the dignity of the Son of God through his resurrection from the dead (Rom 1:4). In other words, on the first Easter Sunday the status of Jesus underwent a fundamental change. The opening paragraph of the letter to the Romans marks the moment in the history of Christian literature when Jesus was formally proclaimed 'Son of God in power according to the Spirit of holiness' on account of his resurrection from the dead.

In the same way, Paul also emphasized the role of the resurrection in the relationship between Jesus and his followers. He expressed his thought through the medium of the mystical, or sacramental, concept of baptism. Paul did not view baptism merely as a Jewish rite of purification by water. For him the pool symbolized the tomb where the body of Jesus had lain and where the resurrection took place. So when the candidates to be initiated into the Christian mystery were submerged in the baptismal waters, they mystically united themselves with the sin-effacing death of Christ. Afterwards, when they rose from the pool, they believed they started a new life issued from the resurrection of Jesus and became children of God.

Do you not know that all of us who have been baptized into Christ Jesus were baptized into his death? We were buried therefore with him by baptism into death, so that as Christ was raised from the dead by the glory of the Father, we too might walk in newness of life (Rom 6:3–4; *cf.* Col 2:12).

This birth to a new life was animated by the Spirit of God emanating from the resurrection of Jesus.

If the Spirit of him who raised Jesus from the dead dwells in you, he who raised Christ Jesus from the dead will give life in your mortal bodies also through the Spirit which dwells in you (Rom 8:11).

A little later on, the centrality of the resurrection in the life of the faithful is expressed with even more emphatic succinctness: 'If you confess with your lips that Jesus is Lord and believe in your heart that God raised him from the dead, you will be saved' (Rom 10:9).

Apart from the correspondence with the Thessalonians, Corinthians and Romans, the theme of the resurrection from the dead plays little or no part in the rest of the Pauline and deutero-Pauline literature.[3] The epistles to the Galatians, Ephesians, Philippians, Colossians, 2 Timothy and Hebrews use the terms 'resurrection' and 'to rise' only ten times, adding nothing to the meanings with which we are already familiar. The other letters, 1 Timothy, Titus and Philemon, never broach the subject.

One final point needs to be examined before concluding the discussion of Paul's contribution to the topic of the resurrection of Jesus. In 1 Corinthians 15:3 Paul firmly asserts that Jesus rose from the dead on the third day 'in accordance with the scriptures', yet contrary to his custom, he fails to back his statement with a citation. It is possible that the post-biblical Jewish representation of Genesis 22, the voluntary self-sacrifice of Isaac, in which the death and the resurrection of the victim on Mount Moriah is figuratively contemplated, kept on haunting Paul's creative imagination.[4] However, only the deutero-Pauline letter to the Hebrews furnishes positive support to this theory.

By faith Abraham . . . offered up Isaac . . . He considered that God was able to raise men even from the dead; hence, figuratively speaking, he received him back (Heb 11:17–19).

Nevertheless, the absence of an actual Bible quotation in favour of the resurrection of the Messiah suggests that there existed no established tradition among Jews about a dying and risen Christ.

In sum, whereas the idea of the resurrection lay at the periphery of the preaching of Jesus, based on the idea of the kingdom of God, St Paul turned it into the centrepiece of his mystical and theological vision, which was soon to become quasi-identical with the essence of the Christian message.

14

The resurrection of Jesus in the rest of the New Testament

The remaining books of the New Testament contribute remarkably little to the problem of the resurrection. The letters of James, 2 Peter, 1–3 John and Jude are silent on the subject. Only the first epistle of Peter has something new to say and the Book of Revelation contains a single reference to general resurrection.

To begin with the latter, chapter 20 of Revelation offers an idiosyncratic picture of the resurrection with no parallel anywhere in the New Testament. Unlike the Hebrew Bible and post-biblical Jewish literature, it depicts the general raising of the dead not in one, but in two stages. The first resurrection is linked to the return of Christ and benefits only the martyrs, 'those who had been beheaded for their testimony to Jesus'. According to the imagery of Christian millenarian speculation, they are to reign with Christ for a thousand years, during which 'the dragon, that ancient serpent, who is the Devil and Satan', will be bound and imprisoned (Rev 20:2–4). At the end of the millennium comes the second resurrection (Rev 20:5), that of the rest of mankind, both the pious and the impious of the past ages, followed by the last judgement. Those inscribed in God's book of life are to join the beneficiaries of the first resurrection, and the wicked will be condemned to a second death and cast for ever into a lake of fire (Rev

20:11–15). This two-tier concept of resurrection has never become part of mainstream Christian thinking, but inspired esoteric speculations over the centuries.

The first letter of Peter also includes something unattested elsewhere, called the 'harrowing of hell' in English theological jargon; that is to say Christ's descent to the underworld between his death and resurrection in order to rescue the deceased. The idea is associated with the redeeming symbolism of a new birth springing from the resurrection of Jesus (1 Pet 1:3). The principal passage contains an explicit hint at baptism.

For Christ also died for sins once and for all . . . that he might bring us to God, being put to death in the flesh but made alive in the spirit, in which he went and preached to the spirits in prison, who formerly did not obey, when God's patience waited in the days of Noah, during the building of the ark, in which a few, that is eight persons, were saved through water. Baptism, which corresponds to this, now saves you, not as a removal of dirt from the body but as an appeal to God for a clear conscience, through the resurrection of Jesus Christ, who has gone into heaven and is at the right hand of God, with angels, authorities, and powers subject to him (1 Pet 3:18–22).

The letter resumes the main features of the theological canvas of redemption familiar from the writings of Paul: Christ's death expiated man's sin and his resurrection brought about the salvation of the believer through baptism. The novel element in the picture is the saving action that the dead, but already spiritually revived Jesus, performed in the underworld prior to his terrestrial resurrection. Some time between the afternoon of Good Friday and the dawn of Easter Sunday, Jesus visited Sheol, the abode of the deceased, intending to save a special group of sinners. They were the wicked humans of the age of the flood, who failed to amend their ways during the time of repentance granted them by a magnanimous God, while Noah was building the ark. According to Jewish tradition, God would not decree the destruction of this most dissolute of all generations without giving them a chance to repent. Hence Noah, who is described as the 'herald of righteousness' (2 Pet 2:5), was ordered to preach to them and try to bring them to their senses before it was too late.[1] He was not listened to, so all mankind perished except 'eight souls' – Noah and his wife, his three sons and their three wives – who escaped destruction in the ark. The water that carried the ark prefigured baptism and its saving power derived from the resurrection of Christ. We are not told whether Jesus, already filled with the Spirit, was more successful than Noah, but the episode underlines the universal character of the redeeming intention attributed to him by the writer of 2 Peter.

The main novelty of the story is the insertion of a new stage into the sequence of events between the death and the resurrection of Christ: the journey to hell of the soon rising, but not yet risen, Jesus and the extension of his saving gesture to all the deceased, represented by the worst of sinners. This enlarged aim far exceeds Paul's restricted purpose, which was the communication of the fruits of the resurrection to the dead Christians. This generosity of 1 Peter towards the deceased of all ages is remembered by the introduction of this odd detail of the story of Jesus into some of the Church's Creeds. The Apostles' Creed reads: 'He suffered under Pontius Pilate, was crucified, died and was buried, descended to hell, rose from the dead on the third day.'

The Athanasian Creed, in turn, declares: 'Who suffered

for our salvation, descended to hell, rose from the dead on the third day.'

Appendix

'Life' and 'eternal life' in the New Testament outside the Gospels

Our analysis in chapter 7 of the use of 'life' or 'eternal life' has shown that in the Synoptics the terms are synonymous with the 'kingdom of God', and 'eternal life' is seen as the reward for the observance of God's commandments and even more so for the performance of heroic virtue. In the Gospel of John, on the other hand, eternal life is the ultimate remuneration for faith in Jesus, the Son of God. None of the synoptic evangelists ever explicitly links resurrection with eternal life. The latter can be conceived of without the idea of bodily revival. If one is to distinguish between 'life' and 'eternal life', the former would indicate the granting of circumstances that lead towards the kingdom of God, whereas the latter is the prerogative of the established citizens of that kingdom.

Paul frequently refers to 'life' or 'eternal life', but he usually does so without explicitly alluding either to the resurrection of Jesus or to resurrection in general. Twice he introduces the idea of immortality, seen as a sign of spiritual survival (Rom 2:7; 2 Tim 1:10), but as a rule the main contrast is between death brought by Adam and life originating with Jesus Christ (Rom 5:17–18, 20; 6:23). Paul comes nearest to associating life with resurrection when he depicts human bodies as vehicles carrying both the death of the crucified Jesus and the life of the risen Christ (2 Cor 4:10–11).

The three Johannine letters, which never speak of resurrection, generally agree with the Fourth Gospel in joining the notion of faith to eternal life. As for the Book of Revelation, it is rich in symbols such as 'water of life' (Rev 7:17; 21:6, 22:1, 17), 'tree of life' (Rev 2:7; 22:2, 14, 19), 'crown of life' (Rev 2:10; cf. Jas 1:12) and 'book of life' (Rev 3:5; 13:8; 17:8; 20:12, 15; 21:27; cf. Phil 4:3).

All in all, these passages regarding 'eternal life' contribute little to the interpretation of the notion of resurrection.

15

The meaning of the concept of resurrection in the New Testament

After the survey of the biblical and post-biblical Jewish evidence concerning afterlife and the examination of the full New Testament material, what have we learnt about the early Christian concept of the resurrection of the dead in general, and the resurrection of Jesus in particular?

Let it be emphasized once again that most of the Old Testament ignores the idea of the revivification of the dead; that active and effective religious life is seen by ancient Judaism as restricted to man's worldly career and that the inevitability of death and a permanent Sheol entailing a reduced, joyless and as it were Godless existence in a dreamless sleep is accepted as mankind's inexorable heritage.

Yet, while in biblical wisdom this world and the present age are the theatre of the love and worship of God, one detects in Jewish piety of the later centuries of the Old Testament era a secret yearning for a continued relationship after death with the Creator and heavenly Father. We have to wait, however, until the end of the third and early second centuries BC, and in particular until the Jewish experience of religious martyrdom, to encounter the notion of life after death in the form of spiritual immortality or bodily revival. These concepts had been attested, especially under the influence of the Pharisees, from the second century BC onwards, but they do not seem to have become part of the core of Judaism until the second or third century AD and later. Since in the early first century AD the impact of the Pharisees on Galilee was at best limited, the frequently assumed notion that belief in resurrection was an accepted fact among the contemporaries of Jesus cannot be derived from sources reflecting popular traditions current in the Judaism of that age.

As the relevant findings have been listed in passing in the foregoing chapters dealing with the New Testament, all that remains here is to offer a systematic exposition of the meaning of resurrection. This will be done under three headings. The first two relate to theology, but the third will take us to the heart of the matter, the 'event' of the resurrection of Jesus.

Before addressing these three issues, a preliminary question must be settled. How do the various accounts of resurrection, or rather resuscitation, mentioned in the Old and New Testaments (see pp. 30–32 and chapter 9) compare with the resurrection of Jesus and with the eschatological resurrection envisaged for mankind?

Resuscitation is the 'miraculous' continuation of life as it was lived previously, the climax of charismatic healing. By contrast, the rising of the dead (with the exception of the wandering about of 'the saints' in Jerusalem after the earthquake that marked the death of Christ (see pp. 92–3), is considered as an occurrence awaited in the future. It is associated with the expected Second Coming or *Parousia*, and the accompanying universal, final judgement of all mankind which conclude the present age. As for the resurrection of Jesus, it is depicted as a unique phenomenon, both historical and eschatological. It is not seen as the continuation of Jesus' pre-crucifixion life, nor is his resurrected body represented as identical with the one known to his companions. Moreover, his resurrection is treated as the anticipation and cause of the reawakening of the dead at the end of time. In short, the resumed existence of the resuscitated dead brought about by Elijah, Elisha, Jesus, Peter and Paul sheds no true light on the concept of eschatological resurrection. The two fall into separate categories.

1. The significance of the resurrection for the theological understanding of Jesus by nascent Christianity

Contrary to the generally held opinion that the concept of resurrection constitutes the focal point of Christology, the doctrine relating to Jesus, close scrutiny of the New Testament evidence suggests that it forms simply the initial stage of the belief in his exaltation. Christ's complete glorification is seen in his enthronement next to God the Father in fulfilment of the words of the Psalmist, 'The Lord said to my Lord, Sit at my right hand' (Acts 2:24, 32–34, quoting Ps 110:1).

The Gospel of John also gives the impression that the resurrection was simply the gateway through which the incarnate eternal Word of God returned to the Father after the accomplishment of his temporary earthly mission. In his first appearance to Mary Magdalene, Jesus immediately announces that he is going to the Father (Jn 20:17). This turning point in his mission is revealed in the general statement that sums up John's Gospel: 'I came from the Father and have come into the world; again, I am leaving the world and going to the Father' (Jn 16:28). His heavenly homecoming was soon marked by the charismatic pouring out of the Holy Spirit over the apostles, left behind as the witnesses of Jesus.

The same idea is voiced by St Paul, for whom the resurrection is the cause of Jesus' elevation to divine Sonship (Rom 1:4). In short, the apogee of the triumphant Christ is not the rising from the dead, but his heavenly exaltation followed by the dispatch of the Holy Spirit.

2. The resurrection of Jesus in relation to the resurrection of his followers and of the rest of mankind

The resurrection does not appear to have had a major doctrinal impact on the Gospels. Neither the general background material, nor the teaching ascribed to Jesus on the afterlife, is particularly concerned with the matter. Paul is the first to raise the question, but he does so more from a pragmatic than from a theoretical viewpoint. In the early stages of the expectation of the return of Christ, the eschatologically frenzied communities of believers were chiefly interested in their own entry into the kingdom of God by means of a forthcoming encounter with Jesus returning from heaven on a cloud. They were convinced that the *Parousia* was at hand and would happen within their lifetime. They would witness it before their death. All they expected therefore was in effect a change of clothes, the divesting of themselves from their earthly frame and replacing it with a new spiritual body. The resurrection as such did not concern them.

But the problem became a burning issue in connection with the members of the Church who died recently. Did they miss the boat? As such injustice seemed inconceivable, Paul reassured the members of his congregation that on D-day the deceased Christians would join the rest of the living followers of Jesus in their triumphant ascent to the divine kingdom. The supplementary ticket issued to this group of Christians who predeceased the *Parousia* was immediately followed by a request for another, and entitlement to resurrection was extended to pagan associates for whom virtual Church membership was secured through the surrogate ritual of baptism for the dead. However, Paul himself did not explicitly apply the power of Jesus' resurrection to the non-baptized righteous of the pre-Christian age. We have to wait until the first letter of Peter for the extension of the saving plan of Christ in regard to the deceased wicked imprisoned in the underworld (see pp. 132–3).

The New Testament remains divided on the final destiny of the ungodly, namely whether they would be raised to face divine justice and eternal hellfire. The resurrection, when conceived as the reward for holy behaviour, was necessarily confined to saints and martyrs, to the just in general, and the wicked were left behind in the cold of Sheol. It was only when some New Testament writers substituted for the loving and forgiving heavenly Father an iron-fisted Judge that the sinners of the underworld were also summoned to be bodily present before the heavenly tribunal to receive a sentence of destruction in the everlasting flames.[1]

3. What does the New Testament tell us about the 'event' of the resurrection of Jesus?

We have now reached the principal topic of this book, *the* Resurrection. No New Testament text attempts to describe the actual return to life of the dead Jesus. All we have are bits of circumstantial evidence, if they can be called evidence, divided into two classes.

The first entails various accounts of female witnesses who, on the third day after the crucifixion, discovered an empty tomb. They thought it was the tomb of Jesus and their finding was later confirmed by two male apostles. Only one explanation of the empty tomb is offered in the Synoptic Gospels: the absence of the body of Jesus was due to his resurrection. It is based on the testimony heard by the women from one or two mysterious strangers (angels?). In John, on the other hand, the disappearance of the body is attributed both by Mary Magdalene and by Peter to the interference of an unknown third party and not to a supernatural event.

The second category of circumstantial evidence is given in all the Gospels except the shorter ending of Mark. It consists of a series of apparitions to various individuals (Mary Magdalene, Peter, James, Paul) or groups (several women, two disciples at Emmaus, seven, ten or eleven apostles, or over five hundred brethren) at various times (on Easter Sunday, the following Sunday or on later dates) and in various places (in Jerusalem, at Emmaus, on a Galilean mountain or by the sea of Tiberias). The meaning of the visions is not obvious: no one realizes at first in the earliest tradition that the appearing person is Jesus. They variously speak of a ghost or the 'gardener' or a stranger.

Thomas is said to have declined to believe his fellow apostles until he experienced by touch the wounds of the resurrected Jesus, and several apostles on the Galilean mountain continued to harbour doubts concerning the reality of their vision of Jesus.

The empty tomb and the apparitions are never directly associated to form a combined argument. For some modern Gospel interpreters the empty tomb saga is 'an apologetic legend' (R. Bultmann), a secondary attempt to provide some 'factual' support to back individual or collective visions. The fragility of the theory is exposed by its intrinsic weakness. The evidence furnished by female witnesses had no standing in a male-dominated Jewish society. In fact, according to Luke, the apostles poked fun at the women. Furthermore, the identity and number of the witnesses differ in the various Gospels as does their testimony. Yet it is clearly an early tradition. If the empty tomb story had been manufactured by the primitive Church to demonstrate the reality of the resurrection of Jesus, one would have expected a uniform and foolproof account attributed to patently reliable witnesses.

To put it bluntly, not even a credulous non-believer is likely to be persuaded by the various reports of the resurrection; they convince only the already converted. The same must be said about the visions. None of them satisfies the minimum requirements of a legal or scientific inquiry. The only alternative historians are left with in their effort to make some sense of the resurrection is to fall back on speculation, hopefully on enlightened speculation.

Six theories to explain the resurrection of Jesus

One could speak of eight theories, but I have discounted the two extremes which are not susceptible to rational judgement: the blind faith of the fundamentalist believer and the out of hand rejection of the inveterate sceptic. The fundamentalists accept the story, not as written down in the New Testament texts, but as reshaped, transmitted and interpreted by Church tradition. They smooth down the rough edges and abstain from asking tiresome questions. The unbelievers, in turn, treat the whole resurrection story as the figment of early Christian imagination. Most inquirers with a smattering of knowledge of the history of religions will find themselves between these two poles. Some of the explanations of the resurrection are insinuated in the Gospels, others emerge from ancient or more recent history. Let us examine them one by one.

1. The body was removed by someone unconnected with Jesus

According to the Gospel of John, the emptiness of the tomb discovered by Mary Magdalene and later confirmed by Peter and the 'beloved disciple', is at first ascribed to unknown persons. Interference with graves was not unusual, as can be deduced from the curse put on tomb desecrators contained in funeral inscriptions (see pp. 59–60). The circumstances of the burial of Jesus suggest a simple explication. The burial took place in great haste because of the imminent onset of the Sabbath and the body was laid in a new tomb, conveniently situated in a nearby garden (Jn 19:41). It was obviously prepared for someone else. Hence it is not unreasonable to suppose that the person in charge of the burial place – the 'gardener' according to Mary Magdalene (Jn 20:15) – took the first opportunity to move the body of Jesus to another available tomb.

The irregular circumstances of Jesus' interment easily account for such an outside intervention. Normally, the funeral duties were carried out by male near kin, but as there is no sign in the Gospel narratives of the presence of the brothers of Jesus at the time of the crucifixion and all his apostles had gone into hiding, one or several less-close acquaintances, Joseph of Arimathea and Nicodemus, stepped in and performed the charitable obligation on Friday afternoon before sunset. According to John, Nicodemus brought along a large quantity of myrrh and aloes to anoint the dead body. Consequently, contrary to the evidence of the Synoptics, there was no need for Jesus' women friends to visit the tomb at the start of the new week to complete the unfinished funerary rituals.

The innocent transfer of the body of Jesus developed later into the legend of the resurrection. However, the fact that the organizer(s) of the burial was/were well known and could have easily been asked for and supplied an explanation, strongly militates against this theory.[2]

2. The body of Jesus was stolen by his disciples

An emphatic rebuttal of the reality of the resurrection is attributed in the Gospel of Matthew to the priestly leaders of Jerusalem. Allegedly, they spread the rumour, which many decades after the death of Jesus was still circulating among the Jewish population of Jerusalem, that the body of Jesus was spirited away by his disciples to produce the semblance of a miraculous resurrection. This story presupposes that a fraudulent prophecy concerning Jesus' rising from the dead was widely known among Palestinian Jews. However, if the closest associates of Jesus did not expect him to rise, it is hard to imagine that outsiders were aware of a prediction, uttered by Old Testament prophets or by Jesus, about his resurrection shortly after his death. The tale of a mischief perpetrated by the apostles is no doubt a later Jewish gossip circulating in Palestine in the time when Matthew wrote his Gospel. Its value for the interpretation of the resurrection is next to nil.

3. The empty tomb was not the tomb of Jesus

The first two explanations are expressly hinted at in the Gospels themselves. The next derives from more subtle allusions underlying the Synoptics. Mark, Matthew and Luke firmly stress that the Galilean women knew where Jesus was buried. While all the cowardly male disciples kept out of sight, the two Marys (Mk and Mt) or the Galilean women (Lk) watched the burial party led by Joseph of Arimathea (Mk 15:47; Mt 27:61; Lk 23:55). Bearing in mind the attitude of male superiority adopted by the apostles on hearing the report of female witnesses about the empty tomb (Lk 24:11), it strikes as most likely that they suspected that Mary Magdalene and her friends had gone to the wrong tomb. If the rock cavity into which the corpse of Jesus was hurriedly laid was freshly prepared to house someone else's remains, no doubt it was in a location reserved for burials with similar tombs surrounding it. In the semi-darkness of dawn a mistake was easy. A present-day reader would wonder why Peter and his colleagues, who considered the women untrustworthy, did not consult Joseph of Arimathea, who was apparently the owner of the tomb (Mt 27:60). Presumably, in the logic of the Gospel narrative, the apparitions of Jesus soon rendered such an inquiry superfluous. The theory of mistaken identity of the tomb, while not inconceivable, certainly does not impose itself.

4. Buried alive, Jesus later left the tomb

That Jesus survived the crucifixion has been propounded by modern writers and novelists from Hugh J. Schonfield's *The Passover Plot* (1965) and Barbara Thiering's *Jesus the Man* (1992) to *The Da Vinci Code* (2003) by Dan Brown. Less extreme believers in Jesus' survival argue that recovery after crucifixion was possible, as it is attested by Flavius Josephus. In his autobiography, Josephus recalls that on an occasion when he was returning to the capital, he saw many crucified Jews by the roadside. Among them he recognized three of his friends, who were still alive. On his pleading, Titus, the future emperor, promptly ordered them to be taken down and treated by Roman physicians and as a result one of the three survived (*Life*, 420).

Jesus remained on the cross for such a short time that Pilate wondered whether he was truly dead when Joseph of Arimathea asked for his body (Mk 15:44). One may further speculate that the piercing of his side by one of the executioners was a later invention introduced by John (Jn 19:34) to dispel doubts as to whether Jesus was dead. But assuming that a semi-conscious Jesus crept out of the tomb in the darkness of night, what happened to him afterwards? Did he disappear into thin air? Not very likely.

5. The migrant Jesus

The idea of Jesus leaving Judaea after he had recovered from his coma is a relatively modern creation. It is part of the teaching of the Ahmadiyya sect of Islam (formed in the nineteenth century), according to which the revived Jesus left the Holy Land, set out towards the east in search of the lost tribes of Israel, and died in Kashmir in India. In the last century, the rich poetic imagination of Robert Graves brought the post-crucifixion Jesus to Rome.[3] So also did Barbara Thiering's peculiar interpretation of the Dead Sea Scrolls. Her married, divorced and remarried Jesus, father of four children, died of old age in Nero's Rome.[4]

In the absence of real ancient evidence these modern musings need not detain us.

6. Do the appearances suggest spiritual, not bodily, resurrection?

While no apparition of the risen Jesus figures in the original, shorter ending of Mark, the oldest of the Gospels, all the other sources describe numerous visions of Christ by Mary Magdalene (Jn, Mk B), the Galilean women (Mt), the Emmaus disciples (Lk, Mk B), Peter (Lk, Paul), the apostles in Jerusalem on Easter Sunday (Mk B, Lk), one without the presence of Thomas and another, on the following Sunday, in his presence (Jn). Jesus was further seen some days later in Galilee on a mountain by eleven apostles or by seven at the sea of Tiberias (Mt, Jn). Further appearances were witnessed, according to Paul, by more than five hundred brothers, by James, and finally by Paul himself at unspecified times and places.

Four types of vision are listed. 1. In Matthew no concrete

details are given. 2. In John and Luke an unknown ordinary man (the gardener or a traveller) is later recognized as Jesus. 3. Again in Luke and John, a spirit mysteriously enters the apostles' residence despite the locked doors. 4. The ghost later becomes a stranger with flesh and bones, who says he is Jesus and invites the apostles to touch him, and he eats with them.

In order to judge the significance of these appearances, we must try to determine the purpose of the resurrection of Jesus in the mind of the evangelists and Paul. From the fact that no one suggests that he came into contact with people outside the circle of his close followers, we must deduce that for the New Testament writers the resurrection was not meant to enable Jesus to perform any further public act. The forty days' extension of his stay with the apostles, not witnessed by anyone from the outside world, formally contradicts Luke as well as Mark's longer ending (Mk 16:19) as both imply that the Ascension happened on Easter Sunday (Lk 24:50). The alleged need for Jesus' remaining with his disciples to give further instruction about the kingdom of God (Acts 1:3) is rendered superfluous by the promise in John that the Holy Spirit will come to teach them all things (Jn 14:26; 16:13). If this was the case, the resurrection of the crucified Jesus is best seen as the first step on the spiritual ladder that leads to his heavenly glorification (see p. 138). Viewed from this angle, the resurrection becomes a purely spiritual concept without requiring any accompanying physical reality. Spiritual resurrection is best associated with visions and appearances. The strictly Jewish bond of spirit and body is better served by the idea of the empty tomb and is no doubt responsible for the introduction of the notions of palpability (Thomas in John) and eating (Luke and John).

What is the evidential value of such diverse visions perceived by individuals or groups of individuals? In essence, they do not differ from the visions of mystics throughout the centuries. No doubt the New Testament characters believed in the reality of their visions of Jesus. But what about people who were not so privileged and had only the word of 'eyewitnesses' to go by? They depended on a double act of faith: faith in the reliability of the reporters and in the reality of the report. Resurrection as a spiritual entity is appropriately expressed by a vision. Anything more tangible is suspect of hallucination, whether individual or collective.

The theory of spiritual resurrection cancels the need for an empty tomb. The body of a risen but immaterial Jesus could have remained in the tomb, with his bones later collected and put into an ossuary inscribed with the Aramaic name Yeshua bar Yehosef (Jesus son of Joseph). Of course, I do not mean to suggest that the ossuary bearing this name, found at Talpiot in Jerusalem in 1980, and recently made famous by a television documentary, originally contained the remains of the Jesus of the Gospels.[5]

All in all, none of the six suggested theories stands up to stringent scrutiny. Does this mean that the traditional resurrection concept, i.e. the miraculous revival in some shape or form of the dead body of Jesus, is doomed to failure in the rational world of today? Or is there another way out of this conundrum that may offer an explanation, if not for the physical resurrection of Jesus, at least for the birth and survival of Christianity?

Epilogue: Resurrection in the hearts of men

The opening chapter of the Acts of the Apostles takes us
to the Mount of Olives, where the apostles of Jesus wave
goodbye to their Master. They believe, without compre-
hending it, that he is no longer in the tomb and is on his
way to the Father in heaven. It is of little importance
whether this spiritual spectacle was witnessed on the third
day after the crucifixion or forty days later. What matters
is that within a short time the terrified small group of the
original followers of Jesus, still hiding from the public
gaze, all at once underwent a powerful mystical experience
in Jerusalem on the Feast of Weeks (Pentecost). Filled with
the promised Holy Spirit, the pusillanimous men were
suddenly metamorphosed into ecstatic spiritual warriors.
They proclaimed openly the message of the Gospel, and
the charismatic potency, imparted to them by Jesus during
his ministry, which had enabled them to preach, heal and
expel demons, burst into life again and manifested itself in
word and in deed. The formerly terrified fugitives cour-
ageously spoke up in the presence of the authorities and
healed the sick in public, at the gate of the Temple itself.
The reality of the charisma opened the apostles' eyes to
the mystery of the resurrection. The spiritual healing power
of belief lay at the basis of the teaching, curing and exorciz-
ing ability of Jesus in his life. According to the evangelists,

he often told the sick who had been restored to health: 'Your faith has healed you.' During his life, Jesus managed to pass on this spiritual power to his disciples so that they could exclaim with joyful amazement: 'Lord, even the demons are subject to us in your name' (Lk 10:17).

According to the New Testament, the chief act of the resurrected Christ in his heavenly glory was the dispatch of the Holy Spirit. 'This Jesus God raised up', Peter announced to the Jewish crowd in Jerusalem. 'Exalted at God's right hand, and having received from the Father the promise of the Holy Spirit, he has poured it out' over his disciples (Acts 2:32). The impact and guidance of the Spirit empowered the apostles and disciples to act as witnesses of Jesus. They did so through charismatic deeds: 'In my name' – Christ is said to have declared – 'they will cast out demons, they will speak in tongues; they will pick up serpents, and if they drink any deadly thing, it will not hurt them; they will lay their hands on the sick, and they will recover' (Mk 16:18).

The scene being set, let us now consider from an existential, historical and psychological point of view the original Galilean followers of Jesus during the short period following the first Easter Sunday. The tale of the empty tomb and the apparitions of the lost Lord momentarily illumined their dark despair with a ray of hope. Doubts nevertheless lingered on. However, when under the influence of the Spirit their self-confidence revived, prompting them to resume their apostolic mission, they felt increasingly sure that they were not acting alone, but that Jesus was with them. So, when they again started to preach the gospel 'with authority', as their miracle-working teacher did in Galilee; when they realized that in *the name of Jesus* his charisma was working again, their doubts melted away in the inward certainty that the crucified Master was close to them, as in the old days.[1] The helping hand that gave them strength to carry on with their task was the proof that Jesus had risen from the dead.

Nowhere has this inner transformation been more movingly portrayed than in the haunting final paragraph of a famous book, *On the Trial of Jesus*, by my late friend Paul Winter:

Sentence was passed, and [Jesus] was led away. Crucified, dead, and buried, he yet rose in the hearts of his disciples who had loved him and felt he was near. Tried by the world, condemned by authority, buried by the Churches that profess his name, he is rising again, today and tomorrow, in the hearts of men who love him and feel he is near.[2]

The conviction in the spiritual presence of the living Jesus accounts for the resurgence of the Jesus movement after the crucifixion. However, it was the supreme doctrinal and organizational skill of St Paul that allowed nascent Christianity to grow into a viable and powerful resurrection-centred world religion.

Resurrection in the hearts of men may strike a note of empathy even among today's sceptics and cynics. Whether or not they adhere to a formal creed, a good many men and women of the twenty-first century may be moved and inspired by the mesmerizing presence of the teaching and example of the real Jesus alive in their mind.

Notes

THE NATIVITY

1. According to the theory advanced by the nineteenth-century German scholar Hermann Usener (*Das Weihnachts-fest*, 1889; 2nd edn 1911), and developed by the Belgian Benedictine Dom Bernard Botte (*Les origines de la Noël et de l'Epiphanie*, 1932), the Nativity of Christ was assigned the date of the winter solstice on which day the worshippers of the Persian god Mithra celebrated the birthday of the sun.

2. *Scottish Journal of Theology* 41 (1988), pp. 177–89.

3. *A Critical and Exegetical Commentary on the Gospel according to Saint Matthew* (Edinburgh), 1988, p. 252.

4. Ibid., p. 221.

5. *New York Review of Books*, 29. 6. 1978, pp. 39–42.

6. *The History of the Synoptic Tradition*, 1963, p. 291.

7. *The Historical Figure of Jesus* (London, 1993), p. 85.

8. 'The Virginal Conception of Jesus in the New Testament', *Theological Studies* 34, 1973, 566–7.

9. *To Advance the Gospel: New Testament Studies*, (New York, 1981), 61–2.

10. Curiously, the name Panther/Pantera/Pandera is attested in the period as that borne by Roman soldiers, and epigraphic evidence, dating to AD 9, refers to one particular Tiberius Julius Abdes *Pantera*, a Sidonian archer in a Roman legion stationed in far distant Germany. See A. Deissmann, 'Der Name Panthera', *Orientalische Studien Th. Nöldecke gewidmet*, 1906, pp. 871–5. The possibility that Panthera was the father of Jesus has been revived by James D. Tabor in *The Jesus Dynasty* (Simon & Schuster, New York, 2006).

11. *Hitler's Table-Talk* (Oxford, 1988), pp. 76, 721.

12. See Jane Schaberg, *The Illegitimacy of Jesus*, Sheffield, 1995.

13. 'The Titulus Tiburtinus', *Vestigia* 1972, Beiträge zur Alten Geschichte 17, Munich, p. 600.

14. See G. Ryckmans, 'De l'or (?), de l'encens et de la myrrhe', *Revue Biblique* 58 (1951), pp. 372–6.

15. See Roger David Aus, *Matthew 1–2 and the Virginal Conception: In Light of Palestinian and Hellenistic Traditions on the Birth of Israel's First Redeemer, Moses* (University Press of America, 2004).

16. See Morton Smith, *Jesus the Magician* (Gollancz, London, 1978), pp. 46–50.

THE RESURRECTION

Foreword

1. See p. 284.

2. Geza Vermes, *The Nativity: History and Legend* (Penguin, London, 2006) (pp. 1–166 of the present volume).

3. For faith wrapped in scholarship, see the 800-page-long monumental *The Resurrection of the Son of God* by N. T. Wright, Bishop of Durham (SPCK, London, 2003).

4. For a recent example, see Robert M. Price and Jeffery Jay Lowder, *The Empty Tomb: Jesus beyond the Grave* (Prometheus Books, Amherst, NY, 2005).

Prologue: The Christian notion of resurrection and its antecedents

1. *Natural History*, 7:55, 150.

2. Philostratus, *Life of Apollonius*, 4:45.

2. Death and its sequels in ancient Judaism: Paving the way for resurrection

1. For the exception of 1 Enoch, see pp. 336–7.

2. 'Exploit the present day'.

3. Biblical and post-biblical antecedents of the resurrection and ascension of Jesus

1. According to an ancient Jewish belief, attested in rabbinic literature, the departed soul, still longing to return to the body, continued to hover over it for three days (GenR 100:7; yYeb 15c). Resurrection on the third day may somehow be connected with this idea.

2. The sequence of events given in the Hebrew Bible is preferable to the account of the Septuagint, where it is said that the prophet lowers himself on the boy seven times without sneezing, or to the Aramaic Targum, where Elisha, and not the boy, sneezes seven times.

3. A similar resuscitation is attributed by the Hellenist Artapanus to Moses, who by pronouncing into Pharaoh's ears the name of God, caused him to drop dead, only to bring him back to life again (Eusebius, Praep. Ev. 9:27. 24–25).

4. Whilst hailing Elisha as a thaumaturge, Josephus plays down his part in the resuscitation of the son of the widow of Zarephath and attributes the miracle to God, who 'beyond all expectation brought the child back to life' (*Ant* 8:327).

5. This designation derives either from the Latin *metator*, probably signifying an angelic surveyor, or more likely the great scribe who stands beside the divine throne, from the Greek *ho meta thronon*.

5. Jewish attitudes to afterlife in the age of Jesus

1. Reference to the biblical origin of resurrection is missing from some important manuscripts of the Mishnah. To those excluded from the future world are to be added the readers of heretical books and magical healers as well as those who pronounce the sacrosanct name of God, and the Epicurean, someone who despises religion.

2. The population of Palestine in 1926 under the British mandate was 865,000. If we discount that of Transjordan

and about 100,000 Bedouin, we arrive at about 600,000, and it is unlikely that the density of the population was higher in the first century AD than shortly after the First World War.

3. Steven Fine, 'A Note on Ossuary Burial and the Resurrection of the Dead in First-Century Jerusalem', *Journal of Jewish Studies* 51 (2000), pp. 69–76.

4. *La croyance des Esséniens en la vie future* I (1993), p. 199.

5. *Ancient Jewish Epitaphs* (1991), p. 114.

6. *Jewish Symbols in the Graeco-Roman Period* IV (1954), pp. 71–98.

7. L. Y. Rahmani, *A Catalogue of Jewish Ossuaries in the Collections of the State of Israel* (Jerusalem, 1994), nos. 815 and 829, figures 127–8.

8. J. B. Frey, *Corpus Inscriptionum Iudaicarum, Vol. I, Europe* (1936), *32, p. 550.

7. The teaching of Jesus on resurrection and eternal life

1. The one significant Synoptic text indicating universal resurrection in view of the reward of the just and the punishment of the wicked is Matthew's story of the last judgement (Mt 25:31–46). It has no parallels among the parables safely attributable to Jesus. To this may be added Mk 9:43–48; Mt 18:8–9; see p. 367.

2. Geza Vermes, *The Authentic Gospel of Jesus* (Penguin, London, 2004), pp. 348–9.

3. Vermes, *The Authentic Gospel of Jesus*, pp. 287–8, 89–90.

4. The expression 'for the gospel' has the same meaning, since it is short for 'for the gospel of the kingdom' (see Mt 4:23 and 24:14 and some ancient manuscripts of Mk 1:14).

5. The four instances (out of twenty-five) where in John eternal life is explicitly connected to raising the dead have been noted earlier in this chapter (see pp. 364–6).

8. Predictions of the resurrection of Jesus

1. John, attempting to reduce the odium incurred by the disciples, claims that Jesus had obtained safe conduct for them from the soldiers sent to arrest him (Jn 18:8).

9. Resurrection accounts in the New Testament regarding persons other than Jesus

1. *Cum*, or rather *qum*, as attested in the best ancient manuscripts (Sinaiticus, Vaticanus, etc.), is the incorrect ending of the imperative second person singular. It is the masculine form applied to a feminine subject. This represents the loose Galilean dialect, apparently spoken by Jesus and his associates. Some other codices replace *qum* by the grammatically correct *qumi*, thus trying to improve or make more literate the language used by Jesus.

2. Legends circulating in the Eastern and the Western Church represent Lazarus as bishop of Cyprus, or even as the bishop of Marseilles in Southern France, where he arrived by boat together with his sisters Mary Magdalene and Martha.

10. The Gospel accounts of the resurrection of Jesus

1. For a more detailed discussion of the burial of Jesus see pp. 245–84.

2. Possibly the wife of Zebedee and the mother of the apostles James and John: see Mt 27:56).

3. Such an extended earthly stay of the risen Jesus is reasserted in the Acts of the Apostles: 'For many days he appeared to those who came up with him from Galilee to Jerusalem' (Acts 13:31).

4. If authentic, a segment of the Testimonium Flavianum of Josephus may be relevant here as indicating a belief in a kind of spiritual resurrection: 'When Pilate, upon hearing him accused by men of the highest standing amongst us, had condemned him to be crucified, those who had in the first place come to love him did not give up their affection for him' (*Ant* 18:64). To this purportedly genuine statement of Josephus, a Christian interpolator, borrowing from the New Testament, later added: 'On the third day he appeared to them restored to life, for the holy prophets had foretold this

and myriads of other marvels concerning him.' It has been suggested that the apocryphal Gospel of Peter, a Greek composition probably written in the late second century, contains some primary source material. See J. D. Crossan, *The Cross That Spoke: The Origin of the Passion Narrative* (1988). Nevertheless, even a perfunctory glance at the text proves that it is dependent on the canonical Gospels so that its treatment here would be a waste of time.

5. *The Resurrection of the Son of God*, pp. 5–6.
6. *Der alte und der neue Glaube* (1872), p. 72.

11. Initial evaluation of the accounts of the resurrection of Jesus

1. Josephus' reference in the Testimonium Flavianum to the resurrection of Jesus is considered by all modern experts as a Christian interpolation. 'On the third day he appeared to them restored to life, for the holy prophets had foretold this and myriads of other marvels concerning him' (*Ant* 18:64).

12. The resurrection of Jesus in the Acts of the Apostles

1. David wears the same prophetic mantle in the Dead Sea Scrolls, where his poems are said to have been 'uttered through prophecy' (11Q Psalms col. 27:11).
2. The same argument, using the same quotation of Ps 16:10, is attributed to Paul in his sermon in the synagogue of Antioch in Pisidia (Acts 13:26–39).

13. The resurrection of Jesus in Saint Paul

1. Little is known about Paul's previous contact with the Jerusalem Church. He speaks of his initial violent hostility towards the Jesus movement (Gal 1:14), and the Acts of the Apostles refers to his presence at the stoning of the deacon Stephen (Acts 7:58). For a fuller sketch of Paul's career, see Geza Vermes, *The Changing Faces of Jesus* (Penguin, London, 2000), pp. 59–75.

2.   In a similar vein, two Church members, Hymenaeus and Philetus, godless chatterers according to Paul, also confused some believers by advancing the view that the resurrection had already occurred (2 Tim 2:16–18).

3.   The deutero-Pauline letters, attributed by scholars not to Paul, but to his disciples, include Ephesians, Colossians, Hebrews, and the Pastoral epistles addressed to Timothy and Titus.

4.   Vermes, *The Changing Faces of Jesus*, pp. 84–6.

14. The resurrection of Jesus in the rest of the New Testament

1.   Josephus, too, is familiar with Noah's attempt to persuade his contemporaries to change their minds. 'But Noah, indignant at their conduct and viewing their counsels with displeasure, urged them to come to a better frame of mind and amend their ways; but seeing that, far from yielding, they were completely enslaved to their pleasure of sin, he feared that they would murder him and, with his wives and sons and his sons' wives, quitted the country' (*Ant* 1:74). The same ideas are also attested in rabbinic literature.

15. The meaning of the concept of resurrection in the New Testament

1.   As has been shown in chapter 14, the Book of Revelation advances the idea of double resurrection, the first bestowed on those who sacrificed their lives for Christ and enjoyed renewed existence for a thousand years, and the second affecting the rest of dead mankind who would receive their just deserts of eternal life or a second death in the lake of fire.

Some Jewish religious thinkers have remained hesitant when faced with the idea of eternal damnation colliding with the concept of a merciful God. A nineteenth-century Russian Jewish legend associated with the saintly Rabbi Hayyim of Volozhin goes so far as to advocate universal salvation.

According to this tale, when Rabbi Hayyim died, he was told that he could enter heaven at once. As a true son of Abraham, he began to bargain with God's representative. He first stipulated that all his pupils should also be granted immediate entry, then all the Jews and finally all the Gentiles. The heavenly negotiator could not agree to the last demand on the grounds that God had not yet decided about the coming of the Messiah. So Hayyim decided not to cross the gate of heaven and continued to pray outside until the Almighty agreed to the salvation of the whole human race. See Louis Jacobs, *A Jewish Theology* (Darton, Longman & Todd, London, 1973), p. 322.

2. Ancient tombs were, of course, often broken into by robbers looking for money, jewels or other valuables. If real, the hundred pounds' weight of precious ointments mentioned in the Fourth Gospel might have seemed attractive to the criminal confraternity of Jerusalem.

3. *Jesus in Rome* (London, 1957), pp. 12–13.

4. *Jesus the Man* (New York, 1992), p. 160.

5. Another epitaph with the carving 'Jesus, son of Joseph' was discovered in 1926 by Eleazar Lipa Sukenik. For the inscriptions see L. Y. Rahmani, *A Catalogue of Jewish Ossuaries in the Collections of the State of Israel* (Jerusalem, 1994), no. 9; Amos Kloner, 'A Tomb with inscribed ossuaries', *Atiqot* 29 (1996), pp. 15–22; James D. Tabor, *The Jesus Dynasty* (HarperCollins, London, 2006), pp. 22–33.

Epilogue: Resurrection in the hearts of men

1. It is noteworthy that even rabbinic literature records that an early Jewish-Christian, Jacob of Kfar Sama, offered to heal the sick 'in the name of Jesus' (tHullin 2:20–22).

2. *On the Trial of Jesus* (2nd edn, Berlin/New York, 1974), p. 208.

Select Bibliography

Classical sources

Josephus, Flavius, *The Jewish War – The Jewish Antiquities – The Life – Against Apion*, in *Josephus with an English Translation*, vols. I–IX, by H. St J. Thackeray and L. H. Feldman, Loeb Classical Library, London/New York, 1926–65

Philo of Alexandria, in *Philo with an English Translation*, vols. I–X, by F. H. Colson and G. H. Whitaker, Loeb Classical Library, London/New York, 1962

Tacitus, Cornelius, *Annals with an English Translation* by J. Jackson, Loeb Classical Library, London/New York, 1937

Allison, Dale C., *Resurrecting Jesus: The Earliest Christian Tradition and its Interpreters* (T. & T. Clark, New York/London, 2005)

Aus, Roger David, *Matthew 1–2 and the Virginal Conception: In Light of Palestinian and Hellenistic Judaic Traditions on the Birth of Israel's First Redeemer, Moses* (University Press of America, Lanham, MD, 2004)

Avis, Paul (ed.), *The Resurrection of Jesus Christ* (Darton, Longman & Todd, London, 1993)

Barr, James, *The Garden of Eden and the Hope of Immortality* (SCM Press, London, 1992)

Barton, Stephen and Graham Stanton (eds.), *Resurrection: Essays in Honour of Leslie Houlden* (SPCK, London, 1994)

Blinzler, Josef, *The Trial of Jesus* (Mercier Press, Cork, 1959)

Brandon, S. G. F., *The Trial of Jesus of Nazareth* (Batsford, London, 1968)

Brooke, George J., *The Dead Sea Scrolls and the New Testament* (SPCK, London, 2005)

Brown, Raymond E., *The Virginal Conception and the Bodily Resurrection of Christ* (Paulist Press, New York, 1973)

—, *The Birth of the Messiah* (Doubleday, New York, 1993)

—, *The Death of the Messiah*, vols. I–II (Doubleday, New York, 1994)

Bultmann, Rudolf, *History of the Synoptic Tradition* (Blackwell, Oxford, 1963)

Catchpole, D. R., *The Trial of Jesus* (E. J. Brill, Leiden, 1971)

Charlesworth, James H., et al. (eds.), *Resurrection: The Origin and Future of a Biblical Doctrine* (T. & T. Clark, New York/London, 2006)

Cohn, H. H., *The Trial and Death of Jesus* (Weidenfeld & Nicolson, London, 1972)

Crossan, J. D., *The Historical Jesus* (HarperSanFrancisco, 1991)

Cullmann, Oscar, 'The origin of Christmas' in *The Early Church* (SCM Press, London, 1956)

Davies, W. D., and Dale C. Allison, *The Gospel According to Saint Matthew, Volume I* [International Critical Commentary] (Edinburgh, 1988)

Davis, Stephen T., Daniel Kendal and Gerald O'Collins (eds.), *The Resurrection: An Interdisciplinary Symposium on the Resurrection of Jesus* (Oxford University Press, Oxford, 1997)

Dunn, James D. G., *Jesus Remembered* (Wm. B. Eerdmans, Grand Rapids, MI, 2003)

Elledge, K. C. D., *Life after Death in Early Judaism: The Evidence of Josephus* (Mohr Siebeck, Tübingen, 2006)

Evans, C. F., *Resurrection and the New Testament* (SCM Press, London, 1970)

Fitzmyer, Joseph A., *The Gospel According to Luke (I–IX)* (Doubleday, New York, 1981)

—, 'The Virginal Conception of Jesus in the New Testament' in *To Advance the Gospel* (Crossroad, New York, 1981)

Fredriksen, Paula, *Jesus of Nazareth, the King of the Jews* (Knopf, New York, 1999).

Gibson, Shimon, *The Cave of John the Baptist* (Arrow, London, 2005)

Goodman, Martin, *The Ruling Class of Judea* (Cambridge University Press, Cambridge, 1987)

James, Montague Rhodes, *The Apocryphal New Testament* (Clarendon Press, Oxford, 1924)

Meier, John P., *A Marginal Jew*, vol. I (Doubleday, New York, 1991)

Millar, Fergus, 'Reflections on the Trials of Jesus', in *A Tribute to Geza Vermes* (JSOT Press, Sheffield, 1990)

Moule, C. F. D., *The Significance of the Message of the Resurrection for the Faith in Jesus Christ* (SCM Press, London, 1968)

Nickelsburg, George W. E., *Resurrection, Immortality and Eternal Life in Intertestamental Judaism and Early Christianity* (expanded edition, Harvard University Press, Cambridge, MA, 2006)

Price, Robert M. and Jeffery Jay Lowder (eds.), *The Empty Tomb: Jesus beyond the Grave* (Prometheus Books, Amherst, MA, 2005)

Puech, Émile, *La croyance des Esséniens en la vie future: immortalité, résurrection, vie eternelle? Histoire d'une croyance dans le judaisme ancien* I–II (Cerf, Paris, 1993)

Sanders, E. P., *The Historical Figure of Jesus* (Allen Lane, London, 1993)

Schaberg, Jane, *The Illegitimacy of Jesus* (Crossroad, New York/Sheffield Academic Press, Sheffield, 1990/1995)

Schneemelcher, Wilhelm, *New Testament Apocrypha: Gospels and Related Writings* (Westminster John Knox Press, Nashville, 1991)

Segal, Alan F., *Life after Death: A History of the Afterlife in Western Religion* (Doubleday, New York, 2004)

Sherwin-White, A. N., *Roman Society and Roman Law in the New Testament* (Clarendon Press, Oxford, 1963)

Sloyan, G. S., *Jesus on Trial* (Fortress Press, Philadelphia, 1973)

Smith, Morton, *Jesus the Magician* (Victor Gollancz, London, 1978)

Stauffer, Ethelbert, *Jesus and His Story* (SCM Press, London, 1960)

Stewart, Robert B. (ed.), *The Resurrection of Jesus: John Dominic Crossan and N. T. Wright in Dialogue* (Fortress Press, Minneapolis, 2006)

Tabor, James D., *The Jesus Dynasty* (Simon & Schuster, New York, 2006)

Usener, Hermann, *Das Weihnachtsfest* (2nd edn, Friedrich Cohen, Bonn, 1911)

Vermes, Geza, *Jesus the Jew* (Collins/SCM Press, London 1973, 2001)

—, *The Changing Faces of Jesus* (Penguin, London, 2001)

—, *The Authentic Gospel of Jesus* (Allen Lane, London, 2003).

Winter, Paul, 'The Cultural Background for the Narrative in Luke I and II', *Jewish Quarterly Review* (1954), 159–67, 230–42, 287

—, *On the Trial of Jesus* (W. de Gruyter, Berlin, 1961, 2nd edn 1974)

Wright, N. T., *The Resurrection of the Son of God* (SPCK, London, 2003)

Index